W9-AMR-968

PALATINE PUBLIC LIBRARY

3 1265 01389 4805

OFFICIALLY
WITHDRAWN

Oct 2013

THE EYE OF
THE MAMMOTH

NUMBER THIRTY-EIGHT

Jack and Doris Smothers Series
in Texas History, Life, and Culture

STEPHEN HARRIGAN

The EYE *of the*

MAMM●TH

SELECTED ESSAYS

FOREWORD BY

NICHOLAS LEMANN

PALATINE PUBLIC LIBRARY DISTRICT
700 N. NORTH COURT
PALATINE, ILLINOIS 60067-8159

UNIVERSITY OF TEXAS PRESS *Austin*

Publication of this work was made possible in part by support from the J. E. Smothers, Sr., Memorial Foundation and the National Endowment for the Humanities.

Copyright © 2013 by Stephen Harrigan
Foreword © 2013 by Nicholas Lemann
All rights reserved
Printed in the United States of America
First edition, 2013

Requests for permission to reproduce material from this work should be sent to:
    Permissions
    University of Texas Press
    P.O. Box 7819
    Austin, TX 78713-7819
    http://utpress.utexas.edu/about/book-permissions

⊗ The paper used in this book meets the minimum requirements of ANSI/NISO Z39.48-1992 (R1997) (Permanence of Paper).

LIBRARY OF CONGRESS CATALOGING-
IN-PUBLICATION DATA

Harrigan, Stephen, 1948–
   The eye of the mammoth : selected essays / by Stephen Harrigan ; foreword by Nicholas Lemann. — 1st ed.
      p.   cm. — (Jack and Doris Smothers series in Texas history, life, and culture ; no. 38)
   ISBN 978-0-292-74561-2 (cloth : alk. paper)
   I. Title.
   PS3558.A626E94   2013
   814'.54—dc23
                            2012035503
doi:10.7560/745612

CONTENTS

––––––––

PART FOUR

WHERE IS MY HOME?

FOREWORD

Nicholas Lemann

When Stephen Harrigan started publishing the essays in this book, the anointed mid-twentieth-century giants of Texas letters, Roy Bedichek, J. Frank Dobie, and Walter Prescott Webb, had passed from the scene. Their rebel child, Larry McMurtry, was in physical and psychological exile in Washington, D.C. And in Texas, the literary world, unofficially but firmly led by John Graves, insistently conceived of Texas as a rural civilization, not too far removed from the frontier. This view certainly worked on the page, but it did not conform with the demographic reality of the state or with the lived experience of most Texans. Because so much of its countryside was dry and spare and its city limits were so generous, Texas, if simple percentage of the population was the measure, had become one of the most urban states in the country—though it was first-generation urban, like Dreiser's Chicago, and that made all the difference psychologically. If you were comfortable with the identity of a Texas writer, as Harrigan always has been, then it was your assignment to deal with this uncomfortable truth.

I don't know that Harrigan ever conceived of his literary mission in exactly this way, but over the years he certainly accomplished it. It was a happy accident that from the beginning he had a primary home for his reportorial and essayistic work in *Texas Monthly*, a commercial magazine operated by people who care deeply about editorial quality, and who for economic reasons as well as personal preference had to figure out how to create a large, mainly metropolitan audience to which the idea of what it meant to be distinctively Texan was important.

In the early years of *Texas Monthly*, Harrigan wrote about just about everything, but he was the primary holder of the nature account, and a good portion of this work is reproduced here. One could argue that the natural world is unaware of state boundaries, but in retrospect Harrigan was using natural subjects partly as a way of working out the question of Texas identity. It's noteworthy that he often wrote about designated natural areas in Texas, like parks and beaches; these are not the primary point of contact with the natural world for a frontier or agricultural society. In that sense these essays are implicitly about a modernizing Texas, even though that is not their direct subject. Often Harrigan found a recognizably Texan main character, an expert who guided him through the place he was writing about. And, in his customary calm, clear, lyrical voice, he always found a way to communicate his profound fascination with and love of his home state without ever venturing into boosterism. Padre Island doesn't have to be the Amalfi Coast for us to treasure it, or for us to be able to understand it as an aspect of who we are.

Texans of my generation (I'm from Louisiana, where the distinctive obsessions are different) often remember receiving the admission of Alaska to the Union as a crushing blow—Texas wasn't the biggest state any more! As a defining quality, the bigness of a place poses a problem to a serious writer. Small almost always is easier to make work on the page, because it entails creating an enclosed world; merely insisting that something is big doesn't confer life on it. Harrigan's Texas is certainly big in the sense that it provides him with a very broad range of material to write about, but he is an intimate writer, one who doesn't need the artificial help that comes from claiming importance for his subjects. He makes us care deeply about the particular and specific. In so doing, in the aggregate, he is making a powerful argument to Texans: you can love Texas, and you can identify deeply as a Texan, without having to yield to the stereotype of Texas bragging. Even to yourself! The ways Texans live, what they think, where they go, how they speak, is distinctive. It isn't superlative, and it isn't generic either. The state is a collection of places that Harrigan sees for what they really are and loves anyway, and together they make a culture, which he loves also.

What Harrigan has always seen clearly is that Texas, at least during his adult life, has not been another country, as it was briefly in the early nineteenth century; on the contrary, it is the most American, or Middle American, of places—a state big and central enough that its governor will naturally think he ought to be president. Texas is enormously various, as one sees in Harrigan's work, encompassing desert and beach and plain and mountain and forest; Latin America and the Great Plains; immigrant culture, native culture, and longtime resident culture. It is also typical, in the sense that one is never very far away from the statistical national center in how people choose to live and in what they believe. It's no use pretending that the picture of a family with children, living a middle-class life in a suburb—a single-family house with a small yard, two cars in the driveway, a daily commute to an office job—is somehow profoundly un-Texan. It's how the plurality of Texans live, and that has to be accounted for. Harrigan's unassuming, honest writing and his unobtrusive, lapidary way of constructing essays makes it easy for him to acknowledge these difficult (by light of Texas literary tradition) truths, casually and without making a big show of it. And the ordinariness of Texas means that Texans can leave home base and range freely throughout the world, with curiosity and interest, without that project carrying any taint of disloyalty or insecurity. Harrigan does that regularly in these pages, bringing a wide range of places into the particular world of his writer's consciousness.

Finally, though, in order to be as significant a writer as Harrigan is while also being identifiably Texan, you have to be able to make at least an implicit claim about what Texas is, and this leads almost inevitably to consideration of the Texas past. Harrigan has done this throughout his career, including in his fiction, and we see copious evidence of it here. He doesn't burden us with the details, but offstage, for decades, a kind of border war has been raging among historians of the West, between an older (well, by now mainly deceased) generation that saw the conquest of the frontier by Americans of European descent as heroic, and two or three subsequent generations that have emphasized ecological despoliation, ethno-cultural oppression, and economic exploitation. With great deftness, Harrigan's work pulls together the best aspects of both camps. Nature and indigenous populations are at the heart of his territory as a writer, but, damn it, it's simply impossible to be a Texan and not be moved by the old legends—the Alamo and the cattle drives and all that. Harrigan has delved into this material to create a more usable and more accurate past for Texans with relatively gentle and humane inclinations. That is a great gift.

One of the fascinating aspects of the historical culture of the American West is how little space there was between at least some aspects of historical action and historical mythmaking. Buffalo Bill shuttled back and forth between the frontier and the theater. Movies, television, and other forms of popular culture, energetically springing off from Texas history into quasi-fantasy, are inescapably a part of what it means to be Texan. And most of the leading Texas-resident writers, including Harrigan, have made part of their living from this process by creating Hollywood versions of larger-than-life Texas events for a mass audience. This can be done honorably and memorably (think of *Lonesome Dove*, or *Apollo 13*), or not, and Harrigan is completely clear-eyed about which is which, but he memorably and funnily demonstrates here that the reality of Texas tradition and its mythologization form a never-ending, mutually reinforcing feedback loop. All attempts to disaggregate them will be quixotic, and it's perfectly all right to consider them together.

A writer's life—especially the life of a writer as dedicated and prolific as Stephen Harrigan—has a lot of aspects. In most cases, books are generated from within and represent, to some extent, a conscious design, or at least what the writer most wants to say at that moment. The kind of essays reproduced here are usually produced on assignment. An author has some freedom to suggest assignments to editors, or to decide which proffered ones to accept or reject, but it's a more responsive, less planned form of literary production than writing books. So it is a special pleasure to see how much, over the decades, Harrigan has pursued a unified mission in his reporting and essay-writing.

Was it by design, or was the larger project something neither he nor his various editors were aware of, assignment by assignment? I don't know, but however he got here, this is a coherent body of work, and a large achievement. It's as good a picture as we have, not only of Texas during the past generation, but, more importantly, of what being a Texan has meant.

PART ONE

MUSIC IN
THE DESERT

MORNING LIGHT

M orning is the time of day when we are least receptive to the lessons of Copernicus. We may understand that our earth is a sphere revolving in the light of the sun, that it moves furiously through space neither forward nor backward, neither into nor out of time, with no apparent purpose and no fate other than entropy. But still a part of our intelligence greets each new day as if celestial mechanics had never been discovered, with a primitive confidence that the sun rises solely for us, to light our way and to warm our blood.

A good Texas morning may contain an unaccountable trace of melancholy, but I think it runs counter to human nature to face the rising sun and feel despair. Our most memorable mornings may have little to do with rousing atmospherical effects; they may be mute and cold, or sodden with stalled Gulf air. We might not even notice that day is coming, never glance at the gauzy whitish circle of the sun as it rises behind a wall of cloud. But we can sense the gathering confidence around us, the world's resolve to come into its fullest expression.

Let's say it is six a.m. From the sixty-fourth floor of the Transco Tower, the city of Houston is an endless field of individual lights—porch lights, bathroom lights, headlights—that shimmy in the heavy atmosphere. In the center of that field, monolithic and black as carbon, are the buildings of downtown. Not a single beam of light escapes from their windows, and there is no sunshine yet to give them any texture or relief. Along the horizon, running from south to north, is a thin flourish of cloud beginning to turn orange.

Already the cars are massing on the freeways, and from this height, in this meager light, they appear as a mysterious organic form. There is no question that an alien visitor would immediately identify the dominant life form on earth as the automobile, a creature of unfathomable motives and ceaseless energy, content to circle the dark, burned-out core of its city.

At the distant point where Richmond Avenue intersects the horizon, the sun comes up, seeping over the flat coastal prairie with a steady motion, bright as a welder's torch. It is a swift and simple event, unannounced by spectacular back-lit clouds or probing rivulets of light. The sun's plainness is beautiful.

As it rises, the sun seems not to cast its light but to hold it in, making the dawn so gradual as to be almost beyond notice. The glassy office buildings, which on another morning might flare dramatically in the rising and subsiding sunlight, merely pass soberly into day. Even when illuminated, Houston is still somnolent, still rich with strangeness, as the compact sun rides the horizon and the nearly full moon withdraws, losing its wattage and melding into the blue of the sky. Straight below, sixty-four stories down, is a billboard that in this transitional moment seems oddly provocative: "Coke Is It." Is it? If it is not It, what is?

In the neighborhoods below, those people not asleep or already behind the wheel are rising from their beds and moving through their houses. Some of them possess a light-headed serenity, some lurch and stumble and wait for the tide of light to sweep them into awareness. One by one, they are turning off their porch lights, their bathroom lights, and soon the whole city seems to have shaken off its collective dream and regained its grasp.

Say it is the same morning, half an hour later. Six hundred miles to the west it is still dark. Standing on a peak in the Davis Mountains, an observer can look out onto a great volcanic plain and see no man-made light at all except for an occasional pair of headlights that cross the bare landscape like a moon rover. There is no wind, and no sound. Shooting stars are visible in the sky, and the moon has disappeared behind a ragged cloud. The landforms themselves—the products of ash fall and lava flow—are indistinct, just hazy shapes in the dark sump below.

Blocked by mountains, the sunrise never quite happens. The dark simply lifts, and the eastern sky turns radiant in its coloration. But the moment when morning occurs is as impossible to pinpoint as the moment when a soul leaves a dying body. Gradually the world seems less threatening, less solitary, less ancient. Birds begin to rustle in their nests, coyotes trot along the valley roads, and hawks soar above the fractured lava peaks, riding the day's first warm updrafts.

By this time it is morning all over the state, and even those who remain asleep can feel its effects. It is a light wash over their unconscious minds, a subtle reduction of urgency and detail in their dreams.

In a quiet Fort Worth neighborhood a mother has been up since five o'clock. It was her milk coming in that woke her, but when she walked into the baby's room to feed him, she found him still asleep, almost the first time since his birth that their bodies had been out of phase. Two months old, he lay there with his eyes clenched tight, his little fingers slowly fanning the air like the tentacles of a sea anemone. His blanket was trussed up about him just so. She wondered if he was dreaming. Did he even know enough of the world yet to construct a dream? She had read that at his age he was amorphous, a creature of sensation. He did not know himself to be distinct. She wanted to think it was her face he saw in his dreams—the emblem of his contentment, the rising sun of his scaled-down world.

Now it is an hour later and the baby has still not stirred. She might have gone back to bed, but she is used to the early morning by now, and this unexpected time to herself is a luxury she does not want to fritter away in sleep. She pours herself a bowl of cereal and thinks about garnishing it with sliced fruit, like the illustration on the box. Finally she decides against it—too much trouble and too much mess. The baby will surely wake up any minute. She can count on her two-year-old daughter to sleep till seven and on her husband's eyes to snap open exactly at seven fifteen. As he does every morning, her husband will bound from the bed into the shower and be dressed in five minutes. He likes to be either asleep or awake and ready for action. In-between states make him nervous. He does not even own a bathrobe. She has never understood this—she loves to bask in her own drowsiness.

She watches television while she eats her cereal. A third-string local announcer is talking to a woman about a combination poor-boy art fair and fat stock show. He keeps nodding his head and muttering "uh-huh," all the while looking like he might suddenly reach over and strangle his guest just to relieve himself of his awful boredom.

After a few minutes of this she turns off the television and walks outside to see if the paper has come. The morning is hazy, and the dewy grass is cold beneath her bare feet. She picks up the paper and hurries back to the warmth of the sidewalk. Something holds her there, keeps her from turning back into the house. She is on the verge of some kind of thought; she can sense a vague opportunity forming for her in the still air. For that one second she feels as if she could slip into a trance.

But then the baby's crying distracts her. She goes back into the house and picks him up, smelling his sour milk breath, feeling her engorged breasts reacting to his outraged demands for nourishment. She walks outside to nurse him on the front porch, hoping to find that moment again. A large white dog walks briskly and purposefully down the center of the street, his head full of ideas. She can hear the sounds of garbage trucks, the yammering noise of some handyman's power saw, the raucous courtship call of a grackle.

Then another sound: a mourning dove, its notes low and hollow and disturbingly evocative. It's a sound that reminds her of Girl Scout campouts, of early morning ground fog and bone-chilling cold and an odd, not unwelcome feeling of loneliness. Her baby lifts his head as if in response to the birdsong. Perhaps they are on the same frequency. Perhaps the sound, which is so tantalizing and ungraspable to her, meshes perfectly with his unformed intelligence. For a moment she envies her baby, because that is what she wants for herself: just to be here, just to be part of the morning.

ON THE EDGE

In the darkness, in the semi-wilderness, we tuned the radio to 1610 on the AM dial.

"*Bienvenidos,*" an unctuous male voice said, "and welcome to Big Bend National Park. We're glad you're here! Vast vistas and sweeping panoramas are just two of the things that make the park unique."

The voice was familiar. It sounded like the same guy who came over the car radio on the outskirts of Disney World, directing drivers to parking lots named for the Seven Dwarfs. Now here he was, filling us in on the park rules and accommodations. I turned the radio off—I did not need to know where to hook up a motor home—and looked out the window. The "vast vistas and sweeping panoramas" were not visible at night, but I thought I could feel the landscape open and contract as we drove through it. Out in the darkness were great set pieces of geology—grabens and laccoliths and cuestas—pure fundamental forms that somehow made their presence known. A sign on the side of the road pointed off to Dog Canyon, through which Lieutenant William H. Echols had passed in 1859 with a train of twenty-four camels. The road itself followed the same route as the great Comanche War Trail, a thoroughfare that had once been trampled into definition a mile wide. We passed landmarks I could not see but had read about—Green Gulch, Pulliam

Bluff, a mountain that supposedly formed the profile of Alsate, the famous Apache chief who was betrayed by the Mexicans and sold into slavery with his people. All of this was invisible, all of it taken on faith.

The road planed upward, and my ears cleared sharply, without effort. The truck's headlights caught a small group of javelinas—dusky, spectral shapes that made me think of tiny prehistoric horses. Several miles later some creature a few inches long skittered across the road.

"Pocket mouse," George Oliver muttered from the back seat, almost to himself. He was sitting upright, alert as an owl, his eyes fixed vigilantly on the road ahead. He had been that way ever since we left Austin, nine or ten hours earlier. He was looking for dead animals on the highway, roadkills that had not yet been completely flattened, had not yet moldered and seeped into the asphalt. There were, of course, lots of them: dogs and cats, deer, jackrabbits, porcupines, armadillos, skunks, mice, squirrels, and even great horned owls. Every few miles George would say, in his reserved, rather apologetic manner, "If, uh, it wouldn't be too much trouble, there's a pretty good hog-nosed skunk coming up here on the left," and O. C. Garza, who was driving the truck, would say with the elaborate courtesy one usually reserves for extreme cases, "Hey, no trouble at all. Can't pass up a good hog-nosed skunk."

Then the four of us would pile out of the car and stare down at a smushed pile of fur and bone and sun-blackened viscera. Sometimes the unfortunate creature's carcass would be too far gone and George would leave it, maybe taking its head along in a Ziploc bag for further study. More often he knelt to the task, taking out his forceps, searching the carcass for ectoparasites—lice, mites, ticks, and wingless parasitic flies—and then dropping them into vials of alcohol held by Linda Iverson, his unskittish associate.

George Oliver was a freelance zoologist who worked as a consultant for various state and federal conservation agencies. His main interests were reptiles and amphibians—herps, he called them—as well as birds and mammals. The ectos were a sideline, something he had fallen into. He sent the parasites to a colleague in Iowa for identification. The results of this research were sometimes published, with Oliver as junior author, in obscure entomological journals.

I knew George from another discipline. Some years ago, when I was editing a poetry magazine in Austin, he had appeared at my door one day with a group of remarkably accomplished and strangely moving poems studded with off-the-wall references to natural history, poems that took note of turtle plastrons and pikas and "the piss ritual of copulating porcupines." He looked much the same now as he had then. He still wore his straight brown hair below his shoulders, and in his field clothes—which included flat-bottomed work boots and an old straw cowboy hat that fit his head imperfectly—he managed to violate every precept of wilderness chic.

We kept climbing, heading up into the Chisos Mountains, the park's heartland. The Chisos are also known as the Ghost Mountains, for Alsate and others who are still supposed to haunt them, and for their basic demeanor. I was anxious for morning, so I could see them.

I was casually familiar with the region, having camped in the Chinati and Davis Mountains and floated down the lower canyons of the Rio Grande in a canoe, but my efforts to visit the park itself had been consistently thwarted. Now I had made it—in January, at the height of the off-season, before the desert bloomed and the weather turned fair and the campgrounds and trails became congested with college students on spring break, with hard-core backpackers, and with the birders who come every spring and summer from all over the world to catch a glimpse of the Colima warbler, a rather ordinary bird that has the distinction of occurring almost nowhere else on earth.

During 1944, the year the park officially opened, there were 1,409 visitors. In recent years the number has been edging up toward half a million. It is a popular place, but it exudes a certain gravity that makes it seem less an outdoor playland than a genuine public trust. The people who have been there, or who plan to go, or who simply take comfort in the fact that it exists, speak of it reverently, longingly. For thousands of harried urban dwellers throughout the state it is a recharge zone, someplace pure and resolute, an imaginary ancestral home.

Such reactions to the Big Bend—the *despoblado*, as the Spanish called it—are modern luxuries. For centuries it offered little but suffering and frustration. It was a cursed, unfathomable desert country with a single, unnavigable river and a confusing welter of isolated mountains

formed from the broken linkage of the Rockies and the Sierra del Carmens. It was a great knurl in the landscape that obstructed the natural
grain of commerce and habitation.

The present boundaries of the park comprise about eleven thousand square miles of this wilderness. The Big Bend is formed by the
Rio Grande, where it pivots suddenly northward from its southeast-
erly course, cutting through a series of magnificent and nearly unapproachable canyons. The river is the southern boundary of the park,
which rests securely in the center of its immense crook. On the United
States side of the Rio Grande is the northern expanse of the Chihuahuan Desert, whose dominance of the park is broken by scattered, free-
standing mountains with names like Mule Ear Peaks and Cow Heaven
Mountains, and by the high bastion of the Chisos range, which rises
over seven thousand feet above sea level. In the Chisos there are stands
of Douglas fir, aspen, and ponderosa pine, stranded there when the lowlands turned to desert; and there are still black bears in the Chisos, too,
as well as a shaky population of peregrine falcons.

None of these creatures appeared within the beam of our headlights.
We saw another mouse or two and a flattened kangaroo rat that George
did not feel was worth climbing out of the truck into the thirty-degree
cold to inspect.

It took us almost an hour to drive from the park entrance to the
Basin, which was five thousand feet up in the Chisos. The Basin is the
place where most of the park's amenities are concentrated, a picturesque little aggregate of buildings—lodge, restaurant, store, ranger station, campground, and amphitheater. All of this was closed when we
arrived. We could see little more than the glow of the Coke machines
and a few lanterns alight in the campground. The campsites were
rented on the honor system: one put two dollars in an envelope, left the
envelope in a receptacle, and then cruised around looking for a vacant
site. At most other times of the year we would have had to reserve a
site months in advance, but in the dead of winter there was plenty of
room. We pulled up to a picnic table, unloaded the truck, and did our
best to secure our tent stakes in the rocky ground. O. C. and I would be
sleeping in my tent, a little green job about as water-repellent as cheese-
cloth. O. C.'s own tent offered better protection, but it was considerably

heavier, and since we would be backpacking we had decided to leave it in the truck. Though he had doubts about the wisdom of this plan, O. C. remained unruffled. He was the perfect traveling companion: tireless, omnivorous, utterly adaptable to any social or climatic conditions. He did not grow moody or sulk, and did not seem to mind when other people did. He was built like a tree trunk, and in his bearded winter phase he looked compatible with the country, like one of Pancho Villa's soldiers decked out in hiking knickers.

Once both tents were up, we crawled into them, numb from the cold and from the all-day drive across half of Texas. The wind gusted all night, snapping the fabric taut and shaking droplets of condensation onto my forehead. I was reminded again of how my love of sleeping outdoors was merely a romantic illusion, that in fact I did not *sleep* outdoors, but rather lay on the ground waiting for morning, occasionally lapsing into a semiconscious state in which I moved about in my sleeping bag like an inchworm until I had found and unwittingly settled upon the most uncomfortable portion of the immediate terrain.

O. C., of course, dropped off right away. He was a machine. I listened to his light snoring and checked my watch every hour. When it read 7:30 I unzipped the tent flap and drew it back to get my first look at the park. The scenery was extreme, what little of it was visible through the clouds. Then I realized that the clouds *were* the scenery; we were on their level. They moved through the Basin swiftly and gravely like a dense current, leaving little eddying pockets in the hollows and drainages of the mountains. The sun was not yet up, and the light in the Basin was cold and steely. The peaks themselves, revealed intermittently through the clouds, were monstrous and abrupt. They surrounded us completely, a perfect bowl except for one giant chink to the west, a natural drainage known as the Window. The Basin had begun as a great cyst, a dome of bedrock rising beneath the more recent deposits of volcanic ash and sandstone. Erosion undermined the softer rocks in the dome, collapsing the center and leaving a ring of mountains. Some of the mountains were smooth, having been eroded through to the original intrusive rock. Others, like Casa Grande, the most imposing fixture in the Basin, were dominated by blocks of lava that were reminiscent of the temples found on the summits of Central American pyramids.

George and Linda were awake, looking sadly at their tent, whose rear half had blown down during the night. Next to it stood a century plant, twelve feet high, each branch holding out its withered platelet of flowers. All about the camping area stood taut mountaineering tents from which people were beginning now to emerge, bleary and silent, walking to the full-service restroom trailing the untied laces of their hiking boots.

Despite the collapsed tent, Linda Iverson was in high spirits. She stood about braiding her blond hair and looking south to the highest elevation of the Chisos, where we were headed. She was twenty-six, a native of Minnesota who had happened upon Austin and taken up residence there, working for a while as a waitress in a restaurant that specialized in omelets, and then enrolling in the university.

We spent the next few hours taking the tents down and rearranging the loads in our backpacks. The sun finally made it over the mountain rim, and the essentially monochromatic winter landscape was subtly enhanced by its presence. The peaks ringing the Basin were just as imposing in the full sunlight as they had been when they were veiled in the clouds, but they were more accommodating to our perspective. They were closer than I had thought and not quite so sheer. I wondered how hard they would be to climb.

We ate breakfast at the restaurant and then browsed in the little gift shop. I bought a half-dozen polished rocks for my daughter and put them in a plastic coin purse that read Big Bend National Park. We made two more stops: at the park store, which featured racks of Harlequin romances and freeze-dried food; and at the ranger station, where a genial, middle-aged volunteer park ranger in a yellow felt vest gave us a "backcountry permit" that looked like a luggage tag, and admonished us to carry plenty of water, since the springs were dry.

The backcountry we meant to explore was known as the High Chisos Complex, a fourteen-mile loop along a well-maintained trail that would take us along the South Rim of the Chisos. It was a walk that could be made easily enough in a day by a casual hiker, or by a tourist riding up the trail in a train of sure-footed, sleepwalking horses, but we planned to take our time and spend as many as three or four days. Consequently, we were loaded down with water and food. We hoisted our packs in the Basin parking lot and ambled off to find the trail. There were roadrunners on the asphalt, pyrrhuloxia and house finches in yucca plants outside the lodge, and on the fringe of the Basin we saw six or seven mule deer, surprisingly heavy animals with strikingly large ears.

The trail looped about pleasantly in the foothills for the first mile or so and then grew progressively steeper until it got down to business in a long series of switchbacks. The Basin dropped away all at once, as if it had been jettisoned, and every time I looked back I was astonished at how far we had risen. The mountains across the valley looked sheer, the vegetation sparse and grasping, but the slope we walked on was well-timbered with juniper cedar, piñon, and oak, plus an occasional madrone tree with its strange reddish-orange bark that looked like oxidized metal. I felt the weight of the water in my pack, which was scientifically designed to distribute its tonnage along some imaginary force field high above the shoulders. I secretly pined for my old Boy Scout Yucca pack, which was secured to a wooden frame with a diamond hitch, whose weight was felt directly and not as a vague, unaccountable sensation, as if some invisible beast were perching on the hiker's neck.

Every few yards George would crouch down and look off into the brush, at a brown towhee kicking through a pile of leaves, at a nondescript rodent he identified as a Texas antelope ground squirrel, at an acorn woodpecker. "Take a good look at his eye," he said. "There's something about that yellow ring around their eyes that makes them look insane."

We stopped more often as the trail got steeper. Looking down through binoculars I could see the Day-Glo backpacks of a group far below us, but they were the only other people I had seen. We had come two or three miles, but I had given up trying to gauge the distance. I was merely relieved when the trail began to level out, passed over a saddle, and led to a broad mountain meadow carpeted with stipa grass. We walked past a pair of fiberglass outhouses and then veered off into the meadow and dropped our packs in a bower formed by the drooping branches of an alligator juniper. Then we took off our shoes and attended to our separate lunches. I watched with revulsion as O. C.

opened a can labeled Potted Meat Food Product, spread the contents onto two pieces of rumpled white bread, and then proceeded to eat his sandwich with inexplicable pleasure. I opened a can of chicken spread, which was not much more appetizing, and ate a few dried apricots.

After lunch we set up our tents and then followed George around as he laid out a series of small aluminum live traps, baited with peanut butter and rolled oats. Trapping is of course rigidly controlled in the park, and collecting permits of any kind are hard to come by. George was, in his way, a fastidious ecologist. He trapped his animals alive, measured them, checked them for ectos, then released them in the same spot. He worried that this procedure might traumatize the creatures, a concern that would strike most conventional zoologists as eccentric, if not absurd. I had once watched a group of zoology graduate students at work in the field and had been appalled at the slaughter. They set out traps (brand name: Havahart), recovered the small mammals that entered them, injected them with sodium pentothal, eviscerated them, cleaned the carcasses with cornmeal, stuffed them with cotton, and arranged the resulting specimens in a laboratory tray with others of their kind.

"Most people are into this collecting syndrome," George said. "I've had people outright say that my data were no good, that there's no way you can get the proper identification from a live rat. These guys who go out and kill tend to be descriptive rather than interpretive biologists."

When the traps were baited and set, we made our way up the slope of Emory Peak, which loomed at the east end of the meadow and whose summit—at 7,835 feet—was the highest elevation in the park. There was a cave somewhere in the peak that George had heard about, the maternity colony for the Big Bend long-nosed bat. We worked our way up the steep slope of the mountain, above which sat the stark lava cap, jointed into long parallel blocks that had formed under the heating and cooling effects of Cenozoic weather. George found a group of snails under a dead agave plant, large round striped snails that he arranged on the palm of his hand and stood for a moment admiring. They were named *Humboltiana agavophila*, for the great German naturalist who had discovered them as well as for their affinity for agave composts.

George replaced the snails and we trudged upward again. The face of the cliff, when we arrived there, looked massive—there were no doubt dozens of caves in the seams of the rock. George set out and in a matter of minutes had found the cave entrance he was looking for, a high vault obscured by brush. Inside, the cave was dry and strikingly angular, made of smooth, collapsed boulders that fit together like masonry. There was a damp, ammonia-like smell—guano. George squatted down under a low ceiling and motioned the rest of us forward, with his finger on his lips.

"I've found two hibernating Townsend's big-eared bats," he whispered, pointing to a furry clump on the ceiling. "I am going to attempt to get some parasites off them while they're still asleep."

It struck me as an ominous, eerie statement. "I am going to attempt to drive this stake through the vampire's heart while he is still asleep." I wasn't sure I wanted any part of it, but I watched, enthralled, as George reached up and plucked the two bats from their roost in one bare hand.

"Yeah," he whispered again, looking down almost tenderly at the bats. "They're hibernating all right. They're very cold. Feel them."

I knew that he had been inoculated against rabies. I reminded him that I had not. He said that the Townsend's big-eared was "not a bad rabies bat." I reluctantly poked one of the bats with the end of my finger—it was indeed cold—and then wiped the finger on my pants leg.

Linda crouched nearby, holding a vial for the parasites. The bats were too drowsy to feel fear as George spread their wings and probed around with his forceps, occasionally blowing softly on the fur to expose a mite or a louse. The bats had very long, fibrous ears—like the feelers of a moth—that converged in the center of the face, creating an expression of alien wrath. When hibernating they ordinarily kept one ear retracted, but the more George handled them the more that ear began to rise. By and by the bats shook off sleep and grew active. One of them twisted his neck around, made a strange whining sound like a tiny disengaged motor, and bit George on the finger, which did not distress him in the least.

He was glad to discover two species of parasitic flies, which he held up for our inspection; they looked like pieces of grit caught in his forceps. A moment later he replaced the two bats on the ceiling as if he were hanging ornaments on a Christmas tree. Once their feet were securely rooted to an almost microscopic irregularity in the smooth rock, the bats flapped their wings once or twice, cloaked them around their bodies, and then, astonishingly, went back to sleep.

There were more bats farther back in the cave, which rose upward in a series of lofts to another entrance fifty or sixty feet above us. In some places a few square feet of roost accommodated dozens of bats, aroused now and watchful, with both ears extended. None of them were the long-nosed bats that George had held out a faint hope of seeing. He searched the cave floor for a skull or some other evidence of the species' presence, but when the light outside began to fail he had to give up the effort.

Back in the meadow I lay in the grass, exhausted, studying a hummingbird nest that had been constructed on an agarita branch. The nest was about the size of a plum, perfectly formed and covered with lichen that resembled a ceramic glaze. Up on Emory Peak the sunlight ebbed and flowed, playing across the surface of the rock.

Emory was William H. Emory. He headed the 1852 U.S. Boundary Survey Team, which made one of the half-dozen forays by engineers and geologists into the Big Bend, attempting to establish roads and trade routes. The region was no more hospitable to them than it had been to the Spanish, who had tried for 250 years to secure their authority along the frontier of Nueva Vizcaya. They sent *entrada* after *entrada* into the wilderness, searching for gold, souls, slaves, and finally for lines of defense against the Apaches. The surveyors met with the same problems—a grave lack of food and water and constant threats from the Indians—and they suffered in the detached way of scientists, sketching their maps and tending their instruments while almost senseless with thirst.

It was the Indians who made the best use of the Big Bend. The Apaches were driven into the region by the Comanches, and the Comanches were in turn driven there by the Americans. Both tribes adapted, learning when the land could be depended upon to sustain life, when the springs were running and the *tinajas*, the water holes worn into the bedrock, were full. The Mescalero Apaches traveled with their water stored in thirty-foot lengths of animal intestines that they entwined around their packhorses. They established *rancherías*—periodic camp-sites—here in the Chisos, in this very meadow. Every year in May, dur-ing what they called the Mexican moon, the Comanches would follow the war trail down from the high plains, raiding the Mexican villages on the other side of the river and living primarily on the spoils.

All of that carnage and enterprise seemed now to have faded away, absorbed into the rock. Over these very mountains had swarmed Chisos Indians, Apaches, Comanches, bandits from both sides of the border, prospectors, businessmen, scalp hunters, refugees, Texas Rangers, min-ers, Pancho Villa, and General Pershing. Now there was the occasional happy hiker.

Before dinner the four of us passed around a canteen and a squeeze bottle of biodegradable soap and washed the bat guano off our hands. On my little Svea stove we cooked freeze-dried Chili Mac and made hot chocolate with crunchy, dehydrated marshmallows. After that, though it was early, there was little to do but go to sleep. It was very cold, and the sputtering gasoline stove neither warmed us nor drew us into con-versation. When we turned off our flashlights the night was complete: there was nothing visible or audible in it. There was simply its presence, the same night that had presided over the Chisos since they had risen through the crust of the earth.

By eight o'clock the next morning the sun was way below Emory Peak, and the wild grass in the meadow was as cold as steel wool. The clouds moved across the peak in droves, or in fast, spritely shreds that reminded me of spirit forms.

In the middle of the field George Oliver was already at work, comb-ing the fur of a yellow-nosed cotton rat with his forceps. "I'd like to find another flea," he was saying. "It'd be great to find another flea or a louse."

He discovered his flea after ten minutes of picking over the rodent and inserted it into the vial Linda held out. He let the rat go, watch-ing for a moment as it scrambled through the grass to its burrow, and moved on to check the next trap, which was also full. "It's like opening presents on Christmas morning," he said.

Almost all of the traps were inhabited, either by yellow-nosed cotton rats or by harvest and white-ankled mice. George measured each one carefully, writing in his notebook the length of its tail and feet and body, and then checked it over for ectos. The rodents crouched and shivered in his grasp. Some bit him, and others sat still as he parted their fur with his breath.

George was delighted with the traps' success. He mentioned that his hands were numb from the cold, but otherwise he seemed happily preoccupied. He belonged here. His home in Austin was a minimal, transitory place, a rented house with a mattress on the floor and a few pieces of furniture that no one had bothered to haul to the dump. It was a *ranchería*, a foraging base.

I wandered about with my binoculars and watched a raucous group of sleek blue Mexican jays. I saw a woodpecker and a wren, some kind of wren. In my secret heart I knew I could barely tell one bird from another, or one tree or shrub or flower from another. I required constant tutoring; I needed a course in Remedial Basic Knowledge. Every trip I made into the wilderness seemed to subtract from my already meager store of information. I envied George Oliver his field identification skills—"Look! There's a white-throated swift. Its markings remind me of a killer whale"—because they were so obviously not just skills, but gifts.

I was restless. Even here, on the second day of a recreational camping trip, outfitted and made shamelessly comfortable by a technology that would have stupefied one of those early explorers, I wanted to move on, to cover ground, to get it over with. I fingered the polished stones in my pocket, anxious to take them home. That was my problem: an absurd, pervasive homesickness. I knew I would have to keep one step ahead of this feeling, to outmaneuver and contain it. But to do so was a bother, and seemed out of keeping with the grandeur of this place that I wanted to love and in fact *did* love. I desperately wanted my emotions to be in pitch with the landscape.

During the morning the temperature dropped steadily. We ate lunch in my tent, and afterward I broke into my store of Del Monte chocolate pudding, the one food item that experience had taught me was absolutely indispensable for backpacking. By the time we had gathered up our camp, slung it up on our backs, and headed out the trail for the

South Rim, it was three o'clock. It must have been about thirty degrees, and it grew colder with every foot of altitude we gained.

We moved into the clouds, following a canyon where all the trees were covered with frost. Another mile or so after that the trail opened onto a plain where the grass had been worn down into the sod by hundreds of horseshoes and Vibram soles. A few hundred feet farther on, where the plain ended, was the most magnificent sight in Texas. The South Rim is a sheer lava bank that looks out upon what a casual observer might take to be a sizable portion of another planet. I walked up to the rim itself and felt a flourish of wind behind me trying to shove the surface area of my backpack forward as if it were a sail. I took a few steps back and studied the view. The Chisos, the high, self-contained bastion in the center of the park, dropped and then surged outward to meet the desert and a field of remarkable landforms. Far off in the haze was the Rio Grande, and I could see the other mountain groups—Punta de la Sierra, Chilicotal, that part of the Sierra del Carmens known as the Dead Horse Mountains—as clearly as on the three-dimensional model at park headquarters. The mountains presented a tableau of arrested motion, an everlasting instant of geological time. The ancient rocks rose and subsided like waves; they pulsed with light, and the light itself seemed generated by the power of the wind.

We walked on for another mile or so, following the rim, stopping every now and then to look out at the new perspectives it offered. We made camp in a little grove just off the trail. There was frost everywhere and the wind was intense. Little snowdrifts accumulated in the creases of our clothes. O. C. and I put up the tent, and then I tried without success to light the stove in the wind. I was sapped. We climbed into the tent and resolved to wait out the cold. I was wearing my long johns, several layers of clothing, and a bulky coat filled with some miracle synthetic; I was bundled up in my sleeping bag, which was rated to ten degrees above zero; and I was shivering uncontrollably. I had *never* been this cold. It was growing dark. We would be lying here with our teeth chattering for fourteen hours.

"You know," O. C. said, "I halfway think we ought to walk down tonight."

I had been halfway thinking the same thing. The Basin was six and a half miles away, a long walk in the dark, but it was mostly downhill. In another few hours we could be sitting in a heated room in the lodge watching television. We considered it for a while and then pulled down the tent and wadded it up inside my backpack. George and Linda called out from their own tent that they were comfortable enough to wait the cold out, and would meet us in the Basin in a few days.

We got our blood circulating. The trail led out along the rim, then cut into Boot Canyon. It turned dark almost immediately, but we could see well enough with our flashlights to maintain a good pace. We followed the canyon down to Boot Spring, where there was an empty horse corral and ranger hut and a few picnic tables at which we sat and wolfed down some canned goods. Then we started off again, following the contour of the canyon, passing the Boot, a free-standing column of rock whose dark shape was strangely delineated against the night sky. Soon we came upon the steep, never-ending series of switchbacks that led back down to the Basin. We rambled down them, rarely speaking, overcome by monotony and fatigue. We could see the Basin far below us, a grouping of lights that never seemed to come nearer. It was one of those occasions when it was possible to lose all belief in progress, in time itself. I knew I would be walking down this hill forever, and when my feet finally did hit the asphalt I had the feeling I had simply appeared in the Basin in some ghostly form, that my real self was back up on the switchbacks, wandering in the void.

I lay on my back on a little swath of curbside greenery in the parking lot, looking up at the stars and removing pieces of ice from my beard. The lodge was full, so we drove to the campground and set up O. C.'s tent, an advanced apparatus that was supported by a cat's cradle of flexible aluminum poles and was as roomy inside as a pavilion. I lay down in profound weariness, as washed out, as eroded, as the landscape.

In the morning we hobbled up to the restaurant for pancakes. There were only a few people there: toothy, radiant young women in down vests and their ruddy, bearded companions, with whom they played footsie under the table in hiking boots that weighed five pounds apiece.

All at once the Basin seemed like a metropolis, alive with opportunity. I went into the store and looked at the cans of food displayed there, weirdly fascinated by everything I saw. To get our legs working again we climbed a small mountain, and in the afternoon we drove forty miles west to Santa Elena Canyon, descending all the way through desert, through the very scenery we had viewed from the South Rim. All along the way were strange formations, dikes and rills topped with free-standing rocks like the spine plates of a stegosaurus. There was an area quaintly identified as the "jumble of volcanoes," a place of low, bone-white hills strewn with nuggets of red volcanic rock that looked as if they had been unloaded there by a dump truck the day before.

Santa Elena Canyon is a deep gorge cut by the Rio Grande through the Mesa de Anguila, a corridor 1,500 feet high that simply stops in its tracks at the junction of the Rio Grande and Terlingua Creek. At this point the river makes a right-angle turn to the southwest, leaving a great floodplain on the American side.

The mouth of the canyon—with its concrete walkway and observation stanchions—is considered a must-see spot for visitors to the park, but in the middle of the winter few people were there. A hundred yards back into the canyon there was a stunning silence, or rather a stunning suggestion of silence, because I could hear a dim, thrumming sound, a constant tone that might have been a bird call echoing through the canyon or the operating sounds of some faraway piece of machinery. The whole thing was extraordinarily, soporifically peaceful. The river was as calm as the rock walls it reflected.

For the next several days we hung around the Basin, taking our meals there and driving back and forth through the park in the truck. It was as if, after a life of consequence and rigor, we had fallen into a decadent lethargy from which we could not escape. The food in the restaurant was consistently acceptable, and as we sat at our table, staring out the picture windows at the brute scenery, we came to recognize the other regulars. Most of them were retired couples wearing identical quilted jackets or vests with patches obtained at the other stops they had made on the national park circuit. They sat at their tables in comfortable silence, the wives with a look of loving forbearance, an air of humoring their husbands on this vast itinerary, this connect-the-dots odyssey of natural wonders. The windows of their motor homes were covered with decals—Yosemite, Royal Gorge, Mammoth Cave. There was no place for these big, lumbering vehicles in the prevailing back-country ethic. Hikers came down from the mountains, their blood puri-fied, their spiritual priorities in order, only to encounter the noxious fumes of a motor home. And yet there was something guileless and credible about these people; they were staking their last years of life on the notion that in these government-certified vistas there was some-thing profoundly worth their attention.

One day we drove east, into a stark low-elevation desert sparsely covered with creosote bushes and agave and candelilla plants. Near the river we took a road that was little more than a jeep trail and followed it north until it dead-ended on the top of Cuesta Carlota, a low, regular ridge that put me in mind of an earthen dam. On the other side of the cuesta was Ernst Basin, a desert savannah bounded on the east by the Sierra del Carmens. The brush on the basin floor was thick, and there was a barely noticeable trail of greenery running through it.

We walked down on the other side of the ridge, following an unmain-tained trail that frequently disappeared into the hard alkaline soil, marked only by occasional piles of rock. I was looking for a place I had read about in one of George Oliver's poems—"Syzygy at Ernst Tinaja."

M. A. Ernst had been a storekeeper and public official around the turn of the century at the little town of La Noria, a few miles north of here. He was ambushed one day as he rode home on his horse, shot in the back by parties unknown or at least never convicted of the crime. Later he was found leaning against a Spanish dagger plant, still alive and holding his intestines in place with one hand. He had written a note for his wife, who did not find it until just after he died: "Am shot. . . . First shot hit, two more missed."

The trail snaked back into a deep canyon that cut through the cuesta to the basin. We followed it toward the desert and came across not one but a series of *tinajas*, swirling, polished depressions in the limestone that were all but dry. We stopped by the largest of them and watched the water bugs swimming in the few inches of water that remained. Compared with the outright grandeur of Santa Elena Canyon, it was nothing special, but the magic of place is an arbitrary phenomenon—I felt comfortable here, among the bleached, rococo rock forms. I would have liked to stay there all day, but the sun was going down and I was not sure we would be able to find the trail again in the darkness. Still, it was tempting. We were nearing the crepuscular hour, when javelinas would begin to snort and rise from their wallows, ready once more to face the desert gloaming.

That night George Oliver and Linda Iverson walked down from the South Rim and pitched their tent next to ours in the campground. They had had a good time, had climbed to the summit of Emory Peak and had experienced continued success with the traps. No sooner had the two of them touched ground in the Basin than they wanted out again, back into the solitude of the wilderness, back into their natural habitat. We ate some chili and then got into the truck and drove to the Grapevine Hills, a weird, haunted region composed of seemingly random piles of soft, scruffy rock. In the darkness we could see the haphazard silhouettes of the formations. It looked as if they would collapse at any moment, but they were obdurate and, to the fleeting perceptions of the creatures who beheld them, timeless.

For a moment I felt suddenly displaced, removed from the scene by a new wave of homesickness. It took more of my attention to combat it than I was willing to relinquish. I decided that one way around this intrusive emotion might be to think of Big Bend as home. I did. It worked immediately.

We stood on a bed of sand in the center of the canyon. We were the only people around for twenty miles.

"Maybe I can attract a predator," George Oliver said. He put the back of his hand up to his mouth and made a sound that he hoped approximated the cries of a small rodent in distress. It was a terrible, high-pitched wailing and squeaking sound. For a long time it had no effect, and George finally put his hand back in his pocket and turned to go.

"Wait!" Linda whispered. "I think I hear something."

The four of us stood still and listened. We could hear it faintly now, the sound of a predator moving toward us through the brush.

THE SECRET LIFE
OF THE BEACH

A white-tailed hawk has spent the night at the summit of a solitary live oak behind the dunes. There is dew on the hawk's wings; he is sluggish and cold. He turns around and around on the branch, positioning himself to catch the warmth of the sun rising into a clear sky over the Gulf.

The tree on which the hawk sits bends elaborately leeward. It stands at the center of the island in a kind of valley, a deflation flat, between the stabilized dunes near the beach and a bare active dune field that backs up to the narrow lagoon separating the island from the mainland.

The isolation of the tree suits the hawk. It gives him a sense of prominence, from which he derives a sense of security. Even at rest, uncommitted to anything except basking torpidly in the early morning sunlight, the hawk gives off an impression of awesome capability and utter indifference. He looks out over the grassland, blinking. His stolid body is clearly marked: a warm gray above, with rufous streaks on the wings, and a clean white underside and tail, which is traversed at the tip by a precise black band.

When the sun is a little higher, he begins his diurnal rounds, rising from the tree with a few powerful surges of his wings and almost immediately entering an up-draft. The hawk artfully conforms to the movement of the warm air, letting it support him, adjusting the tension in his wings for direction and height. The same economy that guides his flight guides his will: there is neither wasted motion nor wasted thought. The hawk's mind is as clear as the air in which he flies. He scans the ground and notes without concern the high-packed burrows of pocket gophers, the scattered yellow flowers of beach morning glory, his own reflection in the water of a tidal pool. Far below him on the highway that runs the length of the island lies a dead mother possum, surrounded by the three embryonic forms that were knocked from her pouch when she was struck during the night by a car. The possum babies are pink, with black, skin-covered bulges of incipient eyes and well-developed forelimbs, which they had used to climb from their mother's vagina to her pouch, knowing the way by the trail of saliva she had deposited.

None of this concerns the hawk. It is movement that excites him. The sharpness of his vision, the expert trim of his body in the air—sensations that would produce a state of rapture if transferred to a human being— are part of the package of the hawk, instruments for locating snakes and rabbits and frogs. But within the range of his vision the narrow island is encompassed: it revolves around the steady axis of his perception. When the hawk flies north the open Gulf is at his right wing tip and the muddy lagoon at his left.

The island is little more than a mile wide and only a few hundred yards from the mainland. Though it is twenty miles long, its northern and southern boundaries are almost abstract landmarks, the sites of natural passes that barely interrupt the continuity of a long strip of offshore islands that shadows the Texas coast for some two hundred miles, from the Brazos to the Rio Grande. This island, like the others that make up the chain, is a barrier island, a sandbar that serves as a buffer between the turbulence of the open Gulf and the calm estuarine waters. Above its base of Pleistocene mud the island is an accumulation of sediment washed down from rivers, fanned along the coast by currents, and pounded into a semblance of geological form by the surf. The island's shoreface is paralleled by three submerged bars, with deep troughs between them, that are the last easily discernible features of the sea bottom before it planes out for its long, monotonous drop along the continental slope. The smooth, wind-generated waves of the ocean, coasting along the consistent upgrade of the bottom, trip over the outermost bar, regenerate somewhat in the trough, and then break and reform again for the next two series, finally reaching the shore itself with a weary, slouching motion. Because of the bars the surf is predictable but sloppy, the waves rebuilding and expending themselves all in a distance of a few hundred feet.

The beach itself is several hundred feet wide, and beyond it are the high and stable foredunes, secured by spartina grass and sea oats from the constant scouring of the wind. The grass flats behind the dunes are stable too, in their way, having been eroded down to ancient sand deposits whose surprisingly regular stratigraphy has been spoiled by the ceaseless disturbance of burrowing animals and rooting plants. But beyond this savannah the dunes are clean and virginal, expanses so utterly without shade or protection that practically no living thing interferes with their architectural purity. The dunes are lower than the foredunes, and blindingly white. And though constantly moving, they are not arbitrary forms. Their complex structure is implied by the wind ripples and slip faces that mark their surfaces. Beyond the dune field is a tidal flat, overgrown with marsh grass, that shelves with no particular demarcation into the lagoon and the deep mud that underlies it.

All this is within the field of the hawk's exquisite vision. High up in the sky the full moon is still visible, as pale as a cloud. At this time of the day the moon is simply a receding ornament, but its effects upon the creatures of the island are profound. All of the waters of the world fall a little toward the moon, as gravity demands. The oceans bulge outward, lagging in their momentum as the earth spins beneath, generating immense longitudinal waves that, when they reach land, are known as tides.

It is high tide now, on this island a visually unspectacular event, since the water rarely rises or falls more than a foot or two. The swash line—the farthest boundary of the surf—has advanced several yards up the beach, leaving a string of muddy, deflated foam and a new wave of detritus: broken shells, mangrove pods from the Yucatán, worm tubes, parts of crabs, plastic rings that once held six-packs of beer together, seaweed, lightbulbs, gooseneck barnacles slowly dying of exposure on a piece of driftwood.

To the creatures that live within the surf zone the tide is a critical occurrence. Most of them live either beneath the sand or somehow secured to it and would be helpless if dislodged. They have no way of controlling themselves in the violence of the waves, no way to go in search of the tiny planktonic forms upon which their existence depends. The tides bring the plankton to them, and the creatures use whatever means they have for extracting it from the environment. Sand dollars, traveling just beneath the sand of the outermost trough, trap the plankton in minute spines that cover their sturdy, chambered bodies and move it along to their mouths. Nearly microscopic creatures called larvaceans construct a kind of house around their bodies, with which they trap and filter protein. Bivalves like the coquina clam open their shells just enough to send up a siphon to draw in the plankton.

In their makeshift burrows just inside the surf a colony of coquinas is monitoring the violence of the waves above them. They can feel the power of the water, and the relative cessation of that power, by the intensity of the tremors it sends through the unstable sand in which they are buried. The clams read the disposition and duration of each wave. They hold themselves down in the sand by extending a powerful muscle, known as a foot, from their shells and then clenching it to give them purchase in the shifting sediment of the bottom.

A wave breaks above them, shaking the tiny clams in their burrows. They are aware of the calm of the receding wave, and they are impelled to reduce the tension in their feet and use the muscle instead to boost themselves up above the sand, where they extend their siphons and suck in the water, with its oxygen and nutrients.

Sometimes they miscalculate and rise out of the sand to find themselves fruitlessly siphoning the open air, having been stranded on the beach by low tide or an especially powerful outgoing wave. At such times the tiny, pastel-colored clams look like a handful of pebbles half buried in the sand. But the illusion is momentary: the coquinas turn the sharp ends of their wing-shaped shells downward, extend their feet, and hitch themselves down into the security of the wet sand.

They are such dim, shapeless creatures within their shells; they are hardly imaginable, hardly recognizable as living beings. The shells are the calcified secretions of the clam, built layer by layer like the flowstone of a cave. The creatures themselves are as impalpable as the shells are exact: a blob containing viscera, gills, muscles that control digestion and motion, and muscles that hold the wings of the shell shut with remarkable tenacity to protect the helpless protoplasm inside. The clam's brain consists of a few specialized ganglia strung out along a neural cord. The creature has no eyes, no sense of smell, no hearing. Yet in some way it is as ardent about its existence as the bottle-nosed dolphin that has ridden the tide over the highest bar and is chasing a school of mullet now in the trough. Within the intertidal zone, as well as upon the island itself, there are no degrees of existence, only a range of mysteries, secrets of perception that every species withholds from all others.

Coquina clams live for about a year if they do not fall victim to the wide range of predators that swarm or swim or walk within the surf. Bottom-feeding fish like drums or croakers cruise above the sand, probing with the barbels on their chins for buried mollusks and then popping the creatures into their mouths with impressive speed. Willet feed on the coquinas in the receding waves, grabbing the still-extended feet of the clams in their bills. With a twist of their heads, the birds then snap the adductor muscles that hold the shell together. Coquinas also fall prey to other mollusks, carnivorous snails that have the gift of locomotion.

One such creature is making its way now toward a colony of coquinas. It is a shark's eye, named for the center point in the whorled design of its shell. The shell rides on the back of the mollusk, which is an almost liquid mass of such volume that it is difficult to imagine how it could ever work itself back inside. Far in advance of the shell are the creature's tentacles, and below them, almost invisible, are two "eyes," blotches of sensitive pigment through which it can sense gross changes in the quality of light. The mollusk glides along on its foot, secreting a film of mucus to smooth the way. Its flesh is formless and almost transparent. The shark's eye burrows easily into the sand and comes out again, unimpeded by the underwater terrain. Though its tentacles are waving rhythmically ahead, more than just the sense of touch they provide guides the snail. It is drawn forward by the smell of the clams, a sense that comes to the snail through a minute organ near its gills.

It tracks the clams relentlessly and thoughtlessly, pulled along by its own appetite. The coquina that it will destroy is unaware of its presence and unequipped to escape anyway. Perhaps in the seawater it draws through its siphon the clam can detect the one-part-per-billion presence of the snail, but such an advance warning cannot mitigate its helplessness.

The snail closes in so slowly that its victim's death seems ordained, and the action itself monumental, as if the mollusks were two landmasses drifting together. When the snail finally reaches the clam it unhesitatingly smothers it with the mass of its body and bores a hole through the shell, rasping in a circular motion with the minute denticles in its mouth. When the hole is drilled the snail inserts its proboscis and begins the process of absorbing the clam. It takes hours to accomplish this, and all the while the other members of the coquina colony pop up and down in accordance with the rhythm of the waves.

Strewn all along the beach are the empty shells of coquinas and cockles, each with a neat hole drilled through it. The evidence of predation and destruction is everywhere. The sea brings an astonishing variety of creatures, pulverized or whole and dying, onto the beach. A hardhead catfish washes up onto the sand, its sharp dorsal fin rising up and down with the heaving of its gills; a yellow sea whip, a thin rope of polyps uprooted from its anchoring place, ends up entwined on the beach with the tendrils of a Portuguese man-of-war; a small sprig of brown sargassum floats up on the tide, the host to a doomed and incredibly diverse community of hydroids, nudibranchs, crabs, shrimps, worms, and fish.

Perhaps nowhere else is the fact of death so obvious and unremitting. The most imposing feature of the seashore is the spectacle of life worn down and out, pummeled into its component parts. The dynamic of the littoral is a constant process of disintegration, a process evident even in the sand itself, whose grains are the result of the seemingly infinite weathering and grinding of rocks.

Most of the active life of the beach is hidden, secreted away in burrows or calcified tubes, covered with sand, cemented to or tunneled into driftwood. The only consistently visible creatures on the shore are birds. Standing at the surf line, looking seaward with concentration, is a mixed population of laughing gulls and rather large, stocky terns—Caspian terns. The gulls are in their summer plumage, their heads hooded with black. The terns' heads are white, but with a black crest flattened back against their heads by the offshore wind. When they are not standing on shore the terns fly low and fast over the water, their wings canted sharply backward. They are diving birds, with the characteristic of dropping into the water as if they had been suddenly shot out of the sky. Whenever a tern manages to catch a fish in this fashion he must then defend it in an exhaustive aerial dispute with the gulls, who are more aggressive and persistent and are capable of running a tern almost to ground.

But standing together on the beach, the terns and gulls are at peace, narcotized by the rhythm of the surf. Sanderlings poke around near their feet, and just above the water a frigate bird soars, a strange dihedral kink in each wing and a quality of reserve in the manner in which it simply bends down and extracts a fish from the waves. There are black skimmers out there too, and spring migrants—swallows and Baltimore orioles and a Chuck-will's-widow—that have flown all the way across the Gulf with instinctive reckoning and endurance.

Within the crowd of shorebirds there are occasional desultory episodes of mating. A male tern bobs his head, struts about, and hops onto a female's back, grabbing her by the neck and then flapping his wings and squawking. When it is over the male hops down and looks out to sea again, his fervor of a moment earlier completely forgotten.

It is the mating season for other vertebrate inhabitants of the island as well. Back behind the dunes a keeled earless lizard skims over the loose sand as lightly as a water bug. The lizard skitters forward for a few feet and then stops, bobbing his head in much the same way as the birds on the beach, advertising himself to whatever females may be around. The lizard is preoccupied with the urge to mate. His skin has broken out in black nuptial bars that run along either side of his body. Somewhere in the same dune field there is a female, but she is already gravid from an earlier encounter with this same male. She is, however, still flushed with her own mating display—an understated suffusion of yellows and oranges where the male has his black bands. Her body is swollen with the eggs she will soon deposit without ceremony into the sand.

The male lizard continues to bob his head, casting about in the vast dune field for another mate. Then he moves on, unfulfilled but undeterred, over the crest of a dune and out to a bed of hard sand where his long digits leave no tracks but where the prints of coyotes, foxes, and skunks are deeply impressed. Beneath a mat of vegetation at the edge of a clear expanse of dunes, the lizard stops, filled with the primal knowledge that to cross the barren sand would be suicidal. Overhead, the white-tailed hawk is circling, stable in the thermals, scanning the brush for a signal, for a movement such as the lizard will give when he bobs his head in autonomic longing.

As the day wears on, the lizard becomes progressively less active, finding relief from the heat in the shade of the dune grass. During the afternoon most of the terrestrial inhabitants of the island are likewise holed up, waiting for the cycle of predation and opportunity that the coolness of the evening will bring about. The cycle continues, of course, in the ocean, and in the tidal marshes at the back of the island, where hermit crabs stagger about beneath the weight of the abandoned gastropod shells they have taken over, to which they have fitted themselves almost as firmly as the original inhabitants. The crabs are, for the most part, very small, their hind parts carefully contorted into the inner chambers of moon shells and whelks. Only their claws are visible, and with these claws they pull themselves along the mud bottom of the flat or up the sheer faces of rocks.

When, at length, the sun begins to go down, the hermit crabs are not aware of it, but to many other creatures the coolness and the beginning of darkness are signals to come out of their torpor and hiding and into their nocturnal wakefulness.

In the grasslands midway between the dunes and the mud flats there is a large, brackish pond and several acres of outlying marshland. In a red-winged blackbird's abandoned nest, slightly elevated in the vegetation beside the pond, a rice rat is nursing her five offspring. It is dark in the nest. The rat has reinforced it with bits of grasses and sedges and left a solitary side entrance that lets in some of the fading light. The babies are two days old, and already they are active and demanding. In only a few days they will be on their own, making exploratory trips from the nest and then, on the tenth or eleventh day of their lives, being booted out by their mother. The rat will then mate again and lose no time in driving away the male whose presence she has endured only for the sake of procreation. None of this, of course, does the rat plan. It simply happens, and for now she is wholeheartedly a mother, as devoted to the little squirming forms at her belly as it is in her power to be.

But the babies are draining her reserves of strength and she is hungry. Before they are quite finished she stands up on her whispery little feet and drops out of the door of the nest. She scoots around a miniature inlet of the pond and wanders for a while through the thick jungle of the marsh grass before returning to the shoreline. She finds an insect to eat, a small crab and a jackknife clam, and then, because she is so hungry from the nursing, feeds for a while on the partially decomposed carcass of a lizard. She works her way up and down the muddy fringes of the pond, and then her hunger drives her farther back into the vegetation than she would normally go. Suddenly, in some unspecific way, she is alarmed; she quivers for a fraction of a second, her heart seizes up, and then every muscle and nerve of her body come together in one great convulsive leap as a pair of fangs plow into the sand where a moment earlier she was standing.

The rat does not bother to follow the shoreline now. She splashes headlong into the water and submerges, holding her breath and swimming beneath the murky water. She careens off the shell of a turtle and, closer to shore, swims between the legs of a reddish egret. She makes it to the opening of her nest with an easy leap and lies inside on her belly, with her heart pounding and the baby rice rats trying to burrow down to her nipples.

The massasauga rattlesnake that put the rice rat through such trauma is moving away from the marshland and into the drier grass flats. The failure with the rat has cost him no loss of momentum or determination. His passage over the loose sand is swift and rhythmic. He can see and hear and sense heat, and yet another sense originates in his tongue, which he sends out ahead of him to record the particulate density of prey in the air. This information is stored on the tongue and processed through an organ at the back of the mouth. The resulting knowledge comes to the snake as taste. Already now he is receiving an intimation, the subtlest bouquet of kangaroo rat. The sensation gets stronger, until it is accompanied by the thumping of the creature's feet, a noise that the snake hears through the ground. He positions himself in a coil just off the kangaroo rat's path. He is very still and trancelike. The massasauga is a small snake, and for a rattlesnake has a small mouth. But then his venom—a neurotoxin—is much stronger than most other rattlesnakes'.

When the kangaroo rat comes down the path the snake strikes him in mid-stride, injecting the venom and then removing the fangs before the rat has even had time to become aware of the danger. Once he has registered the fact that he has been struck the rat leaps high into the air and hops away at top speed. The massasauga does not follow or seem concerned. He simply stays where he is, gathering his body together in a loose coil, resting until some internal timer tells him that the poison has done its work.

For long minutes the snake does not stir, and then finally he begins crawling in the direction of the rat. He moves his head from side to side, flicking his tongue and catching a strong taste of rat urine and fear. About a dozen yards down the path he finds the rat on the ground, convulsing. When the body is still the snake moves up to it, running his tongue along it and then slowly opening his jaws to take it in. But then the rat makes one last effort, leaping from the snake's mouth, landing a foot away, and then twitching until he is still again. This time the snake waits awhile before finally moving in to begin the process of swallowing the rat headfirst.

Back at the pond several dozen diamondback terrapins have risen to the surface, their heads stippling the smooth surface of the water. The heads appear disembodied, and in their fixed, identical expressions they have a hallucinatory quality, as if the mood expressed in those reptilian faces were the true disposition of the pond. The turtles secrete saltwater from their eyes, take in air through their nostrils, and bask indolently in the last remaining light of day. Soon they will swim over to the bank and bury themselves in mud for the night.

At this late hour the pond and the surrounding marsh are congested with bird life: willet, avocets, Louisiana herons, black-necked stilts, American bitterns. They are all feeding, after their fashions, or stalking about, or simply standing still in the water, breathing in the calmness of twilight. Except for the bird cries and the sudden flights of blackbirds and terns across the pond, the marsh is mute and still, the blood of its creatures at low tide.

Now, as if entering a stage that has been set for them, come two roseate spoonbills. They are soaring low above the marsh, banking and teetering and coasting in the invisible element of the air. Their pink plumage, deepened by the quality of the remaining light, is gorgeous and alien. The spoonbills cruise low over the shallow marsh water, ease down within a foot of each other, and begin feeding with their heads submerged, moving their odd, spatulate, primitive beaks through the mud. There is a strong but tranquil breeze rippling the surface of the water where they stand and ruffling their feathers. The burst of color they bring to the subtle camouflage shading of the marsh is startling; the color of the spoonbills seems a mistake, or a conscious provocation, or some sort of benevolent gift. Even after the sun has gone down the birds are charged, for a long moment, with its light.

In the darkness the massasauga moves across the highway, the kangaroo rat still an undigested bulge in the center of his body. The asphalt has retained heat and the rattlesnake pauses to absorb it. All at once he hears a monumental commotion from the substratum that actually shakes him a little from side to side. The snake's concern is uncomplicated and cold, but very real. He tries to get away but moves forward just exactly enough for a moving car to crush his head. Some moments later a solitary coyote, after checking the highway for headlights, walks out and picks the snake up in his teeth, then carries the carcass to the side of the road and eats it, heartened by the bonus of the kangaroo rat.

Darkness has come over the beach with little transition. A cottontail rabbit moves about the shoreward face of the dunes, which is pocketed with the fresh burrows of ghost crabs. From one of these burrows a crab emerges, extending its reticulated limbs and wiping the sand from its eyes with its antennae. The crab needs to replenish the seawater it stores within its gills; it is short of breath. It moves across the sand and down to the swash line, positioning itself there for a low, spent wave from which it can extract the water it needs to survive its terrestrial life. Hundreds of other ghost crabs are doing the same thing, or foraging about near the surf for smaller crabs and for stranded coquina clams whose shells they can chip away with their claws.

Several of the crabs stop to feed on the long tendrils of a beached Portuguese man-of-war. There are other men-of-war in the surf, helpless to control their fate in the choppy waves. Beyond the outermost bar, however, is a large flotilla of these creatures, their purple sacs driven by the wind across the surface of the water. The men-of-war are not individual animals, they are strange aggregates of other organisms, all of them too highly specialized to exist on their own. Small fish swimming through the man-of-war's trailing tentacles are injected with a powerful toxin and then eaten by the countless solitary forms.

For all its biological divisiveness, the man-of-war's will is single. In some way it recognizes the danger to its existence from the prevailing wind and adjusts the puckered "sail" on the top of its gas-filled float to compensate, allowing itself to tack steadily seaward.

As the man-of-war fleet moves away from the beach the tendrils trail across the form of a pilot whale dying of natural causes at the edge of the bar. Unlike the men-of-war, the whale brims with awareness, though he is old and emaciated and no longer alert to his dying. He has been drifting aimlessly for days, and the overpowering loneliness and fright he had felt earlier have been replaced by waves of delirium interrupted by lucid moments of resignation. The whale is twenty feet long, his deep black color unrelieved by markings of any kind. He can feel the breakers trying to lift his bulk over the bar, he can feel his bulbous forehead scraping on the broken shells in the sand bottom. The vertigo he feels brings with it a not entirely unpleasant suggestion of diffusion, and he sees his own death as a process of absorption by the sea.

A half mile away the white-tailed hawk, perched in his tree, can make out the slick black form of the whale in the waves. He can see also the bioluminescence in each wave face, the collective glow of millions upon millions of protozoan forms. The hawk understands neither of these phenomena, but all that the hawk does not know is irrelevant. It is what he knows that counts. The same is true for the manta ray cruising outside the surf, for the mole tunneling beneath the dunes, for the beachcomber walking along the swash line. They know what they need from the island, and they sense that although the sea continually prograzes and erodes it, its life is a greater constant than their own.

GOING INTO THE DESERT

There are two ways to look at the desert. You can see it contriving to extinguish life or straining to support it. It all depends upon your mood, and in the desert your mood depends upon water. One of the first symptoms of dehydration is a loss of morale, a disquieting awareness that the landscape has suddenly turned hostile. But to someone who has had plenty of water to drink, whose thoughts are not gloomy, the desert can appear bounteous.

When I was in the Chihuahuan Desert recently, hiking through the volcanic outwash plains or along limestone ridges sodden with midday light, I found myself obsessively scanning the ground for the translucent maroon blooms of the strawberry pitaya. The flowers of this cactus are meant to attract bees and other pollinators, but in that blanched landscape I was hungry for color too. And I knew that on some of these plants the fruit would be ripening. I had more than enough water, and I usually carried oranges as well, so it would have been more considerate of me to pass the fruit by and leave it for the cactus wrens or carpenter ants. But I was not feeling quite so refined. In the desert, the temptation to seek out moisture is irresistible.

I usually found half-a-dozen blooms on each cactus, though the flowers of the ripe fruits had shriveled to crepe. At that stage the fruits themselves no longer needed protecting, so the dried needles covering the purplish skin could be dusted off with a finger. Peeled, the fruit was a mushy gray ball studded with what looked like poppy seeds—nothing you would think to eat under ordinary circumstances. But the tart pulp tasted, as advertised, like strawberries, or close enough, convincing me that the desert was in some sense benevolent, that for all its austerity it supported pockets of beauty and opportunity. It was an inhospitable place that made me feel welcome.

The Chihuahuan Desert is vast but obscure. Unlike American deserts such as the Sonoran, with its shadeless forests of saguaro cacti, or the Mojave, with its parched playa lakes, the Chihuahuan has no clear emblem to fix it in the popular imagination. (A friend once told me that whenever he hears the words "Chihuahuan Desert" he pictures a pack of hairless, yipping dogs running through a field of sand dunes.) But like the Sonoran and the Mojave—like the Great Basin, the Sahara, the Namib, the Atacama, the Kalahari—the Chihuahuan is a region of low rainfall and high temperatures, where evaporation exceeds precipitation, where water is the most precious thing imaginable.

There is no real agreement about where the Chihuahuan Desert begins and ends. It is not so much a place as it is a condition. Meteorologists fix its borders according to annual rainfall, biologists according to certain plant or animal associations. Those of us who have no need to be precise about the matter can see the desert's reach clearly enough. It's a great, arid swath that extends from the southern borders of the Mexican state of Coahuila all the way up to White Sands National Monument in New Mexico. On some maps it dominates almost all of Texas between El Paso and the Pecos River. On others it is not quite so extensive, but by any reckoning the Chihuahuan covers an immense portion of the Trans-Pecos.

Some ecologists say it consists of 175,000 square miles, making it the largest desert in North America. We may believe them if we like, but the Chihuahuan is so various, so clearly not just one thing, that talk of scale and size can begin to sound irrelevant. In the bajadas and bolsons, in the creosote flats and gypsum dunes, the desert is ferociously real. But you might find yourself in a high mountain oasis filled with evergreens and clouds, or beside a deep, clear pool fringed with luxuriant grass, and wonder just what the desert has to do with these places at all. It is correct, say the ecologists, to think of the badlands and the lush islands as all of a piece, as part of the same biome, the same xeric province. When described in such ecospeak terms, the desert can seem ambiguous. But when you travel to the low, hot, waterless places, its hold is unmistakable.

In the extreme lowlands, hardly anything grows higher than your waist, and when the sun is high its light falls hard and straight. Beneath this burdensome light the desert floor has the feel of a sea bottom—a place ruled by a crushing atmosphere, where life is stunted and scarce. It is not an easy place to love at that time of day, when everything visible seems washed out or fixed in some monotonous middle distance.

"Here in the desert you have to train yourself to look for detail," Alan Brenner, the education director at the Chihuahuan Desert Research Institute in Alpine, told me one day as we walked along in such a landscape. "The big picture is spectacular, and the little picture is spectacular, but the picture in between is daunting to most sensibilities."

The flat plain was paved with volcanic cobbles, and the in-between picture that Brenner spoke of consisted almost entirely of creosote bush, the world champion desert scrub. These spindly, tensile plants, with their tight little leaves, fanned out in every direction, as evenly spaced as the trees in a fruit orchard. There was something hypnotic in their regularity. Like clouds that arrange themselves in sky-spanning columns, the creosote seemed to hint that nature was filled with infinite patterns that the human eye could not quite detect.

Creosote is an invader. It makes its way into environments where other plants have given up hope, sends out its shallow roots, and thrives. Creosote began its conquest some time after the last ice age, when what is now the Chihuahuan Desert was a woodland filled with piñon, juniper, and oak. As the ice sheets retreated and the climate began to dry out, the forests tended to give way to desert grasslands and finally to desert scrub. How desolate any particular region became depended largely on its elevation, with the high mountain environments surviving as relics of a greener time.

In the lower elevations, where piñon and juniper feared to tread, the field was left to things like creosote and cacti that had a decided preference for godforsaken ground. A cactus deals with its arid surroundings by soaking up water in times of plenty and storing it within. Because a cactus must protect that store of water from evaporation, it is cautious about opening its stomata, the minute pores on its surface through which it gathers carbon dioxide.

Creosote, on the other hand, is so efficient at slurping up every molecule of moisture in the vicinity that it has no need to store water. Furthermore, its small, waxy leaves help prevent evaporation, making it feasible for the plant to be on-line during the hottest part of the day. When a drought comes and not even the wily creosote can find water, it drops its leaves and hunkers down. One theory about why the plants are so evenly spaced holds that the dead leaves contain a chemical that may suppress other plants that might be trying to gain a foothold beneath them. Another opinion is that a creosote bush extracts so much water from the soil that nothing else can survive within its immediate radius.

As I walked through the creosote that afternoon, the temperature rose above one hundred. I was used to humidity, so the dry heat was disconcerting. I had no sensation of thirst, and because the sweat evaporated almost immediately from my skin I was barely aware that I was perspiring. But while walking in that environment I was losing about a quart of water an hour, and whenever I went too long without topping off my body moisture I could feel my mental acuity begin to deteriorate.

Things can go wrong quickly in the desert if the water the body loses through evaporation isn't replaced. A friend of mine, when he was seventeen, came close to dying of dehydration when he got lost near the Chinati Mountains. Only a few hours after drinking the last of his water, he remembers, he began to feel dizzy and depressed. By late that afternoon he was having hallucinations. "They were very, very vivid," he recalled. "In the first one my dad appeared on horseback and asked me if I was exhausted. He was dressed exactly the same as when I'd last seen him. I could hear his horse. It was so incredibly real that when he disappeared I was madder than ever."

By evening he had begun to lose his motor control and could not even manage to bring his hands up to break his frequent falls. He fell asleep twice but each time began immediately to dream about water. In the dreams he would raise the water to his mouth, but just as he was taking a drink he would swallow in his sleep. The pain in his throat was so bad it woke him.

He tried to drink his urine but could not make himself do it. His swollen tongue hurt as if he'd bitten it. All he could think about was what it would be like to take a drink. When he was found the next afternoon and the great moment finally arrived, his throat was so swollen he could not swallow—the water just trickled down so that he could barely feel its presence. It was hours before he was even able to experience the sensation of relief. For two days he lay in a room drinking pitchers of iced tea.

Humans can adapt to desert life only by caution, by careful attention. Our surest survival strategy is an instinct to stay out of the sun. This is a trait we share with many other desert creatures, no matter how specialized their own evolutionary tactics have become. The kangaroo rat, for instance, spends its days beneath the earth in a deep burrow, whose opening it carefully plugs with dirt to keep out the searing heat. It sleeps with its tiny paws in front of its snout in order to trap the refuge's precious humidity and hold it close. The creature comes out at night, a nervous, bounding thing with a twitching nose. Its head in proportion to the rest of its body is immense, equipped with voluminous cheek pouches that are meant to be filled with seeds. The legs appear spindly but are strong enough to launch the kangaroo rat in sometimes spectacular leaps across the starlit desert floor. The tail is long and thick, often tufted at the end; it is used for balance and to keep the rat stable in midair as it smites rivals with its feet.

In its evolutionary repertoire, the kangaroo rat has one extraordinary trick: it does not consume water. There are other desert inhabitants—rabbits and so forth—that rarely drink "free" water but get their moisture allotments from fruits and succulent plants. But the kangaroo rat is a far step ahead. Deep in its industrious little body, mixing the starches from seeds it consumes with the oxygen in the air, it manufactures its own water. All animals do this to some degree but at nowhere near a level that would be sufficient for survival. The kangaroo rat, however, is phenomenally thrifty with the water it produces. It hardly sweats, and its urine is five times as concentrated as that of humans. Under extreme deprivation in heartless laboratory experiments, a few kangaroo rats have been induced to drink water, but in the normal course of their lives they never need to consider such a drastic measure.

As I walked across the desert I thought of the kangaroo rat, a little organic still that was bundled up in the darkness below my boots. There were other burrows, filled with other slumbering forms that were waiting for the earth to become habitable again. The wolf spider's burrow was small and guarded by a silky rampart that the spider had spun around its circumference. I peered into the larger burrows, trying to imagine what sort of creature was down in the cool and nearly absolute dark: a badger, a cottontail, a rattlesnake; maybe a carnivorous grasshopper mouse, which is in its own way as predaceous and far ranging as a mountain lion, controlling a hunting range of eight acres. There were toads down there and desiccated fairy shrimp waiting for months or even years to be reconstituted by the touch of water.

Lizards darted across my path as I walked through the scrub. Lizards are generally more heat tolerant than snakes, though like all reptiles they have no means of regulating their temperature internally. When it gets too hot or cold, they remove themselves to a more bearable place. For now, the desert floor was fine. One sort—the greater earless—ran in short bursts, pulling up every few feet with their backs stiffened and their black-and-white-striped tails curved upward like the stinger of a scorpion. They held this pose patiently, as if they wanted to be admired.

The more colorful whiptail lizards were swifter, their movements as elusive to the eye as shooting stars. Chihuahuan lizards tend to be small game compared with some that live in the Sonoran. There you have stocky chuckwallas and desert iguanas. The venomous Gila monster never enters the Texas desert, though many Texans still tread fearfully, expecting it to rush out of the brush at any moment and lock its jaws around their flesh. (Although Gila monsters are not within our purview, I can't refrain from passing on these first-aid instructions printed in Peggy Larson's valuable guidebook, *The Deserts of the Southwest*: "Remove the lizard from the bite as rapidly as possible, as the lizard continues to chew venom into the victim while it remains attached.

It may be difficult to disengage the reptile. . . . Its jaws may be pried open with pliers, etc. A strong tasting or smelling liquid [such as alcohol, chloroform, gasoline] may be poured into its mouth, or a flame may be applied to the lizard's jaw. [Refrain from using the gasoline and the flame methods in conjunction!]")

Fortunately, a visitor to the Chihuahuan Desert requires neither pliers nor chloroform. At least some lizards here—a few species of the little whiptails—make up in weirdness for what they may lack in size or notoriety. Members of these species are all females, and they have developed the knack of reproducing themselves without the participation of males.

Such dynasties begin with a materfamilias, possibly the female progeny of a chance mating of lizards from two similar but distinct whiptail species. Like a mule, which is the product of the union of a horse and a donkey, this lizard is a hybrid. But a mule is sterile, whereas a female whiptail can make carbon copies of herself. Nobody's quite sure how she does it. Apparently she produces a chemical that aggravates the membranes of her eggs and makes them cleave, a job that in a more traditional fashion would be accomplished by the sperm of a male lizard. The egg develops, but without the sperm it has no new genetic input, and so out pops a duplicate of the mother.

Sometimes the desert feels as if it is governed by such alien mores, by unfathomable principles and practices, by secrets. But the desert is a human environment, too, the frontier of privation to which we are always peculiarly receptive. We speak of "going into the desert," and we mean nothing less than seeking our true selves. It is a place where one goes to be scoured and purified, to await visions.

One day I hiked across the flats to an isolated promontory of intrusive rock. On a ledge twenty or thirty feet above the ground were petroglyphs, and nearby were narrow grooves that the Indians had cut into the rock and used to sharpen their arrow points and straighten the shafts. The ground was littered with flint chips, and there were deep metates in the rock, some filled with dirty rainwater, that were as smooth and precise as if they had been drilled by a machine. Through my binoculars I looked across the drab flats to the foothills of a desert mountain range and saw, at that slightly higher elevation, the withered bloom stalks of agaves and scattered tufts of death-defying grass. It was a classic Chihuahuan Desert vista, and I thought of how the rock on which I was standing must have been a landmark and a refuge in this region for thousands of years.

The earliest desert peoples here were hunter-gatherers—or, as one author insists, gatherer-hunters, since most of their diet consisted of food that had been found rather than killed. We know this through the study of coprolites, which were discreetly described to me as "fossilized doo-doo." Coprolite samples taken from a rock shelter that was inhabited during the Archaic Period—from about 9000 B.C. to A.D. 1000—indicate that the people who lived there were inspired omnivores. "The eclectic diet was a complete surprise," writes Glenna Dean, one of the archeologists involved in the survey. "We can imagine a daily rodent eaten along with prickly pear pads and one or another type of fruit or crunchy as a side dish—a blue plate 'rat sandwich.'"

Some parts of the desert were more hospitable than others. Near Presidio, at the fertile junction of the Rio Conchos and the Rio Grande, there lived a farming people called the Jumanos, who represented the advancing edge of the Puebloan civilizations of New Mexico and Colorado. But that sort of pastoral existence was beyond the reach of most desert Indians, who foraged on the land and hunted in the high mountains for game.

"The multitude is innumerable in every direction," stated a report to the king of Spain in 1679 concerning the Indian population of the Chihuahuan Desert. The names of these peoples—Tepeguanes, Conchos, Salineros, Cabezas, Tobosas, Coahuileños, Chisos—have slipped from history, but their presence was very real. They lived within the boundaries of Spanish ambition, and they fought hard against the constant press of would-be conquistadores. In the end, many of them were exterminated or sold as slaves to the mine operators of Nueva Vizcaya, but their desert homeland remained, in essence, unconquered. The Spanish could barely tolerate this wilderness, much less hold it as a secure part of the empire. It was the Apaches and later the Comanches who were the true rulers, though finally their reign was vivid but short-lived.

Wagon trails were opened across the desert, linking—sometimes more in theory than in practice—the cities of Chihuahua and El Paso with Gulf ports like Indianola and New Orleans. A railroad appeared. There were a few modest silver strikes, along with quicksilver mines and real estate speculation and factories for rendering wax from the candelilla plant. But none of that could put an end to the desert's isolation or alter its character.

Ranching, however, went a long way toward changing the face of the desert—by creating more of it. The process started during the First World War, when many ranchers, tempted by an improved market for beef, overburdened their land with livestock. The complex desert grasslands turned to simple desert scrub. J. O. Langford, an early homesteader, wrote poignantly of this change. A malaria victim, he had moved with his young family to the Big Bend area in 1909 to recover his health and found a kind of peace in the desert that he was fated never to know again. The border turmoils of 1913 forced him to retreat to El Paso, where he operated a filling station and where his little daughter, who had survived rattlesnakes and bandits in the desert, was electrocuted while playing on a swing. Years later he managed to move his family back to the desert, but it was not the same. "Where once I'd thought there was more grass than could ever be eaten off," he wrote, "I found no grass at all. Just the bare, rain-eroded ground. . . . Somehow, the brightness seemed gone from the land."

Toward midafternoon I found myself on top of a miniature mesa whose summit looked as if it had been hammered flat by the force of the sun. All around me grew lechuguilla, the fiercest plant in the desert. Its Spanish name translates to "little lettuce," but what it resembles more is an armor-plated artichoke. The lechuguilla's leaves are strong and sharp, and on the slopes that the plant favors, its leaves point uphill in palsied, clawlike clusters. To a person picking his way down such a slope, the plants can appear bloodthirsty and grasping. Lechuguilla lives at least three or four years, husbanding water in its thick leaves, before finally erupting in a bloom stalk that can be ten feet high.

I was too late for the lechuguilla's yellow flowers, but the desert slopes were filled with dried-out stalks that either had fallen to the ground or were on the verge of collapse. I picked up a few and used them as poles to set up a tarp. There was no shade for miles, nothing besides the thin lechuguilla stalks capable of casting a shadow, and I didn't realize until

I slipped under the tarp how deeply I wanted to be out of the sun. I was overcome by a comfort that in any other climate I would have considered marginal.

I lay there all afternoon, torpid and unthinking. Nothing moved along the ground except for a desert millipede, a chain of compressed coils and feathery legs bound together by some animate need. The shadow of a turkey vulture passed over my foot, and I looked up to see the bird not far overhead, suspended in the air with no more consideration than it took for me to lie on the earth.

Turkey vultures are not really desert birds. They're equally at home in the tropics, where their acute sense of smell—rare for vultures—helps them locate carrion beneath dense forest canopies. But you cannot imagine the desert without their forms cruising overhead, soberly patrolling for signs of death.

Young turkey vultures are said to make good pets. They like to be handled and follow their owners around like dogs. And there is something about the look of a fledgling buzzard that exerts a strange pull on the human heart. Its downy, ungainly body contrasts disturbingly with its naked head, which makes it seem as cold-blooded as a pirate. A vulture, of course, is no more malevolent than any other creature, but not many people can afford it anything but grudging tolerance. We don't like the way it makes its living in general, and there's always the faint worry that one day it may be practicing its trade over our remains.

For such a task it is splendidly endowed. Its wings are useless for aerial pursuit, but perfect for hovering in the thermals, from which the vulture scans the panoramic stillness below. A turkey vulture's feet are equipped with claws, but they're not strong enough to grab a bird in flight. They're for holding on to a carcass while the vulture probes inside, ripping and chomping with its heavy-duty bill. It should come as no surprise that the vulture has a powerful digestive system. Chicks grow up eating regurgitated carrion provided by their parents and are able to process seemingly implacable items like bone and hide in a few days. Even with that iron stomach, though, the turkey vulture occasionally gets queasy. When stressed or frightened, it throws up. This happens frequently on highways, where birds working a road kill tend not to notice an oncoming car and have to scramble frantically to get airborne. The prudent thing for a driver to do in this situation is slow down, since vulture vomit is one of the foulest substances on earth. I'm told that if a vulture upchucks on your windshield you might as well sell the car.

At the other end of the avian spectrum are the minute lucifer hummingbirds that venture into the desert to feed on the nectar of flowering plants. During my long siesta I kept my eyes on a blooming century plant—rare for this low elevation—that stood in dramatic isolation fifty yards away. I was waiting for a hummingbird to stop by, but none ever did, and the more I waited, the more unlikely it seemed that such a fragile little bird could fly across this austere landscape without being fried in midair by the sun.

Unlike vultures, which loll about on desert updrafts and hardly move their wings except to alter their course, hummingbirds are an unceasing eruption of energy. It makes your pulse race just to watch them. Their own wings churn the air like rotors, and while the wings whizz frantically about its body the little bird is stabilized, able to hover in front of a flower and draw nectar into its long, grooved tongue, which, when not in use, lies coiled in the hummingbird's cranium like a fire hose.

The aerodynamic maneuvering is costly, and a hummingbird spends a good deal of time refueling. Though they supplement their diet with protein, using a forcepslike bill to pluck spiders from webs, hummingbirds subsist primarily on nectar. In the case of the century plant, they feed mainly on leftovers, since this particular agave has established an agreeable relationship with the Mexican long-nosed bat. The bats have even more prodigious tongues than hummingbirds do, made of erectile tissue that can become swiftly tumescent. A biologist, Donna Howell, has filmed bats feeding on agave flowers, and the slow-motion footage reveals a great amount of indecorous slurping. The bats are favored customers of the century plant, because during nocturnal feeding flurries they scatter pollen to other flowers or collect it on their fur. Howell found that the bats always leave a certain amount of nectar behind; they receive a message through some inscrutable channel that the energy expended in draining the flowers is greater than the fuel intake. The amount of nectar left in the flower is negligible for the bats, but it's well worth a stop the next day for the hummingbirds, who are used to tanking up microliter by microliter. The precise hummingbirds are no help in pollination, but the century plant, perhaps in some fashion exhausted after its nighttime rendezvous with the bats, does not seem to begrudge them.

It is only when the sun is low on the horizon that the desert takes on texture, becomes alluring in a conventional way. The shallow, sun-washed drainages begin to appear deep and inviting, places of refuge. The bleached arroyos that in the full light of day are nothing but impediments, that seem to crisscross the desert floor without logic, suddenly are charged with significance and possibility. Subtle contours in the land become apparent, and in the variable light the solid components of the desert seem to shift and change shape like clouds. The wind is up. The temperature is down. The body, whose resources have been preoccupied all afternoon with preventing heatstroke, begins to make adjustments. As evening deepens, you can feel the blood enlivening your brain once again, and you feel that, instead of coming to the end of a tiring day, you are rising from a long and stupefying sleep.

A little nighthawk, a poorwill, flies low over the scrub, emitting plaintive bursts of song. There is a watery, musky smell—the diluted essence of skunk—that indicates a javelina is nearby, blundering about with its inferior eyesight. The subdued colors of the desert fade, except for a strawberry pitaya flower, which continues to burn like a flame until there is no light to support it. Mosquitoes, bred in the drying puddles of a nearby arroyo, circle ceaselessly around your head and bore into your eardrums with their whine. It is the last thing you want in this contemplative landscape, to be annoyed. Tonight the desert is as petty as it is powerful—filled with minuscule, bothersome life as well as silent beasts who keep their thoughts to themselves as they stalk their prey on the ground or from the air. Vega is bright, and Venus rises with the Twins beneath the moon. Half of the moon is in shadow, and half is startlingly clear, glowing with eerie intensity, like the all-seeing eye of an owl. That is the real desert. In comparison with the moon, even the volcanic soil beneath your sleeping bag feels alive and impatient. A large beetle scuttles across your hand, mistaking it for a rock, for one more silent manifestation of the terrain.

The desert rainy season, such as it is, occurs in the summer. The higher elevations can receive as much as twenty inches of rainfall a year, but in the lowlands the total is much less. The Chihuahuan Desert, by and large, lies beyond the reach of serious precipitation. Tucked away in the heart of a huge landmass, the desert is not on the itinerary of the big seasonal storms spawned in the Gulf and the Pacific. The rain systems that come its way are likely to be trapped by the mountain ranges that border the Chihuahuan for almost its whole extent. There the storms are broken up, the moisture-laden air retreating to windward and the rain shadow below receiving only a hot, evaporative wind.

But in the summer, thunderstorms often find their way to the desert. They're brief and volatile, drenching the unprepared soil and filling the dry washes with fast-moving sheets of floodwater. All sorts of things crawl out of the ground then, ready to feed and mate, to get on with a life that may have been held in suspension for months. I drove along a desert road recently after a rain. From my open window I could hear the bleating of what were probably spadefoot toads, and millipedes by the hundreds were crossing the road. Perhaps it was my imagination, but they all seemed to be crossing at the same angle; it was as if they were all single expressions of some larger impulse, some thought.

A desert tarantula was crossing the road as well. I stopped the car and watched it. It was about six inches long and moved slowly, probing with a pair of forelegs. Each step it took seemed reasoned. I put my hand in its path, and it crawled up to my wrist before thinking better of it and moving back to the asphalt. Tarantulas are capable of inflicting a painful, mildly venomous bite, but if they are handled with consideration they're extremely forbearing. Their abdomens are covered with a mat of short, fine hairs—irritating to certain predators—which they can shed when provoked.

Odds were that this tarantula, being on the prowl, was a male. If he was sexually mature, he was at least ten years old. His future was cloudy, however, given female tarantulas' propensity for eating their mates.

Tarantulas live on insects and other spiders, but they're fully capable of pouncing on a creature as large as a mouse and knocking it out with their venom. After that, they pump it full of digestive juices and leisurely suck away its insides. The tarantula's mortal enemy is the tarantula hawk, a wasp that stings the spider until it is comatose, then drags it off and uses it as a nest. When the wasp's larvae hatch, they begin to consume the still-living spider, bringing a protracted end to a life that may have spanned twenty-five years.

As I drove I saw roadrunners, hunched forward in a kind of Groucho Marx posture, speed across the highway in front of my car, sometimes taking a short hop to the summit of a scrubby mesquite. A large snake, bright pink, hurled itself at my tires. I jerked the steering wheel back and forth and careened all over the road trying to avoid it, feeling a little put out at the effort. I could have run over the snake and no jury in the world would have convicted me, but when I looked into the rearview mirror and saw it escaping into the brush unharmed I had to congratulate myself on my evasive driving skills. But the larger satisfaction was in not having caused a meaningless death, in not having insinuated my Buick Regal into the desert's balance of peril.

Up ahead a jackrabbit was perched tensely on the side of the road, waiting for whatever signal it needed to break and run. Its ears were enormous—they looked as if they were intended to gather data from outer space. The animal itself appeared gaunt and tested. When it finally took off, it crossed the road with astonishing speed, bounding forward on its immense hind legs. When it reached the other side it ran in zigzags through the creosote and vanished under my gaze.

A jackrabbit is not a rabbit. It's a hare. Unlike rabbits, which are born naked in burrows, hares come into the world covered with fur, their eyes open, their minds already factoring the chances of escape over open ground. Jackrabbits survive by vigilance and speed. They live alone, sleeping in little scraped-out depressions in the earth called forms. They're vegetarians, and the tiny indentations you often find along the edges of prickly pear pads are evidence that a jackrabbit has been feeding there.

Further on, another shape crossed the road. This was a canine, and I almost gasped at the thought it might be a wolf. Its haunches were scrawny, but it was larger than any coyote I'd ever seen, and it had a thick, reddish ruff at its neck. Its wildness was breathtaking. As it scrambled over a rise it reminded me of one of those wolves in Disney cartoons who appear on a mountaintop, ragged and lordly, in a flash of lightning.

But it could not have been a wolf. The last wolves in the Chihuahuan Desert disappeared, as far as anyone can tell, sometime in the early seventies, shot or crowded out or poisoned by sodium fluoroacetate. What I saw doubtless was a big coyote, but I didn't want to make myself believe it. I stopped the car and got out, savoring the image, and saw something even more arresting.

At first it seemed to be a rainbow, hovering low in a desert hollow three hundred yards away. It had rained a short time earlier, and the air was charged and complex, so a rainbow would not have been out of place. But that was not what this was. I could make out a few subtle gradations of the spectrum, but the phenomenon itself was a wonderful green light that had none of the phantom qualities of a rainbow. It was so well defined that I felt I could walk up to it and size it with a tape measure. I watched it, expecting something more. It was exactly the sort of supernatural light I had imagined as a boy in Catholic school, a backdrop from which the Virgin Mary might appear and say, as she always did in her apparitions, "Do not be afraid, my child."

The intricate atmospheric conditions that were causing this light could not be sustained for long, and in a moment it simply vanished, like water evaporating on a hot rock. I stared at the little arc of sky where it had been, greedy for something more, for some further revelation. I found it hard to take such a numinous display in passing. There was nothing mystical about it—it was neither hallucination nor vision—but when it was gone it lingered happily in my imagination, and I felt myself woven a little deeper into the fabric of the desert.

After several days of hiking around in the desert I began to wonder what it would be like to walk again in a landscape where every footstep did not have to be a considered proposition. One afternoon, on a rugged talus slope near the entrance to a narrow canyon, I came to the conclusion that it was not worth the effort to walk anymore. I felt like a contortionist as I tried to dodge the profusion of thorny plants surrounding me. Lechuguilla, prickly pear, pencil cactus, bloodroot, catclaw acacia, ocotillo—they were all savagely defending their precious stores of moisture, and I was sick of it. At that moment the desert was unsettling and grim, a place that preferred death over life. The bristly plants clung defiantly to the desert's surface, but if the desert itself had any one desire, it was to become a void.

To a degree, that is the course of things. The Chihuahuan Desert is threatened with "desertification." The more it is abused and degraded, the more it becomes a desert. To understand the tragic nature of this process, it's important to remember how intricate an environment a desert is. Deserts are second only to rain forests in their ability to support a wide variety of terrestrial species. They have a range of climate and topography that creates more ecological niches than could exist in a temperate zone. But this natural diversity is fragile, and when it is stripped away, the desert loses all character and relief and becomes a monotonous, barren land.

The threat comes from every direction. The grasslands are overgrazed, and in their place rise creosote and mesquite. Cowbirds that follow cattle onto the ranges lay their eggs in vireo nests, where the raucous cowbird chicks persuade the vireo mothers to feed them instead of their own young. A real estate development destroys bat habitat, and because there are fewer bats to pollinate the century plant, its population declines. Running water is channeled or used up. Imported vegetation like salt cedar dries up a spring with its powerful hydraulics. The steady economic pressure on ranchers forces them to sell their land, which is subdivided for development. More wells are drilled, more water is depleted. More pesticides and contaminants are cycled into the food chain.

The Chihuahuan Desert Research Institute, which is headquartered in a portion of the science building at Sul Ross State University in Alpine, has been gamely trying to educate people through the years about the desert's variety and fragility. It's not an easy job, because the desert has no real constituency. People look out their car windows at the endless creosote plains and see emptiness. What they are looking at, however, is not the real desert in its vital and complicated glory. What they are looking at is what the desert has become.

There on the talus slope, hemmed in by spines and needles, I was feeling less appreciative of the desert than I might have been. Maybe my cautious steps were a little exaggerated, but I was in one of those moods. The desert did not seem hostile, simply unconcerned about my welfare, and that was enough to make me feel vulnerable and alone.

So far, it had been a wet summer for this part of the desert, and the ocotillo plants I encountered—tall shrubs made up of dozens of thorny stems—were filled with leaves. A north wind began to whip the stems into motion, and I looked up to see the sky filled with separate thunderstorms, moving as ponderously as supertankers in a crowded harbor. All at once the atmosphere began to deepen, and the scraggly, denuded mountains in the distance turned steel blue. I moved down to the flats, thinking to get back to the car, which was four miles away across the pathless scrub. I expected at any moment to be caught in a downpour, but soon it became apparent that it wasn't going to rain, that the great thunderheads were merely going to shuffle about on the horizon and disappear.

So I sat down to watch the spectacle of rain flirting with the desert. I took my Walkman out of my backpack, listened to Elvis Costello's "Imperial Bedroom" for a while, then switched to Schubert. The music brought the desert up a notch, or so I imagined. It imposed feeling and reason on a landscape that otherwise could be frighteningly neutral. Protected by Schubert, I perceived the desert's scale and stirrings in human terms. It seemed to want music as much as it wanted rain, and I felt that if I turned up the volume, life would explode from every burrow, from every pore in the calcified soil.

But after a point—when the ants near my feet appeared to be marching with renewed purpose and the wiry creosote stems were swaying in rhythm—the orchestration got to be too much. I took off the earphones and shrank right back into place—just one more creature with an overworked evaporative system, with no greater understanding of the desert than what my senses were able to tell me. Two Scott's orioles were singing to each other across the flats. When I stood up I startled a grasshopper on a nearby mesquite, who took flight with a whirring sound that resembled the rattle of a snake. It reminded me to be cautious walking back. The thunderstorms were far away now, and the excitement had gone out of the atmosphere. There was only the sun, holding forth as usual. I took a long drink of warm water and felt just fine.

ISLA DEL PADRE

An old man who was hanging out at a bait stand in Flour Bluff asked me if I was driving to Padre Island and if I would give him a ride across the causeway. His face was badly sunburned, and he wore an old corduroy sport coat and a cap with gold braid on the bill.

"They call me Half-Acre," he said as we started across the laguna. "I worked for army intelligence during the war. Still do, in fact." He looked out the window as a great blue heron that was standing at the water's edge spread its wings, executed a deep curtsy, and shoved itself aloft. Behind the bird a board sailor was hotdogging in the shallows, riding with his feet on the rim of the board and pointing the sail ahead of him, clew first, like a weapon.

I wanted to ask Half-Acre if he had ever gone across on the old causeway, whose wooden pilings were still visible in the shallow water, but he was busy talking about Russian submarines, coded messages, and a Walther handgun that he had stolen from Hitler. Up ahead was the Intracoastal Waterway, and soaring above it was the elegant span that replaced the swing bridges I had known as a kid. At the top of the new bridge I let my eyes drift from the road and looked out over the Laguna Madre—the Mother Lagoon. Its surface was marked by oyster reefs and spoil islands, and to the south the mild, milky-blue water bled into the horizon. Ahead, where the road touched down again, was Padre Island.

"I'm a doctor, too," Half-Acre was saying. "Psychiatrist. I've worked with the finest psychiatrists in the world. They'd send me their toughest patients, the ones they couldn't help. I was able to cure them all but one, and I married her. She got her head blown off, though."

I was trying to decide whether to inquire further when we reached Half-Acre's destination, another bait stand, on the narrow shell bank between the causeway and the water. He thanked me for the ride and walked inside, leaving me to wonder if anywhere in the world there was a better environment for such a grizzled old salt than Padre Island.

"A wretched, barren sandbank," wrote a doctor who was shipwrecked here in 1846, "destitute of animals, and nothing found existence here, but disgusting sand crabs, and venomous insects."

No longer wretched, no longer barren, no longer destitute, the island is still, in its mysterious essentials, much the same place that castaway described. It is the world's longest barrier island, running for 115 miles along the Texas coast and guarding the fertile waters of the laguna from the open Gulf. At its north end, near Corpus Christi, it is sporadically developed. There is a county park, a few beachfront condos and hotels, a back-island residential community with canals and an open-air church—all of it giving way soon enough to Padre Island National Seashore, which is a wild stretch of 67.5 miles acting as a psychic counterbalance to the booming resort city of South Padre Island at the southern end.

Even so, "island" seems too grand a term for the place. It is, in fact, a sandbank, half desert and half mosquito-ridden grass flats, a wayward spit of land that, depending on your circumstances, could be either a purgatory or a paradise.

My circumstances that April day were pretty good. I was outfitted. Since I was going to journey down the length of the island, over dicey shell beaches and stretches of soft sand that could ingest a car up to its headlights, I had rented a four-wheel-drive Blazer. I had a Sears tent designed by Sir Edmund Hillary, a few cans of Sweet Sue Chicken 'n Dumplings, four bottles of Gatorade on ice, and a fishing license that I had sworn out at a local 7-Eleven.

Here, near the tip of the island, the tidal flats were overgrown with condominiums, and the island road was lined with sales offices, convenience stores, and windswept shell boutiques. I headed off north, to Access Road 3, an old haunt. The access road led to the beach just below Corpus Christi Pass. At one time, the pass was a natural channel, as much as thirty feet deep in some places, that cut across the width of the island and separated Padre from Mustang Island, which runs north from this point twenty-three miles to Port Aransas. The pass is only a remnant now, a wide break in the dunes that has filled in over the years with hard-packed sand and a few stray tidal pools, but its topographical importance still holds. This is where Padre Island officially begins.

Today was a Sunday, but the sky was overcast and there was a lingering trace of winter in the air that had kept most of the weekend beachgoers home. The few cars on the beach were widely spaced, parked broadside to the surf. Despite the overcast, people were doggedly sunbathing, stretched out on their hoods with their faces turned to the Gulf.

In the old days, that was about as crowded as Padre Island ever seemed to get. I remember being aware as a child of its vast desolation. It was a place that compelled attention but withheld comfort. The relentless wind, the noise of the surf, the salt sting of the water in my eyes—all those things seemed vaguely hostile. I had not been to any other seacoasts, but I imagined them as tamer, less isolated, less demanding. With more effort than ever seemed worthwhile, my mother would set up a folding metal table and tablecloth on the lee side of the car, and during the long afternoon we would fish or body-surf or sit in the car eating potato chips, glad to have a place of refuge. I felt hounded by the wildness of Padre Island, but in the evenings I began to be seduced by it. We would sit in folding chairs as the moon came up, not bothering to move as the evening tide sluiced below us, the chairs sinking and shifting into the unstable sand. The insufferable wind by then had modulated to a cool sea breeze, and the waves were more regular and subdued. The track of the moon on the water was so bright and solid it looked like it could support your weight. The adults, sipping their drinks, would be moved to platitudes about beauty and infinity. The children were naturally suspicious of such sentiments, but like our elders we were both lulled and aroused by the spectacle before us. I would stare out beyond the whitecaps, expecting at any moment to see something really good: a breaching whale, or the suddenly exposed hull of a sunken caravel. Looking out to sea across that blinding streak of moonlight, I thought of Padre Island as a rare place, a place where some cosmic payoff was always near at hand.

Since those days the island has, as its promoters say, "come a long way," but its identity remains rooted in age-old solitude. Behind the imposing beachfront developments at the north end, along the tidal shore of the laguna, you can still find the sites of Karankawa camps—grass flats littered with arrow points and shell tools and bits and pieces of the Indians' distinctive pottery, which they decorated with the natural asphaltum found on the beach. In those calm backwaters the Karankawas scavenged for clams and whelks; they set up weirs and picked off the trapped fish with their longbows. At night, on spots such as these, they built driftwood bonfires and drank tea made from yaupon leaves that left them overstimulated and prey to visions.

The Karankawas, according to an early settler, were "the Ishmaelites of Texas, for their hands were against everyman and everyman's hand was against them." From Cabeza de Vaca onward, almost every white man who encountered those extraordinary people was struck by their exceptional height, by their expert skill as archers and canoeists, and finally by their absolute defiance of the new order. They had no use for horses and firearms, yet they fought the invading hordes with such skill and savagery that even such a mild-mannered soul as Stephen F. Austin ultimately found it necessary to call for their extermination.

In the end, that is what happened to them. No Karankawas exist today to give an accounting of themselves, and the folklore that has arisen about them has been filtered through hundreds of years of Anglo contempt. They are said to have been cannibals who enjoyed tying their victim to a stake, slicing off pieces of his flesh, and eating it before his eyes. One tall tale has them raiding villages and carrying off the children to eat as trail snacks on the journey back home. Another writer chastises them for their guttural language and even asserts that they had trouble pronouncing their own name.

So much about the Karankawas—their appearance, language, dress, weapons, attitude—was so strikingly different from other Texas Indians that they seem to have been an alien presence. One theory, espoused by Herman Smith, the staff archeologist at the Corpus Christi Museum, is that they were not North American Indians at all but Caribs from the West Indies who, sometime before Columbus, had made their way in dugout canoes from Antigua to the Texas coast.

The Caribs were the Vikings of the Caribbean, a ferocious, seagoing people who raided from island to island, who were tall and naked like the Karankawas, and who were such skilled swimmers and bowmen that they could loose arrows while treading water. Smith speaks of the Karankawa arrival in Texas as an invasion. "These guys came across Padre Island like John Wayne at Iwo Jima, and whatever other Indian groups were around then were flat out of business."

The Karankawas didn't stay in business that long either, but their presence on Padre was inerasable. Driving between a row of collapsed beach umbrellas and the seawall that guarded the Holiday Inn, I could feel some archaic power of place, an almost physical sensation that drifted across my skin like the blowing sand.

Surfers were gathered near an old wrecked fishing pier, looking out at the waves with their boards still in their cars, waiting for some promising sign before they committed themselves. One of the surfers had a parrot perched on his shoulder, and as I drove slowly by I overheard him telling a girl that the parrot did not just mimic words but could carry on an intelligent conversation in six languages.

Half a mile beyond, Bob Hall Pier protruded out into the surf on its concrete pilings. The original pier had been made of wood, and in my memory it was longer, so that in walking out to its end you could sense the choppy shallows giving way beneath your feet to the ocean deeps. I remembered hooking a large stingray out at the end of Bob Hall, and I could vividly recall the steady, unflinching pull of its wingbeats. The fish was not merely trying to get away; it was communicating its outrage, and when I saw its strange kite shape break the surface I felt as if I had committed some awful trespass against nature.

Hurricanes—Carla, Celia, Beulah, and finally Allen—had destroyed the old pier, and if the new structure was not quite as evocative, at least it appeared that it would last. The pier was part of what used to be called Nueces County Park. It had recently been named Padre Ballí

Park, in deference to the priest from whom the whole island took its name. José Nicolás Ballí was the son of well-heeled Spanish colonists who had settled in the Rio Grande Valley in the late eighteenth century. His mother was a powerful and deeply religious woman who passed on to her son a facility for not drawing too fine a distinction between material and spiritual comforts. "Padre Ballí left," one modern author cheekily writes, "unmistakable evidence of a carnate existence."

Certainly the priest worked as hard at accruing capital as he did at saving souls. Sometime between 1800 and 1805 he applied to the crown for a grant to the unclaimed strip of land off the coast that Alonso Alvarez de Piñeda, searching for the Strait of Anian, had first named Isla Blanca. When his request was granted, he turned the island into a cattle ranch, placing his nephew in charge while he returned to the comforts of the mainland. The padre lived on the island only once, when he needed a refuge during the Mexican revolution of 1821, an event that assuredly did not favor the interests of an aristocratic Spanish priest. After the revolution, Ballí managed to reaffirm his original grant with the new government in Mexico, but he died soon after, leaving behind a succession of heirs whose hold on La Isla del Padre grew, over time, more and more tenuous.

I drove from Padre Ballí Park back onto the road that led down the center of the island to the national seashore. Soon the filling stations and beachwear emporiums gave way to the dunes and hummocky grasslands that covered the island between the beach and the laguna. Padre was wide here—two miles across—and the swaths of seacoast bluestem, unmarked by trees, looked limitless and pure.

The national seashore is 67.5 miles long, extending all the way to Mansfield Channel. It was created in 1962, after long and sometimes rancorous debate from private landowners and developers who were just beginning to realize the island's potential. A few miles from the entrance, the road I was traveling took a dogleg to Malaquite Beach, the park's only concession to the traditional beachgoer. Malaquite is half a mile long, a cultivated stretch of shoreline that is closed to automobile traffic.

The beach was almost deserted today. I went up to the big pavilion that housed a snack bar and bathhouses and looked out toward the

Gulf, admiring the spotless sand and the wide expanse of blue water that began just outside the turbulent green of the surf. The snack bar was closed, as was the visitors' center, and the pavilion itself—only fifteen years old—was already an eerie relic, its concrete supports eaten away by the corrosive air.

From Malaquite on, there was no road at all. If you wanted to go farther, "down island," you had to have a vehicle that could pull you through the treacherous sand and shell banks that formed Padre's limitless beach. I drove the Blazer down to the waterline and pointed it south, planning to travel near the surf as long as the sand held firm.

Beyond Malaquite the beach was wide, and the shoreline slipped unobtrusively beneath the foamy, played-out waves that minutes before had broken with considerable power against the outer bar. The dunes were low and scruffy, fringed with waving sea oats and low-level creepers like fiddle-leaf morning glory. But between the beach and the dunes something was wrong. I kept thinking as I drove along that it could not possibly be this bad, but I was gradually forced to believe it. Padre Island National Seashore had, in the years since I had last ventured this far, become a vast trash heap.

Most of the garbage had been compressed by wave action into one long strip, but it was difficult to find a square foot of beachfront that did not host an aluminum can or a beady chunk of Styrofoam. And it went on forever, a spectacle every bit as riveting as the natural vistas that I had driven down here to admire.

I was not naive. I was familiar enough with the island to understand that the pristine, undisturbed seashore it is advertised to have is largely a copywriter's dream. Because the middle section of Padre lies at the point of convergence of two longshore currents, it provides a continuous reading of the state of the Gulf. Things wash up here—shells, tree trunks, coconuts, rafts of sargassum, buoys, floats from fishing nets, bottles, even treasure. But the waves make no distinction between picturesque sea wrack and garbage, and the same forces that bring us doubloons and conch shells also deposit sopping mattresses and broken light bulbs.

Scattered along the beach that day, I later learned, were 142 tons of trash. The problem was most acute along the sixty miles of the national seashore. Only about four miles of beachfront are routinely kept clean, a job that falls to probationers from the U.S. District Court in Corpus Christi, who patrol the areas north and south of Malaquite Beach each week, picking up litter by hand. The National Park Service cannot begin to afford the cost of keeping the rest of the island clean, and so it is left to sink under the weight of a constant accumulation of bleach bottles, packing materials, egg cartons, bedsprings, and indissoluble plastics in an infinite variety of forms.

Island tourists are responsible for only a small percentage of the trash. The great majority comes from offshore—from oil and gas operations, from commercial shipping, and from the increasing pollution of the rivers that empty into the Gulf. Drop a paper cup into the Mississippi River in Hannibal, Missouri, in November, and it's likely to end up on Padre Island in January.

The laws governing ocean dumping are anemic. Most vessels in the Gulf of Mexico are restricted from tossing their garbage overboard only if they are inside three miles from shore, and even inside that narrow zone, it's easy enough for a crafty despoiler to evade the law.

I traveled on, with a heavy heart, in four-wheel drive. The corridor of trash and sargasso in the center of the beach was as unvarying as a traffic median. There were inordinate numbers of construction hard hats, rubber gloves, and the disembodied limbs of Third World baby dolls. Occasionally I would see a fifty-five gallon drum standing on end with a yellow sticker warning the curious not to approach. Such drums could be found all up and down the seashore. They were filled with solvents, antifreeze, drilling fluids containing dangerous heavy metals. They too came from the Gulf, from drilling platforms or passing ships— "moonlight dumpers." The National Park Service, at a price to the taxpayer of one thousand dollars per drum, periodically sent men in moon suits to remove them, identify their contents, and dispose of them.

So the two most dominant features of Padre Island were trash and toxic waste. It was enough to drive me to think about radical remedies—decommissioning the national seashore, for instance, and hoping that the resulting flood of demanding condo owners would see to it that the beach was kept clean. But that was a surly thought and only a cosmetic solution. No real change would come unless an enforceable ban on dumping could be extended far beyond the three-mile limit and ports were required to have waste-disposal facilities for ships that would otherwise dump their refuse at sea.

About fifteen miles past the park boundary, the composition of the beach began to change from sand to shell. This was Little Shell, a region whose surface was graded with fragments of coquina clams. The shell looked solid, but it shifted and gave way and provided uncertain footing for my vehicle's businesslike tires. The water washed over the shell in rounded cusps, and cormorants stood at the swash line on their heavy webbed feet, holding their wings out to dry. In the distant haze ahead I could see the island curving a bit, outward toward the Gulf.

At the fifteen-mile marker, near a giant fuel tank that was slowly oxidizing on the beach, I decided to make camp. There was a little draw where the dunes were blown out that looked like a good place, so I went to work clearing the site of garbage. When that was done I set up my new tent, which promptly took off into the air like a hang glider. Obviously, Sir Edmund Hillary had never camped on Padre Island. I was finally able to anchor it by setting six-gallon water jugs into the two windward corners.

That accomplished, I set off exploring. A pass had been dredged here several times in the forties and fifties as a way to regulate the salinity in the laguna, but the pass always closed in soon after it was finished, and now all that was left of it was a low, grassy valley that led through the dunes. A string of ponds followed the old course of the pass, and they were peopled with willets and shovelers and a little blue heron who loped ahead of me as I walked, hiding in the cattails until I flushed him out again.

Flies came to attack me. They were slow and easy to swat, but there was such an endless supply of them that I gave up my goal of walking to the other side of the island, a mile distant. Instead I climbed a high dune and looked out toward the laguna, which from that distance was merely a broad, shimmering mirage. A little to the south, in the center of the laguna, was a landmark called the Hole. The Hole was deep, and the water that surrounded it was so shallow that sometimes it would evaporate, leaving great numbers of fish swimming in a natural trap. Louis Rawalt, who spent most of his life on the island, described how on such occasions one person could take two or three thousand fish.

Rawalt came to the island in 1919 when he was twenty-one. He had been gassed in the First World War and was told not to expect to survive more than six months. He decided to live out his life on Padre, which he did, although he did not die until he was eighty-two. He made a living by fishing and beachcombing, traveling up and down the island in his Model T. He once found a Mayan figurine that dated back to 4500 B.C. Another time, walking in the dunes, he came across the hull of a Spanish galleon.

As I walked back to my camp I remembered Rawalt's account of the day he had caught five hundred pounds of redfish while surf casting at Little Shell. I hadn't fished since high school, but I had brought along a rod and reel from those days; its monofilament line had turned as yellow as old newspaper. Why not give it a try? I got the rig out of the truck, clipped off the old leader, and put on a stainless steel hook and a fancy surf weight that would help keep my bait on the bottom, where the wily redfish prowled. The bait was dead shrimp. I remembered how to puncture them just under the rear fins—fragile as dragonfly wings—and let the hook travel through the body, bending the shrimp to its shape.

Now what? I waded out into the gut past the first bar. The water was not warm, and the waves were high enough to slam me in the chest and make me think about my footing. Standing on the next bar, I cast out ahead into the deeper water, trying to remember if this was the way you were supposed to do it. After five minutes I was looking at my watch. The body blows from the surf were not conducive to patience. Serious surf fishermen—I had passed a few of them on my way down—sat in lawn chairs and drank beer, their rods set into metal holders. But I had decided I would either do this like a sportsman or eat Sweet Sue Chicken 'n Dumplings for dinner after all.

Crabs were down there nibbling at my bait. They sent up delicate tremors through the brittle fishing line. After a while, because I was bored, I began to reel them in, admiring the tenacity with which they held onto the shrimp with one claw as they rose into the air.

Unable to recall a single instance in which I had actually caught a fish in the surf, I gave up and walked back to the truck and waited for night. When it came, moonless and chilly, I built a driftwood fire and watched the sparks, driven by the offshore wind, bound off into the dunes. They moved so swiftly that they seemed alive and willful, as if each glowing speck leapt out of the flames with a destination in mind.

The headlights of a jeep traveled down the beach. Its passage was marked as well by a regular series of percussive sounds—*pop-pop-pop*—as its tires hit the inflated sacs of beached Portuguese men-of-war. Except for the jeep, the beach was deserted. Offshore I counted nineteen lights. Half of them—the steady ones—were drilling platforms. The others were shrimp boats, trawling out beyond the bars where the shrimp were feeding in the dark water.

It was the sort of night that, long ago, would have appealed to those individuals who were in the business of wrecking and looting ships. Wreckers—some of whom were former pirates in the service of Jean Laffite—found the remote beaches and treacherous shoals of Padre Island to be a perfect location for their endeavors. They would typically attach a lantern to the end of a long pole that had been strapped to the front leg of a donkey, then lead the animal in tight circles on the beach. A captain at sea would read the distant, bobbing point of light as a buoy and steer his craft to the harbor he assumed it marked. By the time he realized his mistake, he would already have run aground on the outer bar.

The waters off Padre were dangerous enough, even without the services of wreckers, and hundreds of ships foundered there. One of the island's most notable castaways was John Singer, whose schooner, the *Alice Sadell*, broke apart in the surf in 1847. Singer and his wife, Johanna, built a shelter from the remains of the *Alice Sadell* and, while they waited for rescue, discovered that they liked the island well enough to stay. Singer—whose brother was the inventor of the sewing machine—apparently had some capital, and over the years he built up a considerable ranching operation. At the site of Padre Balli's old Rancho Santa Cruz, Singer constructed a house from mahogany timbers, a blacksmith shop, and corrals. He and his wife had six children. When

Johanna grew tired of island life, she put on a pair of canvas mittens and rowed a flat-bottomed skiff across the laguna and then traveled by oxcart to the relative splendor of Brownsville.

During the Civil War the island was part of the Confederate blockade. Because the Singers were openly pro-Union, they were forced off. In a panic they placed their fortune—sixty-two-thousand dollars worth of jewelry and old Spanish coins—in a screw-top jar and buried it in the dunes. After the war they came back to the island to retrieve it, but it was the old story: the sands had shifted, the landmarks had disappeared, the treasure was lost. Singer searched for it for a year. His wife died. Finally he gave up and sailed for South America. Treasure hunters have been searching for Singer's ranch headquarters, the Lost City, ever since. A Brownsville man is said to have found it in 1931, but before he could locate the screw-top jar the sand had engulfed the site again.

When the fire died down I took a walk along the beach, the darkness so intense that I almost collided at one point with a giant cat's cradle of driftwood. I could not see the surf, but I could sense its movement, the constant crawl and slouch of the waves that could seem, from one moment to the next, either a threat or a comfort. The sound of the waves was constant, too, but I had long since stopped discerning it. It was the aural baseline; above it was silence and, just occasionally, the panicky whining of coyotes.

A friend to wildlife, I left some scraps out for the coyotes and retired to the tent, listening to its fabric snap and billow in the wind. The tent had a floor, so I didn't worry about sand crabs, but sand drifted in through the mesh windows, and I could feel it falling on my face like pollen. I didn't mind. The air was pleasantly rank—salt air—and I banished my outrage at the despoiled beach and let my mind wander, coasting into sleep on a childhood memory of bodysurfing, recalling the sensation of soaring in those smooth waves just before they broke.

By eight o'clock the next morning I had packed and driven twenty miles farther down the beach to Big Shell. The large cockleshells that covered the surface of the beach were streaked with pale bands of color. Unbroken sand dollars were everywhere, and dozens of Portuguese men-of-war huddled together in one spot, the wind having blown them all along the same course. I took an inventory of the unnatural flotsam as well. Within a five-foot radius of where I was standing were a turquoise detergent bottle, a shredded egg carton, a bottle of Lea and Perrins sauce, a pair of light blue Fruit of the Loom jockey shorts, a milk carton, a plastic bag, a club soda bottle, three light bulbs, a container of Lemon Pledge, a ski rope, a sandal, a tuna can, three beer cans, a can of Puncture Seal, an oil filter, and a carton of Acadia buttermilk from Thibodaux, Louisiana.

I looked up in time to see an osprey dive deep into the surf and then shoot up like a subsurface missile, a mullet in its beak. A hundred yards down the beach a sea turtle was washing in. Its head was gone, and though the carcass was fresh enough to bleed, the flesh that was left was gruesome and moldy and hung like a tattered curtain covering the hole where the head had been. More than likely the turtle had been decapitated by a shrimper who had accidentally hauled it to the surface and wanted to ensure that it did no more damage to his nets.

The turtle's shell was about three feet in diameter. I took a good look at the arrangement of the scales on its plastron and then ran a make on it with my reptile book. It was a Kemp's ridley, a threatened species believed to have nested on Padre Island early in this century. Eight years earlier a project had been started to reintroduce the turtles to the island. Eggs were collected from the ridleys' breeding ground in Mexico and buried in Padre Island sand. When the hatchlings emerged they were allowed to flap down the beach—thus imprinting the place on their consciousness—and then scooped out of the water. A year or so later, after growing to the size of saucers, they were tossed out into the Gulf. The hope was that their homing instincts would return them to Padre, but nobody would know, until the first hatchlings reached sexual maturity, if the project would succeed. Meanwhile, more and more turtles were washing up dead.

A high, conspicuous dune was nearby, blown out in the center like a volcanic crater. I wondered if it might be Black Hill, the site of one of the old line camps from Pat Dunn's ranch, but when I walked back into the dunes to investigate I could find no trace of the corral that was supposed to be still standing.

Pat Dunn—Don Patricio to his vaqueros—ran a cattle ranch on Padre

Island for almost fifty years. He came out here with his two brothers in 1879, when he was twenty-one years old and the Kings and Kenedys were starting to put up fences on their vast mainland holdings. Forgotten and nearly inaccessible, Padre remained open range. It was in many ways an ideal location for a cattle ranch. Fresh water was available if one dug deep enough in the dunes, and the Gulf on one side and the laguna on the other served as natural boundaries. The narrow strip of land made the logistics of a roundup simple, and cattle were easy to spot in the almost treeless grass flats.

Dunn was thoroughly accommodated to island life. He built a home out of lumber found on the beach, furnishing it with chairs salvaged from a wrecked steamer. When a 125-pound tin of hardtack washed ashore he developed an unnatural fondness for its contents and hoarded it for years. He was kind to his cattle, preferring that his cowboys catch them by hand because he thought roping was cruel. The cattle in turn flourished, adapting to the island so completely that Don Patricio called them "sea lions." They licked dead fish for salt and wallowed in the asphalt deposits and supposedly ate crabs off the beach. To get them to market they had to be swum across the laguna, and from such peculiar trail drives there grew persistent stories of drovers lassoing redfish.

Over the years Dunn acquired title to almost all of Padre Island, selling it in 1926 for $125,000 to Colonel Sam Robertson, who dreamed of turning it into a major resort until a hurricane blew away his improvements. Dunn moved to Corpus Christi. He maintained a suite in the Driscoll Hotel and was driven around by a chauffeur, but he seemed less content than in the years when he nibbled hardtack on Padre Island.

"If the Lord would give me back the island now," he groused after he sold out, "wash out a channel in Corpus Christi Pass thirty feet deep, and put devilfish and other monsters in it to keep out the tourists, I'd be satisfied."

A shrimp boat was aground on the beach at the thirty-mile marker. Its name was the *Majestic Clipper*, and it was canted to one side, its port outrigger dipping into the surf. The *Majestic Clipper* was a large seagoing vessel, maybe eighty feet long, and on the otherwise featureless shoreline it took on scale, so that it seemed to have the dimensions of an ocean liner.

While I was inspecting the boat, a man looked down from the bow, tossed a rope over the side, and shimmied barefoot down to the sand.

"*Hola*," he said when he landed. He told me he was from Brownsville and was the only member of the crew still aboard. Everyone else had left the day the *Majestic Clipper* tangled a line in its prop and ran aground. But the captain had ordered him to stay on board so that nobody could claim salvage rights. That had been nineteen days ago, he said, in a tone that implied it was no fun to be a castaway. For one thing, it was hard to sleep in a boat that was tilted at a forty-five-degree angle.

He stood back, peeling an orange that I had given him, and looked at the boat as if he were studying his predicament for the first time. "Maybe the captain will come this week," he said, then shrugged. "Maybe not."

I left the shrimper some more fruit and drove on, reminded anew of Padre's reputation as the graveyard of the Gulf. The history of the island is in large part the history of shipwreck, and the evidence of its fatal magnetism is never far from sight. Some miles past the *Majestic Clipper* were the ruins of the *Nicaragua*, a coastal steamer that was driven aground during a storm in 1912. The rusted boilers of the ship rose prominently from the surf, their presence tampering with the normal course of the waves and causing a surge that periodically left one or two other jagged hulks of steel exposed.

Ten miles beyond the *Nicaragua* were the granite jetties of Mansfield Channel. A truck chassis had subsided into the sand at the edge of the boulders, and a pile of soft drink cans had been effectively sandblasted by the high winds until their labels were effaced and they shone like a precious metal. I climbed onto the jetties and walked out fifty yards or so, watching the sea lice scatter around the boulders and listening to the suction of the water in the crevices below. Mansfield Channel, built in the late fifties to provide the mainland village of Port Mansfield with access to the Gulf, was the terminus of the national seashore, though Padre Island itself ran for another forty miles on the other side. The channel was wide, and the water here was blue. A shrimp boat, flying the skull and crossbones, was moving through the jetties out to the Gulf, its wake disturbing a small sport-fishing boat, *Yesterday's Wine*, that was anchored near the channel marker.

A terrible thing happened here in 1554. Of all the shipwrecks that have occurred on Padre Island, the loss of the Spanish treasure fleet is the most lurid and unforgettable, the event that forever fixed the island's reputation as a savage and alluring place.

"Woe to those of us who are going to Spain, because neither we nor the fleet will arrive there," a Spanish priest named Juan Ferrer is said to have proclaimed as his ship left Veracruz. "Most of us will perish, and those who are left will experience great torment, though all will die in the end except a very few."

Such dire predictions were not out of character for Fray Ferrer, who was so full of strange and cryptic pronouncements that he had been summoned back to Spain by the emperor to "give an account of his dreams and fantasies." His fellow passengers were noblemen and merchants who were sailing home with their families, bearing the fortunes they had made in New Spain. The four ships that sailed from Veracruz were heavily laden as well with the crown's revenue from the enterprises of its colony. *Santa Maria de Yciar*, the only ship whose register still exists, carried more than fifteen thousand pounds of silver, most of it in coins stored in casks.

The ships were to sail to Havana, where they would join a larger fleet for protection in the Atlantic crossing. But twenty days out of port they were struck by a violent spring storm. One of the ships managed to make it to Havana, but the other three, running before the storm, were blown all the way back across the Gulf and broke apart within a few miles of one another on the shore of Padre Island.

About three hundred Spaniards, many of them women and children, survived the wrecks. For reasons that are unclear, they decided to abandon the shelter and provisions that could have been salvaged from the ships and undertake a march to the Spanish settlement of Pánuco, which they thought lay two or three days to the south. What lay between them and Pánuco, however, was not only the whole southern half of Padre Island but three hundred miles of marshy coastal lands on the other side of the Rio Grande. For seven days they walked south under the open sun, eating what shellfish they could find and licking the leaves of plants for moisture, unaware that they could find fresh water by digging in the dunes.

Finally they were approached by about a hundred Indians (likely Karankawas) who offered the Spaniards food and then stood by suspiciously as they ate. It dawned on the castaways that they were trapped, and as the Indians watched they began quietly to prepare themselves, readying the two crossbows and various other weapons that they had salvaged from the wreck. When their hosts attacked they were able to repulse them, but as they continued their march the Indians dogged their steps, picking off stragglers with their bows and arrows.

In twelve days they reached the Rio Grande. Crossing the river on makeshift rafts, they lost their crossbows. Soon after, two Spaniards were captured by the Indians and then released when they had been stripped of their clothes. That incident gave the castaways hope that all the Indians wanted was their garments, and in desperation they took off their clothes and cast them on the sand.

Naked, debased, defenseless, the Spaniards marched on. The priests sent the unclothed women in advance, where the men could not see them. One chronicler reports that some of the women dropped dead from shame.

When the women and children reached the Rio de las Palmas they barely had time to drink before the Indians attacked, shooting from a distance with their powerful bows. "The wounded child would run toward the mother for help," we are told, "but the wound was felt by the mother as if it were her own."

By the time the men came upon the scene, all of the women and children were dead. The men walked on, two hundred of them. On the other side of the river fifty of them were killed. The remainder walked for twenty more days, picked off one by one until their hopeless trek to Pánuco ended in annihilation.

There were two survivors. A priest named Fray Marcos de Mena, left for dead in the dunes after being struck with seven arrows, somehow revived enough to continue the journey. He went for four days without food or water, and when he collapsed at night sand crabs picked at his wounds. Muttering prayers as he staggered down the beach, he finally reached Pánuco. The other survivor, a soldier named Francisco Vásquez, broke off from his companions and walked alone back to the wreck site. He was there only a few days before he was rescued by the salvage fleet that had been hastily organized once word of the loss of the treasure ships reached Veracruz.

The salvage crew set up a camp on Padre Island, and for months divers, using only lung power, brought up load after load of silver *reales*. At the end of the project, only half the treasure had been recovered. The rest sank into the sand bottom, along with the ships' timbers and fittings and the personal effects of the doomed passengers.

For four hundred years silver coins have been washing up on the beach north of Mansfield Channel. When the channel was made, the dredge passed right through the final resting place of the *Santa María de Yciar*, destroying the site but bringing to the surface, among other relics, one of the ship's anchors.

Such discoveries narrowed the field of search for treasure hunters, and in 1967 a salvage firm from Indiana located the wreck of the *Espíritu Santo* and began hauling up artifacts. The search was promptly shut down by Jerry Sadler, the Texas land commissioner, who argued that the treasure belonged to "the schoolchildren of Texas." A long-running legal contest sent the salvage firm back to Indiana, and the state, in the guise of the newly formed Texas Antiquities Committee, moved in to claim its prize. In the early seventies the committee launched a full-scale underwater archeology project, burrowing through the sea bottom to find anchors, astrolabes, fragments of timber, verso cannon, and crucifixes.

And of course treasure. The archeologists brought up bullion disks and gold bars and hundreds of silver coins, but when the project was over a great deal more was left buried in the sand. Under the antiquities law all of it belongs to the state. Pocketing anything—coins, cannonballs, corroded spikes—is a crime punishable by a fine of up to a thousand dollars and a jail term of up to thirty days.

"Treasure is there for all, for you and you and you," writes one splenetic author. "But now, in the event you do manage to unearth one of these fast-eroding coins . . . YOU ARE REQUIRED BY LAW to take it to someone sitting in their air-conditioned office and GIVE it to them."

Treasure hunters still converge on Padre, despite the antiquities law and despite the certainty that their metal detectors will be confiscated if discovered by a park ranger. "If you find anybody camped two miles north of the jetties," a treasure hunter named Dave told me, "I can guarantee you, they're hunting."

I had met Dave at a hotel bar in Corpus. The meeting had been arranged by intermediaries, as carefully as if it were to be a meeting with a mob boss instead of an outlaw hobbyist.

"My position is this," he said. "Once you establish the historical significance of a site and the kinds of finds that are going to be made, why not go ahead and let people find the relics? The archeologists don't have any use for these coins. They're not going to tell them anything they don't already know.

"I don't feel like a criminal, but the first couple of times I went down there I was scared the whole time. I've seen people get so worried they make themselves sick to their stomachs."

Dave hunts mostly in the winter, after high tides or storms. He drives down in the daytime, sets up camp, and hunts all night, sweeping his metal detector over the sand and illuminating his way with a single flashlight. If he sees a car coming or anything suspicious he turns off the light and hides the detector in the dunes. He has never been caught, and he knows of only one person who has been arrested on Padre Island since the antiquities law went into effect. Even so, he's paranoid.

He looked around warily and took out of his jeans pocket several plastic bags containing coins he'd found on the beach. The silver pieces were dark gray, their edges ragged and worn thin. They were coins from the 1554 shipwrecks, minted in Mexico City in denominations of two and four *reales*. The names of Carlos and Johanna, the rulers of the Holy Roman Empire, were imprinted in a circle around a rendering of the pillars of Hercules. "Usually when you find a coin," he said, with a glance at a passing waiter who seemed a little too interested in our conversation, "there'll be so much tar and debris on it, it'll look just like a piece of tar."

Dave said that he finds coins, usually a few a night, on two out of three trips down to the island. In the last six years about two thousand coins from the 1554 wrecks have been found on the beach by treasure hunters. Almost all of them have been in denominations of two or four *reales*. A few three-*real* pieces have been found, but they're very rare. One of those, in good condition, might sell for six hundred dollars.

"Back in the fifties and sixties there were some people who supposedly made a lot of money digging up coins off the island and selling them in Mexico, but it's not really profitable anymore. I wouldn't ever sell any of these coins anyway. One day, I suppose, I'll put them in a museum somewhere."

I picked up one of the coins and ran my finger along its worn surface, thinking about how this blackened, wafer-thin object had once been part of the wealth of New Spain. Now, four centuries since its loss, it was something considerably less than a piece of treasure and more than a souvenir.

Today, walking by the jetties, I scanned the ground ahead, almost unconsciously looking for a flat disk of tar that might hide such a coin. I found nothing, of course, which was probably for the best, because in my heart I was not sure I would be able to obey the antiquities law that forbade me to touch it.

M ansfield Channel was a major obstacle in my journey down the island. There was no bridge or ferry to take me across, and swimming or hitching a ride on a boat would have meant leaving the Blazer behind. I thought about how formidable this body of water must seem to the illegal aliens who use the island as a route north from Mexico. They have to cross the deep pass clinging to inner tubes.

The only feasible way for me to get to the other side was to drive back to Corpus, fly to South Padre Island, and then proceed northward on the island until I reached the opposite shore. A week later that was where I was, sitting across the channel on the jetties, eating lunch and watching a pod of dolphins in the pass. They were feeding in a school of mullet, close enough to where I was sitting that every so often one of them would raise an eye above the waterline and look at me.

From that point south, the island was privately owned, but there was little to distinguish it from the national seashore until one reached the condominium towers of South Padre Island. There was no road on this part of the island either, so I had rented a three-wheel all-terrain vehicle and driven up from South Padre on the beach.

The ATV had been more fun than I had expected, and as I sat on the jetties, studiously observing the dolphins eating their mullet, I could not keep my eyes from the bright yellow vehicle parked on the beach. Soon I was roaring off again down the swash line, popping men-of-war with my knobby tires and leaping over piles of sargassum. Ghost crabs, their eye stalks fully extended in alarm, zipped into their burrows at my approach.

Except for a few more drums of toxic waste, the trash problem on this side of the island was not as severe, and the wide beach grew cleaner and the water clearer the farther south I headed. Over by the low, unsecured dunes the sand was surprisingly firm. Coyote tracks were imprinted there, and the ripple marks the wind had made in the tightly packed sand reminded me of the dense cloud patterns of a mackerel sky.

The island was narrower here, and the dune fields were more likely to be breached by hurricane passes. I veered off into the mouth of one pass, opening my machine up all the way on the hypnotic flats. The laguna was no more than a mile and a half away, but the landscape was so featureless that the distance seemed infinite. I passed over the flats at full throttle, in a kind of dream state, like a person falling through the air. I picked up the tracks of some cloven-footed animal—a javelina, probably—followed them to the edge of the dunes, and then took off into the open again, down-shifting as the sand became softer toward the far side of the island.

I had heard stories of vehicles such as mine dropping out of sight into deep beds of quicksand out on the flats. I wasn't convinced that the stories were true, but as I drew closer to the laguna, I paid particular attention to the consistency of the sand, worried that I might suddenly hear a slurping sound and find that it was all over. The bare flats were decorated with shell now, and there were a few isolated hillocks of back-island dunes. A carpet of blanched sea grass bordered the waterline, and a flotilla of little pink bryozoans was just drifting into shore. I waded out into the shallow water, not much liking the feel of the ooze beneath my feet, and looked without success for snail tracks. A formless, wraithlike creature, maybe an inch across, moved with surprising speed just beneath the surface, but I lost it when I took another step and clouded up the water.

Standing in the laguna, I was on the property of the State of Texas.

In 1940 Texas had pressed a claim to the island itself, contending that the original Ballí grant was invalid. The suit was titled *State of Texas v. Ballí et al.*, and even though the state lost the suit and the Ballí grant was affirmed, it was the et als., not the Ballís, who carried the day. The padre's descendants had, practically speaking, long ago lost ownership to people like Pat Dunn, who moved onto the island and acquired title by right of possession.

The defendants in the Ballí case included real estate developers and land speculators, people who had a stake in bringing to reality the long-cherished fantasy of turning Padre Island into the Gold Coast of Texas. With the state's claim denied, there was nothing to stand in the way of the boom.

But the state did derive some benefit from the suit. It managed to set the western boundary of the island according to a survey conducted by J. Stuart Boyles. The Boyles line was more or less consistent with the observable shoreline, and so it left almost the whole of the Laguna Madre—and its potential for oil and gas revenue—in the possession of Texas.

Private owners have been sniping at the Boyles line ever since in an effort to extend their title westward into the laguna. In 1969 they commissioned another survey, by M. L. Claunch, that concluded that the mean high water line of the Laguna Madre was considerably westward of the place where Boyles put it. In 1980 a group of developers sued the state, claiming ownership of a part of the submerged land between the Boyles and Claunch lines. The state, wanting to avoid the expense of a lengthy trial, gave in, a position it has since regretted. Nowadays at the General Land Office the Boyles line is regarded as a sacred boundary. If it is breached further, they say, Texas could lose half of the laguna.

Padre Island's boundaries have always been elusive, its ownership always vague. It has been a difficult place to grasp with any instrument other than the imagination. No doubt I was trespassing on somebody's land as I made my way back to the public beach easement, but I gunned my ATV without remorse. The island was vacant and still, and there was a certain natural primacy in just being here. I liked the way that Padre Ballí had originally taken possession. He had picked up rocks and thrown them in the four directions, and then bent down and drunk the water of the Laguna Madre. Those were gestures that seemed designed not to appease the bureaucrats of Spain but to appease, in some way, the island itself.

Ten miles down the island, the beach narrowed to a strip of sand guarded by a high balustrade of dunes. The dunes formed a series of peaks, a miniature mountain range rising thirty feet into the air. On the highest peak someone had planted a cross made of driftwood, and when I climbed up to inspect it and saw the view from that spot, I felt light-headed with appreciation. On one side was the abbreviated beach and the green Gulf water, so transparent that I could see a shoal of fish beneath its surface, an oscillating blue circle that swept slowly northward. The inland side was protected by dunes. The greenery began at the summit where I was standing and swept downward in a series of swales that ran all the way to the gleaming whiteness of the tidal flats. The carpet was broken only by several small ponds, brackish and short-lived, that nevertheless appeared as deep and cold as glacier lakes.

I had no idea if the cross was there merely to mark the view or if had some deeper significance. The view was enough, though. This was the spot. I suppose I believed at that moment that Padre Island was, in some unfathomable fashion, alive and aware, and that this was its pulse.

But there's nothing like a ride on an ATV to clear your head of mysticism, and soon I was yahooing down the beach again. In the haze ahead loomed the fabled city of South Padre Island, and as I entered its jurisdiction I observed the speed limit and adjusted my attitude. I was here just after spring break and a few weeks before the summer tourist season, and so the place had a downtime feel—not appealingly logy like a genuine coastal town, just a shade vacant and remote. Its buildings—its Bahia Mars and Canta Mars, its Windsongs and Bali Hais—rose upward in sometimes shocking vertical counterpoint to the low-lying sandbar that supported them. I could almost feel the island sinking under their weight.

Thirty years ago South Padre had been little more than a Coast Guard station and a collection of fishing huts. Now, in full flower, it had the feeling of a city that had come up too fast. And yet I always found it a hard place not to like. Perhaps I was just a sucker for its furious fun-in-the-sun mores. Across the laguna sat Port Isabel, with its shrimp fleet, its hardware stores, its Union Carbide plant, as if South Padre had willfully shoved all the grimy and workaday demands of existence onto the mainland. It clearly preferred the role of grasshopper to Port Isabel's ant.

I checked into a room at the Hilton and walked out onto the beach to sample the aquaculture. It was a clean stretch of sand that recorded the footprints of joggers and the tracks of the big graders that swept up and down the beach removing garbage. Dunes were struggling to be born in the gaps between the high rises, but elsewhere the familiar island zones had been obliterated and there was only the gorgeous, foreshortened beach.

Lying there, I read more lurid accounts of Karankawa cannibalism. "In this manner," the author of my book noted, "the Indian tribes would kill the survivors for food. Instead of shopping at the supermarket, they did their food shopping in this manner."

I digested a few more pages of such lore and then ventured into the surf. The firm sand at the waterline was nearly free of shells, and the shore dropped off cleanly. Past the second bar I was already over my head. The waves formed and broke elegantly, and I was struck by how much more comfortable I felt than I usually did in Padre surf. There was nothing here: no Portuguese men-of-war, no seaweed, no strange drifting blobs tickling the hair on my legs. I floated on my back, my eyes closed, relaxing even my perpetual vigilance of sharks. There was no menace in this water or even any inconvenience. But I surprised myself by missing the trash-strewn beach north of here, where the trash itself now seemed like an index of wildness, of the island's unruly and unprotected essence.

The next day I joined up with a group of travel writers who were being wooed by the South Padre Island Tourist Bureau. We went for a morning cruise in the Laguna Madre and then boarded a bus for a look at a new condo that Ben Barnes and John Connally had built in the center of town. The building was called the Sunchase. Its two gleaming white towers, each a halved pyramid, rose up and up into the Padre

Island sky, suggesting, we were told, a bird in flight. The towers were crowned by twin penthouses. "Obviously," our guide said as we filtered into the south penthouse, "Mr. Barnes and Mr. Connally think this will be the next Miami Beach of the Southwest."

The penthouse was unfurnished, as stark and correct as an art museum. It had recently been sold for about seven hundred thousand dollars. The Sunchase straddled the island in such a way that from any one of the penthouse's deep windows or balconies you could see both the Gulf and the laguna. The island beneath us was such a narrow, feeble thing that I felt like a sailor in a crow's nest looking down at the deck of his ship.

"The amenities here," the guide informed us, "include a dry sauna, a steam bath, racquetball, and tennis. In addition to this building, last year we started Sunchase Mall. We think this will be a nice amenity for this building and a nice amenity for South Padre Island in general. We hope there will be some nice restaurants there, and that will be a further amenity."

It became clear as our tour of South Padre Island progressed that the whole city was in itself a gigantic amenity, a way to make this unforgiving sandbar not only habitable but luxurious. In a curious way the city was distancing itself from the island, building up and away from it instead of embracing it. The island was more and more peripheral to the great free-floating resort colony it had spawned.

Next we went to see the Turtle Lady. "Now, she's not a crazy lady who dresses turtles up in clothes," our tour leader told us as we began to file out of the bus. "Well, she *does* dress her turtles up in clothes, but that's just for the small children, to keep them interested."

The Turtle Lady's real name was Ila Loetscher. She lived in a house on Gulf Boulevard whose foyer was dominated by wooden troughs filled with circulating seawater in which maimed sea turtles swam about. The Turtle Lady wore a white blouse with puffy sleeves under a black vest that said "Save the Ridleys." Her goal in life, she explained breathlessly, was to make the world safe for Kemp's ridleys like the one I had seen washed up on Big Shell.

Her means of raising consciousness on that matter was, to say the least, peculiar. From one of the troughs she picked up a turtle the size of a serving platter and held him upright in front of her. "His name is Lynn," she said, "and he wants to say hello."

The turtle flapped his front flippers.

"What do you do, honey," she asked him, "when you want to be kissed?"

Lynn laid his head back in a languid manner. The Turtle Lady kissed him on his bony beak.

"It only took me a week to train this little child to do that," she said. "You give him love first, and he will knock himself out trying to please you."

She held the turtle out to us. "Anybody else want to kiss him?"

When we demurred, she led us out into the backyard, where larger turtles—ridleys and greens and hawksbills—were kept in concrete tanks. Several of the turtles were missing flippers. Another had been brought to the Turtle Lady in a coma after he had eaten fish coated with tar.

"They are very loving little creatures," she said, gazing blissfully into the tank. "Every night these two go to that corner together and put their flippers around each other. So I know they dearly love each other. Of course they dearly love us, too."

She picked up a female turtle she called Dave Irene and said, "Okay, let's play our game." The Turtle Lady pretended to chew on the turtle's flipper, then began smooching her on the neck, smearing lipstick on the creature's white, wattly skin. "She could play this game all day long," the Turtle Lady said, though Dave Irene's reactions were not noteworthy. It is difficult for a sea turtle to look any way but indifferent.

On the way out I sneaked a peak in a downstairs closet. There, on hangers, was a row of frilly dresses in infant sizes. Turtle clothes. There were tiny sombreros too, and tiny little beds.

In the background I could hear the Turtle Lady cooing. "That's right," she said. "Uh huh. You're Mama's little baby, aren't you?"

Driving around town later on my own, I noticed a statue of Padre Ballí that faced the incoming traffic on the Queen Isabella Causeway. When I asked how it had gotten there, I was told to talk to Johnny Ballí.

Johnny Ballí is Juan José Ballí, a great-grandnephew of the padre and a resident of Brownsville, where he is a border inspector for the Alcoholic Beverage Commission.

"It took five years of my life to get that statue up," he told me over a Whataburger in Port Isabel. "But it was worth it. When I was going to school I remember telling my teachers in history class that I came from the family that owned the island. I was always laughed at. Now my nieces and nephews can get up in history class and say, 'My family once owned this island, and there's a statue to prove it.'"

Ballí had wanted to meet in Port Isabel rather than South Padre because he didn't like the idea of spending money in establishments that were effectively fleecing him of his inheritance. "This is a family," he said, "that got a royal grant, and then we got a royal screw. It burns my ass to know that other people are enjoying something that doesn't belong to them. It's our birthright—it's ours!

"You'll have to excuse me if I get angry when I talk about this. I tend to get a little excited. But I'm not running in a popularity contest here. If somebody gets pissed off, piss on 'em!"

Just exactly what happened to the Ballís' hold on Padre Island is unclear. *State of Texas v. Ballí* proved the validity of the original Spanish grant, but long before that the waters had been muddied. Non-Ballís had been buying and selling the island for generations, and if today's descendants of those usurpers did not have an unsullied claim, they had something more powerful on their side: reality.

Just thinking about the way things had turned out made Johnny Ballí squirm in his booth in outrage. But if he hadn't gotten his family's land back, he had been remarkably successful in making sure that nobody around ever forgot the name Ballí. In 1977 he fired his first salvo by standing up at a Cameron County commissioners' meeting and announcing that as a member of the Ballí family he was claiming possession of Padre Island. For five years he haunted the courthouse, lobbying for a statue of his ancestor. He rallied other members of the family. Two hundred strong, they once marched to Padre from Brownsville. Another time a group of militant Ballí heirs blocked off the causeway leading to their ancestor's island. In 1981 Johnny Ballí won his battle for the statue. Cameron County spent forty thousand dollars to appease the

Ballís, although Johnny is miffed that few of the dignitaries invited to the unveiling bothered to show up.

"It's like standing at a bakery window," Johnny said, "just looking outside. Look what I'm bucking, man—people like John Connally. Big John himself. But maybe if I became filthy rich he could become my buddy. I know how to spend a million dollars just as well as the next guy. Hell, I've got good taste!"

We drove back over the causeway to look at the statue. The padre stood with his arms outstretched, a crucifix in his right hand. He was saying, according to Johnny, "Welcome to my island."

"The greatest moment in my life was the day my father saw that statue," Johnny said. "When it arrived here from Italy, they took us out to the warehouse to see it. It was up high in a big crate, and they had us get on a forklift so they could lift us up to see his face. My dad, he couldn't believe it. He saw it and he just broke down and cried."

Padre Island ended a mile or so south of the statue. Just past the causeway, at the Cameron County line, the resort glamour of South Padre began to trail off. Here there were water slides, video parlors, campsites of crushed shell where forlorn little pup tents were sandwiched between duded-up RVs. Widow's walks made of salt-stained lumber had been attached to the tops of some of the mobile homes in Isla Blanca Park, and as I drove along I could hear the barking of seals from a nearby mom-and-pop oceanarium.

I got out and walked along the jetties that guarded Brazos Santiago Pass. Nearby, in an almost empty pavilion, a band was playing in competition with the tape decks from the cars parked on the access road. High school kids promenaded from car to car, a behavioral logic as deeply encoded as that of the ruddy turnstones that were scavenging among the jetties for crabs.

I looked north, up the island that was Johnny Ballí's birthright. The view was not all that good—there was the steady pressure of development on this end, the scandalous state of the beach on the national seashore. I counted on Padre Island to withstand those abuses, not knowing if it could. It seemed strange to me that this insubstantial sandbar could have had such a constant, lifelong hold on my imagination. Watching the mild waves slide onto the beach, I felt inarticulate, subdued—ready, like that ancient priest, to cast rocks to the four winds, to drink the water of the laguna, and claim the island as my own.

"THE TIGER IS GOD"

When tigers attack men, they do so in a characteristic way. They come from behind, from the right side, and when they lunge it is with the intent of snapping the neck of the prey in their jaws. Most tiger victims die swiftly, their necks broken, their spinal cords compressed or severed high up on the vertebral column.

Ricardo Tovar, a fifty-nine-year-old keeper at the Houston Zoo, was killed by a tiger on May 12, 1988. The primary cause of death was a broken neck, although most of the ribs on the left side of his chest were fractured as well, and there were multiple lacerations on his face and right arm. No one witnessed the attack, and no one would ever know exactly how and why it took place, but the central nightmarish event was clear. Tovar had been standing at a steel door separating the zookeepers' area from the naturalistic tiger display outside. Set into the door was a small viewing window—only slightly larger than an average television screen—made of wire-reinforced glass. Somehow the tiger had broken the glass, grabbed the keeper, and pulled him through the window to his death.

Fatal zoo accidents occur more frequently than most people realize. The year before Tovar died, a keeper in the Fort Worth Zoo was crushed by an elephant, and in 1985, an employee of the Bronx Zoo was killed by two Siberian tigers—the same subspecies as the one that attacked Tovar—when she mistakenly entered the tiger display while the animals were still there. But there was something especially haunting about the Houston incident, something that people could not get out of their minds. It had to do with the realization of a fear built deep into our genetic code: the fear that a beast could appear out of nowhere—through a window!—and snatch us away.

The tiger's name was Miguel. He was eleven years old—middle-aged for a tiger—and had been born at the Houston Zoo to a mother who was a wild-caught Siberian. Siberians are larger in size than any of the other subspecies, and their coats are heavier. Fewer than three hundred of them are now left in the frozen river valleys and hardwood forests of the Russian Far East, though they were once so plentiful in that region that Cossack troops were sent in during the construction of the Trans-Baikal railway specifically to protect the workers from tiger attacks. Miguel was of mixed blood—his father was a zoo-reared Bengal—but his Siberian lineage was dominant. He was a massive 450-pound creature whose disposition had been snarly ever since he was a cub. Some of the other tigers at the zoo were as placid and affectionate as house cats, but Miguel filled his keepers with caution. Oscar Mendietta, a keeper who retired a few weeks before Tovar's death, remembers the way Miguel would sometimes lunge at zoo personnel as they walked by his holding cage, his claws unsheathed and protruding through the steel mesh. "He had," Mendietta says, "an intent to kill."

Tovar was well aware of Miguel's temperament. He had been working with big cats in the Houston Zoo since 1982, and his fellow keepers regarded him as a cautious and responsible man. Like many old-time zookeepers, he was a civil servant with no formal training in zoology, but he had worked around captive animals most of his life (before coming to Houston, he had been a keeper at the San Antonio Zoo) and had gained a good deal of practical knowledge about their behavior. No one regarded Miguel's aggressiveness as aberrant. Tovar and the other keepers well understood the fact that tigers were supposed to be dangerous.

In 1987 the tigers and other cats had been moved from their outdated display cages to brand-new facilities with outdoor exhibit areas built to mimic the animals' natural environments. The Siberian tiger exhibit—in a structure known as the Phase II building—comprised about a quarter of an acre. It was a wide rectangular space decorated with shrubs and trees, a few fake boulders, and a water-filled moat. The exhibit's backdrop was a depiction, in plaster and cement, of a high rock wall seamed with stress fractures.

Built into the wall, out of public view, was a long corridor lined with the cats' holding cages, where the tigers were fed and confined while the keepers went out into the display to shovel excrement and hose down the area. Miguel and the other male Siberian, Rambo, each had a holding cage, and they alternated in the use of the outdoor habitat, since two male tigers occupying the same space guaranteed monumental discord. Next to Rambo's cage was a narrow alcove through which the keepers went back and forth from the corridor into the display. The alcove was guarded by two doors. The one with the viewing window led outside. Another door, made of steel mesh, closed off the interior corridor.

May 12 was a Thursday. Tovar came to work at about six-thirty in the morning, and at that hour he was alone. Rambo was secure in his holding cage and Miguel was outside—it had been his turn that night to have the run of the display.

Thursdays and Sundays were "fast" days. Normally the tigers were fed a daily ration of ten to fifteen pounds of ground fetal calf, but twice a week their food was withheld in order to keep them from growing obese in confinement. The animals knew which days were fast days, and on those mornings they were sometimes balky about coming inside, since no food was being offered. Nevertheless, the tigers had to be secured in their holding cages while the keepers went outside to clean the display. On this morning, Tovar had apparently gone to the viewing window to check the whereabouts of Miguel when the tiger did not come inside, even though the keepers usually made a point of not entering the alcove until they were certain that both animals were locked up in their holding cages. The viewing window was so small and the habitat itself so panoramic that the chances of spotting the tiger from the window were slim. Several of the keepers had wondered why there was a window there at all, since it was almost useless as an observation post and since one would never go through the door in the first place without being certain that the tigers were in their cages.

But that was where Tovar had been, standing at a steel door with a panel of reinforced glass, when the tiger attacked. John Gilbert, the senior zookeeper who supervised the cat section, stopped in at the Phase II building a little after seven thirty, planning to discuss with Tovar the scheduled sedation of a lion. He had just entered the corridor when he saw broken glass on the floor outside the steel mesh door that led to the alcove. The door was unlocked—it had been opened by Tovar when he entered the alcove to look out the window. Looking through the mesh, Gilbert saw the shards of glass hanging from the window frame and Tovar's cap, watch, and a single rubber boot lying on the floor. Knowing something dreadful had happened, he called Tovar's name, then pushed on the door and cautiously started to enter the alcove. He was only a few paces away from the broken window when the tiger's head suddenly appeared there, filling its jagged frame. His heart pounding, Gilbert backed off, slammed and locked the mesh door behind him, and radioed for help.

Tom Dieckow, a wiry, white-bearded Marine veteran of the Korean War, was the zoo's exhibits curator. He was also in charge of its shooting team, a seldom-convened body whose task was to kill, if necessary, any escaped zoo animal that posed an immediate threat to the public. Dieckow was in his office in the service complex building when he heard Gilbert's emergency call. He grabbed a twelve-gauge shotgun, commandeered an electrician's pickup truck, and arrived at the tiger exhibit two minutes later. He went around to the front of the habitat and saw Miguel standing there, calm and unconcerned, with Tovar's motionless body lying face down fifteen feet away. Dieckow did not shoot. It was his clear impression that the keeper was dead, that the harm was already done. By that time the zoo's response team had gathered outside the exhibit. Miguel stared at the onlookers and then picked up Tovar's head in his jaws and started to drag him off.

"I think probably what crossed that cat's mind at that point," Dieckow speculated later, "is 'Look at all those scavengers across there that are after my prey. I'm gonna move it.' He was just being a tiger."

Dieckow raised his shotgun again, this time with the intention of shooting Miguel, but because of all the brush and ersatz boulders in the habitat, he could not get a clear shot. He fired into the water instead, causing the startled tiger to drop the keeper, and then fired twice more as another zoo worker discharged a fire extinguisher from the top of the rock wall. The commotion worked, and Miguel retreated into his holding cage.

The Houston Zoo opened a half hour late that day. Miguel and all the other big cats were kept inside until zoo officials could determine if it was safe—both for the cats and for the public—to exhibit them again. For a few days the zoo switchboard was jammed with calls from people wanting to express their opinion on whether the tiger should live or die. But for the people at the zoo that issue had never been in doubt.

"It's automatic with us," John Werler, the zoo director, told me when I visited his office a week after the incident. "To what end would we destroy the tiger? If we followed this argument to its logical conclusion, we'd have to destroy every dangerous animal in the zoo collection."

Werler was a reflective, kindly looking man who was obviously weighed down by a load of unpleasant concerns. There was the overall question of zoo safety, the specter of lawsuits, and most recently the public anger of a number of zoo staffers who blamed Tovar's death on the budget cuts, staffing shortages, and bureaucratic indifference that forced keepers to work alone in potentially dangerous environments. But the dominant mood of the zoo, the day I was there, appeared to be one of simple sadness and shock.

"What a terrible loss," read a sympathy card from the staff of the Fort Worth Zoo that was displayed on a coffee table. "May you gain strength and support to get you through this awful time."

The details of the attack were still hazy, and still eerie to think about. Unquestionably, the glass door panel had not been strong enough, but exactly how Miguel had broken it, how he had killed Tovar—and why—remained the subjects of numb speculation. One point was beyond dispute: a tiger is a predator, its mission on the earth is to kill, and in doing so it often displays awesome strength and dexterity.

An Indian researcher, using live deer and buffalo calves as bait, found that the elapsed time between a tiger's secure grip on the animal's neck and the prey's subsequent death was anywhere from thirty-five to ninety seconds. In other circumstances the cat will not choose to be so swift. Sometimes a tiger will kill an elephant calf by snapping its trunk and waiting for it to bleed to death, and it is capable of dragging the carcass in its jaws for miles. (A full-grown tiger possesses the traction power of thirty men.) When a mother tiger is teaching her cubs to hunt, she might move in on a calf, cripple it with a powerful bite to its rear leg, and stand back and let the cubs practice on the helpless animal.

Tigers have four long canine teeth—fangs. The two in the upper jaw are tapered along the sides to a shearing edge. Fourteen of the teeth are molars, for chewing meat and grinding bone. Like other members of the cat family, tigers have keen, night-seeing eyes, and their hearing is so acute that Indonesian hunters—convinced that a tiger could hear the wind whistling through a man's nose hairs—always kept their nostrils carefully barbered. The pads on the bottom of a tiger's paws are surprisingly sensitive, easily blistered or cut on hot, prickly terrain. But the claws within, five on each front paw and four in the hind paws, are protected like knives in an upholstered box.

They are not idle predators; when they kill, they kill to eat. Even a well-fed tiger in a zoo keeps his vestigial repertoire of hunting behaviors intact. (Captive breeding programs, in fact, make a point of selecting in favor of aggressive predatory behavior, since the ultimate hope of these programs is to bolster the dangerously low stock of free-living tigers.) In the zoo, tigers will stalk birds that land in their habitats, and they grow more alert than most people would care to realize when children pass before their gaze. Though stories of man-eating tigers have been extravagantly embellished over the centuries, the existence of such creatures is not legendary. In the Sundarbans, the vast delta region that spans the border of India and Bangladesh, more than four hundred people have been killed by tigers in the last decade. So many fishermen and honey collectors have been carried off that a few years ago officials at the Sunderbans tiger preserve began stationing electrified dummies around the park to encourage the tigers to seek other prey. One percent of all tigers, according to a German biologist who studied them in the Sunderbans, are "dedicated" man-eaters: when they go out hunting, they're after people. Up to a third of all tigers will kill and eat a human if they come across one, though they don't make a special effort to do so.

It is not likely that Miguel attacked Ricardo Tovar out of hunger. Except for the killing wounds inflicted by the tiger, the keeper's body was undisturbed. Perhaps something about Tovar's movements on the other side of the window intrigued the cat enough to make him spring, a powerful lunge that sent him crashing through the glass. Most likely the tiger was surprised, and frightened, and reacted instinctively. There is no evidence that he came all the way through the window. Probably he just grabbed Tovar by the chest with one paw, crushed him against the steel door, and with unthinkable strength pulled him through the window and killed him outside.

John Gilbert, the senior keeper who had been the first on the scene that morning, took me inside the Phase II building to show me where the attack had taken place. Gilbert was a sandy-haired man in his thirties, still shaken and subdued by what he had seen. His recitation of the events was as formal and precise as that of a witness at an inquest.

"When I got to this point," Gilbert said as we passed through the security doors that led to the keepers' corridor, "I saw the broken glass on the floor. I immediately yelled Mr. Tovar's name . . ."

The alcove in which Tovar had been standing was much smaller than I had pictured it, and seeing it firsthand made one thing readily apparent: it was a trap. Its yellow cinder-block walls were no more than four feet apart. The ceiling was made of steel mesh and a door of the same material guarded the exit to the corridor. The space was so confined it was not difficult to imagine—it was impossible *not* to imagine—how the tiger had been able to catch Tovar by surprise with a deadly swipe from his paw.

And there was the window. Covered with a steel plate now, its meager dimensions were still visible. The idea of being hauled through that tiny space by a tiger had an almost supernatural resonance—as if the window were a portal through which mankind's most primeval terrors were allowed to pass unobstructed.

Gilbert led me down the corridor. We passed the holding cage of Rambo, who hung his head low and let out a grumbling basso roar so deep it sounded like a tremor in the earth. Then we were standing in front of Miguel.

"Here he is," Gilbert said, looking at the animal with an expression on his face that betrayed a sad welter of emotions. "He's quite passive right now."

The tiger was reclining on the floor, looking at us without concern. I noticed his head, which seemed to me wider than the window he had broken out. His eyes were yellow, and when the great head pivoted in my direction and Miguel's eyes met mine I looked away reflexively, afraid of their hypnotic gravity. The tiger stood up and began to pace, his gigantic pads treading noiselessly on the concrete. The bramble of black stripes that decorated his head was as neatly symmetrical as a Rorschach inkblot, and his orange fur—conceived by evolution as camouflage—was a florid, provocative presence in the featureless confines of the cage.

Miguel idly pawed the steel guillotine door that covered the entrance to his cage, and then all of a sudden he reared on his hind legs. I jumped back a little, startled and dwarfed. The top of Miguel's head nestled against the ceiling mesh of his cage, his paws were spread to either side. In one silent moment, his size and scale seemed to have increased exponentially. He looked down at Gilbert and me. In Miguel's mind, I suspected, his keeper's death was merely a vignette, a mostly forgotten moment of fright and commotion that had intruded one day upon the tiger's torpid existence in the zoo. But it was hard not to look up at that immense animal and read his posture as a deliberate demonstration of the power he possessed.

I thought of Tipu Sultan, the eighteenth-century Indian mogul who was obsessed with the tiger and used its likeness as his constant emblem. Tipu Sultan's imperial banner had borne the words "The Tiger Is God." Looking up into Miguel's yellow eyes I felt the strange appropriateness of those words. The tiger was majestic and unknowable, a beast of such seeming invulnerability that it was possible to believe that he alone had called the world into being, and that a given life could end at his whim. The truth, of course, was far more literal. Miguel was a remnant member of a species never far from the brink of extinction, and his motivation for killing Ricardo Tovar probably did not extend beyond a behavioral quirk. He had a predator's indifference to tragedy; he had killed without culpability. It was a gruesome and unhappy incident, but as far as Miguel was concerned most of the people at the zoo had reached the same conclusion: he was just being a tiger.

THE BAY

The wind is light, an idle spring breeze, but it gusts forcefully across the bay, turning the water's surface into a field of percolating whitecaps. A short distance from shore, an unladen tanker coasts through the chop, heading up past Morgan's Point to Buffalo Bayou and the Port of Houston. Its wake loses definition among the unruly wave patterns and ends up as a tired riffle that washes against the eroded shoreline—against piers and bulkheads and stretches of protective riprap formed from old car bodies and pieces of concrete culvert. There is a vague, watermelon-like scent in the air—the smell of fish oil and fish blood released from the bodies of shad or mullet as they are torn apart by predators that have herded them into a roiling, panicky mass. On the edge of the Ship Channel a shrimp boat, winching in its nets, is almost obscured by a cloud of laughing gulls. The gulls are in their breeding colors, their bright red beaks shining like enamel in the clear air.

Galveston Bay can sometimes appear picturesque; it could not be truthfully described as beautiful. Its waters are shallow and murky, an opaque green marbled with currents of resuspended mud left behind by the passage of boats and pipeline dredges. Its shorelines are drab and abrupt. Much of the western margin of the bay is dominated by a petrochemical skyline, a hazy gridwork of twisting pipelines and flaming towers. Nowhere else is there such a concentrated display of the raw wealth that built Texas or of the price the natural environment has paid for that wealth. The bay has been despoiled for so long, has been used so hard, that it has developed a perverse allure. Ross Sterling, the governor of Texas from 1931 to 1933, once built a scaled-down replica of the White House for himself near La Porte. The view he most admired from the roof terrace of his dream home was the lights of the refineries on the opposite shore.

Galveston Bay is a working bay. Take away the shipping, the refining, the whole thrumming human presence, and there is still a feel of industry about it. The bay is a mighty thing, a self-adjusting biological engine that runs day and night, season after season, constantly generating and absorbing life. It is the largest estuary on the Texas coast, the seventh largest in the United States, a vast nursery and feedlot where all manner of marine larvae, spats, and fingerlings pass their perilous youths. Even the people most concerned about preserving the bay have grown accustomed to speaking of it in terms of its productivity, as a resource, as if in order to justify its existence it must compete with the commerce surrounding it. At a time in which the salvation of the oceans has suddenly appeared as one of the planet's highest priorities, Texas still thinks of its poisoned waters with a sense of dollars lost instead of a sense of shame.

On maps, the bay has the shape of a mashed butterfly. One wing is made up of a gracefully curving shoreline that includes the entrance to the Houston Ship Channel on the west and the Trinity River delta on the east. The other wing, flattened and truncated, is known as East Bay and runs east behind the Bolivar Peninsula. Trailing the butterfly is a long, narrow tendril—called West Bay—that makes up the inward shore of Galveston Island. It all amounts to six hundred square miles of water sitting in a shallow basin of mud. Fresh water enters the bay from the San Jacinto River and, to a much greater extent, from the Trinity, whose drainage area pulls rainwater and runoff into the bay from as far away as Fort Worth. From the sea, the saltwater tide flows in through the mile-wide gap where Galveston Island and

Bolivar Peninsula fail to meet, a narrow but vital thoroughfare known as Bolivar Roads.

This mixture of salt water and fresh water in the bay is a hospitable one. It gives rise to an almost inconceivable abundance of life, millions and millions of pounds of harvested sea creatures, flapping and scuttling about on the decks of sport boats and commercial vessels. The catch is so abundant that oysters and crabs from Galveston Bay are eaten on the shores of the Chesapeake Bay.

But the bay is decidedly not what it once was. John James Audubon came to Galveston Bay in 1837, when Texas was still so new a republic that one of the few things a tourist could buy was a Mexican skull picked up off the battlefield of San Jacinto. Audubon was not in the best of moods on this trip. He had lost twelve pounds, his legs were swollen, and the mosquitoes, he wrote, "were annoying enough even for me." But his mind was as engaged as ever. He took note of the birds that had been forced down in their northern migrations by a powerful storm, reported finding a new species of rattlesnake, and discovered a large swordfish stranded on a sandbar that, when cut open, produced ten wriggling young.

The abundance and beauty of the bay seemed to revive him. "Ah, my dear friend," Audubon wrote in a letter, "would that you were here just now to see the Snipes innumerable, the Blackbirds, the Gallinules, and the Curlews that surround us;—that you could listen as I now do, to the delightful notes of the Mocking-bird, pouring forth his soul in melody as the glorious orb of day is fast descending towards the western horizon;—that you could gaze on the Great Herons which, after spreading their broad wings, croak aloud as if doubtful regarding the purpose of our visit to these shores!"

If it was the Eskimo curlew that Audubon was referring to in his letter, that bird is now almost extinct. It was once one of the most abundant shorebirds on Galveston Bay. Eskimo curlews were called doughbirds because the thick, fatty meat of their breasts was as pale and soft as dough. They were killed by the hundreds of thousands—their plump breasts splitting open when they hit the ground—packed in barrels, and sent back east. The last one seen in the vicinity was spotted on Galveston Island in the early sixties.

The bottom of the bay, in Audubon's time, was carpeted with sea-grass meadows, great swaths of turtle grass, and eelgrass that fixed the sediment and kept the water clear. He would have seen stands of pri-meval cypress where there are now container docks; expanses of short-grass prairie, with vultures nesting in the prickly pear, where there are now coastal bermuda and asphalt. He might have seen manatees idling below the surface, as smooth and slow as dirigibles.

All of that is gone, all but the bay itself. If it is no longer the wonder that filled Audubon's heart, it remains a marvel of resilience. How could it even still exist, after all the life that has been extracted from it, all the chemicals and wastewater sludge and brine that have been pumped into it, all the development that has taken place on its shores? More than half of the chemicals produced in the United States come from the area around Galveston Bay. Thirty percent of the nation's petroleum industry is located there. Twenty percent of the people who live in Texas live somewhere along the bay's margin. Municipal and industrial waste-water is discharged into the bay from 1,151 registered treatment plants. Beneath the surface are 251 miles of dredged channels, 247 miles of pipeline. The water contains DDT, aliphatic hydrocarbons, aromatic hydrocarbons, organophosphates. There is chromium, copper, lead, nickel, zinc, and mercury. Fifty-one percent of the bay is permanently closed to shellfish harvesting because of bacterial pollution. Ninety-five percent of the seagrass has disappeared. Bulkheads and marinas are replacing the cordgrass marshes that incubate marine life and prevent erosion. Poachers are collecting and eating the eggs from the few scrag-gly islands where shorebirds still find it congenial to nest. And there are two looming projects—the deepening and widening of the Houston Ship Channel and the completion of the Wallisville reservoir near the mouth of the Trinity—which some environmentalists believe could seal the fate of the bay.

"Your article may be an epitaph," Ted Eubanks, the president of the Houston Audubon Society, told me one day as we stood on the hypnotic expanse of Bolivar Flats, observing piping plovers through a spotting scope. "The destruction of Galveston Bay is running full speed."

Eubanks, who owns a trucking business in Houston, delivered this dire prophecy with his usual air of ominous reason. I recognized his opinion as being on the alarmist end of the scale, a surly, brokenhearted lament of the sort that I had heard dismissed, more than once, as "emotional." But in the long history of human abuse of the bay, emotion has been a conspicuously absent quality. Galveston Bay was always there to be exploited—its original beauty so subtle as to be hardly noticed during the raucous coming-out party of the Texas economy.

Optimists argue that twenty years ago the bay was in much worse shape. The nearly unimpeded dumping of municipal and industrial waste in the Houston Ship Channel had turned the water into an oxygen-depleted witch's brew of toxic compounds and sewer sludge— "the only ship channel in the world," Lloyd Bentsen has quipped, "to have an octane rating." The Ship Channel is still far away from being a swimmable and fishable stream, but the passage of the Clean Water Act in 1970 and a growing environmental awareness helped curb the blithe excesses of industry. The Houston Ship Channel currently has a dissolved oxygen rating of one, a step up from the anaerobic zero it used to be but far from the five required for "contact-recreation." ("Fish can live in category-one water," an employee of the Texas Water Commission told me, "they just can't scoot around much.") And after decades of dreadful wastewater problems, the City of Houston has finally entered into a compliance agreement with the water commission that, ten years and one billion dollars from now, will have reduced significantly the flow of untreated sewage into the bay. The problem is that those gains have been hard-fought and incremental; meanwhile, the bay has continued to suffer torrential assaults from every imaginable direction.

Here at Bolivar Flats, at the seaward margin of the bay with the renewing ocean tide sluicing past, it was still possible to imagine a coastal wilderness. There were immense numbers of avocets and black-necked stilts feeding in the shallows, and beyond them a raft of white pelicans wavered like a mirage in the hazy, heat-refracted light. The piping plovers—representing ten percent of the dwindling world population of their species—stood about on one leg with their beaks under their wings, or shuffled the sand with their feet in an attempt to uncover the boreholes of worms.

Eubanks was worried about a proposal to remove sand from Bolivar Flats and transplant it to the chronically eroded Galveston beaches.

That was the last thing the plovers needed. Their nesting areas on the eastern seaboard were already seriously threatened by development, and now their critical wintering habitat on the flats was in jeopardy too. It was only one more example, one more way in which some modest industrial or recreational enhancement imperiled the vitality of the bay.

"It's real subtle, it's real incremental," Eubanks said. "We're just picking away at the bay. Every marina, every bulkhead, every little sewage plant, every gallon of effluent—it all has its effect. If you asked me right now, I'd say that in thirty years this bay is going to be a saltwater bathtub."

A bay like Galveston Bay has a limited allegiance to the ocean. Some bays are all salt, simple nicks in the shoreline filled with undiluted seawater. Galveston Bay is more complicated. It depends upon the Gulf of Mexico but at the same time defends itself against it, controlling the intrusions of the open sea through the nearly closed gates of its marine passes.

The bay seeks a certain balance: enough salt water to sustain marine creatures, enough fresh water to keep them safe from saline-dependent predators. The big oyster reefs, for instance, tend to be concentrated in the center of the bay, where the saltwater content is characteristically around twenty parts per thousand. That is a congenial enough environment for oysters—which can survive in waters as low as ten parts per thousand—but the salt mixture is too thin to support the various snails and parasites that prey on them.

The ratio of fresh water to salt water is preserved not by delicate adjustments but by erratic and wholesale fluctuation, by floods and storms and by powerful, unseen currents that move beneath the surface. A spring freshet can bring one hundred thousand cubic feet per second of fresh water into the bay, driving the salt water back into the Gulf. During the drier months of the fall the salt water creeps back, exposing the oyster reefs and brackish marshes to a host of predators that could not normally tolerate such feeble salinity.

By contrast, the routine tides in Galveston Bay are marginal events. In the upper parts of the bay the tide is usually measured in inches, though near the mouth it can be as great as three feet. Compared with the wind, the tide is negligible. The bay's fetch—the vast, unobstructed tabletop it presents to the atmosphere—provides a light wind with room to maneuver and grow, allowing it to build waves and send them snowballing across the water's surface. The bay is so susceptible to the effects of wind that a strong winter front can push half—literally half—of its water out into the Gulf.

It is not just the wind that moves the water. The bay is full of mysterious currents that rove silently beneath the surface like some undetectable species of leviathan. These are called density currents—the result of the constant mixing of fresh water and salt water. Because salt water is dense, it sinks to the bottom of the bay and forms a wedge that flows beneath the lighter fresh water, generating a current in the way that a discrepancy in atmospheric pressure generates wind. The greater the depth, the greater the inrush of salt water. The bay's natural depth is anywhere from three to ten feet, but the Houston Ship Channel—which cuts through the bottom of the bay like a giant furrow—is a forty-foot-deep corridor that acts as a saltwater conduit, allowing water from the Gulf to be drawn deep into the bay.

As an estuary, Galveston Bay depends not only on a proper salinity ratio but on the safe harbor its marshes provide for the voyaging planktonic forms that will one day grow into mollusks or fish or anemones. From a distance—as you drive along the Interstate 45 causeway leading to Galveston or across the tidal rivers and bayous farther north—the wetlands that remain along the margins of the bay resemble a lush green mat, as solid and vivid as Astroturf. Up close, they are a mass of solitary spiky plants, thick-bodied stalks of grass that rise from the water like the trees of a flooded forest. The plants are smooth cordgrass, *Spartina alterniflora*. They thrive here, where hardly any other vegetation does. They reproduce by rhizomes that tunnel through the submerged mud. Their cells are dense with salt, giving them the osmotic muscle to suck fresh water from the briny swamp in which they stand.

The cordgrass is hardy but imperiled. Bulkheads, marinas, docks, boat slips, power plants, refineries, parking lots—almost any way in which the bay's resources are customarily tapped leads to the depletion of its primogenitive wetlands. Without the cordgrass, the waves undercut and erode the shoreline; they carry off the land itself—a ranch pasture, the precious square inches fronting a vacation home—and add it into the sediment stew of the bay.

One afternoon I went on a tour of a cordgrass reclamation project near Anahuac, along the eastern shore of the bay, with Bob Nailon, a county extension agent, and Eddie Seidensticker, who works for the Soil Conservation Service. As a team they displayed a touching enthusiasm for the wonders of *Spartina alterniflora*, and kept finishing one another's sentences as we drove in a pickup to the sites where they had been replanting cordgrass. This side of the bay, which consists of a blunt peninsula that finally tapers down to the little fishing and oystering community of Smith Point, seemed light-years away from the heavy industry across the water. We traveled through undeveloped savannahs and spindly forests of Chinese tallow, passing boat slips where Vietnamese fishermen were trailering boats filled with crab pots. The land around here belonged to a few ancestral ranching families, and it had an air of deliberate isolation. Plans to connect Smith Point with Clear Lake City via hovercraft had been lingering in the air for a few years, but it seemed as if they would linger indefinitely.

"What we're trying to do," Seidensticker said as we drove along a ranch road that paralleled the eroded shoreline, "is reestablish the estuarine zone that used to be here."

That zone was definitely long gone. The shore was an ugly heap of riprap that had not succeeded in keeping the bay from eating the ranch acreage. Up ahead, however, we stopped at a place where the Soil Conservation Service had replanted cordgrass thirty years earlier. The contrast was startling. To our right was a ruined shoreline where the bay water washed through rusted car bodies and tires and buckled sections of concrete that the landowner had deposited over the years in a vain attempt to hold back the wave action. To our left was an appealing expanse of *Spartina* extending thirty or forty yards into the bay, the water smooth except for a little passing shiver caused by a school of fish.

"See," Nailon explained, "the grass acts as a shock absorber. It stops the waves before they impact the bank."

"And when you compare the unsightliness of this," Seidensticker said, indicating the riprap, "to that . . ."

I didn't know whether to be comforted by the comeback of the cordgrass or merely appalled that for so long people had thought so little of the bay that the idea of tossing old car parts into it was perfectly acceptable. Nailon and Seidensticker, however, stood there admiring the cordgrass with the deep contentment of gardeners who had raised a flawless crop of tomatoes. The grass was protected from wave action by a fence made of nylon parachute webbing. When the area was first replanted thirty years ago, no wave barriers had been put up, and Seidensticker and Nailon regarded it as serendipitous that the fledgling cordgrass had survived.

"If you've got a small area of fetch," Seidensticker explained, "if you don't have very much open water, this stuff's easy to grow. But here on Galveston Bay we're talking about a fetch of eight to ten miles. You get a wave three or four feet high, and it just knocks it out."

Originally, they constructed their wave barriers out of used Christmas trees. Seidensticker recalled those days as being "labor-intensive." The parachute webbing was a better solution, cheaper in the long run and more effective. And through trial and error they've learned not to transplant grass in clumps, which disturbs the substrate and makes it more difficult for the grass to take hold. Now the high school and college students who do the planting are instructed to insert each stem individually, setting it lovingly into a six-inch hole poked into the mud.

I borrowed a pair of rubber wading boots from Nailon and walked out into the marsh, noting how firm the sediment was close to shore and how mushy it felt as I walked farther out into the less-established fringes, where the wave energy was stronger and more apt to rile the bottom. Standing at the edge of the marsh, I tracked a series of six-inch-high waves as they moved from the open bay into the *Spartina*. It was a surprisingly beautiful thing to see, the way the unruly waves were tamed bit by bit as they passed through the marsh, growing smaller and more elegant until finally they no longer existed. The waves that hit the outlying stems of cordgrass with such bluster never even touched the shore; they just slouched with their filtered water into a clear backside pool whose firm bottom was crisscrossed with snail tracks and the molted shells of crabs. The thick stalks of the cordgrass were decorated with periwinkle shells, the snails clinging above the waterline and feeding on the algae deposited by the tide. In time the periwinkles would be eaten by redfish and black drum, the fish imbibing the shells and grinding them to powder in a special organ, tough as a drill bit, harbored deep in their throats. And when the cordgrass itself broke down, it would be eaten by microorganisms that would, in turn, feed the zooplankton and infant fish sheltered in the marsh.

Part of that zooplankton consisted of oyster larvae. At this stage of their lives oysters are known as veligers, simple transparent forms that ingest diatoms as they waft through the submerged cordgrass. There are a lot of them. A single female oyster is capable of producing five hundred million eggs in a single year. During spawning season the males are hard at work as well, pumping like underwater geysers and sending out clouds of sperm to mix with the drifting ova. Only a small percentage of the eggs are fertilized, and the resulting veligers have only a dim chance of surviving into oysterhood. After twelve or fourteen days the veligers begin to spat, settling to the bottom of the bay and feeling with their single blob of a foot for a receptive hard surface—known as cultch—on which to settle. Most of the downward-drifting veligers never find a cultch site. They sink into the soft mud like doomed paratroopers. Those that survive land, more often than not, on the shells of other oysters and become part of the reef, cementing themselves for life and depending on the currents and tides to bring them food.

In times of floods and heavy rain the oyster population suffers heavy casualties, since prolonged exposure to fresh water saps them of vital minerals. But in the long run fresh water is the oysters' salvation, since it keeps away predatory snails and parasites that could, if uncontrolled, destroy all the oysters in the bay.

"Oysters can be destroyed by a flood, but they'll come back faster than the predators will," says Sammy Ray, a marine biologist with Texas A&M at Galveston. "The last thing you want in an estuary is a stable situation. Show me an area where oysters are not threatened by floods, and I'll show you an area where you don't get consistent oyster production."

Galveston Bay produces two-thirds of the oysters harvested in Texas, though as a shellfish industry, oystering runs a distant second to shrimping. Oyster season lasts from November to April, and most of the oyster fishermen are shrimpers during the rest of the year. As a business, oystering is problematic. Oysters are easy prey, but their numbers can fluctuate wildly, and oystermen are constantly under scrutiny from a host of regulatory agencies. The health department has permanently closed more than half of the bay to oyster harvesting and closes other areas when rainfall and runoff threaten to foul the water. (Since oysters are sedentary filter-feeders, they are perfect bacterial sumps—"miniature sewage-treatment plants," one scientist described them—and in even mildly polluted waters they can bank enough germs to greatly enhance a diner's chances of contracting hepatitis.) In November 1987, in a decision that generated much controversy and bitterness, the Texas Parks and Wildlife Department decided that the reefs were in danger of being fished out and closed the oyster season altogether.

"This is a very typical day in terms of politicking," Joe Nelson told me one day near the end of the oyster season when I visited his operation in Smith Point. "Every day you're fighting for your life."

Nelson's grayish slicked-back hair and flattened nose gave him a dangerous-looking countenance, but he was friendly and related his bureaucratic trials with a touch of exasperated humor. His problems that day had to do with the health department and its decision to close part of the bay after a recent rainfall.

"See," he said, "they took a sample on Tuesday and closed the bay on the assumption that it would be bad. Well, the sample came back Thursday, and it was good, but that was no guarantee that the water wasn't bad on Friday, Saturday, Sunday, and Monday. So then they assume that the water was bad all the way up to Monday and that by now the oysters haven't had time to cleanse themselves. The point is, there was no verification that the water was bad when they closed it, and by the time they find out whether it was or not, it'll be twelve or thirteen days before we're back to work."

As I was straining to understand all of that, Nelson took me on a tour of his dockside facilities, the freezers and shucking tables and piles of fly-infested oyster shell that would be returned to the bay to provide new cultch.

"I've been playing with oysters ever since I was six or seven years old," Nelson reflected, idly sorting through a pile of oyster shell. He said he was born in Galveston in 1936, trundled into a suitcase a few days later, and brought home to Smith Point on a boat.

"Everything was water here," he remembered. "There was very little done by road. We got electricity here in '49. Got phones in '59. Got a shell road in '47 or '48.

"All this shoreline along this bay front where we're at—you could go out there and pick up all the oysters you wanted to deal with. If the tide was low, the chain of reefs would start at Ellum Grove and go all the way to the Ship Channel. There were so many reefs, there were only three passes through the bay—Barrell Pass, Moody's Cut, and the Ship Channel. Then the shell dredges came in and removed all these shell reefs and barrier islands."

The oysters began to decline as more and more dredging and development altered their habitat. Lake Livingston, built on the Trinity in the sixties, reduced the flow of fresh water at about the same time that a newly dug fish pass on Bolivar Peninsula increased the ratio of salt water. Meanwhile, more and more of the shallow-water reefs were declared off-limits by the health department.

These days Nelson's oyster crews spend their time working reefs that Nelson leases from Parks and Wildlife. The work involves not just dredging up oysters but also sometimes shuttling them around, moving them from a section of the bay the health department considers polluted to cleaner water, where they can be purged for two weeks and then harvested for sale.

Joe and his brother, Ben, took me out in a boat to see one of the oyster dredges. The water in the boat slip was a dark green, like a gumbo overloaded with filé powder. As soon as the prop started turning, the mud roiled up to the surface.

"When I was a kid," Joe lamented, "you could see bottom in four, four and a half feet of water. This bay was like a crystal. You could herd redfish, watching everything that was going on. You'd see flounders down there, stingarees. That was before all the sulphur boats destroyed all the grass beds. And you've got bottom down here that's never firmed up from all the dredging."

We pulled out of the channel, the Vingt-et-un Islands on our right and the open bay ahead. The Nelsons' leases were in East Bay, just around the point, their boundaries marked with saplings that rose six feet out of the water and gave the locations a spectral, swampy look.

Over the roar of the engine Joe and Ben hollered complaints into my ear about bureaucratic interference. In fifteen minutes we pulled up to a long barge-like vessel with an overhead awning. The boat was just then hauling up its dredge, which resembled a massive enclosed rake. We went aboard and watched the crew break apart the clusters of oysters on the sorting table. An oyster has to be three inches long before it's legal, and many of the smaller ones were cemented to the shells of the keepers. Mixed in with the clusters were the cone-shaped shells of the predator snails called oyster drills, and many of the oysters themselves were infested with tiny sponges that had bored into their shells and left a signature resembling that of a ringworm.

The Nelsons took along a dozen good-sized oysters when they returned to their boat. While Ben steered, Joe pried one open with a pocketknife.

"See how yellow it is here?" he said, pointing to the swollen protoplasm of the oyster, its heart pumping beneath a glaze of mucus. "He's done started to release his gonads. When he's caught for too long in fresh water he'll feed on his body fluid, use up all his gonadal material to support his life.

"An oyster's always doing one of two things. He's either laying down shell or he's using up shell. See those little brown spots there? That's where a predator's trying to come in and he's laying down shell to prevent it."

Joe stood for a moment studying the oyster. "You know, the more I learn about him and his reproductive cycle, his great ability to withstand predators, his ability to shrink his shell up when conditions aren't right—he's just an amazing creature. I can take this oyster out of the shell and leave him on the half shell and he'll start laying down a crust of a shell on there. As far as I know I'm the only one who's ever experimented with that. I've had 'em stay alive for six weeks on the half shell. He'll be ugly as the devil, but at least he's alive and well."

Joe looked admiringly at the oyster one last time and then slurped him off the shell.

On the way back to Smith Point the Nelsons complained anew about

Parks and Wildlife and the way the health department habitually closed the bay at the first hint of rainfall ("Every time a cow pisses on a flat rock," Ben said, "we get alarmed"), but their mood was high as they downed the rest of the oysters.

"This is the only way to live," Joe said, prying apart another shell as Ben opened up the throttle. "Salt water in your face all day, every day of your life."

The main channel of the Trinity River enters the bay through a green delta land braided together with dozens of wandering, nameless streams. Here, miles above the bay itself, are standing lakes bordered by cypress, the water bubbling with methane gas when you disturb the fecund bottom with an oar. Alligators plunge into the water at the approach of a boat, sending an agitated streak of mud outward from the bank.

This is the country—bayous and swamps and verdant lowlands— that feeds the bay. Down these streams, over these grasslands, comes the crucial freshwater inflow, bearing with it the plant detritus that provides the diet of the zooplankton waiting in the *Spartina* marsh. Anything that alters or interrupts this flow threatens, in small or large measure, the fundamental character of Galveston Bay.

No one knows for sure just how great an effect the construction of the Wallisville reservoir might have on the bay, but driving a stake through the heart of this project has been a cherished goal of environmentalists for decades. As originally conceived in the late fifties, Wallisville was a nineteen-thousand-acre reservoir that would have inundated almost the entire delta of the Trinity River and provided the first lock for the Trinity River barge canal, a wildly ambitious notion then in vogue whose purpose was to connect Fort Worth to the sea. The U.S. Army Corps of Engineers began construction on the dam and the lock in 1966 and was just about finished in 1973, when a federal judge, agreeing with the Sierra Club and other plaintiffs that the Corps' environmental impact statement had been inadequate, issued an injunction. The Corps went back to the drawing board and returned with a modified proposal, one that would reduce the impounded acreage to one-fourth of what it had been in the original plan. The justification for the dam had been changed, too. Since the Trinity barge canal had been shelved, the dam was now billed as a means for controlling saltwater intrusions into the water supply of the rice farmers along the lower Trinity. After years of courtroom intrigue, the injunction was finally lifted, but in the meantime the federal government—which under the Reagan administration regarded water-supply issues as a local responsibility—had backed out of its original agreement to foot most of the bill.

For the dam to be finished, somebody needs to pay for it. The City of Houston, whose water supply would benefit from the reservoir, is the likeliest entity to pick up the tab, but for now the project is dormant once again, and there are a lot of people who would like to see it never wake up.

"It's not an environmental disaster," insists Bill Wooley, the chief planner of the Corps of Engineers. "You've got to remember, this dam is only four feet high. It's not a Grand Coulee. Unfortunately the word 'dam' at the mouth of the Trinity sets off an emotional reaction in people that we'll be stopping the flow. But it's like putting a teacup at the end of a hose. Once that teacup is full, the rest of the water runs around."

A retired real estate agent named John Cheesman took me upriver one day in his custom-made johnboat. He was anti-dam and he seldom passed up the opportunity to show a reporter or interested visitor the site of the impending debacle. When we were a few miles upstream from Anahuac, a squall passed over the boat and Cheesman broke out a pair of sou'westers. In the wake of the squall there were terns and white ibis flying over the channel and mullet slipping out of the water with effortless velocity.

"How big the reservoir is or isn't is irrelevant," Cheesman said, as he turned off the main channel. "The point is you're destroying the dynamics of the river, you're changing the nature of the water. Think of all that vegetative matter in the Trinity River bottom. As it dies, the floodwaters of the river come in and flush it out into the bay. Sure, water will still pour out over the top of the dam, but all the plant detritus—the food base for those juvenile crabs and shrimp in the bay—will settle down to the bottom."

He steered the boat into the marsh grass and cut the motor when the bow hit solid ground. Ahead of us, a few paces away, were the remains of the original Wallisville dam. It was a harmless-looking thing, a long ribbon of concrete that appeared to be no higher than a curb. The lake that would result from the dam, if it were ever built, would be no deeper in most places than four feet.

"It's not the kind of thing," Cheesman offered sarcastically, "that looks like a monument to man's ingenuity."

I was struck by how such a modest structure, located miles upriver from the entrance to Galveston Bay, could have such potentially profound effects on that massive body of water. For all the degradation it had endured, the bay had always seemed somehow impervious to me. I had assumed that when it came time for the bay to die, it would die of some titanic environmental insult that would be worthy of its grandeur. But I realized, standing here on the low concrete spillway of the abandoned dam, that the end would probably not be that dramatic. Galveston Bay was like a beating heart whose veins and capillaries were being closed off, almost unnoticeably, one by one. In the end no one would be able to tell exactly when or why the blood stopped flowing.

The bottom of Galveston Bay, if you could remove the water to inspect it, would appear to be crisscrossed with deep gouges. These are the avenues upon which the commerce of the bay travels, the channels through which heavy oceangoing vessels move along like slot cars on a toy roadway. In Audubon's time the bay was navigable only at high tide, and it was a common occurrence for boats to run aground on the bars and oyster reefs. In 1870 a six-foot-deep channel was cut through the shell islands in the middle of the bay, and dredging has been going on ever since. The Houston Ship Channel, which runs from the buoy outside of Bolivar Roads all the way to the turning basin at the far-inland Port of Houston, has been steadily deepened over the years to accommodate ever-larger classes of vessels.

Improving and maintaining navigational waterways is the work of the U.S. Army Corps of Engineers. The Corps loves its work. It exists to implement plans—to build, to dredge, to shore up, to move earth, and to divert water. At the behest of the Port of Houston, the Corps is now planning to deepen the Houston Ship Channel by ten feet—to a total depth of fifty feet—and to increase its width to six hundred feet.

The port and the Corps maintain that in order to be cost-effective the channel must be accessible to larger vessels. They also contend that the present width of the channel is a potential safety hazard (though collisions and groundings have declined in recent years as a result of a downward trend in overall tonnage).

"It cannot be allowed," says Jim Blackburn, an environmental lawyer and the chairman of the Galveston Bay Foundation, a newly formed alliance of individuals and corporations whose purpose is to monitor the welfare of the bay. "You're talking about sixty-nine million cubic yards of dredge soil in open disposal. They're going to cover eleven thousand acres of Galveston Bay—that's five percent of the bay—with four feet of muck. All of it uncontained, not diked."

The project, according to its opponents, will markedly increase the turbidity of the bay, disrupt the habitats of benthic creatures like worms and clams that form the base of the bay's food chain, and create a conduit that would enhance the saltwater flow from the Gulf. The process of deepening the channel also has the potential of digging up and redistributing toxic pollutants that have settled down peacefully over the decades into the soft sediment.

Waiting for me back at the Corps office in Galveston were the five volumes of the environmental impact statement on the Ship Channel project, hundreds of pages in which the Corps' in-house biologists, chemists, and environmental managers coolly rebutted the grim predictions of lasting harm that the deepening and widening would bring down upon the bay. The Corps' critics—a category that included much of the membership of the Galveston Bay Foundation—regarded those conclusions with skepticism if not outright hostility. It was painfully obvious that the Corps did not meet its payroll by not building things. "The U.S. Army Corps of Engineers," reads a snide bumper sticker, "Ruining Tomorrow Today."

"Okay, we're not the Sierra Club," Ed White, a public affairs officer with the Corps, told me as we motored up the Ship Channel in an air-conditioned launch. "We're a pragmatic organization, and we're in the position where it's real easy to make us out to be a villain. But our people live here, they work here. This," he said, indicating the vast gray fabric of the bay ahead, "is our recreation area as well as everyone else's."

The boat emerged from the protection of the pass into the open bay, cruising above an invisible crossroads where the Houston Ship Channel, the Galveston Ship Channel, the Texas City Ship Channel, and the Gulf Intracoastal Waterway all converged at the bottom of the bay.

"It gets real busy around here," Floyd Kuykendall, the captain of the launch, said. "You got three or four ferries coming in sometimes. Ships coming in, ships going out."

Shrimp boats lined the channel, and we passed shell barges and drilling rigs and gas wells. A tanker, the *Mobil Vanguard*, slowly bore down upon us from the opposite direction.

"If we were a ship that size," White said, "we'd be heading straight for its nose, and at the last minute we'd veer off and depend on that bow wake to keep us apart. That's because the channel's so narrow. You can imagine what would happen if one of us miscalculated. That's one of the main reasons we have for wanting to widen the channel."

The west shore of the bay, as we cruised by Texas City, was studded with anti-scenery—Monsanto, Arco, Union Carbide. Farther up, the landscape softened somewhat, and as we approached Kemah and Seabrook we could see expensive sailboats pouring from the mouth of Clear Lake. At Atkinson Island, across from Morgan's Point, Kuykendall pulled up at the dock, and White and I got off to look around. The island was a low shell bank that over the years had been enlarged considerably by the dumping of dredge material (the Corps does not like to use the word "spoil"). A circulation channel had been cut through the center of the island, and a gas pump station with its unlit burn-off stack stood at the southern end like a lighthouse. White and I stood on a fetid little beach, looking out over the circulation channel, the noise of the pumping station in the background. The dredge material beneath our feet felt as mucky as quicksand, and the paltry tide of the bay had chipped out a little bluff crowned with sea wrack and trash. White pointed to a congregation of plovers just around the point.

"Those birds have found something to feed on," he said. "This is a real good environment for wildlife."

He had a point, since some spoil islands in the bay have become critical habitats for beleaguered shorebirds, but I was saddened by a deeper implication. I thought of Audubon—"Ah, my dear friend, would that you were here just now to see the Snipes innumerable, the Black-birds, the Gallinules, and the Curlews that surround us . . ."—and realized that one measure of how relentlessly we had abused Galveston Bay was our benumbed willingness to regard this bogus, pitiful little island as a blessing.

Standing there, I was not particularly filled with hope. It seemed to me that the ruin of Galveston Bay had, from the beginning, been a done deal. It was not clear whether Wallisville and the Ship Channel projects would ever be completed or what effects they would have on the bay if they were. But they embodied an attitude toward the Texas environment that was a long way from dying out, an attitude that at its root accepted the welfare of the bay as a secondary consideration and not as an essential premise. Perhaps the design of these and other projects could be fine-tuned enough that the damage was negligible, but in the end that was not the point. We needed to do something besides ameliorate harm; we needed to restore the bay, to reach some sort of psychic point where we could no longer allow ourselves to believe that there could be, for example, four acceptable categories of polluted water. Finally, the greatest threat to Galveston Bay was our historic inability to regard it not just as a material resource but as a spiritual one.

Time and again I drove the perimeter of the bay, from the isolated mud flats of San Luis Pass to the dense industrial canals leading to the Port of Houston. I liked the bay best in the morning, when the water was so still that boats seemed to glide across its surface like sleds on ice. I rode back and forth on the Bolivar Ferry, watching pods of dolphins as they traveled into the bay from the open Gulf. Once I visited the rookery islands in West Bay, where the salt cedars were stratified with nesting birds—great blue herons on top, white ibis, roseate spoonbills, and common egrets below. At the shoreline royal terns were gathered together in the family grouping that biologists label a creche. A fledgling reddish egret, too young to take precautions, grazed my ear with the tip of its wing; it looked like a cartoon bird, with its wobbly flight and the baby plumage growing in haywire tufts from its head.

In some essential way, however, the bay continued to elude me. There was no prominence from which to view it, and most of the municipalities that depended for their economic health on its proximity seemed to look away from it, oriented instead toward the inland complex of highways and office buildings that the bay's bounty had helped create. It was, I began to realize, a backyard bay whose grandeur was hard to glimpse.

Wanting a more intimate acquaintance, I decided to go fishing for speckled trout in Trinity Bay, several miles downstream from the mouth of the river. My guide was Gene Campbell, a forty-year-old native of Baytown who had been fishing these waters since he was a kid.

The water in this part of the bay was fairly clear—two and a half feet of visibility—and the shoreline was dominated by great homes set back on green manicured bluffs. After running north for ten minutes, Campbell cut the motor and let the boat drift idly in the outgoing tide. Below us, out of sight, an oyster reef ran perpendicular to the shore.

"Trout are visual feeders ninety percent of the time," he said, running a hook through the tail of a live shrimp. "They're on sight attack. They don't feed well unless they can see. That's why we look for water with some visibility to it."

We could see cabbageheads a foot or so under the water, drifting seaward in the tide. Mullet were popping up everywhere. One of them headed straight for the boat, bounding in and out of the water like a skipping stone, and when the fish saw the boat, it changed course in midair. Campbell got a strike right away but lost the trout. When he reeled in his hook the shrimp was still on, folded into a U shape, its rows of feet barely waggling.

Campbell speculated that a young trout had probably attacked the bait from behind, folding it over to avoid the sharp horn projecting from the shrimp's head. Older fish wouldn't have been so delicate. A full-grown trout tends to wolf down fish, including other trout, up to a foot long.

They are serious predators, which I didn't fully appreciate until I boated one a few moments later and looked down its bony yellow gullet. Two long, pointed teeth—made for gripping rather than slashing prey—hung down from its upper jaw. The fish made a desperate croaking noise, expelling air from its bladder, and continued to croak after Campbell tossed it into an ice chest.

We caught five or six more fish, all of them trout. The fish were biting, but they were picky.

"The tide's slowing down now," Campbell said. "They're getting less active and more selective."

He decided to move off the reef and head for the open, hoping to encounter a slick or a "mudball," which would indicate a school of fish feeding with more abandon. The sky was overcast, however, and growing darker, and without the sunshine to highlight a slick, it was difficult to read what was going on beneath the surface.

"We'll go up on that well," Campbell decided. "See if we can't pick up a few fish before we get shoved out of the bay by this storm." He anchored about twenty yards away from a small offshore rig, and we cast toward the wellhead. The bottom there, he explained, would be reinforced with shell, creating a small patch reef attractive to fish. Campbell reeled in a substantial trout, but after that we had no luck.

"A lot of times at these wellheads," he explained, "we'll catch one fish, and that's it. It may be because there's just one fish there. The question I have is, What's he doing there by himself? Is he a sentry? A bait scout? They're school fish. They have no business being by themselves."

At this time of the year the trout were through spawning in the warm water along the shore. Unlike redfish, which move out into the turbulence of the Gulf surf to spawn, trout are lifelong denizens of the bay. Born in the marshy fringes, they school up and move out into open water after eight or ten months, following the salinity gradients and moving into deeper or shallower water as the temperature suits them. They prey on shad or other fish, and during the fall, when the year's hatch of white shrimp scuttles forth out of the marshes, the trout are there waiting for them, causing the frightened shrimp to leap out of the water like grasshoppers.

"The little fish are the easiest to catch," Campbell said. "They eat more often, their metabolism's faster. A ten-pound trout'll eat a two-pound mullet and digest it for a week. A little one-and-a-half- to two-pound trout, though, he'll eat eight shrimp a day. That's eight feedings, eight chances he'll take your hook."

The sky grew darker as we fished the wellhead, and we could see lightning striking the ground near Smith Point. We reeled in our lines and ran ahead of the storm, stopping near an oil separator to try once more before going in. But the storm was coming on fast, and the sound of the separator's compressor was lost to the increasing rumble of thunder. The air was charged and calm. Static electricity caused our fishing lines to bow upward from the surface of the water.

"Notice how we've got the bay to ourselves?" Campbell said. I looked and saw that there were no other boats on the water. The storm clouds were rapidly engulfing the shoreline and contracting the horizon, so that the refineries and offshore rigs were no longer visible. All that we could see was the gray, marly surface of the bay, beginning to rile as the wind came up out of the stillness. The bay seemed in command of all this atmospheric power—it seemed ageless and, though I knew better, inviolable. I reeled in my line slowly, not wanting to go, and listened as the last dying trout flapped about desperately in the ice chest.

———

SWAMP THING

I was at an impressionable age when I saw my first snapping turtle. I was ten, standing on a low earthen dam in central Oklahoma and casting with a child-sized Zebco into a gloomy lake not much bigger than a stock pond. The lake had a prehistoric feel to it. Dead trees rose from the water, the bare limbs swaying and creaking. The water itself was muddy and still. It looked as if it had been sitting there, immune to evaporation, since the beginning of time.

I had fouled my line on enough of those trees to begin feeling cranky and put-upon. And on the occasions when my plastic lure did reach the water—disappearing like a space probe into the toxic brown clouds of an inhospitable planet—it reported no signs of life. I was about to reel in the line when some unseen force gave a brutal tug that pulled my cork deep below the surface. The pressure from the bottom of the lake kept the fishing line as taut as a bowstring.

I was scared. This thing did not feel like a fish at all. I knew, as I cranked on the reel, that I had hooked something powerful and hostile, something that did not wish to be disturbed. The muscles in my arms were quivering with exhaustion by the time the creature finally appeared. I saw its head first, and then a neck so long I thought it was a snake, and finally the undersized shell, so small when compared with the thrashing mass of the body itself that it looked like a saddle on the back of a dragon.

Not knowing what else to do, I continued to reel in the line. The turtle was hooked in the mouth, and in its anger it kept flinging out its neck and snapping its jaws. It was the most ferocious, the most unworldly thing I had ever seen. The back of its head bristled with spiky warts, its shell was covered with algae and slime, and the skin of its front legs dragged the ground in loose, grotesque folds. As I hauled the turtle up the dam, it grasped the dirt with its sharp claws and contested every inch. But then, sensing a little slack in the line, it lunged forward with such force that its front legs cleared the ground. Paralyzed with awe, I stood and watched as it lumbered hissing toward me, its reptile eyes fixed on mine, its neck coiling and striking. I remember thinking, *It's coming to get me!*

My uncle, who was chopping firewood nearby, came trotting down the slope of the dam with an ax. Of course, I realized, this thing would have to be killed. It was an evil that must be vanquished. My uncle tried to cut off its head, but the turtle was quick and could retract its neck faster than the ax could fall. It died instead from a blow to the shell. After it stopped moving he scooped it up with the blade of the ax and tossed it back into the lake. Watching it sink, I began to cry. It was not pity I felt, but disgrace. That such a savage, primeval beast could be destroyed by a thoughtless child seemed to me a mistake, a cruel imbalance of nature. Until I encountered that snapping turtle, it had never occurred to me that the existence of another creature could be a greater wonder than my own.

I see them all the time now. When I'm strolling across the Congress Avenue bridge in Austin, I can often spot snapping turtles in the lake below as they paddle along the banks just beneath the surface. Snappers are immediately distinguishable from the other turtles that inhabit the lake—the red-ears, cooters, and stinkpots. For one thing, you never see snapping turtles basking on tree limbs or swimming companionably alongside your canoe. They prefer to linger in the dark ooze, now and then extending their necks like snorkels to take a breath from the surface. Their tails are thick, long, serrated, semi-prehensile. (Snappers in fast-moving water have been known to grasp a submerged branch with their tails to keep from being swept downstream.) Their bodies are squat, and the forward edges of their shells ride high above their necks like the collar of an ill-fitting coat. Except for the eerie parchment-yellow color of their eyes, they are dark all over.

In the early summer the females crawl out of the water to lay their eggs, their carapaces thick with drying mud. Hiked up on their stubby legs, their necks extended, their long tails dragging in the dirt, they look more like dinosaurs than turtles. The females are on their way to build a nest somewhere nearby. They will dig a hole in the dirt and deposit twenty or thirty eggs, guiding each one into position with the hind feet like fussy hostesses arranging canapés on a tray. When all the eggs are laid, they will fill in the hole with dirt and then tamp it down by crawling back and forth. Their trip to the nest site and back will probably add up to less than half a mile, but for these awkward aquatic turtles it is an epic journey through an alien world.

Last summer, driving with my family to Houston, I saw one stalled with fright on the highway in the pine country just outside of Bastrop. I pulled the car over and we all got out to look at it. I told the kids to stand back, half afraid this low-lying reptile would leap up and grab one of them by the throat. But the turtle kept still, its neck tucked into its shell. It looked craven and terrified. A car roared by in the opposite lane and the turtle hugged the asphalt with its claws.

I wanted to get the turtle off the road, but that childhood encounter had made me a coward, and I was unwilling to reach down and touch it. I had read that the only safe way to pick up a snapping turtle is by the rear legs, or by the rear edge of the shell, "holding him well away from your body." An agitated snapper has an extensive biting range. It can fling its neck to the side like a whip and strike a target far back on its flank. This turtle was placid, but I didn't expect it to stay that way if I put my hands on it. It would, I thought, explode with rage. It would wriggle violently, release a gaseous cloud of musk, and lunge with its bony beak at my fingers.

I scooted the turtle forward with my foot, and it began to crawl across the highway. Seeing no cars coming from either direction, I decided that the turtle would probably make it without my intervention, and gathered the family back into the car. Driving away, I watched in the rear-view mirror as it lumbered forward with excruciating slowness.

"Oh, no!" my wife called out as a car suddenly bore down upon the snapping turtle. The children cringed and hid their eyes. But the car passed harmlessly over the snapper, which continued on its journey, a dark slouching shape older than any human thought.

It surprised me how much we all had feared for the turtle in its moment of peril. Over the years, I had managed to conquer my atavistic revulsion to certain animals. It was nothing to me now to handle a snake or to brush with my finger the silken fur of a living bat, but a snapping turtle was still a kind of nightmare creature, and a part of me did not want to accept the idea that it was as vulnerable as the rest of creation. I knew that characterizing nature in this way was an ageless human fallacy, but I still could not quite get over the sensation that snapping turtles were the enemy. Their outward appearance was the manifestation of their grim consciousness. Snapping turtles lived, it seemed to me, in a constant state of wrathful agitation. They were like the souls of the damned—irredeemable, and loathsome even to themselves.

"A savage, cross-tempered brute." That's the way one biologist, in an otherwise unemotional volume on reptiles and amphibians, describes snapping turtles. "The general aspect," another authority queasily reports, "is so sinister that it imparts more of the feeling inspired by a thick-bodied, poisonous serpent than that of a turtle."

Snappers are ferocious, but it's important to remember that they are that way for a reason. They are not simply dyspeptic. Snapping turtles are underwater predators; they are attack vehicles. They lie in wait and strike at passing fish, or they paddle up to the surface and seize ducklings by the feet. Their strike has to be fast, the grip of their jaws tenacious.

Out of the water, a snapping turtle's small shell is an imperfect refuge, and so its best defense is to attack. "I have seen it snapping," a nineteenth-century naturalist wrote, "in the same fierce manner as it does when full-grown, at a time when it was still a pale, almost colorless embryo, wrapped up in its foetal envelopes, with a yolk larger than itself hanging from its sternum, three months before hatching."

Folklore says that when snappers bite they will not let go until it thunders. Not true, but they do like to hold on to their claim. They are also very efficient scavengers. This trait was supposedly once used by an Indian in northern Indiana, who exploited a snapping turtle, tethered to a long wire, to locate the bodies of drowning victims. And one of the worst practical jokes I ever heard of was perpetrated by a friend of mine when he was a rowdy adolescent. He put a baby snapping turtle into the purse of his friend's mother.

There are two kinds of snapping turtles, both of which are native to Texas. The common snapping turtle—*Chelydra serpentine*—is the smaller and more aggressive species. Its range extends throughout the entire eastern half of the continent, all the way from Canada (where it has been observed walking on the bottom of frozen streams beneath the ice) to Central America. It lives everywhere—lakes, rivers, swamps, even brackish tidal streams—but its prime habitat is sluggish, muddy water. Common snappers are not behemoths. The largest one ever caught in the wild weighed slightly less than seventy pounds, though one captive turtle that was kept in a swill barrel for two months ate its way up to eighty-six pounds.

Those figures are nothing compared with the mighty *Macroclemys temmincki*, the alligator snapping turtle. Alligator snappers can grow as large as sea turtles, up to 250 pounds or even more. Their heads are massive and blunt, their eyes lower on their heads than those of common snappers, their shells crowned with three high longitudinal ridges that look like miniature mountain ranges. Common snappers are common, but alligator snappers are increasingly rare. Alligator snapper meat has long been a steady seller in the fish markets of Louisiana, and the turtle population took a nose dive when Campbell's came out with a snapper soup in the early seventies. In Texas, alligator snappers are classified as a threatened species by the Parks and Wildlife Department. They tend to inhabit coastal drainages in East Texas, though they have made appearances as far west as Burleson County.

Unlike common snapping turtles, alligator snappers do not stalk their prey or seize it with serpentine strikes of their necks. They lie in wait, settled motionlessly in the cloudy water like boulders or stumps, their mouths hinged open to reveal a fluttering gob of tissue rooted to the lower jaw. When a fish spots the lure and enters the cavern of the turtle's mouth, it is either swallowed whole or neatly sliced. With this leisurely feeding strategy at their disposal, alligator snappers tend to have a less urgent temperament than their cousins. Though they look even more hideous than common snappers, they are comparatively docile.

Alligator snappers are strong and, in strange ways, agile. There is a report of a three-legged specimen climbing an eight-foot-high cyclone fence. The turtles have been known to shear off human fingers. All sorts of things—small alligators, entire beaver heads—have been found in their stomachs. For years it was a commonplace observation that an alligator snapping turtle was capable of biting a broom handle in two. Peter Pritchard, a Florida biologist who has written extensively on *Macroclemys temmincki*, decided to test this hypothesis. He waved a broom handle in front of a 165-pound alligator snapper to see if it really could bite it in half. It could.

"If common snapping turtles were as big as alligator snapping turtles," an East Texas herpetologist named William W. Lamar told me, "they would take bathers regularly."

Several years ago, when Lamar was the curator of herpetology at the Caldwell Zoo in Tyler, I dropped in to see his alligator snapper collection. The zoo had three specimens, including a baby that was kept in an aquarium tank in the reptile house. The first time I saw it I wasn't sure it was even a living thing. It was settled down at the bottom of the tank, eerily still, its jaws hinged open as if in some epic yawn and its right foreleg raised like a pointer's. The only things moving were the lure inside its mouth and a doomed fish that swam near the surface. Lamar remarked that the snapper looked like a log with a worm on it.

We left the baby still angling for the fish and went outside to look at the larger specimens. Another curator climbed over a fence and waded into a pond. He looked around on the bottom a bit, then reached down with both hands and hauled up a forty-five-pound turtle, lifting it by either end of the shell. The alligator snapper's name was Eugenia. She was dark and mucky and immense, a ghastly apparition from the dawn of time.

Lamar looked down at this strange beast admiringly. Eugenia seemed to me not an animal but an entity—a moving, moss-covered rock. I asked Lamar if alligator snappers were intelligent. What I wondered was: Do they think?

"If one looks at intelligence as the ability to learn functions that are nontraditional," he said, "I don't know. Nobody's ever trained one of these things to dance. A common snapper is lacking in personality to me. They do what they do with a lot of aggressive verve, but they're boring. They're like somebody you'd expect to meet in a casino in Vegas. But my opinion of alligator snappers is they're a lot more receptive to stimuli than most people think. A lot more goes on in their lives than most people imagine."

Some months later I acquired a snapping turtle. It was a baby, a common snapper, hatched from a clutch of eggs that a reptile fancier had discovered on the banks of the San Marcos River. A mutual friend delivered the turtle to me one day in a bucket.

I went to the pet shop and bought a twenty-gallon aquarium, a filter, and a pile of decorative rocks. When the aquarium was all set up and running, I put on a pair of gloves and picked the turtle up from behind. To my surprise, it didn't thrash about and try to bite my hand. It merely kept its head retracted into its shell as far as it would go.

The turtle was only a few inches long, no more than several months old. When I put it in the water, it sank to the bottom like a piece of lead and then began to scramble frantically upward without success. It didn't seem to be able to swim. I reached into the water and set it on one of the rocks, and it craned its neck up, up, up until its nostrils were above the surface. And there the turtle stayed.

"Let's call him Sam," my oldest daughter said, and that became his name, though we never used it. He was always just "the snapping turtle." He would lie there on the rock all day and all night, blinking, breathing. I dropped little pellets of turtle food on top of the water, but the turtle would not eat with me in the room. After I left, the food disappeared.

The little aquarium filter chugged along diligently, and I changed the water once a day, but the moment I put the turtle into the clean water it immediately turned into a fetid bog. I was tired of the maintenance, but I grew oddly fond of the snapping turtle. I found him more interesting than odious. His silent, patient, undemanding presence was somehow restful to me.

Nevertheless, after a few months I had had enough. The whole house was beginning to stink. I decided to take the turtle and release him back into the San Marcos.

The night before I let him go, however, I dropped a few pellets of turtle food into the tank and hid behind the door, watching. I saw the turtle track the food with his eyes as it sank slowly down to him. When a pellet was several inches away he shot his neck out with a startling and unnecessary motion, snapped his dinner savagely in half, then gulped it down with urgent, gagging movements of his throat.

The kids and I took him down to a murky little eddy cut into a bank of the river. I put on my gloves, set him into the water, and he was gone in an instant in a swirl of mud. I suddenly felt an unexpected pang, of what I cannot imagine.

We walked along the bank looking for him. We wanted to say good-bye to this creature that had never had any need or cognizance of us—that just was. I wondered if he would survive. If he did, if he was not eaten by another snapping turtle, if he was not caught on a boy's fishing line, he might live ten or twenty years, spending the winters denned up under cutbanks, the summers loitering in the mud. He would grow up to replace the turtle whose death I had caused so many years ago, and whose savage, unappeasable spirit was still alive, still snapping at me in my dreams.

PART TWO

HIGHWAYS AND
JUNGLE PATHS

THE ROOF OF EDEN

It was evening, the long summer twilight of the Front Range. I sat on the veranda of the Stanley Hotel in Estes Park, Colorado, drinking peppermint tea from a crystal cup while violet-green swallows coasted above the lawn in perfect arcs of flight. The air was cool. I rubbed my hands on the warm teacup and wished I had bought that sweatshirt after all, the one with the words "Rocky Mountain National Park—75th Anniversary" silk-screened below a noble profile of a bighorn sheep.

Seventy-five years. Idly, I did the math—27,393 mountain evenings such as this one. Several hundred evanescent generations of birds and chipmunks and tundra flowers winking in and out of existence upon the Rockies' eternal facade. Measured against the peaks above me, which gleamed like steel in the flaring sunlight, seventy-five years was so small a unit of time as to seem theoretical.

And no doubt in another few nanoseconds of mountain time the sprawling tourist village of Estes Park—with its water slides and taffy shops, its souvenir boutiques selling hand-blown glassware, porcelain gnomes, and full-color busts of John Wayne—would prove to be as transient as alpenglow.

"A concentration of beautiful lateral valleys, intersected by meandering watercourses, ridged by lofty ledges of precipitous rock, and hemmed in upon the west by vast piles of mountains climbing beyond clouds . . ." That was how Rufus B. Sage, probably the first man to write about the area, described its appeal in 1843. Sage was traveling by himself—he was, he wrote, "one of the world-hating *literati*," a man with a craving for cosmic loneliness. It is hard to imagine a better place for him than these immense glacial valleys and knife's-edge summits with their plumes of drifting snow. But the mountains were not entirely uninhabited. The high country still bore traces of rock walls along which Indians had stampeded game. In Sage's time, Utes and Arapahos still raided each other's encampments at the base of the mountains, and enterprising braves would climb alone to the highest peaks, where they would lie in wait beneath piles of brush and grab eagles by the feet. But by and large it must have thrilled Rufus Sage to see how thoroughly the human presence was muffled in a blanket of solitude.

Today, Rocky Mountain is one of the most visited national parks in the country. About 2.5 million people come here every year, most of them passing through the gateway town of Estes Park and proceeding across the national park along the alpine highway known as Trail Ridge Road. The majority of tourists never leave their cars—they just drive on across the Continental Divide, admiring the scenery, on their way to somewhere else. But in summer the trails still teem with world-hating literati, most of them content with even a vestige of "the far-spreading domains of silence and loneliness" that Rufus Sage discovered.

By the time I finished my second cup of tea, streetlights were coming on in the dark hollow of Estes Park, though the peaks above were still spotlighted by the setting sun. I walked through the lobby of the old hotel, stopping to scrutinize the portrait of its namesake that hung near the billiard room. "F. O. Stanley," read the plaque, "Inventor—Industrialist—Lover of Mankind."

Stanley, along with his twin brother, was the inventor of the Stanley Steamer, a sprightly motor car that once hit a speed of 127 mph. One of the cars still stands in the hotel lobby as a curiosity—an elegant contraption with a mahogany steering wheel, lantern headlights, and a winding horn mounted on the side of the car.

Stanley used to pick his guests up at the train station in Loveland—

guests such as Enrico Caruso, John Philip Sousa, and Theodore Roosevelt—and transport them sixteen miles via Stanley Steamer to his marvelous hotel. He was an abstemious sort and only grudgingly set aside one room in which his guests could smoke, a room he himself never entered. As a lover of mankind, he was selective. He would sit out on the porch and turn away guests whose looks he did not find promising.

He died on the porch in 1940, and over the years his hotel went to seed in an elegant and creepy way. (Stephen King spent several nights in Room 237, working on *The Shining*.) Though it has recently been restored, its grand old mustiness has not been tampered with. My room was like an attic bedroom in my grandmother's house—with old-fashioned, two-button light switches, a lumpy four-poster bed, and a constant mountain breeze through the open window.

The next morning I got up early and drove through town on my way to the park. The main street of Estes Park was already crowded with lumbering RVs and mountain bikes. The traffic police wore shorts and baseball caps, and instead of guns they had water bottles strapped to their belts. On the rock facade of a liquor store a climber was practicing his holds, shifting his weight fluidly from limb to limb with slow, spidery motions.

I paid my entrance fee and drove up to Bear Lake. The parking lot was huge, and almost full. Four nuns piled out of the car ahead of me and, with their habits blowing in the breeze, began to lace up their hiking boots. I ambled along the nature trail around Bear Lake. The lake was a quiet expanse of dark, tannic water, its surface protected by the fringing firs and pines. In its waters the sharp, bare peaks above were reflected with eerie fidelity. Longs Peak was the highest—14,255 feet, almost a mile higher than where I stood. From this angle, the peak did not have the soaring splendor of an isolated summit. It was simply the highest in a series of distant waves of gray rock.

But it had always been a commanding goal. A trip to the summit and back, I had been told, takes twelve hours, and for much of the way it is a taxing scramble across boulder fields and narrow mountain defiles with woozy downward vistas.

"It is one of the noblest of mountains," wrote Isabella Bird, who climbed Longs Peak in 1873, "but in one's imagination it grows to be much more than a mountain. It becomes invested with a personality. . . . Thunder becomes its voice, and the lightnings do it homage."

Bird was forty years old when she climbed Longs Peak—"a quiet, intelligent-looking, dumpy English spinster." Her health was not good. She suffered from a chronic spinal condition that she sought to relieve by constant travel. Though she spent only three months in the Rockies, she wrote a classic account (*A Lady's Life in the Rocky Mountains*) of her adventures. Her prose, like her nature, was excitable. She ascended Longs Peak in the company of Rocky Mountain Jim, a rough-but-courtly sort, whose face had been mutilated in a grizzly bear attack, leaving him with only one eye. His ruined face and "dark, lost, self-ruined life" intrigued her. "Desperado," she reported, "was written in large letters all over him."

Her account of the assault on the peak is a masterpiece of throbbing Victorian prose. "Jim dragged me up," the fatigued adventuress wrote, "like a bale of goods, by sheer force of muscle." During the trip, he hauled her with his lariat, severed her entangled frock with his knife, and delivered her to the summit, where they were "uplifted above love and hate and storms of passion, calm amidst the eternal silences."

Rocky Mountain Jim apparently fell gloomily in love with Isabella during the ascent, but when they came back to earth she did not encourage him. "He is a man whom any woman might love," she wrote her sister, "but no sane woman would marry." Bird left the Rockies and went on to more adventures in the Far East. The next year Jim was shot in a dispute, probably over a woman. He died, but for a while it had looked as if he might recover. "It is hard to die," a friend remarked, "in the wonderful air of that great altitude."

I wandered for an hour or so along the trails leading from Bear Lake. A browsing deer looked up at me, folded its ears forward, and snorted as if it had a cold. A weasel rippled across the trail, half concealed itself beneath a boulder, and watched my progress with curious intensity. On the way back to the parking lot I passed through a grove of young aspens, their green, paddle-shaped leaves riffling in the wind and casting a lattice of shadow on the forest floor.

This was the low country, the montane woodlands dominated by ponderosa pine. When I got into my car and drove up Trail Ridge Road,

I quickly passed through the subalpine zone, with its forests of fir and Engelmann spruce, and then past the contorted, wind-stripped trees at timberline to the tundra itself, the vast, sloping, high-mountain carpet with its cushion plants and lichens and pinpricks of yellow flowers.

I stopped the car at an overlook and got out, breathing in the austere air and looking down at a sea of meadows and conifer forests. Feeling light-headed and eager to learn, I joined a tundra walk departing from the Alpine Visitor Center. The ranger was young, with a scholarly air and a neat beard. The brim of his campaign hat sat so squarely above his brow it looked as if it had been adjusted with a carpenter's level. He pointed out alpine avens, skypilot, and the stunted willows eaten by the ptarmigans that winter in the tundra. To illustrate his lecture, he pulled a stuffed marmot out of a plastic bag. The marmot was a shapeless lump of fur, as stiff as cardboard.

"In the winter, while he's hibernating," the ranger said, "you could pick this guy out of his burrow, play a game of football with him, and come summer he'd have no recollection. All he does during the summer is lounge around and pig out till he gets fat, and in the winter he sleeps it off. If Shirley MacLaine is right, I'm coming back as a marmot."

On the way back down Trail Ridge I stopped to observe several living marmots that were lying on the tundra rocks and now and then opening their mouths and chirping like birds. The marmots were obese, and their scrappy fur was as full of dings as a bad carpet, but they were not the comical rodents I had expected. They had a certain air, a nobility of repose that made me think of the stone lions outside the New York Public Library.

That night I set up a tent in the campground in Moraine Park as two black squirrels with long, tufted ears looked on inquiringly. Moraine Park, a commodious meadowland banked by glacial ridges, was scoured out of the bedrock by a creeping tongue of ice. The glacier has been gone for thirteen thousand years, but its mighty work is still thrillingly apparent. The marshlands were dewy. The meandering stream was a garish silver band, and the whole expanse looked glimmering and fresh, as if it had just hours before been hatched from beneath the ice.

There was a slide show that night in the Moraine Park amphitheater, and I followed the other campers as they ambled along the road in the dark. Through the bright windows of the RVs I could catch glimpses of people playing cards, watching TV, or reading paperbacks with florid, die-cut covers. At the amphitheater the ranger stood at a lectern made of rock, a microphone clipped to his tie. Behind him was a projection screen, and beyond that the moraine and the distant tundra slopes. The moonlit peaks looked as rumpled and comfortable as corduroy.

The ranger showed slides of ponderosa pine and bitter-brush, of elk-scarred aspen and broad-tailed hummingbirds. The campfire near his feet burned itself out quickly, and as the program wore on, the darkness increased so that the mountain peaks showed only as a dark, jagged line across the star field. The air was so still and silent that each *ka-chunk* sound the projector made as it advanced a slide seemed to echo with a satisfying heft.

"Someone once said," the ranger concluded in a low and reverent voice, "that next to freedom, national parks were the greatest idea America ever had."

The next morning I was up early to mull that one over. It was first light, and fog pooled in the hollows and distant canyons. Each of these canyons, each tiny fissure branching off from the glacial valley, turned out, when seen through my binoculars, to be a broad avenue leading to the still-unseen heart of the American wilderness. I cherished the notion that I was free to follow any of these gorges, for as far as I wanted to go—to disappear, if I chose, into those foggy valleys.

In 1917, two years after Rocky Mountain National Park officially opened, a college student named Agnes Lowe did just that. The *Denver Post* announced her intention of dashing into the "Garden of Eden" clad only in a toga of animal skins. This was a publicity stunt. Young ladies did not enter the wilderness alone and unequipped in 1917, and two thousand people assembled to watch "the modern Eve" romp off into the mountains.

The next day a man in a robe, billing himself as "the new Adam," announced his intention to follow Miss Lowe into the Garden. He appears to have been crazy, and did not get far before being dissuaded by park personnel. Meanwhile Eve had a few rough days—"Nearly froze last night," she wrote in charcoal on the bark of a tree—but soon adjusted. When a group of hikers encountered her, they saw that she had shed her cave-woman costume and was roaming through the sunshine "à la Nature."

Miss Lowe allotted only a week to her role as Eve, and soon returned to college. But as I walked through the marshy grass in Moraine Park and trained my binoculars upward—up through the dense conifers to the tundra and finally to the crags and spires of naked rock—I imagined she was here still, an ageless alpine nymph giddy with the license of the wilderness.

"I believe there is a God!" poor Rocky Mountain Jim had blurted out to Isabella Bird during their ascent of Longs Peak, as the day dawned beatifically below them. It was an understandable outburst. The park is one of those places whose beauty can affect you like a seizure. Is it any wonder that Jim found himself overpowered with belief, doomed as he was, as he stood there with his beloved upon the roof of Eden?

FEELING FLUSH

We find ourselves in Monte Carlo. From the gaudy turrets of the Casino a swarm of bats spirals up into the evening sky over the gardens and seascape terraces that are filled with elderly women walking arm in arm. It is midwinter, sixty degrees Fahrenheit, just cool enough for their leopard coats, real or faux. The sovereign principality of Monaco—smaller than New York's Central Park—is so minute, so tidy, that it can be taken in with one quick sweep of the eyes. There is the ancient fortress Rock, with the white flag flying above the palace to indicate that the widowed Prince Rainier III, His Serene Highness, is home. The harbor from which Julius Caesar once sailed is filled now with ponderous yachts, and behind it, creeping upward toward a crowning massif, are shopping streets laid out in irregular tiers and switchbacks.

This evening the Mediterranean and the sky above it share the same deepening hue, so there is no perceptible horizon when we look seaward from the Casino's terrace; just a seamless, hazy void. This vast sheet of water is as calm as an ornamental pond, though now and then a seaborne breeze will touch its surface and cause it to lift and fall in faint, suspirating motions.

Soon, on January 27, it will be the feast day of Saint Dévote, celebrating the arrival on these shores, sixteen centuries ago, of the patron saint of Monaco. According to legend, Dévote was a Christian girl from Corsica who had been tortured and killed by the island's Roman governor. Her friends placed her body in a fishing boat and set it adrift, praying for the winds to deliver her to a Christian country for burial. A storm came up, and the little boat would have been lost had not a dove emerged from the dead girl's mouth and guided the craft to this craggy shoreline at the opening of a steep gorge.

Dévote had the posthumous good fortune to end her journey among the faithful. The Monégasques, as the ancestral population of Monaco is known, buried the girl and built a chapel to her memory, and she in turn responded to their kindness with answered prayers and miraculous cures.

But Monte Carlo is no Lourdes. It is, of course, a prime disporting ground for the world's leisured classes and has been ever since Rainier's ancestor Prince Charles III established the Société des Bains de Mer (Society of Sea Bathing) in 1863. Though Charles was certainly interested in promoting Monte Carlo's already fashionable beaches, the SBM had about as much to do with sea bathing as poor Saint Dévote had to do with recreational boating. This was the Victorian age, however, and it would not have been discreet for Prince Charles to announce his real goal of turning Monaco into the gambling capital of Europe.

The casino he built is an amiable Belle Époque monstrosity whose facade is crowded with sculptural flourishes, from winged men to cupids to trident-wielding water nymphs bursting out of their niches. Opposite is the equally ornate Hôtel de Paris; like the Casino it is strangely, sparklingly clean, so free of grime and so unweathered that it looks more like a theme-park replica than the real thing.

The evening's plans call for a cautious bit of gambling. After the sun has set, after we have eaten a bowl of *soupe de poisson* and injured our gums on the sharp crusts of French rolls, we stroll into the Casino, affecting a Continental nonchalance. Inside it is like a wonderfully overripe art museum—a procession of gilded *salles* with murals depicting scenes of pastoral concupiscence. Across the walls and ceilings romp various maidens, shepherdesses, and sprites, either breezily naked or outfitted in swirling, diaphanous garments. Some of them are picking fruit; some are reclining on clouds; some are languorously smoking cigars.

At this time of year the Casino is thinly populated, a fact that only enhances its native aura of exclusivity. But the place feels surprisingly welcoming. Once a visitor has displayed his passport and paid his admission, he is granted the illusion of being a member of the club. Most of the patrons are feeding francs into the slot machines that are clustered in a side room, but the vulgar sounds of these *machines à sous* are swallowed up in the elegant silence of the main gaming hall. Here the only noise is the whisper of the ivory roulette ball traveling in its wheel of polished wood. Only one table is in operation, and the players crowd around it without excitement, as if it were merely a fire that they had been drawn to for warmth. They are, for the most part, a languid and sleepy-looking assemblage of junior aristocrats—young men with mussed or flowing hair, wearing designer sports jackets that are as shapeless as raincoats. They place their bets, casually sip their drinks while the wheel is spinning, and display the same indifference whether the croupier rewards them or sweeps their chips away with a little rake.

I have allotted myself a grubstake of twenty dollars, but I decide it would be an insult to these gentlemen to subject them to the spectacle of my miserly and craven betting, so I merely hover for a while, squinting down at the action as if with a coolly appraising eye, and then it's off to the Loews hotel, in whose rowdier, American-style casino I am able to lose my $20 in an instant without undue embarrassment. There is more action in the Loews casino and no fussy decorum to suppress it. The place is full of middle-class American women sitting on stools and patiently working the slot machines, with onlookers crowding around the jittery shooters at the crap tables. Next door, in La Folie Russe, dancers with whiskers painted on their cheeks are presenting a topless musical number borrowed from *Cats*.

In the morning the sun rises through a sea mist, gradually disclosing the curve of the shore, the hills crowned with self-contained medieval villages and laced with balcony roads, built by Caesar and Napoleon, that lead off into the Italian Alps. No fishing boats bob on the water; no signs of industry or commerce intrude; no sounds are heard except the squawk of Mediterranean gulls. Here, in the pleasure capital of Europe, there is an eerie lack of urgency and motive. One rises in the morning and feels only the call to leisure.

If we were to be serious about getting into the mood of Monte Carlo, we would pass our days in a listless, becalmed state, waiting to dress, waiting to eat, waiting for the Casino to open again so that we could redeem ourselves from last night's stingy betting. But at heart we are bustling American tourists, and so we rouse ourselves and head off to the palace to witness the changing of the guard. To travel on foot from one end of Monaco to the other requires, at a brisk walk, hardly more than an hour, though it's easy to lose your way in the twisted streets or surrender to the impulse to follow some steep, wandering stairway to its hidden terminus. Along the Avenue Princesse Grace, along the Avenue Président J. F. Kennedy, along the Boulevard Albert Premier and the Rue Grimaldi we make our way to the foot of the Rock, the great natural bulwark, whose summit is crowned by a tasteful, rambling palace that looks more like an immense bungalow than a princely castle.

We climb up the steep Rampe Major, the modern city falling away behind us until it is just a cluttered expanse of red-tiled roofs and cream-colored condominium towers. The Mediterranean is hammered flat by the winter sun, and the martial music and pealing bells that accompany the changing of the guard echo across its taut surface all the way to Italy. The ceremony itself is perfunctory, or perhaps just seems so in the heart of the off-season, with so few tourists to witness it. The palace guards wear white spats and blue, velvety helmets. Like figures in a cuckoo clock, they emerge from their hiding places to play their instruments, slap their rifles, and bark their commands; and then suddenly they are gone.

The palace shares the promontory of the Rock with Monaco Ville, the principality's oldest residential area. This is a neighborhood of narrow, sunless streets and cavernous shops selling T-shirts and toy roulette games. One of these streets is home to a wax museum depicting the history of Monaco. The museum is a game effort, but the history of Monaco does not lend itself to vivid tableaux. In scene after scene we follow the waxen princes and lords of Monaco as they shake hands with heads of state, attend palace balls, or walk among their subjects "promoting handicrafts."

The final exhibit is a stiff family grouping of Princess Grace and Prince Rainier and their three young children. The royal family is outfitted in dated seventies fashions that make them look like the Brady Bunch, and the only expression on their faces is a quizzical rictus. And yet, in its artless way, the scene is poignant. Here is the happy home of Their Serene Highnesses, a home still gleaming with fairy dust, magically remote from tragedy and disappointment.

Monaco without Grace Kelly. Ten years after the princess unaccountably lost control of her Rover 3500 on the Moyenne Corniche and sailed past a crash barrier to her death, even the most cynical visitor to Monaco is likely to feel a curious vacancy, the recognition that the principality has been forever sapped of a critical measure of its storybook allure.

The celestial perfection of the royal couple, though, was always something of an illusion. If we can believe her unauthorized biographers, Grace was not a particularly happy princess. She never managed to be comfortable with court folderol or even fully conversant in French. When Rainier asked her in 1966 what she would like for a tenth-anniversary present, she supposedly replied, "A year off." She wanted to act in movies again, but her husband and subjects would not hear of it (Rainier even refused to let her play the Virgin Mary in *King of Kings*), and so she channeled her creative passions into tame pursuits like the promotion of breast-feeding and public performance of light verse. By the last year of her life she was overweight, a bit bibulous, and disinclined to get out of bed in the morning.

To the Monégasque people she is nevertheless a cherished icon. They buried her behind the altar of the cathedral, along with the Grimaldis, the Florestans, the Hippolytes, and many of the other personages on display in the wax museum. Except for the fresh flowers on the marble slab, it would be easy to mistake her tomb for just another medieval resting place. GRATIA PATRICIA, the inscription reads, PRINCIPIS RAINIERII III UXOR.

A few blocks east of the cathedral, towering above the sea cliffs on the south side of the Rock, is the oceanographic museum built by Prince

Albert I to showcase his passionate interest in marine biology. The museum is four stories high and from the outside looks like a hall of justice or some other stern government building. Just inside the entrance is a statue of Albert in his yachting cap, and behind him when I visited was a comprehensive exhibit on the marine subject dearest to a Monacan's heart—the natural history and commercial cultivation of pearls.

The museum is an imposing institution and in fact draws more visitors than the Casino, but thanks to the obsessive interests of its creator it has a quirky, personal appeal. We spend an hour or so in the downstairs aquarium, watching the living nautiluses hover motionless in their tanks, and then saunter through a great hall dominated by the sixty-six-foot skeleton of a fin whale that is said to have met its death at the end of Albert's harpoon. The prince's specimens of aquatic life are arrayed along the second-floor gallery walls—hundreds of clear glass tubes in which blanched and wrinkled sea creatures float upended in preservative fluid. I could stay here all day, gazing at lurid abyssal fish and watching films of the mating habits of eels, but it is time to stroll out once again into the glamorous streets, down into the market of La Condamine and up the Boulevard des Moulins, past shops selling chocolate Nativity sets and bristling wild boars made of silver, past uniformed yacht crews on shore leave and jaunty Euro-cads in sweatshirts embossed with heraldic crests. All the young women we pass are beautiful; all the old women are grave. Monte Carlo is so immaculate, so rich, with such an air of being a private estate that my eyes search hungrily for any hint of despair or poor taste. My spirits lift a bit when I notice a purple plush monkey attached by suction cups to the windshield of a Citroen, and I feel a brief frisson of real life when I happen to glance into the first-floor window of an apartment building and see a fat man standing in his underwear, his arms hanging disconsolately at his sides as he stares at a large clock on the opposite wall.

Ah, but it is just as easy to fall into the spirit of the place. For all its hauteur, Monaco is a source of constant whimsy and surprise. Here is a restaurant called Le Texan, with a huge bas-relief of the Alamo behind the bar and tables filled with European diners giving one another puzzled looks as they try to assemble their fajitas. Here are a monumental statue of a woman's breast and, not far away, a fanciful sculpture of Adam and Eve, in which Adam is presented with slicked-back hair and a pencil moustache. And here is Ringo Starr, striding into Rampoldi to take a seat at the table next to ours, his earring glinting in the subdued light.

Now it is the eve of the feast day of Saint Dévote. In the church that was built at the spot where the saint's boat purportedly made landfall, a morning mass is conducted in Monégasque. The sound of the language—an ancient amalgam of French and Italian—is both fluid and percussive. And in the nebulous pleasure ground of Monte Carlo, where nothing seems quite as authentic as it ought to, this elemental speech hits the ear just right, sounding as natural and authoritative as the shriek of an ocean bird. "Santa Dévota," the congregation sings in this strangely comprehensible language, "gardara nostra Roca, aé la proutegerá de tütu má!"

That night a crowd gathers in front of the harbor, where a small fishing boat with a raised sail sits on a bed of palm fronds, ready to be set afire. Every year the Monégasques celebrate the feast of their patron saint by burning a boat, a tradition that originated centuries ago when a fisherman looted the church of Saint Dévote. When the defiler was apprehended and the relics he had stolen were returned, his boat was burned on the beach.

It is Rainier's duty to light the fire, and after a policeman has doused the boat with kerosene a motorcade of black Rolls-Royces punctually arrives. Out of the lead car emerges a portly, elderly man wearing a white muffler and an air of princely fatigue. Rainier is accompanied by his son, Albert, his daughter Caroline, and his grandchildren. Though they are flanked by security guards, they move through the crowd without any sense of urgency or fuss. The public appearance of Rainier in this minute country has a kind of intimacy about it, as if he were the mayor of a village instead of the prince of a realm. Without words or ceremony the royal family torches the boat, and as it is swallowed in greasy flames they repair to a reviewing stand to watch the fireworks over the harbor.

The famous Monte Carlo fireworks are not a disappointment. The sky shimmers with color, and birds circle in frantic confusion. Tendrils of light, falling with 3-D precision from the night sky, are accompanied by rumbling, sputtering blasts that shake the quay on which we are standing and even, I suspect, the ageless monument of the Rock. For some reason, the cadence of the exploding fireworks puts me in mind of the Monégasque rhythms of the morning's mass, and for a moment I have a feeling about where the soul of Monaco resides: somewhere between the legend of Saint Dévote and the fairy tale of Princess Grace, between the natural majesty of the Rock and the architectural frippery of the Casino.

When the fireworks are over, the prince and his family leave the reviewing stand without comment, wearily shake a few hands, and then, to the applause of their subjects, drive off toward the palace. The smell of gunpowder lingers over the quay, and pale, dispersing columns of smoke still hover in the sky. It is nine p.m. The casinos are open, and dawn is years away.

THE ANGER OF ACHILLES

I wouldn't say it's my favorite painting. That honor—if it is an honor coming from such an untutored critic—would probably fall to some mainstream masterpiece like Vermeer's *The Letter* or Van Gogh's *The Starry Night*. *The Anger of Achilles*, however, stops me in my tracks whenever I go to the Kimbell Art Museum in Fort Worth, and I find I have an affinity for this painting that cuts deeper than textbook appreciation and that continues to surprise me with its strength. When you strike up that kind of relationship with a work of art, it can seem like fate—as if some force is instructing you, for reasons you can't know, to brood over a particular image.

I first saw it a few years ago, when I happened to be in Fort Worth with an afternoon to kill. I was planning to see a matinee of *Raise the Titanic!* but my better self intervened. I could see a lousy movie anytime, but here I was in Fort Worth, and I had never been to the Kimbell. There was a reason for that. I've never been particularly fond of art museums, which have always struck me as too hushed, too decorous. I suppose that, in truth, I have the provincial Texan's deep-seated suspicion of serious culture. As often as not, I feel cowed by art, inadequate and surly. I'm afraid of being taken in, of giving my heart to something that might turn out to be phony, so I tend to hold back, fierce in my ignorance. The museums themselves only reinforce such feelings. In those temples, among the nattering docents and somber, blazer-clad guards, I find myself skulking about like a spy.

But I liked the Kimbell. It was a small place, but it had grandeur, too, with its high vaulted ceilings that made the interior seem as lofty and sumptuous as a desert pavilion. Bathed in natural light, imbued with an unforced and appreciative silence, the museum made me feel that I could, for once, let my guard down and just look at the pictures.

The Anger of Achilles was hanging in the southwest gallery then; they've moved it since. I had been making my way along the wall, politely admiring a group of dark and fusty-looking canvases whose subject matter I can no longer remember, when the *Achilles* seized my attention. It was large and bright, and my eyes were drawn to it as if it were a window that had just been thrown open in a gloomy hallway. I liked the painting at first simply because it was easy. It was colorful and clean, with a plain-spoken, unflinching figurative style. It depicted some scene from classical Greek lore, the sort of subject that I usually found to be high-blown and corny. But this work's sincerity was commanding. Four people were compressed within the tight borders of the canvas. On the left was a young warrior in the act of drawing his sword, but something about the languorous contortions of his body, his bland, unreflective face, made this threatening gesture seem unconvincing. The artist, I thought, had failed with this figure, but part of the power of the painting was the way it triumphed over this central flaw. My eyes rested on the faces of the other three characters, faces filled with such sadness and tragic weariness that I was startled by the intensity of my response, by the way I immediately accepted them not as painted forms but as fellow human beings in distress. On the right side of the frame a man—no doubt a king—motioned to the warrior to put down his sword. In the tight confines of the canvas the king's arm appeared a bit foreshortened, but the rest of him was rendered with such confidence and subtlety that matters of technique receded into irrelevance. I simply watched him—the struggle that was apparent in his eyes even as he stared down his antagonist.

Between the king and the warrior stood a young woman with her hands crossed over her chest, her head angled to one side in the moody, otherworldly pose of a Pre-Raphaelite maiden. But there was nothing insipid about her; her sorrowful distraction was authentic. She had passed through some mysterious emotional turbulence, had triumphed over it, and now anchored this scene with her serenity. Behind her, one hand resting comfortingly on her shoulder, stood an older woman—a queen, a mother—her eyes red from crying, looking at the impetuous warrior with sympathy but also with a kind of contempt for the uselessness of his rage.

I wasn't sure exactly what predicament was being portrayed here, and I stared at the painting for quite a while before even thinking to consult the museum label. *The Anger of Achilles*, it said, had been painted in 1819 by Jacques-Louis David. Achilles is the figure on the left, the youth in the act of drawing his sword. The painting presents the moment when he learns that Iphigenia, his betrothed, is to be sacrificed to the goddess Diana instead of married to him. This is all the fault of Agamemnon, the king of the Greeks and the father of Iphigenia. He has killed a deer sacred to Diana and now, when the Greek fleet is massed at Aulis ready to sail against Troy, the angry goddess has turned the wind against it. She will not be appeased unless the daughter of Agamemnon and Clytemnestra is put to death.

Knowing the stakes, I studied the painting again. A scene that could easily have been theatrical and overwrought was instead almost unbearably calm. Its theme was not so much the heroic clash of wills between gods and men as the mute acceptance of a family tragedy. I was convinced that only a great artist could have made a picture like this, in which the strongest characters were not those who drew their swords in outrage but those who responded with dignity to their own helplessness.

I knew vaguely who David was, but it was not until I consulted an art textbook later that I could recall his other works. He had painted the riveting *Oath of the Horatii* and the gigantic canvas depicting the consecration of Napoleon, both of which hang in the Louvre. And it was David, I realized with some embarrassment at my ignorance, who had created one of the most famous paintings in the world, the portrait of Jean-Paul Marat lying dead in his bathtub.

David painted *The Anger of Achilles* near the end of his life, and thus the painting belongs to a body of work that has been generally dismissed by critics. "Unlike many great artists," states the *Oxford Companion to Art*, "David did not mature with age; his work weakened as the possibility of exerting a moral and social influence receded."

It's true that for most of his life David put his art to passionate use. He was an activist, and he meant for his painting to galvanize and instruct, to figure in the real course of events. He was born in Paris in 1748 and came of age at a time when French taste was beginning to shift away from the pleasant rococo reveries of painters like François Boucher, whose sensual canvases were chockablock with cherubs casting approving looks at pastoral lovers ("Such an inimitable and rare piece of nonsense," Diderot said of one of those paintings).

David admired Boucher, but his soul cried out for something more stringent and consequential. After winning the Prix de Rome and spending several years in Italy brooding over antiquity, he found his niche in "history painting," a genre he infused with the rigorous tenets of Neoclassicism. History painting dealt with noble, ancient scenes. The works were supercharged with moral uplift and bore ponderous titles like *Septimus Severus Reproaching Caracalla for Wishing to Assassinate Him*. In David's hands, history painting was filled with urgent relevance. His *Oath of the Horatii*, which quivers with purpose and commitment, could not be mistaken in its time for anything less than a call to arms for the French Revolution.

In the chaos of that time David rose to dizzying prominence. A self-portrait painted in 1794 shows him unreflective, impatient, his brown eyes blind with fervor. He was a firebrand who embraced the revolution in its full horror and did not flinch. He voted enthusiastically for the execution of King Louis XVI, he cold-bloodedly sketched Marie Antoinette being led to the guillotine, and he served on the Committee for Public Safety, which issued the arrest warrants that led hundreds to their death in the Place de la Revolution. David also threw himself into designing elephantine pageants celebrating the First Republic, in which ornate chariots and revolutionary icons were paraded through the streets and pâpier-maché symbols of monarchy were burned to release flights of doves.

David managed to survive the shifting moods of the revolution, though he narrowly missed going to the guillotine with his denounced friend Robespierre. It was only with the rise of Napoleon that his status and popularity were restored. He flattered the emperor with memorable canvases, including *Bonaparte Crossing the Alps*, which hangs in Versailles, but as Napoleon's court painter he seems to have regarded himself as ill-used and underpaid. When Napoleon fell, David was exiled to Brussels, where he spent the last nine years of his life.

In Brussels in 1819 he painted *The Anger of Achilles*. During his old age he returned to the classical subject matter that had made his reputation, although with the exception of the *Achilles* the subjects themselves were mostly trivial—lounging gods and goddesses and winking cupids that put one in mind of Boucher. With the *Achilles*, David, perhaps for the last time, dealt with themes that were grave and worthy of his troubled experience.

He was offered the chance to go back to Paris, but he chose to stay in Brussels rather than accept the clemency of the monarchy that he despised. "I was old enough to know what I was doing, I didn't act on impulse," he wrote his son about his revolutionary activities. "I can rest here, the years are passing, my conscience is clear, what more do I need?"

The Anger of Achilles was exhibited in Brussels and Ghent. Afterward it was bought by a Parisian collector and kept from public view for more than 150 years. It was acquired by the Newhouse Galleries in New York, which subsequently sold it to the Kimbell in 1980 for a price the museum won't reveal.

When I saw it recently, it was hanging near an exhibit of paintings by Impressionists, who worked in defiance of artists like David and their stalwart meaningfulness. To the Impressionists, a painting like *The Anger of Achilles* must have seemed, for all its undeniable technique, contrived and even comical in its high-minded concerns.

But David was nothing if not high-minded. "It is not only by delighting the eye," he wrote, "that great works of art achieve their purpose, but by making a deep impression, akin to reality, on the mind." By that measure, *The Anger of Achilles* has achieved its purpose, at least with one viewer. It may be a great painting or it may not, but for me it was the painting that took the chill off art, the one that first spoke to me at the moment when I was ready to listen. When I go to the Kimbell now, I no longer feel that museum edginess, because the *Achilles* is there as a touchstone, and my appreciation of it somehow makes me more accepting of the variety of work that surrounds it. But it's to the *Achilles* that I keep returning, marveling at how one of the architects of the Terror could have painted the hurt in Clytemnestra's eyes. Perhaps the impotent Achilles in this picture is in some unconscious way meant to represent David himself, the heedless ideologue who lived long enough to see his zeal reproached and his art booted out of fashion. In his life, David was rash and unthinking, but this painting—an old man's painting—is touched with wisdom. It radiates regret and hard-earned lessons and finally an awful tranquility.

As I stood in front of it on my last trip, another visitor came up beside me. He was about seventeen, and he towered over my head and seemed as big as a parade float. No doubt he was a guard or tackle on a high school football team, an uneasy combination of muscle and baby fat. He was wearing cowboy boots and Wranglers and a huge bull-rider hat slung low over his eyes. For a long time he stared at the painting, his thumbs hooked behind his belt buckle. Then he said, with an air of wonder and appreciation, "Huh."

Later I saw him in the gift shop, buying a postcard of *The Anger of Achilles* and then slipping it into his breast pocket next to a snuff can. There was an innocence in his response to the painting that I trusted, that made me more confident of my own regard for it. Perhaps what led us both to this painting in the first place was the provincial temperament we shared, the Texan fondness for objects that are direct and weighty and without guile. Of all the paintings in the museum, David's *Achilles* comes the closest to having the common touch. I could imagine the artist tackling some myth closer to our own antiquity—Travis drawing the line at the Alamo, for instance—and creating a weird, powerful hybrid of Neoclassicism and Western art.

"This young man works in the grand manner," Diderot wrote in 1781 when David first exhibited at the French Academy. "He has heart, his faces are expressive without being contrived, the attitudes are noble and natural, he can draw."

What was true in the salons of Paris two hundred years ago is true in

Fort Worth today. I thought of David, working in exile in his Brussels studio, his stern mind in repose as the paint touched the canvas. He could not have known that his picture of Achilles would be judged as one of his lesser works, that it would hang in a Texas museum instead of the Louvre. No doubt he would have been disappointed, but he also would have recognized the more important point: that his painting had been true enough, and rigorous enough, to last. The people who admired it now were not the people he had once meant to reach, but he had reached us all the same.

ROCK AND SKY

We know the Anasazi, to the degree that we can ever know them, by what they left behind. The rock walls of the Southwest are still adorned with their fading art: whirling circles, handprints, owl-faced figures. On mesa tops and along canyon trails, the ground underfoot is strewn with thin gray fragments of their pottery. And of course there are the ruins, those shrines to fleeting civilizations and to the permanence of the American landscape.

At Mesa Verde National Park, which includes the most famous of the Anasazi sites, most of the best-known ruins are cliff villages, secreted away beneath the brow of the mesa in crevices that open out onto the deep canyons and distant plains of southwest Colorado. From afar, these tidy dwellings with their weathered masonry are barely discernible from the vaulting cliff faces surrounding them. Chinked tight against the contours of the rock, they look like giant mud-dauber nests. They have an air of camouflage, of natural mimicry, that seems like a deliberate aesthetic, something the inhabitants took pains to achieve. Looking across the canyons at these villages, nestled and disguised beneath their sandstone overhangs, you feel they were never meant to be discovered.

But of course they were discovered. Here, in the least-visited public section of Mesa Verde, on a day with steady rain falling and no hope of sunshine, the cliff dwellings were overrun by visitors who had come to view the haunted remains of the Anasazi culture. My wife and I and our three kids descended to the ruins on paved footpaths, passing below the alcoves of nesting ravens and the shallow indentations in the cliff face that the Anasazi used as hand- and footholds for their precipitous travels to the canyon floor. Some of the tourists stopped at each numbered marker to consult diligently their interpretive trail guides; others merely took in the ruins with a quick sweep of their video cameras and hustled out of the rain. All in all, we were the usual unholy horde of sightseers, trying to absorb at a glance what we should have let seep into our bones. But I felt we were doing no harm. Like the other Anasazi sites I had visited in the last few weeks, this place seemed enclosed in a protective bubble of solitude—self-regarding, unyielding, serene.

The Anasazi left behind literally thousands of such places, scattered throughout the desert washes, canyons, and mesa tops of the Colorado Plateau. They are the best-known unknown people of ancient America. The Anasazi are whom we have in mind when we speak vaguely of "cliff dwellers," that long-ago culture that lived in a universe bounded by rock and sky.

The heart of their civilization lay in what is known today as the Four Corners, where Colorado, Utah, New Mexico, and Arizona come together in a universe of cloud-swept plains and eerie land forms. The ancient magic of this country is a lodestone for travelers. Along the freeways and washboard roads we must have seen three hundred vehicles just like ours—Dodge Caravans crowned with plastic cartop carriers from Sears; children with Walkman headphones staring out the window at moody spires of rock, at Navajo dogs herding their sheep toward the brushy shelter of a summer hogan. There were streams of RVs with the owners' names hospitably written beneath the window or on the spare-tire covers—"The Rudloes," "The Pinckneys," "Hi, We're the Guthries." And there were buses crammed with Italian, Austrian, or Belgian passengers, with Navajo drivers at the wheel. Like us, they were all on the Anasazi tour. They had come to see firsthand these mysterious habitations that suggested an America not just from another time but from another realm of human perception.

The Anasazi's claim on our imagination rests largely on the popular notion of them as "the Indians who disappeared." Their intriguing little cities were already long abandoned when the Navajo filtered down from the mountains in the fifteenth century. The Navajo called the vanished residents by a word that, after centuries of being garbled in the polyglot Southwest, comes down to us as "Anasazi." The original word meant either "the ancient ones" or "the enemies of our ancient ones." But exactly who the Anasazi had been—or what they called themselves—was as much a mystery to the newly arrived Navajo as it is to us.

The archaeological record, rich as it is, gives us only a blinkered understanding of Anasazi life. We have the sense of an industrious, questing people whose world hummed with spiritual energy. The Anasazi built not only cities but roads as well—hundreds of miles of broad thoroughfares that can still be traced across the desert floor. They built underground chambers, sometimes connected by secret passageways to looming castle towers. To provide water to their fields, they constructed a system of irrigation canals, dams, and reservoirs. They wove cotton and made blankets from the feathers of their domesticated turkeys. Journeying to the south, perhaps all the way to the moody, glittering cultures of the Valley of Mexico, they came back enriched with trade goods and knowledge of agriculture. They brought back macaws and tried to keep them as pets, but the jungle birds did not survive in the arid Anasazi country, and when they died they were sometimes buried as lords.

What happened to the Anasazi? That is the great riddle. Were they driven out by enemies? Did their crops fail? Did their political structure break down? Were they abducted by UFOs? No one knows for sure, but the question is not quite as unanswerable as popular lore suggests. The Anasazi, along with their contemporaries in the Southwest—the Sinagua, the Hohokam, the Mogollon—were hunter-gatherers who had evolved into an agricultural society in a part of the world where water was scarce, growing seasons short, and crucial resources finite. As their population grew, they harvested more and more timber for roof beams, cleared more and more land for farm plots. Erosion became a problem, and drought, and then a sudden climatic change in the late thirteenth century brought on longer winters. At some point, it appears, they just decided to move along.

The Anasazi did not exactly disappear off the face of the earth. The majority of them migrated east and south to the banks of the Rio Grande and helped create the various Pueblo cultures that are still vital today. Others moved into Arizona, settling around Black Mesa and contributing to the ancestry of the Hopis. But the legend endures that somehow they were simply winked out of existence, leaving nothing behind but their strange dwellings and the restive spirits that still haunt them.

For anyone with any imagination, it is difficult to prowl among these ruins with an entirely clear head. They do have an irresistible, otherworldly charge. Partly this comes from their natural surroundings. The cliffs of Canyon de Chelly, with their whorled and sweeping expanses of rock, seem to be the fossilized record of a transitory event, like a powerful wind or a surging sea. The broad desert corridor of Chaco Canyon is a more subtle landscape, unremarkable at first sight, but it absorbs and reflects sunlight in ways that can make it seem spectral or even, to certain receptive minds, holy. Then there are the great tabletops of Mesa Verde, which rise in the blue distance like icebergs looming on a flat ocean, or the gaping overhangs, bigger than the Hollywood Bowl, that house the old cities of Betatakin or Keet Seel.

You see these places, and you have an immediate regard for the people who chose to live in them. Whoever the Anasazi were, whatever their pragmatic needs for food and shelter and arable land, they seem to have picked the sites for their houses and cities out of a craving for physical beauty and intimate contact with the landscape. They did not impose. Their residences took the forms that the natural surroundings suggested—built into crevices, bundled up against cliffs, dug into the earth, or carved discreetly into the rock itself. The Anasazi were not ecological saints—they wore out the land in places and stripped it of its resources—but they were attuned to the raw presence of the earth in ways that do not seem possible anymore.

One day when there was a driving rain and the dirt road to Hovenweep National Monument had closed, we pulled up at the Anasazi Heritage Center, near Cortez, Colorado, and browsed among the exhibits for an hour or two until the sky began to clear. The children marveled at a holographic bust of an Anasazi man. When they looked at it from one angle it was a bare skull; from another, a handsome, vacant face. If they shifted their eyes in the slightest, however, the two images came together, so that the man's face and skull appeared as overlapping, transparent clouds. It was like a taunt, a pestering reminder of how distant and unreachable the Anasazi would always be.

But as I looked at the other exhibits, I felt the gap begin to shrink. Anasazi handicrafts are contemporary, if only in the sense that they are timeless. I was drawn to the stately gray or russet surfaces of the pottery, streaked and crosshatched with soft black lines; and to an unforgettable frog pendant, carved out of three thin strips of overlaid shell, decorated with bulging turquoise eyes. One corner of the museum was devoted to a full-scale model of a pit house. This was the sort of dwelling the Anasazi lived in until about A.D. 900 or so, when they began building their houses above ground, on their way to creating the multistoried apartment cities that are their most imposing relics. What struck me about this pit house was how deep it was set into the earth and how secretive and snug it appeared, down to the entrance tunnel that resembled nothing so much as the entrance to an animal burrow.

Even after they began to build their houses on the edge of the sky, the Anasazi still indulged a cultural yearning to be underground. Their pit houses lived on in the form of kivas, the ceremonial cellars that underlay the courtyards of almost every village. In the kivas the Anasazi conducted their rituals, held clan gatherings, and reflected on the foggy times when their ancestors had climbed out of the Lower World through a hole in the sky and emerged here, onto the deserts and mesas of the Fourth World.

In Pueblo Bonito, the largest of the structures in Chaco Canyon, we walked in the late afternoon among the ruins of the courtyard. There were kivas everywhere, unroofed and unexcavated, so that the courtyard resembled a moon surface pitted with meteor craters. Except for the missing roofs, every feature of the kivas was still visible—the hearths and draft deflectors, the benches and pilasters lining the curved walls, the niches that once held sacred paraphernalia. In the floor of each kiva was a shallow round hole known as a *sipapu* (or *sipapuni*), which commemorated the Place of Emergence, the opening through which the ancestors first appeared from below. In Hopi mythology, which presumably echoes the events of the Anasazi creation story, the ancestors sent a scout up into the Fourth World in the form of a catbird they had fashioned from clay and magically coaxed into life. When the catbird reported back favorably, the humans climbed up from the Lower World on a bamboo stalk, and when they had all passed through the *sipapu*, they covered the hole with water.

"Remember the *sipapuni*," these Anasazi pioneers were told by Spider Grandmother, the messenger of the Sun Spirit, "for you will not see it again. You will go on long migrations. You will build villages and abandon them for new migrations. Wherever you stop to rest, leave your marks on the rocks and cliffs so that others will know who was there before them."

The Anasazi did as they were instructed, marking the rocks, building their towns, and then, when it was time, drifting away. But they were not nomads, and you can see in the ruins they left behind an expectation of permanence, as if the builders of these cities believed they had arrived not at a way station but at a journey's end. The construction of Pueblo Bonito alone required, according to one estimate, over a million dressed stones. And the city today—ruined and sagging as it is—looks no more transient than the fractured cliffs that rise behind it.

The children scrambled ahead of us as we wandered through the interior spaces of Pueblo Bonito, their voices growing fainter as they progressed through a bewildering maze of rooms. The doors were low to the ground and shaped like capital T's, the walls cool and stout. Where ceilings survived, the small rooms were as dark as medieval cloisters, but most of the time these two- and three-story buildings were open to the sky, their floors marked by beams of piñon pine still bearing the scars of stone axes. I stopped and tried to call to mind the life of this place—to visualize these small, smoke-darkened rooms in the dead of winter, the sound of human conversation in an unknown language, the guttural mutterings of turkeys, the barking of dogs, the noises of chipping, flaking, grinding, the creaking of looms, the snapping of piñon fires, the hypnotic drone of a singer's voice rising from the ventilation shaft of a kiva.

But seven centuries of silence were too powerful an obstacle for my imagination to penetrate, and after a while I gave up and walked across the park road and climbed down into a huge kiva known as Casa

Riconada. The kiva was almost seventy feet across, and without the roof that had once covered its hearths and banquette it looked like a miniature sports arena or an ancient Roman bath whose waters had long since ceased to flow. I took a seat on the bench and experienced a vague, religious twinge, feeling observed from above, as if this empty kiva served to focus the eye of God.

The Anasazi would not have thought of it that way. In their time this kiva would have been covered with a lattice of wooden beams, its roof paved with field stones, its sacred space enclosed in shadow. They would have looked not up to the sky, but down to the floor, to the *sipapu* from which their ancestors had first entered the Fourth World.

The Fourth World isn't what it used to be, now that it's overrun with vacationing families like my own, searching simultaneously for revelation and a vacant room in the nearest Motel 6. But in spots, in these crumbling walls and kivas that have yet to be deconsecrated by time or abuse, it must be close to the world that the Anasazi beheld. We sit in these ruins and try to invoke them—try to grasp who they were and why we feel their absence so sharply—even as they continue to disappear, climbing up their bamboo stalk to the next hole in the sky.

THE LITTLE MAN'S ROAD

We traveled the Alaska Highway during the summer solstice, driving aimlessly beneath a virtually never-setting sun. My wife played with the radio dial, calling forth Garth Brooks, stray fragments of National Public Radio, or crackly public-service announcements from deep within the Yukon—"Those people who are not bringing moose stew or bannock to the potluck supper are asked to bring a salad."

After only a day or two, I was a starry-eyed cheechako; the word is Chinook for a fair-weather tourist whose head is filled with Arctic romance. Going down the highway, I daydreamed of having my own sled team, with a lead dog whose mind was razor sharp and who knew instantly whether to turn left or right when I said "gee" or "haw." A line from a Robert Service poem, "There are strange things done / in the midnight sun," cycled through my brain, and routine sights along the road—a threadbare moose, a coyote as big as a German shepherd—caused me to break into a wondering grin.

The Alaska Highway, which turned fifty in 1992, was built in a rush the year after the United States entered the Second World War. The highway was the needle that pierced Alaska's wilderness and brought the twentieth century rushing in. Villages burgeoned into cities; native populations faced a barrage of alien mores, diseases, and opportunities; and an endless stream of homesteaders, entrepreneurs, tourists, and cranks from the lower forty-eight discovered a yellow brick road to a gleaming land that had hitherto been distant and unreachable.

The highway that was built in 1942 may have represented a stupendous engineering feat, but in appearance it was almost as primitive as a wilderness trace, an ever buckling asphalt ribbon winding precariously over the seething Arctic terrain. It is hardly a pioneer road any longer, but when you drive along it a half century later you sometimes feel that you are mushing into the unknown. The highway runs for 1,422 miles, from Dawson Creek, in British Columbia, to Delta Junction, Alaska, where it merges with the Richardson Highway for the last leg into Fairbanks. The route it follows takes a traveler through an infinitude of muskeg bogs and taiga forest, across broad glacial rivers and along the shores of glittering green lakes.

But for all its epic sweep, the highway often has the appearance, on a mile by mile basis, of a ramshackle farm-to-market road. It is rarely more than two lanes wide, and some brief stretches remain unpaved. In many places the asphalt is dimpled with a peculiar road hazard known as frost heaves. When the RVs that were always ahead of us suddenly lurched like prairie schooners, we knew that a frost heave was coming up. I would take my foot off the accelerator, easing the tires through the deep ruts, and feel our low-slung rental car rock from side to side like a boat in a gentle chop. The frost heaves slowed us, but the reduced velocity gave my eyes an incentive to linger over the landscape, to look for the white flash in a distant marsh that might be a trumpeter swan or for the humpbacked form of a grizzly bear bounding across a tundra slope.

Sue Ellen and I started out by driving south along the highway—backward, as it were, since the road was originally created to move personnel and supplies from Canadian railheads north and west into the inaccessible reaches of Alaska. We began where the road ended, in Fairbanks. We spent a day there, taking in such sights as there were: a dog-mushing museum, a musk-ox research center, a three-tiered riverboat filled with hundreds of retirees who were afterward spirited off in buses to tour Denali National Park or the Kenai Peninsula. Standing on the bank of the Chena River, we gnawed on salmon jerky and trained our eyes beyond the willows to the faraway horizon, where the snowy peaks of the Alaska Range stood in crowded rows.

The gift shops in Fairbanks were selling Eskimo Ulu knives, protective booties for sled dogs, and earrings made of walrus ivory. Dozens of RVs were encamped in the parking lot of Alaskaland, a forlorn theme park whose main attraction was an open-air restaurant with an all-you-can-eat menu of baked salmon steaks, fried halibut and ribs, and three-bean salad. When we emerged from the restaurant it was ten o'clock at night, but the sun was high and our circadian rhythms were sprung, and there was no reason we could think of not to head down the highway.

The road had four lanes for a while, but beyond the trailing edge of Fairbanks it contracted to two. We had no itinerary, no particular destinations. We just wanted to follow the road for a bit and see what it took us past and what it led us to. Since we were scheduled to fly out of Fairbanks in a week, we drove nearly half the length of the highway to the Canadian city of Whitehorse and then turned around and went back the way we came. For most of the way, pink fireweed bloomed beside the road and legions of black spruce spread out in all directions. We passed the ruins of log cabins built in the gold-rush days, fishing lodges with bleached moose antlers over the doors, and Quonset huts that had been customized by enterprising priests into ornate Roman Catholic churches. There were no real towns between Fairbanks and Whitehorse; just an occasional village with a motel and a good bakery.

We crossed parched riverbeds where the water threaded through gravel channels and dusty piles of uprooted trees. Beyond, raw mountain faces, veined with snow, rose into the sky. Somewhere between North Pole and Tok, we saw our first moose—our first moose ever—standing by the road, saggy and knock-kneed and pondering the traffic. Its thick coat was molting, and the few clumps of fur left looked like dirty carpet samples glued to its flanks. I stopped the car a discreet distance away and watched as it turned slowly from the roadside and walked across the spongy ground to a screen of trees. Standing still, it had seemed comically ill-proportioned, but when it moved it struck me as graceful and solemn. Moose, I remembered reading, are full of surprising traits. They can, for example, plunge underwater to a depth of twenty feet and hold their breath for half a minute. Despite their complacent appearance, they are often ill-tempered and dangerous, and dog mushers and hikers have learned to fear them as much as they do grizzly bears. I watched this moose through binoculars as it stalked away. It turned once to look at us, and I had a foreshortened glimpse of its massive head, the beckoning eyes in a prehistoric face, the long black ears that were as shiny as vinyl.

It took me a few days of driving along the Alaska Highway to understand just how solitary and isolated this road really was and how immense was the surrounding wilderness. One afternoon, when the peaks were obscured by storm clouds and the rain had turned the forest into a forbidding gray screen, it suddenly occurred to me that the Alaska Highway was not simply part of an endless network of roads but the *only* road, the lone track that led through an otherwise trackless land. There were no back roads to speak of, and intersections with other highways were as much as a hundred miles apart. Looking at the map, I realized that if I abandoned the car near Tok and began walking north through the misty spruce forest, I would very likely reach the Beaufort Sea, 450 miles away, before I crossed another road.

"I see it as the Little Man's Road," wrote Interior Secretary Harold Ickes on the occasion of the completion of the Alaska Highway, "the road where Mr. Jones and Mr. Ivanovich and Mr. Chang will help each other fix a flat. I see it leading from the factories and gleaming white houses of America across to Siberia, Asia and Europe . . ."

The idea of an overland route that would take people to Alaska, and beyond the edge of the continent itself, had been brewing since the early part of this century, when E. H. Harriman dreamed of a railroad that would begin in Toronto, cross all of Alaska, and burrow through the Bering Strait to Siberia. But Harriman's railroad was never built, and for four decades afterward travelers who wanted to reach the heart of Alaska came by boat, plane, or dogsled. There was a boomlet of road planning in the 1930s, but the highway was not finally built until after the invasion of Pearl Harbor. When the Japanese attacked the Aleutian

Islands in July 1942, it became even more obvious that the territory of Alaska was a potential avenue of conquest. "The only ground protection from Vancouver to Bering Strait," wrote Jim Christy in his history of the Alaska Highway, "was a cannon that sat on the lawn of the capitol building in Juneau facing the sea and which was used as a flower pot."

A highway was needed to link the existing Canadian and American air bases and to supply ground defenses. It had to be built absurdly fast, and it was. With the support of the Canadian government, the U.S. Army and the Public Roads Administration began surveying the route. The survey parties set out on horseback, accompanied by local Eskimo guides, prospectors, dog mushers, bush pilots—anybody who had an opinion about where the road should go. The first supplies and equipment came up on pack trains, and the advance parties hunted moose and Dall's sheep to supplement their K rations. The thousands of soldiers who followed them were set to work hacking out the road with picks and shovels, shoving down trees with bulldozers, and spanning rivers with log bridges. In the summer they were tortured by mosquitoes that rose from the wetlands; in the winter they were subjected to the ferocious Arctic cold.

In the nearly constant daylight of summer, it was possible to build three or four miles of primitive road a day, but almost every inch of the route presented novel obstacles. The shifting ice bottoms of the glacial rivers had a tendency to destroy bridge pilings. Barrels of antifreeze froze. The mossy muskeg swamps swallowed the logs and gravel that were set down to serve as the highway's foundation, and the thawing permafrost beneath the muskeg created lakes that engulfed the road and the machinery needed to extend it.

Nevertheless, by October 20, 1942, seven months and twelve days after construction began, a primitive version of the Alaska Highway had been laid down. A dedication ceremony was held a month later on the shores of Kluane Lake, in the Yukon. In the blizzardy cold, American and Canadian officials cut a ribbon with a pair of scissors inlaid with Alaskan gold.

My wife and I drove on, grateful for subsequent improvements to that primitive route and always hungry. Our food preferences ran to sourdough pancakes, reindeer sausage, and strawberry-rhubarb pie.

Once or twice we encountered clouds of mosquitoes and had to break out the Avon Skin-So-Soft, but most of the time the insect life left us alone. Hawks appeared in the sky, and we searched in vain for an eagle's nest. When we stopped to pay our respects at the grave of Lieutenant Roland Small, who was killed in a jeep accident in August of 1942 while building the highway, we traumatized a pair of lesser yellowlegs, who obviously had a nest somewhere near this lonely memorial. They dodged about above our heads and called to one another with such panicky bursts of sound that we decided to withdraw and leave them in peace.

Though the highway was crowded with RVs, and though there was a town every thirty miles or so, with its nature museum of rickety stuffed animals or its "trading post" specializing in sculptures made from spruce burls, the human presence seemed like a brushstroke on a vast canvas.

A place called Mukluk Land, outside of Tok, Alaska, was the boldest tourist attraction on the whole highway. It announced itself, with splendid conviction, by means of a twelve-foot-high red mukluk (which, as we cheechakos know, is a sealskin-and-fur boot invented by the Eskimos), which hung over the front gate. Beneath the mukluk were laminated testimonials from visitors. "The highlight of our whole trip!" a couple from Skinner, Oklahoma, declared. "I'm eighty-nine years old," wrote Mamie Sherwood of California, "and I had a wonderful afternoon at Mukluk Land."

We paid our five dollars and were ushered into Mukluk Land headquarters, where a woman demanded that we play a ball-toss game before we could take in the other attractions. I won enough tickets at the game to purchase five Tootsie Rolls, which seemed to make the woman giddy with happiness. She then released us into Mukluk Land proper, where we gazed upon a giant mosquito, an Alaska-pipeline display that consisted of various pieces of old pipe lying around on the ground, and an array of rusted machinery, including a futuristic-looking bus labeled "Santa's Rocket Ship," which was so old and scorched and broken down that it looked like something that had indeed fallen to Earth from outer space. A giant cabbage that we had hoped to see was mysteriously absent, and though we were encouraged to take a dogsled ride, we were disappointed to learn that it would not be pulled by dogs but by an all-terrain vehicle.

Beyond Mukluk Land, the highway skirted the great coastal ranges that rise along the shoreland of the Gulf of Alaska. At a border crossing we were unceremoniously waved ahead into Canada. Though the speed limits were posted in kilometers, the road was the same, still dimpled with frost heaves, still laden with battleship-sized RVs. Sometimes I was reluctant to stop at scenic overlooks, because I did not want all the RVs I had so laboriously passed along the way to get ahead of me again. But more often I willingly surrendered my hard-won lead, content to let the procession pass us by as we sat in the car with the motor idling and stared out at a glacier valley or an unbroken forest, as vast as the sea, surging gently toward a sharp horizon that seemed to be the very edge of the earth.

At one such overlook we fell into conversation with a couple from California who headed up this way every year in their Slumber Queen, driving from Oakland to Seattle to Vancouver to Cache Creek to Prince George and on to Dawson Creek, where they could at last begin their northwest trek on the Alaska Highway. The salmon run would begin in a few weeks, and they were en route to a fishing camp on the Kenai Peninsula, where they could join the grizzlies and bald eagles and other predators that waylay the fish as they travel up their native streams to spawn.

"I like to catch salmon," the man said, "but I like to catch halibut more. A halibut is all muscle. It'll break your arm with its tail. You have to shoot it in the head before you bring it on board the boat."

The woman loved everything about Alaska but the northern lights. She said she had been sick often as a child. Lying feverish in bed, she'd had nightmares involving colored lights that pulsed and changed shape in a menacing fashion. The first time she had seen the aurora borealis, one deep winter night above Fairbanks, it was as if her childhood fears had come alive.

A hundred and fifty miles down the road we pulled up at a historical marker on the shores of Kluane Lake that commemorated the opening of the highway at nearby Soldiers' Summit. It was a sharp, clear day. The weather was a perfect seventy degrees, and Kluane Lake was a brilliant milky blue, its water thick with swirling bands of glacial silt. A pair of bicyclists, burdened with nests of panniers and sleeping bags, pedaled south. When I asked one of them where they were headed, he gasped and said with a rueful smile, "San Francisco." Behind us the mountains rose in tiers. A frontal range guarded the St. Elias Mountains, whose summits reared into the sky with swelling grandeur. Cradled within that natural fortress, hidden from view like some majestic secret, were the ice fields of Kluane National Park. The Sheep Mountain Information Centre was a few miles south, where the deep blue lake suddenly gave way to a dusty plain marked by a watercourse. During the gold rush a prospector rode through this valley on a horse named Slim. The landscape was booby-trapped with pockets of alluvial mud, and the horse bogged down in one near the bank of the river and perished. The prospector, out of grief, respect, or cussedness, named the little river after Slim.

Rising like a wall above the Slim's River valley was Sheep Mountain, where Dall's sheep often can be seen scrabbling along the barren slopes. We scanned the mountain with binoculars but saw none; only backpackers climbing along a faint trail, headed into the icy sanctum of the park. They were carrying their food in bear-proof metal cylinders. The urge to join them, to see that hidden landscape beyond Sheep Mountain, was almost intolerable, and Sue Ellen allowed me to whine about it for a while before suggesting that it was time to get back on the road.

"There's a race of men who don't fit in," I bellowed out the open window, quoting the Bard of the Klondike again as we coasted over the frost heaves. I had always been a snob about Robert Service's poetry, but no more. Anybody who could write a line like "the freedom, the freshness, the farness" deserved his place in literary mythology.

Robert Service was an English immigrant who came to the Yukon in 1904. Thanks to the books of Jack London, who was the first writer to work the Yukon claim, Service was already besotted with the manly esprit of the Arctic. He worked as a bank clerk in Whitehorse and recited verse around town in the evenings. He lacked the motivation to write his own poetry, until one night he was shot at by a bank guard who thought he was a burglar. Out of this experience he wrote "The Shooting of Dan McGrew."

Whitehorse, where Service lived, is a pleasant, touristy town of twenty-one thousand on the banks of the Yukon River. After 750 miles of scattered hamlets and open country, it seemed like a metropolis to us. We visited the *Klondike*, an old stern-wheeler that once plied the Yukon, and then had a decorous lunch in a downtown restaurant. Afterward we went to the MacBride Museum, where we saw the scissors that cut the ribbon on the Alaska Highway during the 1942 festivities on Soldiers' Summit. After the ceremony, the blades of the scissors were separated—one half went to Franklin Roosevelt, one to the Canadian prime minister MacKenzie King—but they were reunited in time for the fiftieth anniversary. Next to them was a telephone. When I picked it up I could hear the howling wind from fifty years ago and the crackly sounds of bands playing "God Save the Queen" and "The Star-Spangled Banner."

From Whitehorse the highway ran southeast another 884 miles to Dawson Creek. We looked longingly in that direction and then turned around to catch our plane in Fairbanks. On the way back, the country appeared even newer and stranger than it had on the way down; it was of such a scale, I thought, that you could never get used to it.

About halfway back to Fairbanks we pulled off the road and found a trailhead leading into the Tetlin National Wildlife Refuge. It took us on a modest loop a mile or so through a forest of black spruce. The trees were stunted and monotonous. Though black spruce are sturdy, patient trees—taking 150 years to grow six feet—they seem, at first glance, to be weedy and characterless and strangely menacing. These dark trees rose above us in teetering ranks, their tight, stunted branches casting no shade, so the forest stood open to the sky. Bohemian waxwings swept from tree to tree, but they were the only birds we saw. We walked on mossy ground that sank under our feet like a played-out mattress. The trail was well surfaced and as broad as a sidewalk, so there was no chance of getting lost, but as we strolled deeper into the spruce forest I began to feel a twinge of anxiety. The skeletal black shapes of the trees fanned outward for probably hundreds of square miles, and I could not tell from the hovering Arctic sun what time of day it was or in what direction we were headed. We were two specks in the Alaskan universe, and the great highway we had been following for a week seemed at that moment to be no more significant than an ant trail. Alaska overpowered it, and us along with it. It seemed to me that this landscape was too big to be diminished by a road. At least that was my hope as we walked back through the black spruce to the place where we had left the car.

MY IGLOO

To build a proper igloo, you need the proper material: a certain kind of snow the Inuit of the Central Canadian Arctic call *aputit-siarveq*. This is dry, strong, surprisingly tensile snow forged by a ceaseless wind and unthinkable cold. In the winter darkness the surface of this snow can set almost as hard as concrete—so hard the hooves of passing caribou leave only a faint track.

When I arrived at the frozen shores of Hudson Bay one April day, the good igloo-building snow was almost gone. One more week, I was told, and the snow's structural integrity would have melted away. But it was still thrillingly cold—twenty degrees below zero Fahrenheit—and the inlet on which we traveled by dogsled was a boundless highway of sea ice. In a few months, the ice would start to warm and break apart, but for the time being it was still frozen fast, a solid six feet in depth, except where the seals who lived beneath the ice had used the claws on the ends of their flippers to scrabble out breathing pockets.

An igloo is a more elaborate construction project than one of these conical seal holes, but not by much. To build one, you need only a pair of hands, one or two simple tools, and a trace of genetic memory. An igloo is a dome, one of the most ancient templates for human shelter. I had been fascinated by domes ever since I walked into the Pantheon in Rome and found myself thunderstruck by its spaciousness and strength, by its mysterious perfection. Domes seem to have a kind of organic inevitability, like clouds. I wanted to see an igloo in the flesh, so to speak, because an igloo is the most organic dome of all, a shape-shifting expression of snow, the quietest, purest building the human mind has ever conceived.

A fifty-nine-year-old Inuit elder named Jack Kabvitok, who teaches shop and wilderness skills for the school system of the little town of Rankin Inlet, had agreed to show me how to build an igloo. It was his dogsled on which we were riding and his voice that occasionally broke the arctic silence, calling out the Inuktitut words for "right" or "left" or "faster" to the seven dogs padding along on the snow in front of us. Jack's English appeared limited to an occasional hearty outburst—"How you doing?" "Hungry yet?"—and my Inuktitut was nonexistent, but had we been able to carry on a running conversation, I doubt that we would have done so; any idle word felt like a violation of the land-scape's presiding quiet.

Our destination was an icebound peninsula twenty miles away. Jack had a cabin there, and that was where he planned to build the igloo. There was no trail to mark the way, except for the tracks left by our little expedition's other sled which, with its lighter frame, was habitually a quarter mile or so ahead of us. This sled belonged to Dyan Gray, a young Canadian woman who worked as a tourism official for Nunavut, the vast self-governing Inuit region that had been carved out of the North-west Territories and was soon due to become an official Canadian terri-tory. On Dyan's sled rode the New York City photographer Aldo Rossi, and on his lap sat Anaqti, Dyan's pampered, malingering dog.

Beneath the ice, the tides in these narrow inlets were still active, and the shoreline was crowded with huge blocks of ice that had been pushed upward by the movement of the water and now shone with an eerie translucence. Mysterious spangles of light danced in the ferocious sunlight. Across the top of the sea ice, the steady northwest wind had shaped the snow into an endless series of contours that resembled fro-zen waves, and the dogsled schussed gently from the crest of one wave to the next, exactly as if it were a sailboat rocking along on ocean swells.

From time to time, we glimpsed towering piles of rock—shaped like men—called *inukshuk*, erected to serve as signposts in the winter blankness. Some of these *inukshuk* were recent; others might have been hundreds of years old, as old as the stone tent rings and V-shaped kayak stands we passed that marked the sites of ancient hunting camps. The igloo—at least in its function as an actual residence—is itself pretty much a thing of the past. Nobody lives in snow houses anymore, but to an Inuit subsistence hunter barreling across the sea ice in his snowmobile, searching for seals or beluga whales, an igloo still makes perfect sense as a temporary shelter. A skilled igloo maker can build one in an hour in an emergency and, once completed, the structure is impressively strong. Unlike a tent, an igloo won't blow down in a roaring wind. A full-grown man can stand on top of it and jump up and down and still not break the dynamic tension that melds the snow blocks into an impervious dome.

Jack learned igloo building when he was ten, back in the days when, according to his wife, Aline, "there were really Eskimos." Igloos were serious business to the native people of the arctic well into this century. A thousand years or so ago, during the Thule period, when the Inuit culture was at its zenith, people had lived in winter structures framed with stone, sod, and whalebone and covered with caribou hides. But this period of prosperity ended when temperatures all over the arctic began to plunge, driving the whales to warmer waters and diminishing the caribou herds. The settled life of the Thule became unsustainable, and the scarcity of bones and skins left snow itself as the only reliable material for winter housing.

In traditional times, igloos were warmed and lit by seal-oil lamps and were built large enough to support sizable families. Often, two or more igloos were joined together with passageways. The inhabitants slept on caribou hides spread on couches made of snow, sometimes sharing the space with pregnant sled dogs or their puppies. When first constructed, an igloo was a gleaming and pristine domicile, but over the course of an arctic winter, smoke from the seal-oil lamps darkened the walls until it resembled, in the eyes of one disappointed European observer, a "witch's cave."

Early in the afternoon, we spotted Jack's cabin in the distance, a tiny dark square in a universe of white. The cabin sat on a subtle rise, a narrow snow-covered peninsula that was almost indistinguishable from the frozen sea surrounding it. Aline had driven ahead of us on a snowmobile, along with her and Jack's fourteen-year-old grandson, Wayne, and the two of them were waiting for us when we pulled up. After the dogs were unharnessed and staked out at intervals along a chain and fed dried whale meat, we retired to the one-room plywood cabin, wiping our snowy feet on a welcome mat made from the hide of a ringed seal. We sat there for a long time in the steamy heat of a portable stove, drinking tea and eating salami, coconut cream pie, and Aline's superlative bannock as the circulation slowly crept back into our fingers.

"Well," Jack said after a time, as he chewed on a frozen shard of raw caribou, "let's go look around."

He slipped into the caribou parka that Aline's mother had made for him, took up an aluminum rod, and led us outside. It was already four in the afternoon, but the sun didn't appear to be going anywhere. It hovered like a white moth above the horizon.

The dogs lifted their muzzles out of the snow and watched curiously as Jack used the rod to probe around the base of the narrow peninsula, searching for snow of the perfect thickness and consistency. He rejected two or three locations. Then, with the end of the rod, he drew a circle about ten feet in diameter.

"Let's make igloo," he said.

To construct an igloo, Jack needed only two tools: an ordinary crosscut saw and a machete-like implement called a *pana*, or snow knife. He knelt and began to saw into the snow at the circle's southeast edge, where the doorway of the igloo would be located. First he removed a deep wedge of snow and set it aside, then began to cut out a block about one and a half feet long by three inches wide. He undercut the block at a diagonal to a depth of about one foot and wrestled it free from the surrounding snow. It squeaked like Styrofoam as he withdrew it. He set the fresh-cut block in front of him and inspected it with a look of growing distaste, finally muttering something to Wayne in Inuktitut.

"Snow's no good," Wayne translated.

The top half of the block was solid, but the bottom half was made of inferior snow that crumbled to the touch. Jack pulled himself wearily to his feet, took up his aluminum rod again and began searching farther down the slope. Fifty yards from the cabin, he found a patch he liked better and once again drew the circle in the snow and pulled up the first block.

"That's better," he said. With the *pana*, he trimmed the bottom of the block and set it in place on the perimeter of the snow circle. Then he shaped the top of the block into a diagonal incline. With each succeeding block, this angle grew steeper, and the igloo's first layer spiraled lazily as it advanced along the circle he had drawn in the snow.

Working without commentary, he continued to saw out the blocks in orderly ranks, building a kind of igloo basement in the process. I sat down on the snow and watched him work. I had intended to lend a hand, but it seemed to be a one-man operation and, anyway, the process was more intricate than I had expected. Clearly there was a science in trimming a block to the exact angle and slope, then shoving the block into place against a neighbor to stand without any adhesive other than severe cold and the laws of physics. When Jack finished the first layer and began the second—"OK," he said, "going up now"—it was easy to imagine the whole thing tumbling down at some point.

Yet up it went. With each layer, the inward angle of the blocks grew steeper, but the spiraling wall never wavered. By the time Jack had erected the third layer of snow blocks, he was almost hidden from sight. His two hands, encased in furry caribou mittens, bustled about all by themselves at the top of the snow blocks like characters in a puppet show.

Jack kept building the shell of the igloo while Wayne filled the cracks between the blocks with snow and Aline came out with a pan of water and started pouring it over the structure. The water quickly froze in the cold air, creating an even stronger seam.

When Jack had completed the fifth layer of blocks, he cut out a door with his snow knife and invited me inside. The door was about the size and shape of the opening to a doghouse and was set beneath the top layer of snow. Entering the igloo was like wriggling into a badger's burrow. Inside, the igloo felt marvelously spacious. The flat arctic light seeping through the blocks of snow made the dome look like some sort of translucent curtain.

"Not much more now," Jack said, grinning, as he heaved another block into place. His hair and eyebrows were heavily flocked with snow. The dome grew higher, and the spiral of snow blocks grew tighter until finally he had to stand on his tiptoes to reach the apex. It struck me, as I watched him, that building this shelter had occurred completely from the inside. At every step of construction, from the first cut in the snow, from the setting of the first block, Jack was screening himself against the freezing wind. The way he was building this igloo around himself reminded me of a caterpillar spinning a cocoon.

Finally there was only a triangular gap at the top of the igloo. Jack bent down, selected an irregular block of snow from the scrap pile that had accumulated on the igloo floor, then lifted it with one hand above the opening and held it up there while he trimmed it into shape with the *pana*. Then, as if he were closing a manhole from the inside, he lowered his hands and set the block into place. All that remained was to cut a small ventilation hole into the keystone. When he had done this, he stepped back, smiled, and announced: "You got igloo."

It had taken two and a half hours, and no doubt he could have accomplished the task in half the time if he had been in a hurry. But he was a methodical and finicky craftsman, and even now that the igloo was completed, he could not leave it alone. He kept walking around the outside, filling in the cracks with snow, smoothing the rough spots, and shooing away Anaqti when she trotted up on the mistaken assumption that this edifice had been built for her.

"What do you want to sleep in that igloo for?" Aline asked Aldo and me a few hours later in the cabin, after we had eaten a dinner of beef steaks and were waiting for the persistent arctic daylight to subside. "It's cold in there. Are you crazy?"

Around ten o'clock, we pulled on our parkas and mittens and went outside. Darkness was still hours away, but a heavy ground fog swirled across the narrow peninsula and the sunlight was strangely obscured, hidden behind a penetrating grayness that resembled night. Down the slope, the igloo was glowing, lit from within by a kerosene lamp Jack had placed on the floor. From a distance, in this strange muzzy darkness, the igloo seemed to hang alone in the firmament, shining with the softest, whitest light I'd ever seen.

When Aldo and I crawled inside, Jack was there spreading musk-ox and caribou skins on two sleeping platforms he had fashioned of snow on either side of the igloo. He had made a kind of end table for each of us as well, had done everything but put a mint on our pillows. He himself had no interest in sleeping in the igloo, though it could easily have accommodated him and perhaps three or four others.

I wouldn't say it was the most comfortable night I have ever spent. Two layers of thermal underwear and a subzero sleeping bag cushioned by the fur of arctic beasts didn't completely dispel the cold. But I felt reasonably safe and cozy, and I experienced enough intermittent dozing to count as a night's sleep. Sometime during the night, Anaqti skulked inside to join me on the sleeping platform, and when I awoke the next morning, she was staring at me with her pale, eerie eyes.

I lay there drowsily for a long time, scratching the dog's ears and examining the interior of the igloo with a beguiled attention to detail. The sun had long since risen from its brief dip below the horizon, and a sedate light shone through the concave wall. I counted fifty individual snow blocks from the archway over the door to the keystone at the top. With the morning light illuminating the blocks from behind, I could clearly make out the pattern of the horizontal striations that marked the succeeding layers of the winter's snow.

I struggled into my snow boots and parka and crept outside. The air was utterly still, the light utterly flat. Thirty yards away, tethered beyond the tidal push-ups on the open sea ice, the sled dogs were still asleep, each one nestled in a perfect mound of snow. A single raven flew overhead, its black plumage slashing across the white sky, its voice piercing the muffled silence. Then the raven was gone and the arctic peacefulness closed over me again: no color, no movement, no sound. A whole world with nothing in it.

I walked up the slope about twenty or thirty feet for a different view, and when I turned around the igloo was gone. In the bluish, washed-out light, which cast no shadow and gave no contour to the land, it had simply disappeared. I peered hard and walked back, expecting the igloo to reappear with each step I took. But by the time my eyes finally found the dome against the background of snow, I was almost close enough to reach out and touch it.

As the morning progressed and the light grew stronger, the igloo became more conspicuous, but it still seemed like a secret place, a hummocky rise in the snow that gave no hint of the beautiful translucent chamber within. Had we dwelled in it for any length of time, of course, it would have become a drippy, smoke-darkened cave. But as we pulled away in the dogsleds that afternoon, I took some pleasure in the realization that this house would remain pristine until it melted away in the spring thaw, and would shine in my memory for long after that, a pantheon of snow.

A SECRET DOOR

"So that's what a sonata looks like," Sue Ellen said. We were standing at the edge of a shimmery chasm in the floor of the Mexican jungle. Shaped like a teardrop, the chasm measured perhaps three hundred feet from one end to the other, and it was filled to its limestone rim with the water of an underground river. The Spanish word for such a sinkhole is "cenote," not "sonata," but I kept myself from correcting Sue Ellen, remembering that in twenty years of marriage she had never been grateful for this particular service. And as malapropisms go, it was inspired. The water in the cenote seemed as pure as music.

We stood there listening for a moment more, Sue Ellen, our three girls, and I, and then we dug our masks and fins out of the gear bag and leapt in. The water, even with the tropical sun to warm it, carried a charge, and the kids surfaced from that first plunge yelling with mock distress that they were freezing to death. I swam down to the center of the pool and looked upward, through twelve feet of water transparent almost beyond comprehension. It gave me a peculiar feeling of satisfaction to see my family snorkeling above me in a V formation, as if they were not in the water at all but sharing the sky with the birds that soared and swooped above them.

This had been my idea: a family snorkeling vacation in Yucatán, the five of us traveling light with our trusty masks and fins, roving from one supernal body of water to the next. It was a backwater tour that I had in mind: no cattle-boat diving on Cozumel, where the Mexican government had just given the go-ahead to dynamite a section of the island's exquisite reefs to accommodate more cruise ships; no parasailing or jet-skiing or rides on giant inflatable bananas pulled by speedboats off the beaches of Cancún. Instead, we would follow the one highway leading out of that unholy resort city, pulling over at some sagging jacal with a hand-lettered cardboard sign out front that read *"Visite el cenote"* or veering onto an unmarked dirt track in the hope that it would lead us to the edge of a sparkling lagoon.

Now, on this bright spring morning in 1995, we stood at the banks of Car Wash, which was the prosaic gringo name that had been bestowed upon the teardrop-shaped cenote. No doubt it bore an ancient Mayan name as well, because in this part of the country, which is without surface streams or rivers, cenotes have always been vital features of the landscape. For the ancient Maya, they were the only access to fresh water, but they served as spiritual portals, too, leading from the Middleworld of surface life to the highly complex Otherworld, an unseen realm of dark waters and shifting heavens.

We spent several hours exploring the cenote, basking on the sunny surface or diving to the bottom, which was not a bottom at all but a broad pinnacle, the summit of all that rock that had long ago collapsed into a hollow cavern beneath the earth. The sinkhole sloped downward on all sides from this cone of fallen limestone, leading into dark underwater rooms that extended into the vast porous tableland of the Yucatán Peninsula. When I took a deep breath and swam cautiously to the brink of one of these caverns, I encountered a sign, ghostly white against the blackness, that warned "Stop—Go No Further—Prevent Your Death." Not far beyond this sign, I had been told, was some sort of ancient temple or fire pit, a reminder of the time when a lower water table had made this a system of dry caves. And 3,500 feet upstream from this altar was a large, submerged cavern called the Room of Tears, so named because one of the divers who had found it supposedly wept at its beauty.

That afternoon, standing on the summit of Nohoch Mul, the towering pyramid at Cobá, I could not get that watery Otherworld out of my mind. Cobá, an extensive Mayan ruin a few miles up the road from Car Wash, had once been an imperial rival to the great city of Chichén Itzá. But Chichén Itzá conquered Cobá and its allied cities in the Puuc hills and endures to this day as one of the most visited Mayan sites. Cobá, not nearly so well known, is still mostly hidden—seventy square miles of shattered, jungle-covered temples, with two mighty pyramids rearing up out of the canopy.

All five of us had started up the broken stairway of Nohoch Mul, but Sue Ellen and our two older girls—eighteen-year-old Marjorie and thirteen-year-old Dorothy—decided to turn around midway up the pyramid, when the climb began to grow frighteningly steep and precarious. Only Charlotte, our surefooted eleven-year-old, made it to the summit with me. We sat up there on a terrace in front of a temple decorated with friezes of the Diving God and looked out over an endless, ragged forest punctuated by several shallow lakes. (In Maya the word "*cobá*" means "water stirred by wind.") The only other thing that broke the flat sweep of the forest was the pyramid known as La Iglesia, which emerged from the canopy a mile away, a pile of rubble half sheathed in vegetation. An iguana sunned itself on the stones below us. It had molted away the scabrous skin of its tail, which now looked as tender as the shoot of a plant. A constant chatter rose up from the dense forest beneath us, made up of who knows what—jays, tanagers, toucans, motmots, spider monkeys.

The world we saw from the top of this pyramid was a nearly seamless forest stretching out to touch the horizon in all directions, a landscape that appeared as timeless and unconquerable as the open ocean. But buried beneath these trees, I had read, were some five thousand unexcavated structures and an extensive network of roads leading out to other vanished cities, roads that Mayan workers had constructed of masonry and white marl that they crushed with giant rolling pins.

And surely there were dozens, if not hundreds, of cenotes down there as well, hidden beneath the forest canopy. The immense limestone shelf that makes up the Yucatán Peninsula is veined with underground rivers, which flow beneath the earth in total darkness and silence, constantly eating away at the rock, carving out an infinity of channels and caverns. When the ceiling of one of these caverns happens to collapse, a cenote is formed and a window is opened onto one of the most secret regions of the planet.

A great deal of that subterranean water flows into the ocean, discharging into the wildly picturesque lagoons that are found all along this part of the coast. We visited several of these lagoons the next day, stopping first at Chac al lal, which was only a short walk from our hotel in Puerto Aventuras. We came by boat, however, coasting in on the ocean swells through a narrow pass into a shallow basin ringed by coral rock. The lagoon spread out before us, an expanse of perhaps five or six acres, its water as searingly blue as the flame of a furnace.

And there, perched at the very edge of the ragged coral shoreline, standing guard over this dazzling waterscape, stood a single Mayan temple not much bigger than a toolshed. There was no plaque or sign to identify this building, to tell us whether it had been a shrine to an ancient Mayan god or a lighthouse or a customs station connected with the coastal trade that once flourished along these shores. In any case, the structure had been a relic for at least four hundred years, and by now it was as weathered as the ironshore shelf on which it had been built.

The lagoon was vacant except for a dozen German tourists who came trooping down the path with their snorkeling gear as we anchored the boat in front of the temple. Like many tourists, they had planned their trip for the most congenial time of the year—the dry season, which lasts from November to April. During these months, the water appears exquisitely clear from above, but when we slipped overboard and looked beneath the surface, it not only was opaque but had a strange visual texture, like wrinkled wax paper. Various fish—sergeant majors and parrot fish—swam in front of my mask lens, but I perceived them only in a nearsighted haze.

"What's wrong with the water?" the kids wanted to know. But there was nothing wrong with it. The peculiar haziness was merely proof that fresh water from those underground streams was pouring out of the rock, mixing unevenly with the salt water surging into the lagoon from the sea. When fresh and salt water meet, they have a tendency to stack themselves, the heavier salt water settling to the bottom, the fresh water riding on top. The plane that separates them is known as the halocline.

Sometimes a halocline is hard to miss, a sharp divide that sorts the water into strata as clearly defined as the rock in a road cut. In this lagoon the distinction was far more subtle, a strange, wavy blending that reminded me of an old episode of *The Twilight Zone* I had seen as a kid, in which a family discovers that their house contains a secret door to the fifth dimension. When they work up the nerve to go through the door, they find themselves in a world of undulating, distorted images, with imperceptible and barely audible figures beckoning them further.

My own family, I knew, felt a little as if they had been dragged into a strange dimension as well. I had originally told the kids we were going to Cancún for spring break, and while this had been true in a technical sense (we would be arriving and departing at the Cancún airport), I had not adequately prepared them for the fact that they would not be spending their days sipping virgin daiquiris at the swim-up bars of luxury hotels or hanging out at Planet Hollywood and the Hard Rock Cafe. They had been cruelly disappointed in these fantasies once before, years earlier, when I accidentally left them with the impression that we would be spending a weekend in fabulous Cancún, when in fact we were going to a sleepy little hideaway on the Frio River called Concan. Once again, we were not going through the main door, but through a secret door, into a world of mute Mayan temples and wrinkly water and endless submerged grottoes.

We wore ourselves out that day, visiting another solitary temple/lighthouse a few miles down the coast and then stopping to snorkel another lagoon or two and to browse along their shorelines for beautiful cobbles of fossilized coral. By the end of the afternoon only Marjorie had the energy to accompany me to Xel-Ha, a national park at a broad lagoon between Puerto Aventuras and Tulum.

The admission fee for Xel-Ha was ten dollars apiece, and "National Park" struck me as a highly suspect designation for what turned out to be an assemblage of swimwear boutiques, cafes, towel rental facilities, and juice bars. The lagoon that spread out in front of all this, however, was the real thing. It was a vast and tranquil sheet of water with a few craggy islets rising from it. The low afternoon sun cast a flat, soothing light across the surface.

When Marjorie and I entered the lagoon, we encountered once again that tricky mixture of fresh and salt water. Here, however, the halocline was more apparent. The fresh water on top was chilly and blurry, but when we dove to six feet or so, we hit a band of warm, clear water, in which schools of big parrot fish were suddenly, magically visible, grazing along the sand bottom of the lagoon. I noticed that the passage of my body through the halocline stirred up the layers, causing them to commingle in eerie ways. When I came across a large barracuda on the bottom, half the fish was clearly visible, but the other half melted away into a gauzy abstraction.

"Admit it, Dad, it's a purse," Dorothy chided me the next morning as we made our way along a rocky path deep into the forest.

"It's not a purse," I said, referring to the canvas shoulder bag that contained several bottles of water and a notebook that I could not handle without soaking the pages with sweat. "I believe Eddie Bauer refers to it as a guide pouch."

"As if you were a guide," she said. "It's a purse."

We had embarked on the first phase of the Indiana Jones Jungle Adventure, a mile-and-a-half walk through a humid tropical forest that led to a cenote known as Nohoch Nah Chich, a Mayan phrase meaning "the Giant Bird House." Nohoch Nah Chich is the main hub in a remarkable attempt to map the underground river systems of this part of the Yucatán. The leader of the enterprise, Mike Madden, the American owner of a dive center based in Puerto Aventuras, had shown me a map that morning of the Nohoch system. When Madden set the rolled-up map down on the floor of his office and opened it, it took up nine feet, and it depicted a fibrous network of caverns, tunnels, and cenotes spreading aimlessly in all directions. Madden and his teams of cave divers have been exploring this system since 1987, using underwater scooters to roam through enormous water-filled rooms that can be 1,400 feet long by 400 feet wide, and then can pinch off to narrow passageways through which a diver has to wiggle like an eel. Except for the occasional distant light of a surface crack or a cenote opening, the caves are perfectly dark, and the divers must swim through them bearing their own light as well as their own air, sometimes carrying 250 pounds of survival equipment. By using the scooters, and by caching extra scuba tanks and lights at critical intervals, they have traveled more than thirty thousand feet in a single dive. There is no telling where the thing begins or ends. It is already the longest underwater cave system in the world. At the time we visited, Madden and his divers had mapped 129,000 feet, painstakingly connecting one cenote to the next, and were on the verge of following the passageways all the way to the sea.

To the degree that this sprawling subterranean complex has a front door, Nohoch Nah Chich is it. Madden started the Indiana Jones tour as a way of allowing casual tourists such as us a relatively safe peek into a lethal and unnervingly beautiful counterworld.

The Indiana Jones Jungle Adventure is a hokey name for an authentically strange experience, though I must admit I did swagger a bit along that forest path, with my Eddie Bauer guide pouch slung over my shoulder and sweat pouring into my eyes from my sodden hatband. The path was an irregular ribbon of coral rock, and the kids seemed to enjoy the challenge of keeping their footing as they hurried along. More than a dozen people were on the tour this morning, along with several horses carrying ice chests and snorkeling gear.

At the end of the path we came to a Mayan farm, where a man named Don Pedro lived with his wife, Doña Rafaela, in a breezy compound of *palapas*, fruit trees, and Brahman cattle. The cenote was on their land, and as we passed the main house—where Doña Rafaela had set up a display of embroidered dresses to sell to the Indiana Jones adventurers—we could see the land disappearing into a deep crater fifty or sixty yards away. The Nohoch cenote was eight hundred feet in diameter and appeared to be completely dry except for a crescent of dark water far below. To reach the bottom of the sinkhole, we climbed down a wooden stairway and then walked across the broad summit of the rubble cone to a wooden platform built at the edge of the water. Above us rose the raw chasm of the sinkhole, the rock festooned with the long stringy roots of the trees that grew along the lip of the precipice. Perpetually shaded by the steep overhang that rose above it, the narrow strip of water here was dark, but achingly clear. Schools of minnows patrolled the area beneath us, and when Charlotte—eating a grotesque Mexican cookie crowned by a bright pink marshmallow—dropped a crumb into the water, the minnows converged on it with the fury of an atomic fusion reaction.

"Where are we going exactly?" Dorothy asked as we pulled on our fins.

"In there," I said, pointing to a dark maw at the base of the cliff face. It looked like the entrance to some theme park thrill ride—the mouth of a cavern with a few stalactites hanging down like fangs, ready to swallow anyone who ventured too close.

The guide, a young woman with a Brooklyn accent, divided the expedition into two groups of ten and passed out an underwater flashlight to every two snorkelers. She explained that we would be swimming into the cavern to a distance of eight hundred feet, beyond the reach of sunlight, traveling a circular course that would bring us out the way we came in. She reminded us that we would not be going into the regions accessible only to cave divers; there would always be air above us.

"Youse guys stay together now," she admonished.

Silently, our little flotilla of snorkelers entered the cavern. We kept our eyes underwater, transfixed by the velvety blue light from the receding sun. I dove to the bottom, looking up at my children paddling above, glowing in that brilliant pane of blue light like figures in a stained-glass window.

But by and by, that light disappeared, and we had only our flashlights to guide us as we floated deeper into the cavern. The rooms we passed through were the size of houses, filled with cantilevered boulders and cave formations that glowed in the flashlight beams with a milky radiance. There were cascading flowstones and stalactites that hung from the ceiling and pierced the surface of the water like daggers. The water's clarity suggested a kind of nothingness, the void of deep space. I swam around and below the children, watchful and a little worried, because the water was so deep, the rooms so vast, and unspeakable dangers so easy to imagine. The kids were all good swimmers, and there were shelves of rock to rest on if they got tired, but just the same, I would periodically take hold of their hands to reassure myself that this strange universe was not somehow tugging them away.

During the next few days we drove up and down the road between Playa del Carmen and Tulum, visiting one cenote after another. Some of them were large, nearly dry craters like Nohoch, with a rim of water at the bottom leading back infinitely into the rock. Others were filled almost to the edge, with the surface so still and translucent it looked as if it had been sealed with a giant sheet of Saran Wrap. When we snorkeled through the waters of these cenotes, the sunlight fell across the boulders below us in waving curtains of light. We saw turtles and golden fish with accordion-pleated sailfins they raised above their backs to catch the sun's rays, and peculiar little diving birds—grebes, I think—that pedaled along underwater for great distances with their enormous feet.

At the entrance to one cenote, we found a dilapidated old school bus. Through its open windows the children had the opportunity to see an ancient hippie, completely unclothed, sashaying down the aisle as he sang a mournful a cappella version of "Paint It Black."

"Okay, we've seen a naked hippie," Dorothy said. "Now can we go to that Xcaret place?"

We had passed the entrance to Xcaret many times in our meanderings up and down the road, had seen the tour buses streaming into it and the colorful billboards advertising the theme park as "Nature's Sacred Paradise." Robbed of Cancún, the kids had focused their hopes on this place, which seemed to offer exactly the sort of exotic synthetic experience their gringo souls most deeply craved.

So Sue Ellen and I relented and we drove into Xcaret, passed through a fake Mayan temple, and paid twenty dollars apiece for a wristband that was our token of admittance. What we found inside was an incredibly well-groomed, well-run, and utterly dispiriting tourist trap. There were uniformed attendants everywhere, and restaurants and gift boutiques, one-hour photo shops, horse-riding demonstrations, botanical gardens, and snack bars squeezed around authentic Mayan ruins. There was a manicured beach and a man-made breakwater to protect it and an enclosure where, for an extra fee, visitors could swim with captive dolphins.

The centerpiece of Xcaret, however, was a snorkeling tour of an underground river that flowed through the park. A few years before, this river—a winding channel that worked its way above and below the surface before discharging into a sparkling lagoon—had been one of the loveliest features of the entire coast, or so I'd been told. But now that it had become part of "Nature's Sacred Paradise," it had been blasted and diverted, its opening to the sea closed off and its aura of beauty and mystery debased.

To enter the underground river, it was necessary to put all our valuables into plastic bags to be ferried to the exit point. We were then required to don orange safety vests, and when we entered the water, we became part of a crush of bobbing snorkelers moving passively along on a gentle current, flailing about with our orange safety vests and wristbands.

"This is stupid!" Charlotte said, and I allowed myself a little thrill of triumph, proud that this trip had helped further what I considered one of the most crucial elements of the children's education: the ability to tell the difference between what is real and what is fake.

My attitude toward Xcaret was partly the environmental hauteur of a privileged American. In this desperate country, where the peso fell each day and showed every sign of falling through eternity, places such as this meant jobs. Still, my mood was low when we left—I was thinking of all the beautiful places we had visited in the past few days that would no doubt someday suffer the same fate as Xcaret.

But when we turned off the road for lunch, heading to a beach and campground known as Xcacel, things began to improve. There was, for instance, a two-headed sea turtle, maintained alive in a shaded tank just above the beach. An old American woman, a fierce advocate of the turtles that crawl ashore on these beaches to nest, put her hands into the tank and lifted out the turtle, which had eight waving flippers and two heads that strained in opposite directions.

"This is Boo-Boo," she said, "and this is Bo-Bo," indicating each of the heads in turn. "They've got two of everything—two sets of lungs, two hearts—but only one rectum. So when one of them wants to go to the *baño*, the other one has to go, too."

We admired the two-headed turtle for a moment more, made a contribution to a fund to protect the turtles' nests from human egg poachers, and then strolled over to an open-air restaurant that overlooked one of the prettiest beaches in the Yucatán. The turquoise water was blinding, an assault of color, and the breeze moved gently beneath the palm fronds, where we sat eating our *pescado tikin xik*.

This beach, the local rumor went, had been sold to the Japanese, so who knew how long before it, too, went the way of Xcaret and Cancún? How long would that Mayan temple on the edge of the lagoon stand there in its pure solitude, and how long would the cenotes we had snorkeled in remain untapped and unpolluted?

I thought of that trip into the perfect darkness of the Nohoch cenote, with the light beams sweeping across the lustrous flowstone and bats flapping in the airspaces above our heads. Ancient Mayan kings had once performed bloodletting rituals, piercing their penises with stingray spines and running knotted cords through their tongues as a way of reaching a level of spiritual intensity sufficient to allow them entrance into the Otherworld. The places we had visited did not require such a cruel price of admission, and though they were off the normal tourist path, they could hardly be considered a part of the secret Mayan cosmos. But sitting and recollecting in the bright glare of the sun, I felt we had at least touched the margins of that ancient dreamscape, and that when we looked back on this trip, it would be in dreams that we remembered it best.

PART THREE

THE SHADOW
OF HISTORY

THE TEMPLE OF DESTINY

I n 1519—almost half a millennium ago—two men stood at the top of
a temple pyramid in the Valley of Mexico, looking out over the Aztec
city of Tenochtitlán. Both men were in the grip of a dream. Hernán
Cortés was thirty-four years old, a tall, lithe gentleman-adventurer
from the Spanish province of Extremadura. His hair was thin and his
beard too sparse to completely conceal a knife scar near his upper lip.
Though his physical and mental energies were boundless, he had the
complexion of a scribe. ("Their bodies were as white as the new buds of
the cane stalk," the Aztecs marveled of the Spaniards, "as white as the
buds of the maguey.") Ever since Cortés and his five hundred followers
had sailed from Cuba for the unknown shores of Mexico, they had been
riding a tide of fabulous luck, and now the tide had delivered them to
the dreamscape of Tenochtitlán, to this beautiful and gruesome city
floating like a water hyacinth in the middle of a lake.

Montezuma II, the ruler of the Aztecs, was fifty-two. In his youth he
had been an honored warrior, but as emperor he was a rarefied being, a
pitiless aesthete who was rumored to dine on young children and fret-
ted over every uncertain portent. For a long time there had been plenty
of worrisome signs: a comet, "like a flaming ear of corn"; a strange storm
in the lake; a captured bird with a mirror in the center of its head. All

of this had helped to convince Montezuma that Cortés was the incarnation of Quetzalcóatl, the banished god whose vengeful return had long been prophesied. Montezuma was terrified of Quetzalcóatl, who promised to depose Huitzilopochtli, the Hummingbird on the Left, the god of war and human sacrifice from whom the emperor derived his power. But Montezuma could not fight a god, and so his only choice was to welcome the intruder with wary courtesy. "No, it is not a dream," he told Cortés at their first meeting. "I am not walking in my sleep. . . . I have seen you at last! I have met you face to face!"

Montezuma was not asleep, but even at this distance the conquest of Mexico seems more dream than history, some abiding pageant of the unconscious mind. Ever since I first read that Mexico City utility workers had discovered the remains of the Great Temple, I had been mad to go there, to see with my own eyes the evidence that this amazing story had really taken place. Could there be a more resonant tourist attraction anywhere in the New World? Here, at the summit of this pyramid, Cortés and Montezuma had stood for a moment hand in hand, and then a few months later the uneasy stasis was broken forever and the idol of Huitzilopochtli was carried down the steep steps, its place in the temple reclaimed by a statue of the Virgin.

Within a matter of months Montezuma was dead, and though Cortés and his followers were forced to flee the city in mortal chaos, they came back a year later to erase it from the earth. They pulled down the pyramid along with the seventy-odd other buildings that had once formed the main ceremonial complex of the Aztecs. The ruins and foundations of those buildings—palaces and temples, monasteries, idol houses where sacrificial victims were dismembered and stewed, a royal zoo and aviary that employed three hundred keepers—were buried beneath the Christian streets. Mexico City's main plaza was superimposed squarely upon the site of Aztec religious and civic life. The city of Tenochtitlán had not entirely vanished, but its shattered remains lay secreted away.

Today the ruins of the pyramid are exposed, and a splendid new museum that interprets the history of the Great Temple rises discreetly behind them. At first glance, visitors might easily mistake the site for an unfinished public works project. The greater part of the pyramid was destroyed, and its base, like so many other buildings in Mexico City—

like the immense listing cathedral fifty yards away—has subsided into the soft ground reclaimed over the centuries from Lake Texcoco. Where once the pyramid was a towering monument, it is now a depression in the earth, an expanse of truncated walls and corridors made of volcanic stones, its decorative stucco facade long since eroded away. Visitors' catwalks lead down from the street and over the unpolished marble floors of ancient plazas and temples and ceremonial quarters. Pieces of massive sculpture are still visible: boxy, snub-nosed serpents' heads, so stylized they look mechanical; grim-faced frogs crouched like sentinels; a wall carving of human skulls.

The ruins represent a complicated process of building and renovation. During the two hundred years of Aztec residence in Tenochtitlán the pyramid was periodically enlarged, and each new phase was built on top of the one preceding it. Much of what is exposed today would have been hidden in Cortés' time; he would have seen only the final phase, the tallest and grandest pyramid the Aztecs ever built, crowned at its summit by massive temples to Huitzilopochtli and Tlaloc, the god of rain.

Bernal Díaz, who was with Cortés and whose chronicles of his adventures are precise and vivid, recalled that the Spaniards climbed 114 steps to reach the top of the pyramid. Once there, Montezuma turned to Cortés and expressed concern that his visitors must be exhausted from the ascent. Cortés replied that he and his men were never tired.

From the temple platform Montezuma showed the Spaniards the view. Tenochtitlán was built on an island in the middle of Lake Texcoco, creating an ingenious imperial fortress connected to the mainland by three causeways whose access was controlled with removable bridges. There were other cities along the mainland shore, and Diaz could see their temples in the distance "like gleaming white towers and castles: a marvelous sight." Montezuma pointed out the aqueduct, which brought fresh water from the springs at Chapultépec, and the canoe traffic flowing along the surface of the lake and through the extensive network of inner-city canals. The Spaniards could hear, from miles away, the murmur of commerce in the central market whose size and splendor eclipsed any they had seen in Europe.

And yet in the eyes of Cortés and his men it was all built upon an abomination. Though they themselves had slaughtered thousands of innocents on their march through Mexico, they could neither comprehend nor tolerate the idea of ritualized human sacrifice. To the Aztecs and the other nations of Mexico, however, sacrifice was a binding tenet of existence. The gods constantly required the nourishment of "precious eagle-cactus fruit"—the pumping human hearts ripped from the bodies of living victims. When the Great Temple was consecrated in 1487, tens of thousands of people—taken by the Aztecs in war or as tribute—were sacrificed. For four days the procession of victims made its way up the steps, as visiting dignitaries watched from galleries that were garlanded with flowers and sedge to protect against the reek of gore. In front of the Hummingbird's temple the priests would seize each victim and bend him backward until his body was as taut as a bow, then the executioner would slice beneath the ribs with a ceremonial knife and in the next motion reach in and tear out the wildly beating heart. The body was then rolled down the stairs, along a stream of blood that made its way down the pyramid in a slow cataract. At the bottom, the limbs were cut off to be cooked with squash for a ritual human feast, and the torsos were tossed to the animals in the zoo.

On their journey to Tenochtitlán the Spaniards had already seen their share of human sacrifice; along the way they had been toppling idols and converting the native priests into acolytes after washing the matted blood out of their hair. Cortés and his men were cruel and hardened adventurers, but they seem to have been genuinely unnerved by the idolatrous bloodlust they saw all around them. Their mission of conquest and greed steadily deepened into a religious crusade. Isolated in a world as unbelievable as a distant planet, they clung desperately to their idols, no doubt realizing that in this dangerous city the subtlest turn of events could place the invaders themselves on the sacrificial slabs.

On the pyramid that day Cortés asked to be allowed inside the temple, and after some thought and consultation the emperor led the Spaniards into the sanctum of Huitzilopochtli. His guests were horrified. The idol of the Hummingbird, Diaz reported, had "huge terrible eyes." Three human hearts were burning in a brazier, and "the walls of that shrine were so splashed and caked with blood that they and the floor too were black. Indeed, the whole place stank abominably. . . . The stench was worse than any slaughterhouse in Spain."

Cortés asked Montezuma for permission to erect a cross on the top of the pyramid, so that the lord of the Aztecs could see how his false idols would tremble in the presence of the true God. Montezuma replied, "in some temper," that if he had known Cortés was going to offer such insults he would never have allowed him into the temple.

Cortés tactfully dropped the subject. Montezuma's hospitality was icy, but it was all that was keeping Cortés and his men alive. Over the next week or so it became clear to the Spaniards just how precarious their situation was. Montezuma protected them only because he thought Cortés was Quetzalcóatl, and he dared not challenge a god. But Montezuma's control over the situation was shaky. There were thousands of Aztec warriors—Jaguar and Eagle knights armed with wooden broadswords faced with cutting edges of obsidian—who had very little tolerance for their uninvited guests. Cortés' predicament was delicate, but his response was astonishingly blunt: he arrested Montezuma in the heart of his own capital.

This outrageous strategy worked for a time. Montezuma was dumbfounded and ashamed, but compliant with the will of Quetzalcóatl. Diaz tells us that the Spaniards treated him with great deference, that during the long, idle hours of his house arrest the emperor argued religion with Cortés and gambled good-naturedly at a game played with smooth gold pellets. "It was not necessary to instruct most of us," Diaz writes, "about the civility that was due to this great chief."

Cortés was now the dictator of a restive Tenochtitlán, and with typical bravado he marched to the top of the pyramid—to the temple of Huitzilopochtli—with an iron bar in his hand. "Upon my word as a gentleman," wrote one of Cortés' soldiers many years later, "I can still see him as he leaped high in the air, hovering over us almost supernaturally as he smashed the iron bar down on the idol's head."

"Who would conquer Tenochtitlán?" reads a fragment of Aztec poetry engraved on a wall of the new Museum of the Great Temple. "Who could shake the foundation of heaven?" The museum itself is filled with artifacts found at the site. The most arresting is a nine-ton monolithic oval disk, bearing in low relief the image of Coyolxauhqui, the treacherous goddess who was killed by her brother Huitzilopochtli when he was born, fully armed, from beneath the writhing serpent skirts of his mother. The dismembered goddess is depicted on the stone as a jumble of body parts, the head angled away from the torso, the limbs sheathed in armor studded with the likenesses of rattlesnakes. Not far from this violent and chaotic sculpture I came upon a sea-shell carved from a boulder, a work of such finesse and serenity that it instantly shattered my old storybook notions about the ferocious gloom of Aztec thought. The shell's beauty was troublesome, and challenging. Who were they, after all, these people who chose the harmless, radiant hummingbird as the manifestation of the deadliest god humankind has ever worshipped?

After an hour or two of wandering through the museum—among the life-sized terra-cotta statues of Eagle Knights, the displays of sacrificial knives, the human skulls with leering stone eyes set into the sockets—I was no closer to an answer than when I came in, and the story of the Aztecs and their conquest by Cortés still seemed like a supernatural event. It was hard to view the story through the eyes of a historian, as a military campaign beset by the usual run of confusion, intrigue, and complicated alliances. On some level Montezuma's perception made more sense: the conquest of Mexico was a clash of gods whose fatal out-come had long since been preordained.

On the first floor of the museum I stopped in front of a model of the Great Temple. The pyramid was depicted along with the scores of other buildings that made up the center of Tenochtitlán. The complex was surrounded by a high wall known as Coatepantli, the Serpent Wall, and the buildings within the enclosure looked sterile and polished. Little human figures had been positioned around the grounds, and when I looked closely I could see lords in their feathered headdresses, armed knights in the guise of their animal totems. The pyramid domi-nated everything, towering and steep, its walls studded with the stone heads of serpents. The exhibit had the placid unreality of a model rail-road layout, but it was still startling to realize that a city like this had once existed.

That city was gone, of course, cursed and obliterated by the con-quering Spaniards. That Cortés and his men survived to wreak such vengeance is one of history's miracles. The arrest of Montezuma had only forestalled the crisis that was building in the city. Cortés was weakening, and he was surrounded by a hostile population that had lost faith in the credibility of the emperor. Finally, when it seemed an attack by the inhabitants was imminent, Cortés persuaded Montezuma to climb onto the palace roof and tell his people to let the Spaniards leave the city in peace. As the lord of the Aztecs stood there in his embroidered mantle and turquoise earplugs, his bottom lip pierced with a crystal tube containing the feather of a kingfisher, he was met with a hail of stones. One of the stones hit him in the head, and when he was brought back to his apartments, he refused all ministrations and languished, as Diaz tells it, until he died.

"Cortés and all of us captains and soldiers wept for him," Diaz says, though some historians believe that the Spaniards, angered by how useless the emperor had become to them, stabbed him to death on their way out of the city.

The Spaniards memorialized their retreat from Tenochtitlán as La Noche Triste, the Night of Sorrow. More than half of Cortés' men perished in this nightmarish battle, and none escaped unwounded. Hacking their way along a causeway, the Spanish were pressed on all sides by thousands of warriors in canoes. The Aztecs removed the bridges in the causeway; Cortés' men fell into the gaps and drowned from the weight of the gold they were carrying, forming new bridges of dead men and horses across which other soldiers made their way to the mainland.

The Aztecs thought they had driven the Spaniards out forever, but the prophecy was still unfulfilled. Cortés managed to rally his men, enlist the aid of Tenochtitlán's enemies, and besiege the city a year later. He built ships and launched a navy on the lake, blockading the Aztec capital and subduing one by one the cities on the mainland that provided it support. Finally he assaulted Tenochtitlán itself. "Such was the slaughter done on water and on land," Cortés wrote to Charles V, "that with prisoners taken the enemy's casualties numbered in all more than forty thousand men. The shrieks and weeping of the women and children were so terrible that we felt our hearts breaking." When Cuauhtémoc, Montezuma's successor, was captured and brought before

Cortés, he tearfully begged to be stabbed. Cortés refused, and patted him on the head.

L ate one afternoon I took a walk from my hotel to the pyramid. I was staying at the Hotel de Cortés, a cool stone bulwark built in the eighteenth century as a home for Franciscan monks who had come to end their days in New Spain after a lifetime of missionary work in the Philippines. In front of the hotel ran Avenida Hidalgo, the street built along the route of the old Tacuba causeway, along which Cortés had fought his way out of the city on La Noche Triste.

I crossed the street and made my way through the alameda, the plaza where, after the conquest, the Spaniards had burned infidels. Now it was a public park draped with willows and bordered by street vendors.

My way took me past the Palacio de Bellas Artes, the national concert hall, which was built in the 1930s and which has already sunk twelve feet into the substrate; through the colonial heart of the City of Mexico, with its sixteenth-century buildings housing banks and *pastelerias* and religious-supply shops where one could buy a statue of a bloodied Christ lying in a transparent casket; onto the zocalo, the main plaza, where a crowd of striking schoolteachers had assembled to listen to speeches and chant their demands.

It was a clear day for Mexico City, but I could taste the particulate in the air, and the demonstration reminded me of the city's desperate, sprawling essence: the eighteen million souls who lived on the surface of the vanished lake, in the despoiled metropolis that spread over the once magical Valley of Mexico.

I walked into the Metropolitan Cathedral, which the Spanish began building in 1573 as a monument to the bloody exorcism that Cortés had conducted in Tenochtitlán. The cathedral was vast and heavy; I could sense its weight. It was not vaulting toward heaven but pressing down upon the earth. The floor was uneven, moving upward toward the nave like a ramp. Everywhere there were altars and chapels, lofts and pulpits, golden encrustations. It was a gloomy place that spoke of the vengeance of the Lord, the heartless triumph of Quetzalcóatl. Here, where the cathedral was erected, where images of tortured saints now resided, had stood the great cranial racks of the Aztecs, the skulls of sacrificial victims strung like beads on an abacus—so many skulls, says Diaz, that it was impossible to count.

When I came out of the cathedral, the teachers had begun to disperse. Vendors were selling comic books and mangoes on sticks, the flesh carved like rose petals. Over by the Great Temple a line of salesmen had set out blankets for displaying their wares. One man had an ancient set of bathroom scales on which a customer could weigh himself for a few pesos. Another demonstrated wind-up plastic scorpions. A boy stood trying to interest passersby in two baby squirrels that skittered along on the pavement, their necks secured by leashes made of string.

The squirrels were so small and so out of place that for a moment they startled me, as if they were some new kind of creature. But they were just one more lingering, exotic element, part of the strangeness that Cortés had finally been unable to quell. Mexico City itself seemed that way, exotic and forlorn. "My heart burns and suffers," Montezuma had said, "as if it were drowned in spices . . ."

I stood at the railing of the excavation and looked down upon the volcanic building blocks and the weathered serpents' heads with their thick ribbons of flicking tongues. I could see braziers and four-petaled flowers carved into the stone, and the remains of the apartments where the Eagle Knights had once gathered to put on their feathered ceremonial dress. They had stood here; it had all happened. Cortés destroyed the pyramid, but he could not eradicate its foundations. And it was fitting, I thought, that the city of Tenochtitlán was now underground, half glimpsed but silently persisting, like some dark but enticing thought that cannot be banished from the mind.

THE MAN NOBODY KNOWS

At seven o'clock in the morning, the valley of the Inn River was still dark. It would take another hour or so for the winter light to begin leaking over the crests of the mountains. Though the sun had not yet risen, the temperature was mild, and the streets of Innsbruck were half submerged in a slurry of melted snow. High, high above the city, along the ramparts of the Alps, the lights of villages and lodges shone like distant stars.

I had come to Innsbruck to learn about the Stone Age man whose mummified body had recently been found in a nearby glacier, and when I glanced up at those peaks I tried to look at them through a Neolithic lens. A traveler walking through this valley five thousand years ago, I imagined, might also have seen clusters of illumination beckoning from villages far away in those mountain meadows. There would have been fewer lights, of course, and they would have flickered rather than held steady, but perhaps they would have filled the hiker's mind with the same sort of awe and isolation I felt today gazing up at the Alps. Measured against those mountains—which looked even deeper and more eternal than the black sky behind them—five thousand years ago seemed very near at hand.

Indeed, it was hard not to think of the man in the glacier as being, in some weird sense, still alive. One of the names the press had given him—besides *Der Eismann, Der Gletschermann, Der Tirolmann,* and *Der Similaunmann*—was Ötzi. This name, derived from the Ötztaler Alpen region where the body had been found, had a mocking, mascot-like ring to it, as if the man were not in on the joke of his own long-ago death. In photographs he appeared hideously deceased but also somehow aware. With his dried-out eyeballs staring blankly out of their sockets, he seemed more than a relic from the past—he seemed like an emissary.

Though the Iceman's body was shriveled, gnawed upon, hairless, and as tough as rawhide, it was otherwise remarkably intact, and its discovery had intrigued scientists and casual newspaper readers around the world. Lying for five thousand years or more in the glacial ice, the body and its effects constituted an almost miraculous time capsule from the waning centuries of the Late European Stone Age, an era more precisely known as the Late Neolithic Age.

The people who lived in central Europe then were farmers and animal herders, hunters and artisans. They tended their crops of wheat or barley and lived in wooden houses with plank floors, with corrals for their livestock nearby. Some of their villages were walled and fortified, some were raised on pilings at the edges of marshy lakes. With implements made from deer antler, they quarried flint for the manufacture of the stone axheads and daggers that would soon be rendered obsolete by the metallurgical revolution that ushered in the Bronze Age.

Late Neolithic Europeans buried their dead in communal tombs made of massive stone blocks. Within these megalithic vaults the dead lay in rows, bundled up like sleeping children, the males lying on their right side, the females on their left. Near them were arranged various tools and treasures for use in the next world—axes, knives, beads of limestone and shell.

Finds of such artifacts are not uncommon. Over the years archaeologists have unearthed many of these burials, with their rows of broken skeletons and formal grave goods. But the Iceman is unique. He died alone, apparently by accident, and lay undiscovered beneath a thick shield of ice as the megalithic tombs crumbled and the world he had known passed away. The things that were found with him were not ceremonial objects but the tools and weapons and personal effects of everyday use. And his body was preserved as a mummy, though not a stately, embalmed mummy like the kind left behind by the Egyptian Pharaohs of the Old Kingdom, entombed in their pyramids during the same epoch that the Iceman was sealed in his glacier. His body had not been preserved by elaborate funerary rituals, but by atmospheric chance, and, when it was found, it was whole.

The Iceman's leathery hide still bore its ancient tattoos, and within his body's desiccated organs there was a potential diagnostic treasure trove of enzymes, food remnants, parasites, and genetic material that might one day be able to shed light on the Iceman's health at the time of his lonely death.

For the time being, he resided in a freezer vault at the University of Innsbruck's School of Anatomy. "No, no," I was told by Werner Platzer, chairman of the anatomy department, when I asked to see him. "It is unpossible!"

Allowing anyone in to see the mummy, he explained, could provoke an international incident. The Iceman's ownership would ultimately be decided in favor of Italy—though the body would remain in Innsbruck three years while scientists completed their testing—but when I visited, it was a matter of dispute between that country and neighboring Austria. The body had been found fifty to sixty miles south of Innsbruck, on a high mountain pass near the main crest of the Alps. This crest is an important watershed—moisture from its southern slopes drains into the Adriatic Sea, while rain and snowmelt on its northern side feed the rivers and streams of the Austrian Tirol. At the end of the First World War, the Treaty of Versailles stipulated that this watershed was the border between Italy and Austria. Later on, the border was fixed by a series of stone markers.

These markers did not, however, follow the exact contours of the watershed; hence the custody battle. The Iceman was found about a hundred yards within the Austrian side of the watershed. If the watershed was the border, he was clearly Austrian. If, however, the true border was represented by the stone markers, then the Iceman belonged to the Italians, since a line drawn between the two nearest markers placed him in the Italian state of South Tirol.

Until the exact ownership of the Iceman was determined, he remained off-limits to the public and the press, and so I had to content myself with looking through a stack of photographs in the university's Institute for Pre- and Proto-History. The office door was decorated with cartoons from Austrian newspapers and magazines whose German gag lines I could not read, but which showed the mummy's wrinkled body propped up in a railway carriage for his trip into the twentieth century, or being pulled apart in a tug-of-war across the Italian-Austrian border.

The first photograph of the body showed it lying face down in a pool of slush, just beginning to emerge from the ice that had contained it for millennia. The back of the Iceman's head was as smooth and round and weathered as some archaic pottery vessel, and beneath it were his wizened shoulders, the scapular bones protruding like a pair of folded wings. Another picture showed him whole, after his removal from the ice, lying on a steel dissecting table at the university. His left arm was flung awkwardly across his chest, rigid as a stick. The skin was stretched taut over his skeleton. Something had long ago chewed away his genitals, but a wad of plant fiber—the lining of what had once been a shoe—still covered his right foot.

I studied the close-ups of the Iceman's ghastly face. Hairless and shriveled, with the tip of the nose and upper lip missing, it still bore the stamp of a particular identity. There was a gap between his front teeth, exposed now by the absence of the lip; in life it would have showed whenever he smiled. His chin was sharp, his eyes were open. The tissue of one eye was white, the other piebald. A blurry blue cross was tattooed on the back of his knee, and there were more tattoos on the small of his back, three discreet columns of horizontal lines.

The Iceman had been found at an altitude of 10,500 feet on September 19, 1991, by a German couple on their way home from climbing Finail Peak in the Tirolean Alps. They spotted the body near a high mountain pass known as the Hauslabjoch, in a field of receding ice that had once been a nameless tributary to the Similaun Glacier. Not far from the Hauslabjoch is another pass, the Niederjoch, which is lower by some six hundred feet. For centuries shepherds from the villages to the south led their sheep over the Niederjoch and down into the long valley, the *ferner*, beyond it. Sometimes, when the Niederjoch was covered with snow, the shepherds would detour to the west and take the Hauslabjoch.

Perhaps that is the detour the Iceman took so long ago. It was no accident that he lay in the path of modern climbers and hikers. The mountain terrain dictated, then as now, where people would walk.

Between his time and ours, however, the tongues of the glaciers had crept up and down these steep mountain defiles, advancing and receding with the rhythm of a tide. When the Iceman tried to climb over the Hauslabjoch, the glaciers were in retreat. The ground he lay on as he was dying probably was clear of ice, but over time the glacier came back and covered it, burying him until he was revealed during the warm autumn of 1991.

Rainer Henn, director of the Institute of Forensic Medicine at the University of Innsbruck, had already examined a half-dozen bodies that had come out of the thawing glaciers that year, including the remains of two climbers lost in 1934. When he entered his office on September 23, there was a note on his desk alerting him to the discovery of yet another victim of the mountains.

By law, Henn is required to remove any such body from the ice, perform an autopsy on it, and determine the cause of death. When he took a helicopter up to the Similaun Glacier, he had no idea that the corpse he was about to inspect was a Stone Age relic.

For four days, ever since the German couple had discovered the Iceman and notified the warden of a nearby mountaineering hut, hikers and climbers had dropped in on the site; some of them had gathered up pieces of equipment or clothing that were lying near the body. Reinhold Messner, the legendary mountain climber, had happened by as well, and had been struck by the apparent antiquity of the body and the strange blue marks on its back. He thought it might be four hundred years old.

"When I came to this place," Henn told me, "the body was still partly covered with ice. I only saw the back of the head and part of the back. I had not the faintest idea how important it was. I only knew that this body must have been completely mummified before it was covered with snow."

Henn and his colleagues began hacking away with mountaineering axes at the ice enclosing the body, and dug a small trench to channel away the slush water that had accumulated in the warm sunlight. In the trench, Henn found a small stone dagger with a long wooden handle.

"When I saw this knife," he said, "I had the idea that this man was very old—I had no idea *how* old—and from this moment I ordered all these people to be most careful while getting the body out of the ice."

The body was wrapped in plastic and taken by helicopter and ambulance to the University of Innsbruck, where it was examined the next morning by Konrad Spindler, the dean of the Institute for Pre- and Proto-History. By now, most of the Iceman's equipment and the remains of his clothing had been recovered as well. There were a few strips of plaited grass, which might have been a shoulder cape or a sleeping mat, and pieces of an animal-hide jacket, finely stitched with threads of twisted grass. There was part of a bow and a leather quiver filled with fourteen arrows, two of which were notched and feathered and the others presumably unfinished. Another leather case, containing a flint scraper, a ball of resin, and a few flint tips, was thought to be a repair kit for the arrows. Then there was the small flint knife that Henn had found and a simple stone amulet, as well as several broken pieces of wood that, when fitted together, suggested a pack frame.

There was also an ax, in superb condition, with a long wooden handle to which a precision blade was still attached with rawhide lashes and some sort of ancient putty. After studying the ax, Spindler had first decreed that the frozen corpse dated from the early Bronze Age, about two thousand years before the birth of Christ, but this estimate turned out to be off by a millennium. The ax blade, with its duck beak shape and low hammered edges, fit the profile of a blade from the early Bronze Age, but it was not bronze, the alloy of copper and tin that transformed the Neolithic world. The Iceman's blade was almost pure copper, probably quarried from a mountainside and pounded into shape rather than smelted and cast—the product of an earlier technology. In addition, carbon 14 tests on the Iceman's body and on the plant fiber lining his remaining shoe confirmed that he had lived between 4,800 and 5,500 years ago.

As a relic, the man could be classified and dated. But it was the sense of something that could never be known—the mystery of his human identity—that moved me when I looked at those photographs. It was odd how a five-thousand-year chasm of time created as much a sense of intimacy as of distance. I found it impossible to think of the Iceman for long without feeling sorry for him, imagining his solitary death and the apprehension, the dread of the family he never came home to.

Sitting in Konrad Spindler's office, I asked him what he had felt when he had first seen the body. A meticulous man in a blue suit and steel-rimmed glasses, Spindler studied the pink message slips lined up in ranks on his immaculate desk.

"At first I did not feel any emotion," he said. "There was too much work to be done." A faint smile played across Spindler's impassive face. "But perhaps later," he said, "I thought of Mr. [Howard] Carter, when he opened the tomb of Tutankhamen."

We talked about who the man might have been and what he might have been doing that autumn on the Hauslabjoch. "Perhaps he was a shepherd with goats," Spindler mused, and immediately I wondered whether the Iceman had a dog to help him with the herd, and whether the dog had died with him or found his way back home.

"There are copper mines in these valleys," Spindler went on. "We have here natural outcroppings of copper. Perhaps he was looking for nuggets. Surely in the winter he must have lived in a settlement in the valley—but we don't know whether north or south. Surely he had contacts with others. The tattoos couldn't be made by himself. They had to be made by another person.

"His bow is unfinished. Perhaps the original bow of this man was stolen or broken, and he went down to the valley and fetched wood for the new bow. Perhaps in the evening as he sat by the fire he worked on the bow.

"His clothes are made from hide, from deer. Very fine and exactly made." Spindler pointed to the stitching on his own suit. "The stitches are very fine. But there are some other stitches that are very raw. So we think maybe this man tore his clothes and repaired them himself, but very raw."

I asked Spindler if he had a guess about what happened to the man.

"I think he died by coldness," he said. "He lost his way, and he died by coldness. In this time—late September—you have degrees under zero Fahrenheit. If you lose your way in a blizzard, you don't have any chance to go on living."

Whatever terrible misfortune befell the Iceman in life, he became, as it was later explained to me, "a very lucky corpse." It is widely believed that the bodies of people who are lost in the deep freeze of a glacial landscape remain as preserved and undefiled as Snow White in her glass casket. In reality, they are transformed in fascinating and gruesome ways—their limbs are sheared off by the movement of the glacier, their fatty tissues turn as pale and hard as plaster. The body of the Iceman underwent its own metamorphosis, but through a series of remarkable occurrences it was in far better shape after five thousand years in the ice than most bodies after a few months.

"You would perhaps like to see some of our other glacier bodies?" one of Professor Henn's assistants inquired when I dropped in at the university's Institute for Forensic Medicine. He led me down the hall and unlocked the door to a small museum of forensic science. It was a strange place. There were rows of jars filled with people's heads floating in greenish preservative fluid, their eyes and mouths gaping open. There was an exhibit of the ropes, dog leashes, chains, and other constrictive devices that had been removed from hanging victims, and in glass cases nearby there were several of the victims themselves, or at least what was left of them after weeks of hanging from a tree limb in the forest.

"Here is how a glacier body looks normally," my guide said, indicating a human form lying full length in a display case. "This one fell into the glacier in 1923. He came out in 1952." The man under the glass was still tangled in his mountaineering ropes, still wearing his boots, crampons, and sweater, but he was broken and disjointed and his head was so shriveled and papery it reminded me of an onion. Inside the ice, subject to cold, humidity, and lack of oxygen, the parts of the body that had once stored fat—the adipose tissues—had turned hard and pale. The organs had long ago rotted away, so all that was left were bones, teeth, fingernails, and this crust of adipose flesh.

Henn joined us and took me to an examining room to show me the body of another climber. "This person came from Vienna," he said, looking down at the torso of a man. "He disappeared in 1934. We found him three or four weeks before we found the Iceman."

The body had most likely lost its lower half when the glacier moved above it, grinding it against the rocks. One of the man's arms was mummified, the hand pinched into a claw and the nails weathered and blackened. But the rest of the body was like a badly chipped plaster statue. Henn told me that when the man had been found, he still had his railway tickets and a membership card to a mountaineering club in his pocket. The climber had been in his robust sixties when he died. Even now his glasses rested on what was left of the bridge of his nose, and a dental plate lay casually on his chest. His face had turned into a shell of stony tissue, but a scrap of beard was still attached to his chin like a piece of coarse sandpaper.

"This is what we usually see," Henn explained, looking down at the body, which looked less like human remains than an oddly shaped piece of soft, crumbly rock. "It was a chain of lucky circumstances that preserved the Iceman in such an outstanding way."

Those circumstances began with the site of his death. The place where the Iceman was found was a flat shelf of rock about two hundred feet wide, with a narrow cavity running through it. This stone trench was ten or fifteen feet deep, a logical place to take shelter in the face of a sudden storm. Presumably this is what the man did, though he died anyway, and afterward foxes or perhaps vultures began to feast on the body. But for some reason they stopped. Maybe another storm came, covering the body with snow and driving the scavengers to lower elevations.

Had it lain there under the snow for long, the Iceman's body would have been transformed, as were the bodies of the climbers in the forensic museum; but something else happened instead. Most likely the dry autumn winds of the Alps—the *foehn*—blew away the first protective covering of snow, exposing the body and leaching it of moisture. Within several weeks it became a mummy—a shrunken, dehydrated, but otherwise perfect husk of the man who had once inhabited it.

The rock trench in which the body lay became a crypt. Over time the ice that had once covered the spot came back, but inside his narrow crevice the Iceman was spared the crushing weight of the glacier.

And because this terrain on the Hauslabjoch pass was flat, the glacier barely moved, so there was no damage from the pulverizing scree that a glacier carries with it when it slowly glides downslope.

Protected from all the elements that would normally have destroyed it—bacteria, scavengers, chemical transformation, the shifting and sliding of the landscape itself—the Iceman's body lay undisturbed in its frozen chamber. When it emerged, it was in good enough shape for Henn to plan an autopsy to determine whether the man died from hypothermia, as Spindler suspected, or from some other cause.

"Legally," Henn told me, "I have to do an autopsy to find out how he died. It will be difficult and take a long time. First, we will find out by computer thermography what is inside. Because the body is so hard, we will have to use not a scalpel but an electric saw. We will make small incisions at the sides so we do not damage his shape."

But the autopsy would be months in the future. In the meantime, teams of scientists from all over the world had begun to analyze the Iceman's equipment, his clothes, even the pollen found frozen in the ice near his body.

"We are looking for all that could be of interest," Platzer told me later that afternoon in his office in the anatomy building. "For instance, parasites—ecto- or indo- parasites. We are looking at what is inside the stomach. And we are looking at the skin, to see if he has the same cells in his skin as we have in ours. It is a very interesting question: Had the man lived outside and was therefore very sunny brown? Had he such cells as are necessary for the sunny brown of the skin? Will we find any antigens? If this man has the same antigens as we do, then the same ills are in his way of life."

I asked once again if I could see the body, but Platzer denied my request with a polite wave of his pipe. He did consent, however, to show me the vault where the Iceman lay. I followed him through the corridors of the anatomy building, an edifice that was as old and grave as a cathedral. Our voices echoing off the high ceilings, we passed somber murals depicting the dissection of the human body and then vast white-tiled rooms where the real thing was under way. Dozens of cadavers lay on tables while lab-coated medical students peeled back skin and cut away snippets of flesh. A fusty preservative smell penetrated every crevice of the building and the wrinkled brown bodies on the tables looked neither older nor younger, neither more nor less dead than that of the Neolithic man who had come out of the glacier.

It was into this bustling postmortem environment that the Iceman had been taken after his five millennia of perfect solitude. In the basement of the anatomy building, Platzer led me through a door marked "*Unbefugten ist der Zutritt verboten*" and into a large room with tile floors and several empty dissecting tables. Against one wall were two stout metal doors whose silvery surfaces had a pattern like crinkled aluminum foil.

Platzer opened the door on the right and showed me the dark, pantry-size chamber inside. "And so, behind the other door," he said, "is the body."

I stared at the rippled surface of the freezer door, wondering what sort of alarms would sound if I betrayed Platzer's good faith and simply reached out, pulled the handle, and opened the vault. What brought me to the brink of this seditious conduct was the knowledge that the Iceman was just a few feet away from me, lying on his back in the sub-zero blackness that replicated his burial chamber in the glacier, his eyes staring at the ceiling, his stiff arm extended across his body. To his Stone Age family and friends, I suppose, he had lived on after his death as a wandering shade, since they had never been able to properly entomb his body and put his soul to rest. Was it *his* restless spirit I felt today in the basement of the anatomy building or merely my own, as I stood there imagining what was waiting to be revealed if I would only open that door?

COMANCHE MIDNIGHT

arie was seven years old today, and the sweat was for her. She arrived at the sweat lodge clutching a baby doll and a bottle of Mountain Dew. Gayle Niyah-Hughes, her mother, had brought along a Care Bear birthday cake for afterward and some prayer ties that she had made herself.

"There's one for me and one for her," she explained, fingering the little pouches filled with tobacco and sweet grass that would be burned in the fire pit so that the smoke would rise like a tangible prayer. "I don't make the best ones, but it probably doesn't matter if they're not perfect. I just wanted to have this for my daughter. It'll mean more to her than having a party at Pizza Hut."

Seven men had gathered to do the sweat and pray for Marie. One of them—judging from the sharpness of his features and the moustache that grew only in two small tufts at the sides of his mouth—was close to being a full-blood Apache. Most of the others were, in varying degrees of heritage, the people I had come to Oklahoma to find: Comanches.

Like many other modern Texans—heirs to the conquest—I could not help regarding Comanches with a romantic cast of mind, as some long-ago blood enemy, as the personification of the frontier itself. The Comanches once dominated much of Texas from the Edwards Plateau to the High Plains. Though in the end they lost it all, the intensity of their defiance is commemorated in the pitiless and self-reliant Texan character.

In my imagination the Comanches belonged to history, and it was easy to think of them as extinct. They were an emblem of barbaric splendor, and as such it was tempting to believe they had not been subdued but had merely vanished like a prairie wind. But the Comanches did not vanish. They are still around, though much of their culture has long since been destroyed or mislaid. They are a people haunted by the richness and vigor of their past, haunted all the more as each new generation devolves farther away—in language, in blood, in logic—from the ancestral ideal. In that sense, they are like everyone else on earth: a people struggling to recall who they were and to understand who they have become.

When the sun was a little lower, Kenneth Coosewoon, the sweat leader, began taking his ceremonial instruments out of a lacquered-wood carrying case the size of a small toolbox. There were bundles of braided sweet grass, an eagle feather, a gourd, and a deerskin pouch containing sticks of wood that he had found glowing one night on a creek bank. Coosewoon wore a black jogging suit and glasses. His grayish hair was long and tied back, and a beaded medicine bundle hung around his neck.

In the old days the sweat lodge was an important fixture in a Comanche camp. It was a center for prayer and purification. Before a young man undertook a vision quest, or a group of warriors embarked on a raid, they would prepare themselves spiritually in the sweat lodge. No one knew any longer exactly what the Comanche sweat ritual had been, so Coosewoon more or less had to improvise. Like many other facets of contemporary Comanche culture, the sweat ceremony was a pastiche of half remembered lore, gleanings from other tribes, and bits and pieces of Christian dogma.

"I never even dreamed I'd run a sweat," Coosewoon told me as he gathered his things together. He was the director of the alcoholism center in Lawton, and several years ago he had gotten interested in the sweat ritual as a kind of therapeutic extension of the Alcoholics Anonymous program. He advertised in the paper for someone who knew the old ways and could run a sweat, but no one answered the ad. Then one day he was praying at the creek bank when he saw the glowing wood. The wood was hot to the touch, and at the moment he picked it up he heard a bird shriek and a big oak tree shake in the wind, and then a spirit spoke to him.

"The spirit said, 'You don't need nobody. You go ahead and run the sweat. Just be yourself. I'll be with you all the time to help you.'

"He said everything would come to me and everything has come to me. I was given stuff little by little. An eagle feather. A gourd. I was given a pipe, but I ain't never fired it up yet. A Sioux medicine man named Black Elk told me to pray with it and respect it and it will tell me when it's all right to fire it up. In the old days we would have had a pipe carrier to work with me on it, but we don't have any of those guys anymore."

The sweat lodge was made of heavy canvas draped over a cured willow frame. It was a low, hemispherical structure whose entrance faced east, the source of wisdom and knowledge. When it was nearly dusk we stripped down to gym shorts or bathing suits and crawled inside. There was a deep pit in the center, and the bare earth surrounding the pit was covered with strips of old carpet. Dried sage hung from the bent willow poles, and Gayle fixed the medicine ties for her and Marie onto the frame above their heads. One by one, seven heated rocks from a bonfire outside were brought into the lodge on two forked branches and lowered into the pit. Coosewoon blessed the glowing stones, brushing them with the braided sweet grass, and then sprinkled cedar over the pit, filling the lodge with its harsh and aromatic smell.

"Grandfather," he prayed, "thank you for the lives of the people in this lodge. Thank you for the earth and for our Indian people, Grandfather. And we ask your help for all the Indians who are stumbling around drunk, Grandfather, who are not walking straight on Mother Earth, Grandfather. And we thank you especially for the life of Marie, Grandfather, and we pray that you show her how to walk firmly on the earth, Grandfather, and show her how to travel the four directions . . ."

When Coosewoon was finished, he said, "Ahoh! All my relations!" and then each person in the lodge prayed in turn. Just when the dry heat from the rocks began to be uncomfortable, Coosewoon doused them with water, and we began to steep in the purging humid air. The others' prayers were direct and unaffected pleas for deliverance—from alcoholism, from broken hopes, from the diabetes that kept loved ones in the Indian hospital, waiting for their legs to be amputated.

"Heavenly father," Gayle said when it was her turn, "I thank you for the life of Marie. When I first saw her seven years ago, Lord, I was *scared* because I know life is so hard, Lord. Lord, I thank you for the life of my husband, even though he's been gone for three years. I know it's wrong to grieve over his death, that I should be thankful for what I have, but it's so *hard*, Lord. Lord, I ask you to bless me and Marie and my children that are still unborn. Help me to understand the ways of our Indian people. Ahoh! All my relations!"

The sweat took place in four stages, with the participants leaving the lodge every half hour or so to replenish themselves in the cool night air. After each break more stones were brought in, and before the water was poured over them they glowed in the pit, the only light in the utter darkness of the lodge. During the second session Coosewoon sang a song that had been given to him by an old woman a few years before, accompanying himself by shaking a gourd.

"Hey! ya-ya-ya-ya—Hoh! nya-no-nya-no," or so the song sounded to me, its primitive rhythm oddly complex and familiar.

The steam made me light-headed and short of breath. And in that dark lodge, filled with ancient music and the smell of sage and cedar, I found myself entertaining the illusion that the last two hundred years of history had never taken place, that the Comanches were still and always would be the lords of the plains.

In the old days the Comanches knew themselves as Nermernuh, a term that—like so many other self-designations of American Indians—has one simple, confident meaning: people. In the sign language used by the Plains tribes, the Nermernuh were represented by a wiggling motion of the hand that symbolized a snake traveling backward. The Utes—their historic enemies—knew the Nermernuh as Kohmahts, "Those who are always against us," and it was a corrupted version of that name that finally prevailed among outsiders.

At the height of their power the Comanches presided over a vast swath of prairie, desert, and mountain foothills that became known as Comancheria. They roamed as far north as Nebraska, and their raids carried them as far east as the Gulf Coast and deep enough into Mexico to encounter rain forests and to come home bearing legends of "little hairy men with tails."

The Comanches were stocky, barrel-chested, prone to nearsightedness. Their faces were broad, with heavy, looming features. The men were vain and superstitious about their hair, keeping it long and greased with buffalo dung, and their ceremonial leggings and moccasins were distinguished by long trails of fringe that dragged on the ground. Comanches filled the cavities in their teeth with dried mushrooms, powdered their babies with cottonwood rot, and directed attention to their war wounds by outlining the scars with tattoos. Boys shot hummingbirds out of the air, snaring them in the split shaft of an arrow. Although there was no prescribed cosmology, the Comanches had a complex and appreciative awareness of a world brimming with spirits and half-glimpsed designs. Unlike other Plains tribes, they did not have an overarching tribal unity. The Comanches were parceled out into bands and each band was an ad hoc government unto itself, led by men who had become chiefs not through any formal process but through the uncontested power of their personalities.

Long before, when they first filtered down out of the eastern Rockies onto the plains, the Comanches had been just another wandering tribe of bandy-legged pedestrians. But when they encountered the shaggy mustangs that the Spanish had brought to the New World, it was as if they had found some long-missing component of their own identity. The Comanches adapted to the horse with breathtaking commitment. They understood better than any other Indians what a powerful new technology this creature represented. The Apaches, for instance, made only limited use of the horse as a war tool, using it to carry them longer distances on a raid but ultimately dismounting to fight. Comanches fought on horseback, seated on rawhide facsimiles of Spanish saddles or hanging low along the horse's shoulder, loosing arrows from beneath its neck.

They learned to breed horses and became wealthy by plains standards. It was not unusual for a Comanche warrior to have a string of 250 ponies, for a chief to have as many as 1,500. The horse made the Comanches dangerous, but they had always been predators. Boys became men, and men acquired status, primarily through deeds of war. Texas history is filled with accounts—some bogus, some not—of Comanche savagery. Settlers who encountered the mutilated bodies of their loved ones—the scalps taken, the genitals ripped off, the entrails baking in the sun—were understandably eager to propagate the notion that Comanches were demons who wallowed in the blackest depths of human cruelty. Torture and ritual mutilation were not confined to the Indians, of course. The difference was that white society had learned to fear and scorn in itself the very bloodlust that the Comanches openly celebrated.

For hundreds of years the Comanches held the plains by right of conquest. They were able to keep Spain from establishing an effective colonial claim on Texas, and they fought the more relentless American juggernaut with desperate ferocity through many bitter generations. But by 1874—the year of the pivotal battle at Adobe Walls—it was pretty much over. Most of the bands—their populations halved by disease, their livelihood and morale shattered by the unimaginable efficiency with which the hide hunters were destroying the buffalo—had already retreated along with the Kiowas and Apaches to the reservation at Fort Sill in southwest Oklahoma. Seven years earlier, at the Treaty of Medicine Lodge, a Comanche chief named Ten Bears—who had visited Abraham Lincoln in the White House and had been shown Comancheria on a great globe in the State Department—had made a speech of defiance that was in tone an unmistakable elegy: "I was born upon the prairie, where the wind blew free and there was nothing to break the light of the sun. I was born where there were no enclosures and everything drew a free breath. . . . If the Texans had kept out of my country, there might have been peace. . . . But it is too late. The whites have the country which we loved, and we wish only to wander on the prairie until we die . . ."

The Comanches knew they were living in an apocalyptic time, and they were susceptible to any sort of messianic logic that could fuel their resistance. A young man called Ishatai—whose name translated to "Coyote Droppings"—rose up among them as a prophet. He was credited with predicting the appearance of a comet, claimed miraculous powers, and asserted with conviction what the Comanches most longed to hear: that the white men could be driven from the plains, that the buffalo could be restored, that life as it had always been understood could resume. Ishatai inspired an avenging alliance of Comanches, Kiowas, and Cheyennes. The first objective was Adobe Walls, an isolated trading post a few miles north of the Canadian River in the Texas Panhandle that had been set up to accommodate the hide hunters and skinners who had come south to annihilate the last great herds of buffalo.

Though Ishatai was a spiritual leader, he did not claim to be a war chief. That role, according to legend, fell to Quanah, a prominent young warrior from the Kwahadi band who was destined to become the most famous Comanche who ever lived. Quanah was the son of a chief named Peta Nocona and the celebrated white captive Cynthia Ann Parker. Cynthia Ann had been seized by the Comanches at the age of nine on a terror-filled day in 1836 when the Indians had raided her family's settlement in East Texas. Her adjustment to Comanche ways was thorough—she married Peta Nocona and bore him three children, including Quanah—but her life was bracketed by shock and heartbreak. After twenty-five years as a Comanche she was recaptured when Texas Rangers raided a camp on the Pease River. Though Cynthia Ann could speak no English, she broke into confused tears when she heard her name. She and her fifteen-month-old daughter, Topsannah, were treated with kindness, and the Texas Legislature even voted her a pension. But her one wish—to be released back onto the prairie with the rest of her family—was denied. When her daughter died she grieved with the wild intensity of a Comanche mother, and not long after that she herself perished from what has variously been described as a broken heart, a "strange fever," or self-starvation.

Quanah was a teenager when his mother was stolen from his world. At the time of the battle of Adobe Walls he was about twenty—a cunning, fearless, embittered warrior commanding a force of perhaps seven hundred men, who, thanks to Ishatai's mystical power—his medicine—believed themselves magically invincible. The Indians arrived at Adobe Walls on a warm June night and attacked the collection of sod buildings in the predawn darkness of the next morning. Adobe Walls was inhabited that night by fewer than thirty buffalo hunters and storekeepers, and Quanah had counted on overrunning them while they slept. But the buffalo men had been up most of the night fixing a broken roof support in the saloon, and their wakefulness spoiled the surprise attack. The defenders managed to barricade themselves in time, though one man was killed as he ran for cover, and two brothers, German teamsters who had been sleeping in their wagon, were discovered and brutally dispatched. The frustrated Indians even scalped the teamsters' dog.

The raid quickly turned into a disaster. The Indians—whose notion of warfare relied on individual initiative and abrupt, feinting charges—were unprepared for a coordinated assault on an entrenched position. The hide hunters, on the other hand, were superb marksmen, accustomed to leisurely potting hundreds of buffalo a day at long range with their Sharps rifles. As warrior after warrior went down, the Comanches and their allies quickly discovered that Ishatai's protective medicine was a cruel illusion. Quanah himself was wounded. Three quarters of a mile away, at the top of a low mesa, wearing nothing but his yellow medicine paint, the prophet Ishatai sat on his horse, watching the fight. His powers had proven so ineffective that they could not even protect a warrior next to him who was knocked from his horse by a spectacular shot from one of the distant buffalo guns.

After a lingering siege that lasted three days, the attackers withdrew, unable to recover their dead. The buffalo hunters cut off the heads of the Indians they had killed and impaled them on stakes. The alliance that Ishatai had put together fell apart, and though Quanah and his band continued raiding for some months afterward, the medicine was gone. That fall, U.S. soldiers surprised a Kwahadi camp in Palo Duro Canyon and captured most of the remaining free Comanches. Then they shot the Indians' horses. Nine months later Quanah and Ishatai led the People, under army escort, onto the reservation. The trek to Fort Sill took a month. A doctor who accompanied the Comanches and joined them on their last buffalo hunt as free men had the time of his life. "I never feel so delighted," he wrote, unwittingly memorializing the vanished joys of Comanche existence, "as when mounted on a fleet horse bounding over the prairie."

"We must have been an ornery group of people," Kenneth Saupitty, the chairman of the Comanche Tribal Business Committee, reflected as we sat one October morning in his office. Saupitty was, in effect, the Comanche chief, though that title had been retired after Quanah's death. ("Resting here until day breaks and shadows fall and darkness disappears," reads his tombstone in the Fort Sill post cemetery. "Quanah Parker, Last Chief of the Comanches.") Saupitty was fifty-one but looked younger. His hair was short, with no gray in it, and his cordial, chatty demeanor made him seem at first acquaintance more like a middle manager than the chief executive of an Indian nation.

The chairman's office is located in a wing of the Comanche Tribal Complex, which sits on a rise just off the H. E. Bailey Turnpike, a few miles north of Lawton. The building has the anonymous multipurpose design of a nursing home or a municipal annex. The day I was there, a Ford Aerostar was parked on the lawn, next to a monument that listed the names of Comanche warriors from Adobe Walls to Vietnam. The Aerostar was a bingo prize that was to be given away the next weekend in a game of Bonanza.

There are 8,410 Comanches. About half of them still live here around the old reservation lands of southwest Oklahoma. To officially be a Comanche, to be counted on the tribal rolls, a person must have a "blood quantum" of at least one fourth. Once enrolled, a member is eligible to vote for the officers of the Tribal Business Committee and to qualify for the various assistance programs and grants that are channeled to Native Americans through the Bureau of Indian Affairs.

Comanches no longer have a reservation. It ceased to exist in 1901, the year the federal government implemented the Jerome Agreement, a scheme by which the reservation was broken up for the benefit of white entrepreneurs and settlers who had long coveted the Indian land. In compensation, each Indian was given an allotment of 160 acres in the hope that this would force the Comanches to become assimilated homesteaders rather than wards of the government. To a small degree, it worked. Most Comanches didn't become farmers of their own allotted lands but leased them out instead. For a time, the lease payments provided a reliable economic base, though with each new wave of descendants the per capita value of the original parcels grew more and more diluted. Of greater importance was the fact that allotment, which brought with it a flood of settlement into Indian country, put jobs for the first time within practical reach of most Comanches.

But whatever prosperity has come to the Comanches has been decidedly marginal. Comanches have all the familiar problems of other Indian peoples, including staggering rates of alcoholism and diabetes. And for all the worldly benefits that came with allotment, nearly half of the Comanches in the Lawton area are unemployed. Those who have jobs—who are fortunate enough to be employed as civilian workers at Fort Sill or as bureaucrats at the Tribal Complex or the BIA—often have extensive kinship obligations that leave them supporting as many as a dozen people on one salary.

The Comanches may have lost their reservation, but there do still seem to reside within them the traces of a reservation mentality. Though they never became tillers of the soil as the whites expected them to, they did cease to be nomads. They clung to the old reservation the way their ancestors might have lingered at a dying campfire. The Second World War, in which many Comanches served, helped to disperse them somewhat, but few of the People became wholeheartedly cosmopolitan enough to take on the alien priorities of the white man's world.

As I visited Comanches I kept sensing a kind of languor, a reliance on certain earthly rhythms that white people do not seem to feel. Many of them were poor, and though they were certainly not poor by choice it seemed to me that as a people they shared a fundamental disinterest in the ideal of wealth. Even the dynamic rhetoric I encountered at the level of tribal government had the air of mimicry.

"I have maintained," Saupitty was telling me, "that we don't have a choice as far as economic development goes. We've got to provide work in some way. We've got a big bingo expansion coming up. We're moving it into downtown Lawton, right off the interstate access. We're talking a fifteen-thousand seater. Then we're going to expand the complex. At this point we're thinking about an amphitheater, maybe a KOA campground, a store that would be an outlet for souvenirs. We've looked at horse racing. Horses and Comanches should be compatible.

"Horses and Comanches," he mused. "You know, we've been told about that by books and movies all our lives." He looked up at a woman who was passing out agendas. "What about you, Joyce, can you ride a horse?"

"I was thrown off once," she said. "Haven't been back on since."

The old Comanche way of life came to an end with such punishing swiftness that, to an outsider, the Comanches of today still seem to be trying to absorb the shock. At one moment the People were running after wild buffalo on the plains, wolfing down the animals' raw livers and gall bladders, and then, in the wink of an eye, there they were on the reservation, wearing shoddy preacher clothes and gouging Mother Earth with plows. If there was ever a group of people not meant to be farmers, it was the Comanches. On the reservation they sometimes chased after cattle on horseback, filling them full of arrows and bullets and then cutting them open and feeding the steaming offal to their children.

Some Comanches, of course, were more flexible than others. Quanah—now Quanah Parker—became a spectacular success in this strange new world and before long was one of the most celebrated and richest Indians in the country. His half white blood, his regal bearing, and his status as a revered former enemy made him a sentimental favorite among his conquerors. A group of ranchers built him a thirty-two-room house whose roof was painted with giant white stars. He invested forty thousand dollars in a railroad, the Quanah, Acme, and Pacific. He had his own stationery, a per diem for official travel, and even a place in Theodore Roosevelt's inaugural parade.

In other ways Quanah hewed to his former life. He had numerous wives, and when he was instructed by the reservation agent to get rid of all but one he responded by saying that was fine with him, as long as the agent was the one who broke the news to the disenfranchised wives. He had no interest in the teachings of the missionaries—Baptist, Mennonite, Catholic, Dutch Reformed—who descended upon the reservation and instead turned to the "pagan" peyote religion that was becoming increasingly important to the demoralized Indian peoples of the Southwest. Quanah initially opposed the allotment program, but he was still regarded by many of his people as a sellout, and they remembered that it was the white men who had appointed him chief of the Comanches.

Comanches are individuals, and Comanche politics is therefore contentious and confused. I was never certain, as I listened to accounts of recent tribal history, exactly which chairman had been recalled when, which members of the business committee had used tribal funds to lease Learjets and start fast-food franchises, which officials stood accused of outright embezzlement. Saupitty himself was recalled—illegally, he maintains—during his first term, in 1980. In reaction, a group of his supporters seized the complex, charging the originators of the recall with misappropriation of funds and demanding an audit. The standoff lasted six months. Some Comanches applauded the activists and camped out in their tepees in support; others threatened an armed assault. The crisis finally dissolved, but not before the Bureau of Indian Affairs suspended all federal funds until the Comanches resolved their differences. Today the affair—the Comanche Civil War—is commemorated by a small plaque that sits in a stubbly field next to the complex. To read the inscription, one has to crawl through a barbed-wire fence.

L ong ago, when the Comanches wandered unimpeded across the plains, they would occasionally happen upon the bones of extinct mammoths. No creature in the People's experience matched the size of those bones, so they surmised that the bones belonged to the Great Cannibal Owl, a malicious entity that carried off human children in the night. The Great Cannibal Owl was said to live in a cave in the Wichita Mountains, an alluring range of granite, laced with streams and abandoned gold mines, that rises as light as a cloud from the Oklahoma grasslands. The country around the Wichitas has a hallowed, ancestral feel to it, but when you drive through it with a Comanche, you cannot shake the feeling that it is, like the rest of Comancheria, a paradise lost.

"Our Comanche people don't like owls," Hammond Motah said as he drove around the base of the Wichitas, listening to the muffled bombardment from Fort Sill's vast gunnery range. "They're taboo. If my wife and I are at home at night and we hear a screech owl outside, we'll run out and chase it away."

Motah managed the print shop at the Comanche Tribal Complex

and also served as the tribe's public information officer. He wore slacks and gray suspenders, and though he was fluent in PR jargon (he spoke frequently of the need to "develop a format" for my inquiries), the more time I spent with him the more I was convinced that his worldliness was only a veneer. In his late forties, Motah had the classic physiognomy of a Comanche: a stout body and a broad, powerful, contemplative face.

Motah studied elementary education at Arizona State, but he taught only briefly, working instead as a planner for other Plains tribes in the northern states. He came home to Oklahoma as something of an activist (he was one of the Comanches who took over the complex), and he had been deeply impressed by the cultural cohesion he had seen up north. It was a source of great sorrow to him that Comanche traditions seemed to be helplessly slipping away, replaced by a cultural crazy quilt stitched together with borrowings from other tribes. That is, arguably, the inevitable course of any society, but the Comanches were particularly vulnerable. As raiders and nomads they traveled light; they carried their culture in their heads. Their beliefs and manners were existential, rooted in action. Without the sustaining momentum of the open range, they began to collapse.

"We're really a vanishing race," Motah said. There was a tear forming in his eye. The Comanche language was dying out. People Motah's age could understand it but could not speak it fluently, and within another generation or so it would be a ceremonial relic like Latin. Young people beginning to dance in powwows were susceptible to fads and fashions, forsaking the old Comanche dances and taking up the single bustles of the northern tribes. Instead of sitting up all night cross-legged at a peyote meeting, singing the old songs and invoking the old spirits, kids tended to hang out in the parking lot after powwows, drinking and smoking dope. Soon, even the definition of a Comanche would have to be revised. Intermarriage among the tribes had been so common since the reservation days that eighty percent of the younger Comanches have no more than one fourth Comanche blood. If they marry someone with less than the minimum blood quantum—a likely occurrence—their children won't be Comanches. "This is the last generation," Kenneth Saupitty had told me, "that our constitution will allow."

Motah himself was married to a Kiowa, and though he and his in-laws got along fine, there were certain Kiowa taboos he had to watch out for. He could not speak directly to his mother-in-law, for example; if he did, his teeth would fall out.

"When it comes to the Kiowas," he told me, "I'm like A Man Called Horse."

Earlier that afternoon, Motah and I had visited the Comanche elder center in Lawton, where senior members of the tribe congregated every day for a free lunch. On the paneled walls were framed photographs of famous Comanches—Quanah with his implacable barbarian expression, Ten Bears in spectacles with a commemorative medallion around his neck. A few women in the front room were working at a quilting frame, but the rest of the elders were in the dining room, eating boiled hot dogs, sauerkraut, and canned beets. There were Halloween decorations on the tables. I sat down and talked for a while with an elder who reminisced about his childhood at the Fort Sill Indian School. He had arrived there terrified, not knowing a word of English. If you were caught speaking Comanche, he said, your mouth was washed out with soap.

Soon my attention was seized by a conversation at the far end of the table, where a woman was saying something about Adobe Walls.

"What'd you say?" an old man next to her asked. "Cement walls?"

"No, *Adobe*," she said and then turned to me. "You ever heard of Adobe Walls?"

"Yes, ma'am," I said. "In fact, I always wondered what happened to Ishatai. Do you know?"

"Who?"

"Ishatai."

"No, I don't know nothing about him."

After lunch we dropped in on a man named George "Woogee" Watchetaker, a former world champion powwow dancer ("I retired undefeated!"), artist, and rainmaker. Watchetaker was seventy-two. He had been born in a tent, back in the days when Comanches were still suspicious of houses and the bygone mores of the plains still had some sway. Back then, he remembered, Comanche men still plucked their eyebrows.

"My dad," he told us, "he made his own tweezers out of tin. He'd sharpen the tweezers with a file and pull his eyebrows out and his side-burns too."

Watchetaker himself had a trace of a moustache and a growth of stubble on his chin. He wore glasses with thick black frames and kept his hair in two long braids tied with rubber bands. He had few teeth. His living room was filled with souvenir-shop Indian art—plaster busts of braves and squaws, paintings of wide-eyed Indian children and mounted warriors praying to the Great Spirit.

"Here about 1969," he said, "I used to be a big drunkard. I used to smoke. The day before Christmas I got tired of it and wanted to quit. I went to bed and watched TV till midnight and then woke up at five-thirty, waiting for the TV to come on again. I was looking out that window when I saw something. It was a figure standing there. It looked like smoke. I wasn't scared or amazed at what I saw. Pretty soon it spoke to me—'George, you know what you been doing is wrong. You got a short time to live. But if you change your way of life, you're gonna be well respected. You'll live a long time. Remember my words. Listen to me.'

"Then," Watchetaker said, making a snakelike motion with his hand, "he just slunk away. I didn't say anything to anybody about what I saw. That evening I played Santy Claus. My craving for drinking stopped just like that."

Not long after that incident, when west Texas was suffering under a drought, Watchetaker was asked to come to Wichita Falls and make rain. He had never professed to be a medicine man and was afraid to put himself on the line, but the spirit spoke to him again and told him to go ahead and try. He went to Wichita Falls, set a bowl of water down in the middle of a shopping-center parking lot, blessed it, smoked over it, and spit water in the four directions.

"And it hadn't been a minute before a bolt of lightning shot across the sky and it started raining. Next day they had big headlines: He done it.

"So I remember the words that that vision has told me," Watch-etaker concluded. "I don't drink, I don't smoke, and my name has been everywhere."

That night there was a moon—a Comanche moon, bright enough to light the warpath—shining on the fields as we drove back to Lawton. Motah told me about the time, a few years back, when he had decided to go on a vision quest. In the bygone days a vision quest was the classic Comanche rite of manhood. A teenage boy would go out into the wilderness, deprive himself of food and water for four days and nights, and wait for his "visitor," usually an animal spirit who would issue instructions and leave the boy with a personal fund of mystical power—his medicine.

For his vision quest, Motah picked a site near a spring and made a circle of sage. He remembers being strong and confident the first day, but by the second day he was so thirsty he could not refrain from licking the dew off some nearby leaves. After a time his parents, both of whom had died years before, appeared to him pleading. "You don't have to do this," they said. "Come with us." But he stayed in the circle. He was taunted by a group of *nenuhpee*, sinister apparitions that take the form of tiny warriors and are also known to modern Comanches as leprechauns. "You're a fake," the *nenuhpee* jeered. "You don't belong here. You don't know anything about the old ways." Several more visitors appeared—some benign, some malevolent—but before the prescribed four nights had passed Motah was so hungry and sick and scared that he crawled out of the circle.

"I went home and slept for two days," he said. "I went to see a medicine man to tell him about my experience. He was extremely interested. He said he hadn't heard of a Comanche going on a vision quest for fifty years."

At the Comanche elder center I had been introduced to Thomas Wahnee, a seventy-seven-year-old retired roofer who was born, he told me, the year Quanah Parker died. Wahnee was a quiet, modest man who gave the impression of being subtly amused by everything he saw. He wore dark glasses and a hearing aid, and a single incisor dangled precariously from his upper jaw. Wahnee was a peyote man. Like many other elders, he had grown up in the Native American Church, attending meetings back in the days when participants still wore buckskin shirts and tied their braids with otter fur. Not all Comanches, of course, followed the peyote road. Most adhered to some variant of traditional Christian worship, while others found spiritual expression by participating in powwows. But the Comanches were the first Plains Indians to acquire the peyote religion, and they played a major role in its dissemination.

Wahnee invited me to attend a meeting of the church, and one cold winter evening I arrived at his house. A growly pit bull was chained up at the side of the house, and in the back yard a tepee stood next to a stock fence.

Ten people, mostly men in their sixties, had gathered for the meeting, and we sat around in Wahnee's house until late in the evening listening to tales of power and witchcraft and medicine. When the fire was built, Wahnee and the elder men led the way into the tepee, carrying their toolboxes (containing gourds and feather fans and other paraphernalia for the peyote rite) like men going off to work a late-night shift at a factory. We circled the outside of the tepee and then went inside and sat down on sofa cushions on a bed of sage.

Wahnee, as the leader, sat to the west of the earthen fire ring. The fire ring was in the shape of a crescent, the ends pointing east. In classic peyote symbology, the crescent represented the path of a man's life from birth to death, but over the years the religion had taken on an admixture of Christianity, and the shape of the fire ring now symbolized, as well, the hoofprint of the donkey that Jesus rode into Jerusalem.

When everyone was settled, Wahnee brought out the sacrament—Father Peyote—and placed it on the fire ring. It was a gray, wrinkly nubbin of cactus, ugly with knowledge and medicine. Wahnee then passed around corn shucks and a bag of Bull Durham tobacco, the makings of the ceremonial cigarettes that were to be smoked during the evening's first prayers. After the smoking and the praying Wahnee distributed a leather bag of peyote buttons and a vial of peyote powder. I ate one button and swallowed some of the powder, afterward rubbing my hands over my head and body as the ritual mandated. The bitter taste almost made me gag and the peyote sat uneasily in my stomach, but I began to gaze contentedly at the perfect glowing coals of the fire.

Then the singing began. Wahnee sang four songs, holding a staff and eagle feather in one hand and shaking a gourd with the other. He was accompanied by a drummer who pounded out a stern rhythm on a No. 6 cast-iron kettle that had been half filled with water and hot coals and then covered with a taut deer hide. Thus constructed, the drum was a little model of Mother Earth herself, a reverberant fusion of water and fire.

When Wahnee had finished with his songs he handed the staff and gourd and eagle feather to the man on his left. Each participant sang four songs, and when the circle was completed they began again and then again. It went on for five or six hours. I stared at the fire, trying to locate some sort of tonal entree into the music, but all the songs sounded indistinguishable to me. Nevertheless, I felt bound up in them somehow, and when each one ended I experienced a tiny wave of sadness along with the sensation that the temperature in the tepee had dropped a few degrees.

At two in the morning Wahnee sang the midnight song—about a band of Comanches long ago who had lost their horses and, while walking along a creek, killed a bear—and then he left the tepee to blow his cane whistle. He blew the whistle in each of the four directions, announcing to the world our prayerful presence there in the tepee. The notes he produced were so sharp and resonant it seemed that they were reaching us from the rim of the earth and that Wahnee himself had been transformed into some sort of magic bird.

When he came back he walked clockwise around the fire and took his seat again in front of Father Peyote. The singing and praying began again and went on for another three hours. At the next interval I asked Wahnee, according to protocol, for permission to leave the tepee for a moment. He nodded his head good-naturedly, and I stood up and made the circle to the east, taking care not to make the mistake of passing in front of anyone who was smoking and eating peyote. The fireman held the flap open for me as I walked out into the night, the songs commencing again behind me. The night was very cold and the sky was clear. There was dew on the grass and it glistened in the starlight. I was not supposed to go back into the tepee until there was a pause in the singing, so for a long time I just stood there and watched it. The tepee's canvas skin was transparent, and the fire pulsed inside it like a beating heart, in time to the drum and the voices.

I wondered for how much longer such vibrant remnants of the old Comanche life would endure. During the time I spent in Oklahoma I kept hearing about someone who, at least in theory, seemed perfectly poised between the Comanche past and the Comanche future. He was a great-grandson of Quanah Parker, and he had gone to Hollywood on a "sacred mission" to make a movie about his ancestor.

I met Vincent Parker for dinner at Chaya Brasserie near Beverly Hills. He would not tell me his age ("That's my secret," he said defiantly. "I have held on to that one little sense of mystery"), but he looked about thirty. He was wearing a Giorgio Armani suit with a matching tie and pocket square, and he carried a topcoat draped over his arm. His olive skin was smooth, and his hair was fashionably long and tousled.

Sipping a glass of red wine, he studied the menu. "I think I'll have the shrimp ravioli," he told the waiter. "The only problem is I hate to change wines."

Parker closed the menu and regarded me with an emphatic gaze, blinking incessantly, as if there was something wrong with his contacts. "I'm a living example of what Quanah Parker wanted," he said. "I am in some respects what he envisioned for his people. He wanted them not only to retain their identity but also to be at ease in this dominant society."

Vincent said he was the great-grandson of Quanah and Chony, the chief's first or second wife, depending on which scholar's opinion you accept. He had grown up in Lawton in a family with eleven brothers and sisters. His parents—who had the good fortune to strike oil on their allotted land—instilled in their children the Parker ambition to master the white man's world.

Vincent graduated from the University of Oklahoma, worked for a time as an aide to Oklahoma governor George Nye, and dabbled in tribal politics, running unsuccessfully for vice chairman after the 1980 takeover. He was keenly aware that his ancestor presided over all his endeavors.

"I told my father I felt different from any of my brothers and sisters. My father said, 'You *are* different. When I look at you, I see *him*.'"

That was powerful medicine. To a Parker, Quanah was hardly a typical mortal.

"He was a way-shower," Vincent said as the waiter brought his shrimp ravioli. "The Christians had their Jesus, the Indians had their Gandhi, and the Comanches had their Quanah Parker."

Vincent had the feeling that he was meant to be a way-shower, but wasn't sure how he was to accomplish it. He spent a lot of time in the Star House, Quanah's famous residence, sitting in his great-grandfather's chair and praying for guidance. One night his mission came to him: he would write and produce a play about Quanah. He secluded himself in the Star House to write the script, and when it was finished he blessed it by fanning cedar smoke over it with an eagle feather. Nine months later, the play premiered as an outdoor pageant in Quanah, Texas, with members of the Parker family making up the cast. The pageant ran for five years, and then Vincent moved to Los Angeles to pursue the goal of commemorating Quanah in a feature film. Bankrolled by his family, he traveled west with a sense of sacred purpose and a wish list. ("Before I left Oklahoma," he said, "I wrote in my journal that I wanted a Gucci watch. I love black and gold. The first day in L.A., I went to Gucci and bought it.")

During his time in L.A. Vincent has worked in various postproduction positions for Walt Disney Studios, learning the industry to prepare himself for his task. With his remarkable tenacity and focus, he has already begun to beat the odds. A documentary on Quanah that he produced has just been completed, and he has come close to putting together the funding for a feature. In his spare time he has dabbled in modeling and has been hired to appear in a commercial for Jeep Comanche, in which he will face the camera and say, "Comanches. My forefathers led them. Now I drive them."

"Sometimes it's hard," he said. "I'll call my father and tell him I have no energy. I get tired of playing the social circuit, putting up with the Hollywood bullshit. At any given moment I question it. I can understand how Jesus wept and questioned his own mission."

On the other hand, it's not so terrible. "Going to dinner at Spago,

Le Dome, and Nicky Blair's. That's my world. I love the wonderful cultural activities that are afforded to me here. People laugh at me because I spend so much time at Tiffany's, but there are so many wonderful things there! I give no apologies for being driven in a chauffeured limousine. Quanah himself had a surrey with silver trim. If he were here today he'd be with me in the limo. What made him effective is the spiritual influence he brought about. If anything, that's what I'm trying to hold on to."

After dinner we walked down the street, toward the Beverly Center, talking about the Adobe Walls song that Quanah had written after the battle and that was one of the few surviving Comanche songs from pre-reservation days. It was a song of mourning, a song of loss.

"I do intend to protect the integrity of this project at all costs," Vincent said, returning to the movie. "I tell producers, 'You're going to continue your careers in L.A. I'm not. I'm going back to these people in Oklahoma, and no amount of money could compensate me for the damage I could do. I cannot sell out!'"

I stared frankly at this improbable person. He may have been just another Hollywood hustler with a messiah complex, but I didn't think so. Beneath his fashion plate exterior, there was something steely about him, and it was not hard to imagine him in another time as an arrogant and fearless warrior, a lord of the plains.

"I'm not playing around out here," he said with sudden passion, as the Beverly Hills traffic surged by us. "I'm on the warpath."

WOLF HOUSE

"I have been asked why Jack London, socialist, friend of the common man, built so large a house," Charmian London wrote in her biography of the husband who had called her "Mate-Woman," and whom she had exuberantly called "Mate-Man" in return. "How shall I say? Jack could not traffic in small things."

When he began building Wolf House, his magnificently rough-hewn lair in northern California's Sonoma Valley, Jack London was at his largest. He was the most famous writer in the world, the author of *The Call of the Wild, White Fang, Martin Eden, The Sea Wolf,* and dozens of other books that he had composed at a scrupulous lifetime quota of one thousand words a day, as if he were still laboring in the canneries and jute mills of his Oakland youth. Working with San Francisco architect Albert Farr, London conjured up a gnarly, rugged domicile of volcanic boulders and unpeeled redwood logs, with thick concrete walls on the inside to discourage the spread of fire and a deep, strong foundation to anchor the structure against earthquakes. He declared it would last a thousand years.

But it did not even last a day. Before its owners could move in, the house they had spent nine years planning and building caught fire and burned down, leaving behind a different sort of monument than the one London had intended: an enigmatic, emblematic ruin. The massive rocky skeleton of the house stands today as the centerpiece of Jack London State Historical Park, which is located about an hour's drive north of San Francisco in a wine-growing pocket of Sonoma County known as the Valley of the Moon. The park is on the site of London's Beauty Ranch, where he and Charmian lived during the last decade of his life. It's a variable landscape of oak savannas and vineyards, spread out below the eastern slopes of Sonoma Mountain. But the ruin itself is enclosed within a dark, mossy forest, which adds to its spectral power, and seems to pose its central question: what happened to Wolf House, and what happened to Jack London?

In 1911, the year construction on Wolf House commenced, London was only thirty-five, and though he still looks fit and tempestuously handsome in photographs from that period he had long since worked and drank and smoked and medicated himself into ruinous health. "I would rather be ashes than dust!" he once proclaimed in a famous credo that has inspired generations of hard-living undergraduates. "I would rather be a superb meteor, every atom of me in magnificent glow, than a sleepy and permanent planet."

And yet the truth is he planned Wolf House as a shrine to permanence. The man who had been an oyster pirate on San Francisco Bay, a socialist firebrand, a gold prospector in the Klondike, a war correspondent during the Russo-Japanese War, and a restless wanderer in the South Seas now gave every sign of being ready to settle down as a gentleman rancher on the extensive acreage he had acquired for Beauty Ranch. "I am really going to throw out an anchor so big and so heavy that all hell could not ever get it up again," he declared.

The house was built around a central courtyard, which featured a deep reflection pool that was to be stocked with bass. Though Charmian had commodious "apartments" on the third floor, most of the other rooms in the house were a testament to the manly vigor and caged-beast working habits of its creator. There was a gun and trophy room, a manuscript vault, a huge library where all the books London had accumulated in his rootless life would finally find a home, and an equally expansive writing room on the third floor. A two-story living room commanded the northwest wing of the house, but where London really meant to entertain his male guests was a hideout on the first level he had christened the Stag Party Room. Finally, London—who was too restless, too untamed, and too much of a snorer to share a room with any woman, even the redoubtable Charmian—built himself a personal "sleeping tower" that perched all alone above the roof of the third floor like an eagle's eyrie.

"It should be thought of, that house," Charmian wrote, "in relation to Jack, not as a mansion, but as a big cabin, a lofty lodge, a hospitable tepee, where he, simple and generous despite all his baffling intricacy, could stretch himself and beam upon you and me and all the world that gathered by his log-fires."

Wolf House took two years to build, at a price of eighty thousand dollars. On the afternoon of August 22, 1913, Jack and Charmian went horseback riding along a ravine at the ranch and looked down at the red-tiled roof of the great house. It was all but finished. Little remained but for the workmen to clear away the debris of construction and for the Londons' heavy, custom-made furniture to be delivered. In only a few weeks they would move in.

"How beautiful—Our House, Mate Woman!" Jack said to Charmian as they sat there on their horses contemplating the building they expected would serve as their home and headquarters for the rest of their vigorous lives.

But near midnight of that same day neighbors noticed a strange glowing presence in the direction of the Londons' ranch. Jack and Charmian were awakened at their cottage, a half mile away from Wolf House. By that time flames and smoke were rearing high into the night sky. Jack had the horses harnessed so they could drive to the fire, but Charmian remembered his lack of urgency in getting to the site. "What's the use of hurry?" he said. "If that is the Big House burning, nothing can stop it now!"

In a matter of hours Wolf House was destroyed. Only a smoking shell of concrete and ruddy volcanic rock remained. Jack did not seem at first to be deeply affected. He occupied himself trying to calm the anguished foreman, who kept crying, "My child! My child!" as the house burned, and in raising the spirits of distraught workers and friends who had gathered to witness the conflagration. To at least one neighbor, it seemed that the strangely cheerful London didn't fully grasp what had happened to him.

It was not until four in the morning, when Jack and Charmian had returned to their cottage and were lying in bed, that the full realization finally descended. "He lay in my pitying arms," Charmian reported, "and shook like a baby."

Jack London State Historical Park incorporates a good deal of London's ranch, including the cottage where he and Charmian lived, the barns and silos and pigpens that were the heart of the ranch economy, and the impounded lake at the summit of a redwood-covered hill that the Londons used for recreation. But it's a good bet that most visitors who come to the park are less interested in acquainting themselves with Jack London's agricultural techniques and visions than they are in seeing the remains of the house he planned and built and dreamed of, and that finally slipped from his grasp at the moment he reached out to possess it.

The path from the parking lot leads pilgrims from grassy meadows into a deep forest glade as somber as a medieval vault. The bright velvety lichen covering the trunks of the live oaks almost glows in this subdued light, as does the lurid orange bark of the madrone trees. There are towhees in the underbrush, and woodpeckers swooping above them, and red-tailed hawks intermittently visible overhead through gaps in the forest canopy.

You come upon Wolf House sooner than you expect to, after about a half mile of easy walking. The ruin does not crown a commanding promontory, but sits almost hidden in the primeval shade of a redwood grove. It is massive, of course, and eerie, but strangely not decrepit. Its powerful superstructure of red volcanic boulders appears sturdy enough that the house could be rebuilt tomorrow. At first glance, it is merely a jumble of towering rock and hollow space, but even a brief acquaintance with the blueprints of Wolf House will allow you to pick out the areas where the great rooms briefly existed.

The site of the Stag Party Room is plainly visible, as is the towering living room above it and the empty concrete pond that dominated the courtyard. What is most impressive about the house is not its size, however, but its insistent jaggedness. None of the volcanic boulders and cobbles that make up its exterior walls was shaped for the purpose. They were cemented into place exactly as they were blasted out of the quarry or picked up off the ground, and to this day their surfaces— weathered and covered with lichen—are startlingly sharp and irregular. It is no accident, you think, that the dream home of America's woolliest major writer would be this cavern of unpeeled logs and unhewn rocks.

What caused the fire? The Londons came to believe that it was arson, perhaps the work of socialists angered and disillusioned over Jack's sudden infatuation with paternal grandeur, perhaps one of the neighbors with whom he was in litigation over thorny water issues. But in 1995 a group of ten fire experts who spent four days investigating the site determined that the blaze most likely started when a pile of linseed-soaked rags, left behind by a workman on the wooden floor of the dining room, had self-ignited in the heat of that August night.

It is difficult to know how hard the loss of Wolf House hit Jack London. In his life he had had more than his share of grand dreams come true, and the visible collapse of this one may evoke more regret in an observer than is really warranted. To all appearances, he seemed to shrug it off and go on with his business. After the fire, still living in the nearby cottage, he maintained his strenuous literary output— completing another six or seven books—travelled to Hawaii and Mexico, and became active in business pursuits as various as grape juice and motion pictures. But, according to Charmian, "The razing of the house killed something in Jack and he never ceased to feel the tragic inner sense of loss."

"I'm going to live a hundred years!" he declared to his wife one robust morning not long after the fire. But he didn't, no more than his house lasted for a thousand years. By November of 1916 his kidneys, ravaged by years of disease and abuse, had pretty much ceased to function, and the lean smoldering appearance that had helped to fix his legend in his readers' minds was gone as well. His body was bloated with the effects of uremia, and his eyes were haunted.

He was thirty-nine when he fell into a coma one night on the sleeping porch of his cottage. Four physicians rushed to the ranch, but they could not revive him, nor could Charmian, who shook him by the shoulders and shouted into his face: "Mate! Mate! You must come back! Mate! You've got to come back! To me! Mate! Mate!"

He was cremated and his ashes were buried on a hilltop at the ranch. There was no ceremony. No one said a word as the urn was placed into the ground: Charmian and the other mourners simply stood there in silence as a light rain fell. Then a heavy red boulder from Jack London's ruined house was dragged up the hill by a team of horses and rolled on top of his grave.

THE LAST DAYS
OF DAVID CROCKETT

Do not be uneasy about me. I am among friends. I will close
with great respects. Your affectionate father. Farewell.

Those are, in a sense, David Crockett's last words. They are the closing lines of a letter written from the unstable Mexican province of Texas on January 9, 1836, the last remarks attributed to him that are not the product of hearsay or dim recollection. In less than two months Crockett would die at the Battle of the Alamo, but this letter to his daughter and son-in-law back in Tennessee carries an almost ecstatic tone of bright hopes and new prospects. Crockett reports his often-problematical health to be excellent. Everywhere he goes he is received as a celebrity, "with open cerimony of friendship" and "hearty welcome." Texas is bounteous, filled with plentiful timber and clear water and migrating herds of buffalo. He has joined the insurgent Texas army and has already picked out the land he will claim in exchange for his service in the fight against Mexico. He wants all his friends to settle here, and he fully expects to be elected as a member of the convention that will write a constitution for Texas. "I am," David Crockett declares, "rejoiced at my fate."

What was that fate? All that is known for certain is that Crockett was killed at the Alamo, a fortified mission on the outskirts of San Antonio de Bexar (now San Antonio) on March 6, 1836, along with the rest of a small garrison that had been besieged for thirteen days by an overwhelming force personally led by the autocratic ruler of Mexico, General Antonio López de Santa Anna. But 175 years later the precise nature of Crockett's death remains a hauntingly open question. Did he die in the fury of combat, iconically swinging his empty rifle in a hopeless last stand? Or was he one of a group of men captured at the end of the battle and then quickly and coldly executed?

Of course, either way, Crockett was still dead—still, in the overcooked rhetoric of the time, among the "spirits of the mighty" who had fallen at the "Thermopylae of Texas." So what difference does it make? Well, as the endless and heated argument over the facts of Crockett's death reveals, it makes the difference between a man who is merely an interesting historical personage and one who is a character of legend, one of those rare names that doesn't just appear in American history but resides in America's core idea of itself.

In 2000 I published a novel called *The Gates of the Alamo*, and I knew when I began research for the book that I was going to have to come to terms with Davy Crockett. Crockett was arguably the most precious intellectual property of my generation. Walt Disney's 1955 television show (and later movie) *Davy Crockett, King of the Wild Frontier* sparked a pop-culture flash fire. *Davy Crockett* was our *Star Wars*, our *Harry Potter*. Something about this character seized our collective imagination. His buckskin outfit, his coonskin cap, and his prowess with rifle and knife and tomahawk all tapped into a child's unformed craving for personal power and independence. And the way Fess Parker played him—laconic, unhurried, amiable but unrevealing—made him come across as a favorite uncle, just the sort of patient, quiet-spoken role model children of the atomic age needed to soothe our apocalyptic fears.

We met him again a few years later, when John Wayne played him—rather well, I now think—in the 1960 epic *The Alamo*. Baby boomers would continue to have an ongoing association with Davy Crockett in movies, toys, comics and—when we reached our cynical, disillusioned years—in revisionist histories. But it would be a misreading of American culture to imply that the baby-boomer claim to Davy Crockett was an exclusive one. Crockett had been his own creation before he was ours. Beginning in the 1820s, when he first stepped onto the national stage as a duly elected congressional curiosity, he had the out-of-nowhere star power of a Sarah Palin. He fascinated the country because in some perceptible way he was the country: the rugged frontiersman, the unstoppable striver looking for success in business, for respect in politics, for ever-beckoning westward horizons.

Those of us who grew up on the movie portrayals by Fess Parker and John Wayne would not have recognized the pilgrim politician who arrived in Texas the winter of 1836. Crockett, whose preferred name was David, not Davy, was forty-nine. Portraits painted of him a year or so earlier show a man with lank black hair, parted in the middle and worn long enough to spill over his high collar. His eyes are dark, his nose is severe and straight, but even with these striking features his face has a kind of dreamy mildness about it. In his only full-length portrait, painted by John Gadsby Chapman, Crockett seems a bit paunchy, but a woman who saw him at a ventriloquist's performance in New York not long after this image was made remarked that he was "quite thin."

Several people recalled that he wore a fur hat on his way to Texas, but their recollections came decades later, long after Crockett's coonskin cap and buckskins had become an iconographic outfit. In real life, he tended to play down the frontier caricature he otherwise cultivated. "He did not wear buckskins," insisted one witness, and a woman who saw Crockett shortly after he arrived in Texas confirmed that he "was dressed like a gentleman."

He was one of the most famous men in America, but in the winter of 1836, celebrity was almost all he had left. Only a year and a half before, the nascent Whig Party had flirted with the idea of running Congressman David Crockett of Tennessee for president of the United States. Crockett was already a folk hero, a man who had carefully overseen the transformation of his backwoods biography—Creek War veteran, bear hunter, roving leatherstocking—into a new American myth of plain wisdom and restless self-reliance. He was a canny and resilient politician who had been elected, reelected, defeated, and reelected again by the citizens of his west Tennessee district. He was also principled, steadfastly pressing the interests of his landless Tennessee constituents, clashing with Andrew Jackson over, among other issues, the president's heartless Indian Removal Bill. But in the end he could not play the game at a level that was shrewd or cynical enough to keep the Jackson forces from running over him.

When he lost his congressional seat in 1835 he had nowhere to land. He was in debt and estranged from his wife. The Whigs had tired of him, his former ally, Andrew Jackson, had squashed him politically, and his last two books—lazy follow-ups to his highly regarded and best-selling 1834 autobiography—were taking up space in his printer's warehouse.

"I told the people of my District, that, if they saw fit to re-elect me, I would serve them as faithfully as I had done," he said to one of his adoring crowds in Texas, "but, if not, they might to go to hell, and I would go to Texas."

In Disney's *Davy Crockett, King of the Wild Frontier*, Crockett's motivation in coming to Texas was marvelously simple: "Freedom was fightin' another foe," went the irresistible song, "and they needed him at the A-a-alamo." John Wayne, in *The Alamo*, was likewise an unambiguous freedom fighter with no goal other than to help the Texans in their noble overthrow of Mexican tyranny. But the real David Crockett was brokenhearted, embittered, and in desperate need of a new beginning. Texas held the promise of financial gain, fresh political opportunity, and a new audience for the semi-fictional character of himself that David Crockett had invented.

In the beginning, it seemed that promise might be realized. The Texian rebels had driven the Mexican Army out of San Antonio de Bexar, the Texas capital, in early December 1835, and soon after Crockett arrived the war entered an uneasy hiatus. With no urgent need to be anywhere in particular, he and the small group of men who accompanied him spent a month or so hunting buffalo and scouting out possible land claims in northeast Texas. When he showed up in the settlements, cannon were shot off in celebration, banquets were held in his honor, and the delighted local citizens tried to enlist him for office. But Crockett knew he had to earn his welcome, and so he took the oath of allegiance to the provisional government of Texas and joined the army as a mounted volunteer.

He rode off to Washington-on-the-Brazos, the seat of the rebel government, to receive orders from General Sam Houston on where to report next. Though he held no rank, a small contingent of men went with him, apparently regarding him as their leader. Crockett's whereabouts for the next several weeks are not precisely known, though he did go to Washington and may have been on his way to the coastal stronghold of Goliad when he was ordered—or took a notion—to join up with the forces in San Antonio de Bexar.

Crockett rode into Bexar in the company of about a dozen men. Entering town on the La Bahia road, he might not even have noticed the broken-down old Franciscan mission that sat in relative isolation on the far side of the river, a forlorn outpost that would seal both his fate and his legend. But it would be another two weeks before the rebels found themselves trapped behind the walls of the Alamo. For now, they were in control of the whole town, though the men of the Bexar garrison were undersupplied and felt as though the Texas government had forgotten about them. John Sutherland, who was sent out as a courier the first day of the siege and hence survived the battle, remembered that Crockett's arrival cheered them considerably. He stood up on a packing crate in the main plaza and told them "jolly anecdotes," and assured them he was there to help in their cause and that he aspired to no rank higher than private. A few days later his presence served as the excuse for a fandango that went on well past midnight, and was only briefly interrupted by the news that General Santa Anna and his army were already on the banks of the Rio Grande and headed for Bexar.

The news of the Mexican advance precipitated an ugly command dispute between William Barret Travis and James Bowie. It would not be unreasonable to assume that the pacific Crockett played some role in smoothing over these tensions, but he refused offers by the volunteers to take on a formal leadership role. He was still Private Crockett when the Mexican forces swept into Bexar on February 23, 1836, and forced the rebels to barricade themselves inside the Alamo.

We know, of course, that Crockett endured the siege of the Alamo and died in the final assault, but hard information about his activities during those thirteen days is maddeningly scant. John Sutherland states that on the first day of the siege Travis assigned Crockett and his men to defend the low palisade spanning the gap between the church and the gatehouse on the south side of the mission. But the notion that Crockett confined himself to one defensive position during the siege is subtly contradicted by a high-spirited letter Travis wrote to Sam Houston on February 25, after the defenders repulsed a probing assault by the Mexicans on the south side of the mission. "The Hon. David Crockett," Travis observed, "was seen at all points, animating the men to do their duty."

This terse observation is, in my opinion, the last really authoritative glimpse we have of the life of David Crockett. Unlike other accounts, Travis's statement was not set down decades later, when it was likely to be corrupted both by the passage of time and the ever-expanding Crockett legend. It was written instead immediately after the events it describes, by a commanding officer indisputably in a position to witness them.

This scrap of information is crucially revealing. It confirms our wishful assumption that Crockett, in his final days, was a consequential man; that despite his insistence that he be regarded simply as a "high private" he was in fact a natural leader to whom men looked for guidance or reassurance. In the last few years the bottom had fallen out of his life, but he was still a man of spectacular achievement who had risen from an impoverished frontier childhood to become a not-implausible contender for the presidency of his country. He was still in possession of his droll fame and easy humor, and as one of the oldest men in the Alamo he had a seasoned perspective that no doubt the twenty-six-year-old Travis found useful.

Susanna Dickinson, who survived the Battle of the Alamo along with a number of other women and children, gave several accounts of the siege in the latter part of her life. In one of these, published in 1875, she recalled Crockett entertaining the garrison defenders on his fiddle, though he also had his fatalistic moments. "I think we had better march out and die in the open air," Mrs. Dickinson reported Crockett as saying. "I don't like to be hemmed up."

Enrique Esparza, who was eight years old during the Alamo siege, decades later remembered Crockett as a "tall, slim man with black whiskers" whom the Mexicans called Don Benito. "He would often come to the fire and warm his hands and say a few words to us in the Spanish language." In Esparza's memory, it seems to be Crockett, not Travis, who is effectively in charge of the garrison and even calls the men together on the last day of the siege to inform them of Santa Anna's unacceptable terms for surrender.

Esparza's boyish recollections are certainly confused, but tantalizingly so. The impression they convey that Crockett played some sort of key leadership role in the defense of the Alamo does not seem to me to be off the mark. A decade or so ago, the late Alamo scholar Thomas Ricks Lindley hypothesized that there was a significant and previously unknown reinforcement to the Alamo in the last few days of the siege, and that Crockett himself slipped through the Mexican lines to meet this new force and guide it back into the Alamo. Among the scattershot clues that led Lindley to this supposition are an item that appeared in the *Arkansas Gazette* several months after the battle claiming that "Col. Crockett, with about 50 resolute volunteers, had cut their way into the garrison, through the Mexican troops only a few days before the fall of San Antonio," and an otherwise puzzling statement by Susanna Dickinson in her 1876 testimony to the adjutant general of Texas. "Col. Crockett," she said, "was one of the 3 men who came into the Fort during the siege & before the assault."

Though I took Lindley's theory and ran with it in *The Gates of the Alamo*, I have to admit it's based on a fairly thin string of evidence and hasn't been embraced by other historians. But like Esparza's probably fanciful memories, it stirs the imagination in productive ways: Crockett had to have been doing *something* during those thirteen days. He was too great an asset, too big a personality, to have mutely settled into the ranks of the rest of those trapped men.

The question of Crockett's activities during the siege of the Alamo pales before the all-consuming mystery of how exactly he died. The death of David Crockett has always excited a weird, primal fascination. For kids of my age, there was something intoxicatingly otherworldly about the final scene in Walt Disney's *Davy Crockett, King of the Wild Frontier*, in which Fess Parker stands on the Alamo ramparts, swinging his empty rifle as an unstoppable swarm of Mexican soldiers creeps ever closer with their bayonets. I remember my flabbergasted realization, at age seven, that Davy Crockett was not going to survive this. The death scene itself—or near-death scene, since the movie faded out before he actually met his demise—was shot on a soundstage, a bit of Disney cost-cutting that created a mood of claustrophobic doom. The shock of Crockett's fate evolved into a rhapsodic fantasy of rifle-swinging martyrdom that few American boys could resist.

With such potent imagery in mind it is easier to understand the howl that went up in 1975 when a narrative of the Texas Revolution written by a Mexican officer named José Enrique de la Peña was published for the first time in English. Peña, who participated in the assault on the Alamo, wrote that after the attack, "Some seven men had survived the general massacre. . . . Among them was one of great stature, well proportioned, with regular features, in whose face there was the imprint of adversity, but in whom one also noted a degree of resignation and nobility that did him honor. He was the naturalist David Crockett."

In Peña's account, Santa Anna, over the pleas and protestations of several of his officers, ordered the immediate execution of these seven men. "Though tortured before they were killed, these unfortunates died without complaining and without humiliating themselves before their torturers."

Despite the fact that Peña was sympathetic to Crockett and went out of his way to credit his courage, the media promoted the new account as shocking evidence that Davy Crockett, the King of the Wild Frontier, had "surrendered" at the Alamo. The die-hard Swingin' Davy crowd could not abide such talk and bombarded Carmen Perry, the translator of the Peña account, with hate mail and outraged phone calls.

But the evidence the traditionalists needed to support their cherished version of Crockett's death consisted principally of a few hyperbolic recollections by supposed eyewitnesses that described Crockett fighting "like an infuriated lion" or surrounded by a "heap of dead." Meanwhile the evidence for the execution scenario continued to mount until most historians gradually accepted it without qualm. After all, the

Peña account was not the only source. There were six others as well, though of wildly varying degrees of believability. The most important of them was a letter written in the summer of 1836 by a sergeant in the Texas army named George Dolson who relates an interview with a Mexican "informant" who was at the Alamo and claimed to have witnessed the execution of Crockett.

In the face of all this evidence, the Swingin' Davies appeared to have lost. The execution scenario had the stamp of orthodoxy. But then, in 1994, a lieutenant in the New York City Fire Department named Bill Groneman published a feisty little volume called *Defense of a Legend* that argued that the Peña account was a forgery. Groneman's argument was generally dismissed by professional historians, but he did raise serious questions about the provenance of the manuscript and credibly reopened the debate over the mystery of Crockett's death.

The controversy has since been the never-ending subject of even more books, dozens of learned articles, radio programs, and documentaries. And when it came time to dispatch Davy Crockett (now played by Billy Bob Thornton) in Disney's 2004 film *The Alamo*, director and screenwriter John Lee Hancock did so in a Peña-esque way, with Crockett defiant but on his knees, his hands bound behind him.

The manner of Crockett's death is now more than ever a mystery. Almost certainly, a handful of men were executed after the main fighting in the Alamo was over, but I don't share the conviction of the historians who still maintain without a doubt that Crockett was one of them. Although I have yet to hear a conclusive argument that the Peña document is a forgery, I am convinced that his rendering of Crockett's death is not much more reliable than the original Walt Disney version. Mostly this is because it just sounds wrong. Peña's almost hagiographic description of Crockett (his "great stature," his "regular features," his "nobility") seems suspect to me on its face, as does his equally overwrought description of William Barret Travis ("a handsome blonde, with a physique as robust as his spirit was strong").

Peña's narrative, like many historical accounts, is most likely a pastiche of direct experience, hearsay, and bombastic opinions. I think the author added the Crockett passage to the story simply to heighten the drama and concoct a death scene for the Alamo's most famous defender. This is what I think is also going on in the other execution accounts. They might be, as some historians insist, mutually corroborative, but they might just as easily be mutually derivative, all of them passing along an overheard version of Crockett's last moments.

So what do we know for sure? We know that David Crockett died at the Alamo. Susanna Dickinson, many years later, recalled that as she was escorted out of the Alamo church as the battle was winding down, "I recognized Col. Crockett lying dead and mutilated between the church and the two story barrack building, and even remember seeing his peculiar cap lying by his side." But there are problems with Dickinson's account, too. It comes to us secondhand, having passed through the pen of an author named James M. Morphis, whose purple prose inspires not much more confidence than Peña's overblown death scene. I much prefer Dickinson's brief and to-the-point testimony to the adjutant general. Of Crockett's death, all that is reported is that "He was killed, she believes."

It took a while for the nation to process Crockett's death. "Colonel Crockett is *not* dead," cheerfully declared a New York newspaper, "but still alive and grinning." Another paper said he was on a hunting expedition and would be home in the spring, still another that he had received grievous wounds but was recovering nicely from them. As late as 1840, four years after the battle, there was a purported sighting of David Crockett near Guadalajara, where he had been taken after being captured at the Alamo and condemned to slave labor in the silver mines.

But he was dead. That is the one fact visible in the fog of his final days. The former congressman from Tennessee was disposed of with gruesome anonymity. His body was dragged onto a funeral pyre with those of the other Alamo defenders, and for three days the stench of burning flesh horrified the citizens of Bexar and brought in circling clouds of buzzards. It was a graceless end, but the beginning of an uncontainable legend. David Crockett, who had come to Texas in search of a new start, had found immortality instead.

TAKING CARE
OF LONESOME DOVE

There sat the town of Lonesome Dove: a dozen grim buildings made of adobe and faded lumber, a single desolate street teeming with dust devils and undercut with dry washes, a vulture coasting above the twilit Rio Grande. The town was perched on a high cutbank above the river, affording it a panoramic view of the mesquite flats on the Mexican side. In the evening stillness I could hear cattle lowing and red-winged blackbirds rustling in the canebrakes, and the percussive sound of a bass launching itself out of the water.

A group of horsemen came riding from one end of the street toward the deep wash that led down to the river. They were seated on antique high-backed saddles and armed with horse pistols and Henry repeating rifles and Green River skinning knives. The horses looked as lanky and weathered as the men who rode them, and the spectacle of them wading into the tranquil river in the charged evening light was so exhilarating that for a moment it was possible to disregard the crowd of camera operators, grips, sound men, lighting technicians, script supervisors, and wranglers that testified to the somewhat dispiriting fact that it was all just a movie.

The riders were halfway across the river when the director yelled, "Cut!" Escorted by a half-dozen watchful wranglers, the actors turned their horses around to the American side and led them back up the bank to the starting position for another take. The pounding of hooves against the soft earth produced a deep, satisfying rumble, and though the actors chatted and joked among themselves as they spurred their horses up the street, the illusion of authenticity would not go away— any reader of Larry McMurtry's vast novel could have stood in this dusty make-believe town southeast of Del Rio and checked off the cast of characters as they rode past.

There was Woodrow F. Call, the emotionally withheld former Texas Ranger whose iron will sets into motion the star-crossed trail drive that is the heart of the story. As Call, Tommy Lee Jones wore a black round-top hat and a white beard that put me in mind—not inappropriately— of Captain Ahab. Behind him rode Robert Duvall as the loquacious and magnificent Augustus McCrae. Then came Robert Urich as Jake Spoon, Danny Glover as Joshua Deets, D. B. Sweeney as Dish Boggett, Tim Scott as Pea Eye, Ricky Schroder as Newt . . . all of them splendidly grungy in their chaps caked with fuller's earth (to provide the illusion of even more trail dust than they had actually accumulated), in their faded bandannas and their sweat-stained hats with artfully frayed and moth-eaten brims.

"Don't they look great?" Bill Wittliff, *Lonesome Dove*'s screenwriter and executive producer, asked as we stood there eating dust. "Don't they look just wonderful?" The mood on the set was high at this hour, with the day's work almost done and the light growing more gorgeous by the minute.

"Getting some good stuff, Bill!" Robert Duvall declared to Wittliff as he moseyed over after the final take. Duvall was startlingly Gus. I had seen him a few nights earlier in *Colors*, and the memory of him as a middle-aged Los Angeles police officer was still strong enough for me to marvel at the swiftness of the transition. It seemed that in a matter of only days he had realigned his body, changed from a bulky cop with a low center of gravity to a rangy, hollow-cheeked cowman with decidedly bowed legs. He was full of an actor's enthusiasms tonight, praising the cinematographer, discussing the pacing of an upcoming scene, describing a passage in a book he'd read about how a group of Texas Rangers, ambushed during a river crossing, broke down and cried like babies at the death of their leader.

Duvall had a wonderful role to play. In the course of this movie Gus McCrae would rescue Lorena Wood (Diane Lane) from the appallingly villainous Blue Duck (Frederic Forrest), slam a surly bartender's head onto the bar of a saloon, engage in two desperate Indian battles, and die a heartbreaking and unforgettable death in Miles City, Montana. These events seemed written already into Duvall's face, into his whole aspect; you could see the claim the character of Gus had not only on the actor's attention but in some magical way upon his being. Tonight, however, he was ebullient. Standing there bowlegged, his thumbs hooked in his gun belt, Duvall lifted himself off the ground in an irrepressible hop.

It was an article of faith on the set of *Lonesome Dove* that this would not be an ordinary movie. Logistics alone moved it out of that category: an eight-hour television miniseries with a budget of almost twenty million dollars, a big-name cast, and a devastating sixteen-week shooting schedule involving dozens of sets, massive location shifts, eighty-nine speaking parts, and up to 1,400 head of stampeding cattle. Though it was destined for the small screen, the film's scale was vast, a throwback to those bygone days when cinematic behemoths like *Giant* and *The Alamo* still grazed in the pastures of Texas myth.

But *Lonesome Dove* was special not just for its scale but for its source material. Larry McMurtry's Pulitzer Prize–winning novel is an epic compendium of Texas history, folklore, and cherished bits of cultural identity. Though the novel borrows elegantly from a variety of sources— trail drive memoirs, the works of J. Frank Dobie, the historical friendship of Charles Goodnight and Oliver Loving, even old movies—its own singular vision is never in question. Overlong, slow to start, *Lonesome Dove* is nonetheless an irresistible book, a ragged classic fueled by McMurtry's passionate regard for his outsized characters and by his poignant reckoning of their limitations. In the space of a few years, it had become the sacred text of Texas literature, and the filmmakers were aware that there were a lot of readers who did not want to see it screwed up.

The role of guardian angel was being played by Bill Wittliff. I had known Bill for years, long enough to appreciate the fit he and *Lonesome Dove* made. In movie jargon, Wittliff was a hyphenate, a writer-producer-director whose credits over the years had included *The Black Stallion*, *Barbarosa*, and *Red Headed Stranger*. Most of his films reflected, in one way or another, a preoccupation with the myths and lingering values of the Texas frontier. Like his friend Larry McMurtry, he grew up in rural Texas in the forties and fifties, when it was still possible to witness firsthand the fading pageantry of the open range. (Wittliff remembers standing at his stepfather's graveside after the rest of the mourners had left, watching a relative open the coffin and reverently slip a pair of boots onto the deceased's feet.)

"I think I was the perfect screenwriter for this," he said, digging into the pocket of his jeans for the key to his pickup. "I really do. The people in the book are all Larry's people, but I knew them, too. I never got jammed even for a second wondering who these people were or what was at their core. That's one of the things that *Lonesome Dove* is about: the fact that we all somehow believe that those are the guys we came from.

"You've read the screenplay," he said to me in a concerned voice. "Do you think it's faithful to Larry's book?"

It struck me that I'd never heard a screenwriter express that particular concern before. But Wittliff was obviously more than *Lonesome Dove*'s screenwriter or its executive producer. He was its custodian. I had stayed up for three nights with his script and found that in its 373 pages it managed to accommodate all the book's vital particulars while discreetly pruning its shaggy story line. Even the changes had a certain scholarly flourish. When Wittliff felt he needed a line of dialogue for Call at the end of the movie, for instance, he lifted a quote from Charles Goodnight, the legendary cattleman on whom Call is partly based.

"The thing I keep preaching to everybody," he said, "is that *Lonesome Dove is* the star. If we take care of *Lonesome Dove*, it'll take care of us."

Taking care of *Lonesome Dove* was not a simple proposition. The stampedes and dust storms, the Indian battles and rapes and hangings and river crossings and seething nests of water moccasins—all that would have been difficult enough to film without the logistics behind it: the wardrobe trucks, prop trucks, catering trucks, and motor homes that had to be moved at every change in location; the highboys, Crank-O-Vators, scrims, dinos, baby stands, and ballasts that had to be set up for each shot; the unforeseen details that had to be tended to (biscuits that were not brown enough to match those in the preceding shot, pipes that would not stay lit, moustaches that would not stay on); and then finally the myriad ways in which horses and cattle could be counted on to display their indifference to a film adaptation of an 843-page trail drive novel.

The director of *Lonesome Dove* was Simon Wincer, a forty-four-year-old Australian with a calm demeanor and a kindly, inquisitive expression. He had risen to prominence recently with a pair of films, *Pharr Lapp* and *The Light Horsemen*, that demonstrated a stylish way with narrative and—equally important—a talent for moving large groups of animals around.

"I'm used to large-scale projects," he said as he flipped through a green binder with the day's storyboard and shooting script. "And this one is as epic as they come. When I came to Texas I realized it was like remaking the Bible."

Though *Lonesome Dove* was a television production, Wincer and Douglas Milsome, his cinematographer, were shooting it like a feature, with sophisticated lighting, moving cameras, and complex staging that required scenes to be shot from up to a half-dozen different angles. The film's fluent intercutting—which would be so thoughtlessly accepted by a viewer's retina—required such laborious repositioning of cameras, lights, and hundreds of accessories that watching it was like watching an army strike camp only to set it up again a few yards away.

One afternoon while the crew was prepping a shot, I went over to talk to Tommy Lee Jones, who was sitting at the base of a six-kilowatt light in the dirt yard of the Hat Creek bunkhouse, idly whacking the ground with a quirt. D. B. Sweeney, who plays the lovesick Dish Boggett, had told me to ask Jones for a recitation of the vinegarroon toast, which Sweeney had termed "a beautiful Texas haiku."

"Hell, yes, I can recite the vinegarroon toast," Jones said. He held up an imaginary shot glass, narrowed his eyes, and declaimed:

"'Here's to the vinegarroon / that jumped on the centipede's back. /

He looked at him with a glow and a glee / and he said, "You poisonous son-of-a-bitch, / if I don't git you, you'll git me.'"

"You can find that in one of Mr. Dobie's books," Jones explained. "*Cow People*, I believe it is."

At forty-one, Jones was at least a dozen years shy of Woodrow Call's unspecified middle age, but in the midday light he looked pretty close. In addition to the white beard, his face was covered with three layers of latex stipple to simulate wrinkles, and above that were artful depictions of burst capillaries and liver spots.

He described the application of this makeup in authoritative detail, and during the days I spent on the set his conversation touched with equal enthusiasm upon the nature of the bicameral mind, the poetry of William Carlos Williams, the lost Jim Bowie silver mine, the proper technique for flanking a steer, and the art of acting.

"The acting's easy," he said. "It's like anything else—like makin' a pan of biscuits—it's all in the preparation. You have to go through life and find those things that accrue to the big bouillabaisse of your brain. Or the little bouillabaisse, as the case may be."

A Harvard-educated resident of San Saba, Jones projected an appealing air of real-world savvy. His interpretation of Call—a man so interior and taciturn that he cannot even bring himself to acknowledge his own son—seemed to be a shade or two less grim than McMurtry's but authentic all the same. Jones said he had based the character partly on his own two grandfathers, and of course he had read Mr. Haley's book about Mr. Goodnight.

Jones had a booming voice that made me think of Shanghai Pierce, the South Texas cattle baron who bragged that his own voice was "too big for indoor use." The makeup and fringe of white beard did their job in making him look older, but they also lent his ornery features an unexpected mildness. On a horse, he was spectacularly convincing. There was about him a certain unstated pride—a reveling—in the fact that he was a Texan, that the character he was playing came to him not just through research but as a kind of legacy, through his own bones.

"In this next scene," he explained as he was called over for rehearsal, "I come ridin' the Hell Bitch in from over there to where Gus is sittin' on the porch. There's five Hell Bitches in this movie—one to buck, one to bite, one to kick, one to drag around, and one just to stand there."

The Hell Bitch, in the book, is Call's prized but unbroken gray mare. This particular scene called for the horse to come charging wildly into the frame with its rider barely in control—one of many occasions in the filming of the movie in which Jones would be called upon to display his horsemanship.

The braking horse was consistently engulfed in a cloud of dust, though a few million more particles of grit were barely noticeable in the endless sandstorm that plagued the production. The crew, whose faces were often obscured by bandannas and surgical masks, had taken to calling the movie Lonesome Dust. Every few takes a water truck would drive by to wet down the swirling earth in front of the house, and an assistant camera operator would spray a product called Dust Buster over the moving parts of the Arriflex lens. One of the wardrobe assistants had discovered a pair of orphaned baby jackrabbits, and when the wind was down she would bring them out of the protective pocket of her camp stool and feed them drops of milk from the end of her finger.

Duvall, as Gus, sat on the porch in his weather-beaten hat and faded red undershirt. He seemed oblivious not only to the dust but to all the people and instruments that were crowded inches away from his face. Unlike Jones—whose attitude toward acting appeared as genial and uncomplicated as that of a high school quarterback who, to be a good sport, had agreed to take the lead in the senior play—Duvall was always taut with concentration. Sitting on the porch between takes, unapproachable and solitary, he muttered his lines under his breath, jerking his head this way or that with the ratchety, quizzical movements of a songbird.

Duvall seemed always to be engaged in some mysterious private rehearsal, some secret summoning act that he employed for even the most cursory scenes. One night I watched as he prepared for a shot that would be merely a cutaway view of Gus walking up to the Dry Bean saloon. Waiting for his cue, bathed in the illumination of a quartz light, Duvall paced back and forth, refining Gus's crotchety stride. Just before "Action" was called he stopped, slapped his thighs, rubbed his hands together, planted his feet, and crouched forward, as tense as a long distance runner at the start of a race.

Occasionally, though, when a scene satisfied him, Duvall would release his grip. "I nailed that scene!" he said after one such take, waltzing past the lights and firing an imaginary six-shooter at the ground. "Pow! Pow! Pow! I nailed it!" At such moments the grizzled and bowlegged Texas Ranger seemed to have fled from Duvall's body like an exorcised spirit, giving it back momentarily to its primary occupant, whoever exactly that was.

The action of *Lonesome Dove* takes place from Texas to Montana, a range of locations that would be prohibitively expensive for any picture, much less one that involves so much livestock and period baggage. Though New Mexico would stand in for many of the more northern locations, one of the things Wittliff insisted upon was that the Texas parts be shot in Texas.

The ranch outside Del Rio on which the production company had set up shop contained fifty-six thousand acres. Within its fence lines were landscapes that could credibly represent anything from desert to brushland to Hill Country glade. Today an impounded stretch of Pinto Creek just upstream from the ranch headquarters was being used as the Canadian River.

The scene to be filmed was described in the screenplay as follows:

EXT. CANADIAN RIVER-MORNING
The Hat Creek cowboys (naked or wearing only long johns, though all are wearing their hats) whoop and yell as they swim the herd across the Canadian River.

It was innocuous-sounding words like those—"swim the herd across the Canadian River"—that presented *Lonesome Dove* with its endless trials in livestock deployment. Down by the creek the Shotmaker—a half-million-dollar four-wheel-drive vehicle with a soaring camera crane—was already in position and workers were shuttling back and forth across the creek in a makeshift ferry in order to set up another camera on the opposite bank.

At the base camp, a quarter mile up the road, some of the actors who were playing the Hat Creek drovers—including Larry McMurtry's son James—stood around in their chaps outside the wardrobe truck, being dusted down with fuller's earth.

In a nearby field Tommy Lee Jones was running the Hell Bitch in figure eights to get her (or him—this particular Hell Bitch was a gelding) into a calm frame of mind.

"Thar's them bovines now," he said, reining up and watching as three hundred head of cattle moved in his direction. The animals' hooves, trotting over the dried brush covering the field, produced a whispery rattling sound that made it seem that the cattle were not bearing down upon the earth with their full weight.

In a perfect world, these would have been Longhorns. But as Jimmy Medearis, the head wrangler, explained to me, Longhorn cattle—particularly cows with calves—are not "maneuverable." For the sake of historical accuracy, Mexican *corrientes* were the next best thing. They were framey, wild-looking beasts with substantial horns, and there were a few in the herd that were as shaggy and humpbacked as buffalo.

The wranglers herded the cattle down to the creek and then escorted them—via a much shallower crossing just upstream—to the top of the high bluff on the far side. Jones, Danny Glover, Ricky Schroder, and the rest of the actors playing the Hat Creek Outfit soon followed.

Jimmy Medearis remained on the near bank, a bag of range cubes hanging across his saddlehorn. He planned to strew the feed into the path of the oncoming cattle to slow them down after the excitement of the crossing. Nearby, an EMT team moved into position.

"This is going to be a hand-on-switch situation," Robert Rooy, the first assistant director, announced. "All three cameras need to be ready. Everybody please clear. Speak up now if you're not ready or forever hold your peace. Stay off the radios, please. No idle chitchat."

There was no apparent motion for a few seconds after Wincer called "Action," but soon a cloud of dust was visible behind the bluff on the other side of the creek.

"Cattle at sixty yards," Rooy said, holding a walkie-talkie to his ear. "Cattle at forty yards. Cattle at twenty yards."

Jones appeared over the bluff first. He was wearing his long underwear and riding the Hell Bitch down the steep embankment with the herd of cattle behind him. The other actors—some of them totally naked except for their hats, others in their long johns—followed, swinging ropes and heyahhing the cattle along to the water.

The herd plunged without complaint into the water and held their stricken faces high while they groped for the bottom with their hooves. Beside them the cowboys struggled to hold on while their horses stroked awkwardly across the narrow creek. In an instant, the pretty green water had changed into a stew of suspended mud and dislodged vegetation.

The crew was applauding as the drovers, sopping wet and buzzing with adrenaline, emerged from the creek.

"That look like a cattle crossin'?" Jones asked Wittliff.

"Damn right it did."

Duvall had not been involved in the river crossing, because in the movie he is waiting for the cowboys on the far bank, having just come back from the various thundering adventures involved in his rescue of Lorena from Blue Duck. In the scene remaining to be shot, he would talk to Call and the others while the cattle crossed the river in the background.

Duvall, Jones, Tim Scott, Ricky Schroder, and D. B. Sweeney retired to their director's chairs in the scattered shade of a huisache and rehearsed the scene in relative peace while the wranglers began recycling the cattle back to the other side of the creek.

"I was sorry to hear about Bill Spettle," Duval said in a recitative, as yet uncommitted voice.

"Same bolt a lightnin' that kilt him kilt thirteen head a cattle," Jones responded, hanging his wet socks up on a limb to dry. "Burned 'em black."

They went through it several more times, waiting for the complicated shot to be set up. When it was ready, Jones and the rest of the drovers who would be emerging from the river rode their horses into the water to get wet again. Duvall sat waiting for them on his horse, enduring numberless pesty adjustments: a makeup man standing on a ladder and combing the hair beneath the actor's hat brim, a camera assistant taking a light reading off his face, a woman from the wardrobe department snapping a Polaroid while another daubed sweat on his back, a boom operator dangling a fur-covered microphone above his head, and a wrangler crouching beneath his horse, holding its tail. Through it all Duvall was as mute and still as an equestrian statue.

All this artifice fell away when the cameras started to roll and Jones and the others rode up from the creek as if they had just crossed with the cattle. The cattle themselves were crossing again for real, and so the background was full of marvelous chaos as Jones and Duvall delivered their lines. The takes were all good, but on the third take something extraordinary happened, something you could not explain. It had to do simply with the way Duvall said the line "I'm sorry we lost Bill Spettle"—the way his voice now seemed to have landed in some new register of compassion and tragic authority.

At that moment I was convinced. Gus and Call seemed utterly real to me, and I was struck with a vague sense of premonition that at first I could not account for. Then I remembered something I had seen the day before, when I had been poking around the set of *Lonesome Dove*. I was in Pumphrey's General Store, admiring the shelves that were stocked with realistic-looking bottles of chill tonic and Chief Two Moons Bitter Oil Laxative, when I wandered into a side room filled with props. Leaning against the wall was a human form, wrapped in burlap and lashed to a board. When I saw that the form had only one booted leg, I realized what it was. It was Gus, who dies of gangrene in Montana and is hauled back by Call to be buried in Texas.

That burlap-wrapped mannequin was an unaccountably poignant sight, as if Gus were real and the body was really Gus. You get confused on a movie set, because for all the chaos and tedium the urge to believe that it is all not just a movie is as strong as it is in a theater. Watching Duvall and Jones speak to each other as Gus and Call now above the noise of the cattle and the whistles and grunts of the drovers, I found myself particularly susceptible. I was sad that Gus would die, sad that Call would end up haunted and bereft, but most of all I was sad because I could not help knowing that the myth they represented, for all its immediacy and ageless power, was still a myth.

When the scene between Gus and Call was finished and the cattle had crossed the river for the seventh and last time, somebody noticed a solitary cow still standing on the other side of the creek.

"I'll get him!" yelled one of the actors, a young bit player still clad only in his cowboy hat and chaps. Swinging his rope, he kicked his horse toward the water.

"Stop!" Jimmy Medearis, the head wrangler, shouted after him. "Let us get him! You guys are *not* cowboys!"

The actor obeyed, but he cast a resentful eye at Medearis. What was the harm in pretending?

HIS FOSTERING HAND

Mount Vernon was more than George Washington's home; it was his project. From the time the Virginia property came into his hands in 1754, when he was a bold and desperately ambitious young major in the Virginia militia, until his death two weeks shy of a new century in 1799, by which time he was the embodiment of American grandeur and rectitude, he never stopped tinkering with the place. For much of his life, Washington was away from home on thunderously urgent business, and so he directed most of the work on Mount Vernon from a certain Olympian remove. But his correspondence is so filled with appraising references to wallpaper, nails, paint, hinges, locks, putty, and glass that the man who emerges from it seems as much a frustrated handyman as the presiding figure of his age.

Even when things were at their bleakest, when his new country was falling apart before his eyes, Washington never lost interest in his fixer-upper on the Potomac River. In September 1776, in one of the first crucial engagements of the Revolutionary War, the colonial army suffered a humiliating rout on Manhattan Island, fleeing in panic from the invading British and Hessian forces as Washington rode among his troops on horseback trying futilely to beat them back into action with his riding whip.

"If I were to wish the bitterest curse to an enemy on this side of the grave," he wrote to Lund Washington, the cousin who managed Mount Vernon in his absence, "I should put him in my stead with my feelings." But in the same letter, penned in a dark hour when his cause seemed hopeless and he felt his reputation sagging into disgrace, Washington was still issuing instructions for work on his dream house. "The chimney in the new room should be exactly in the middle of it," he instructed Lund, with a whiplash change of tone and topic, "doors and everything else to be exactly answerable and uniform—in short I would have the whole executed in a masterly manner."

The homegrown Palladian mansion that Washington continually remodeled on his eight-thousand-acre estate sits on a high bluff above the Potomac. Although it is now just eleven miles downriver from D.C.'s Reagan National Airport, Washington's "Home House" still manages to impart a formidable sense of remoteness and serenity. And if you're fortunate enough to have the place to yourself, as I did one evening thanks to the hospitality of the Mount Vernon staff, Washington seems no more remote a presence than the fireflies on the sloping lawn or the swaying branches of the ages-old pecan tree that towers above the southern wing of the mansion.

I was sitting that night on the piazza, the commodious high-ceilinged ground-level porch that faces the river and runs from one end of the house to the other. It is a beguilingly informal and versatile space that George and Martha Washington often used as an open-air dining room. An extensive veranda like this—which has become a mainstay of North American domestic architecture—might seem to us an obvious way of taking advantage of Mount Vernon's splendid location, but at the time the piazza was built, nothing of the sort had yet been seen in England or the New World. The supremely practical George Washington thought it up on his own.

From the piazza, I looked out over the lawn in the fading light. A gentle, grassy slope led down to a sharp precipice planted with trees; my eye coasted over the leafy canopies of this "hanging wood," past the deer park below and on out to the immemorial Potomac. The only hint of the present century was the steady electric light of a single boat and the reverberating yammer of its engine.

George Washington's father, Augustine, built a compact and unas-suming house here around 1735 that George's beloved half-brother Lawrence substantially rebuilt before his death in 1752. When George subsequently became master of Mount Vernon, he raised the elevation from one and a half to two and a half stories and proceeded to gradually transform the house into an imposing, but never intimidating, mansion with multiple dining rooms and parlors, eight bedchambers, a study, and a cluster of outbuildings, known as dependencies, elegantly bound to the main house by colonnaded passageways. A few of his building sketches survive, and they are plain and clear and sometimes highly inventive. "Washington was his own architect and builder," wrote his wife's grandson, George Washington Parke Custis, "laying off every-thing himself. The buildings, gardens, and grounds all rose to ornament and usefulness under his fostering hand."

Washington spent his whole adult life constructing Mount Vernon, and to a degree it is a simulacrum of his own complex and ever-evolving personality. It is, for example, a monument to privacy and contain-ment. On the outside, there is a sense of grandeur but little ostentation apart from the rusticated sidings he copied from pattern books. Inside, however, in the dining rooms and parlors, one finds a hint of the vain inner self that it was Washington's life's work to tame. The walls in these rooms are painted with insistent theatrical colors—glowering Prussian blue and several eye-popping shades of verdigris green—that were the height of fashion in Washington's day and are as vibrant as the outer walls are austere. The riotous colors serve to remind us that the grave, sober leader who publicly disdained pomp and made a show of turning away acclaim also spent a good deal of effort designing his own uni-forms and obsessively plotting his worldly advancement.

Still, it is the public Washington—so even-tempered, even-handed, and magisterial—who dominates Mount Vernon, just as he domi-nates history. During the eight years he was away fighting the Revolu-tion, he almost never left the army, coming home only for a total of ten days, but with an almost godlike omniscience he monitored the ongo-ing construction on the house.

"What are you going about next?" he wrote to Lund in 1781. "Have you any prospect of getting paint and Oyl? Are you going to repair the Pavement of the Piazza? Is anything doing, or like to be done with respect to the Wall at the edge of the Hill in front of the House? Have you made good the decayed Trees at the ends of the House, in the Hedges, &ca. Have you made any attempts to reclaim more Land for meadow? &ca. &ca."

It was an endless, expensive, constantly expanding project, made possible only by the hundreds of slaves that Washington and his wife owned. Most of these slaves were field hands, but some were skilled carpenters and housewrights. Washington's conscience was troubled, though not tortured, by slavery. He wished to see it disappear "by slow, sure and imperceptible degrees," but in the meantime he needed all that free labor—all those skilled hands wielding froes and beetles and adzes and draw knives—to shape his timbers, to cut his cypress shingles, to mix his plaster and fire his bricks and to bevel and rusticate the pine planks that covered the mansion, giving the appearance of cut stone.

It was not just the mansion that was constantly being repaired and expanded but the whole plantation, with its stables, slaves' quarters, storehouses, kitchens, coach houses, and laundry yards. There was even an innovative "dung repository" for compost. One of the plantation's most intriguing structures was a two-story treading barn. The sixteen-sided structure of this visionary barn approximated a circle. Inside, a horse could walk around and around the circumference of the second story, flailing wheat with its hooves. As the grain was separated from the chaff, it drifted down to the collecting floor below through gaps in the sturdy white oak planking, a process that was much more efficient than treading on open ground. The barn fell into ruin and disappeared sometime near the end of the nineteenth century, but an exact replica was raised in 1996.

After poking my head in the various outbuildings, I strolled through the two remarkable gardens—one for growing fruits and vegetables, one for ornamental flowers—that flank the bowling green extending from the west face of the mansion. It was an intoxicating creation, not just the plants but the beautiful terraced brick walls enclosing them. Even the ancestral privies, with their spacious summer-house feel, were part of Washington's binding vision: the studied harmony of structure and open space that reigned over the entire Mount Vernon grounds.

"I am now I believe fixed at this seat," Washington wrote after his marriage to Martha in 1759, "with an agreeable Consort for Life and hope to find more happiness in retirement than I ever experienced amidst a wide and bustling World."

Washington was fifty-one when he resigned his commission as commander-in-chief of the Continental Army in 1783, but neither the bustling world nor his own bustling nature could tolerate his living a quiet and inconsequential life as a country squire. His years of peace at Mount Vernon were chronically interrupted by bouts of war and political turmoil and by the careful tending his reputation demanded, especially after he reluctantly took the oath of office as our first president in 1789. In the end, that reputation almost totally obscured him. "Washington," Abraham Lincoln once declaimed, "is the mightiest name on earth."

When Washington finally managed to retreat from public life, hundreds of people stopped in at Mount Vernon annually to take advantage of his hospitality. He was a convivial yet somewhat elusive host, frequently slipping away to his bedroom and private study, or to make his rounds of the plantation. "I am not only retired from all public employments," he wrote Lafayette, "but I am retiring within myself. . . . I will move gently down the stream of life, until I sleep with my Fathers."

George Washington sleeps with his fathers today in a brick tomb built to his specifications on a wooded slope between the mansion and the river. In a sense, it was Mount Vernon that killed him. With a throat already raw, he had insisted upon going out on a cold and drizzly December day, eager to mark some trees for removal so that the view of the river from the piazza would be improved.

He went to bed in good spirits that night but woke in the early hours of the morning with a violent inflammation of the throat that slowly squeezed off his breath.

"I find I am going," he said.

He was sixty-seven. Visitors are not allowed in the bedchamber he shared with Martha, and in which he died, but they can look through the door just long enough to take in the Spartan details. When I was on the tour I lingered there as long as I politely could, but when I turned my eyes to the bed on which Washington had died, I felt an unexpected spasm of emotion. It was as if after spending a day at Mount Vernon I had actually come to know the figure who had once lain there slowly suffocating.

"I die hard, but I am not afraid to go," Washington gasped toward the end of his long last day. It was a grim and premature passage, though one would like to hope he took some comfort in the fact that he was dying in a room he himself had built, that he was passing into history within the shelter of his own creation.

THE EYE OF
THE MAMMOTH

ere's the plot of an episode of a 1950s TV show called *Science Fiction Theatre*:

A baby woolly mammoth has been found preserved in the ice of the Arctic Circle. A group of scientists, including a sorrowful-looking female zoologist in a Peter Pan collar, melt the ice and stare in wonder at the prehistoric creature lying motionless on the floor. Could it possibly still be alive, in a state of suspended animation? The scientists administer a "galvanic shock," and the baby mammoth miraculously scrambles to his feet. But something is wrong: he misses his mother. He begins to pine away until the zoologist, whose own child has died, rushes to comfort him.

But then she is injured in a car wreck, and by the time she recovers and gets back to the baby mammoth, it's too late. The weakened, heartbroken creature greets her with a forlorn bleat from his trunk and falls over dead.

"Funny, isn't it?" the zoologist says as she dabs at her eyes with a handkerchief. "Crying over an animal that should have died half a million years ago?"

When I tracked down this show recently and watched it for the first time since boyhood, it looked itself like an artifact of the Ice Age. The images on the DVD transfer were faded and skittery. The mammoth was played by a baby elephant wearing plastic-looking tusk extenders and scraggly tufts of hair glued to its head. But I had no trouble recalling the story's haunting effect on me. Deep into adulthood the memory lingered: a lonesome lost creature imprisoned in time, a frozen heart made to beat again, a block of ice like a window through which the light of prehistory still dimly shone.

Back in the fifties in Abilene, as I sat in my cowboy pajamas watching *Science Fiction Theatre*, it did not occur to me to find this scenario far-fetched. I had a calm certainty that in my lifetime a mammoth would indeed be brought back to life. As it turns out, I might have been right. A number of frozen mammoths have been extracted from permafrost over the past century, and though they are very much dead and cannot be reconstituted by a galvanic shock, their nuclei could conceivably be inserted into the egg cells of an elephant, which would act as a surrogate mother. A group of Japanese scientists recently predicted that by 2016 the world may witness the birth of a baby mammoth.

If it happens, it will be a reunion of sorts, since humans and mammoths go back a long way. In Texas, the people we know today as Paleo-Indians were hunting mammoths a mere ten thousand or eleven thousand years ago. By that time, the glaciers that had once covered much of North America were long gone. And they had never extended this far south, so there is no chance of finding a frozen mammoth in Texas, much less one in suspended animation. But mammoth bones are everywhere: emerging from eroded cutbanks, plowed up in farmers' fields, unearthed in construction sites.

These bones are from *Mammuthus columbi*, the Columbian mammoth, not the woolly mammoth that was featured in *Science Fiction Theatre*. Columbian mammoths ranged further south than their cold-weather cousins, throughout the Pleistocene grasslands and woodlands of North America, all the way down to what is now Mexico. They were larger than the woolly mammoths, reaching up to fourteen feet high, with domed heads and huge, sweeping tusks.

Sixty or seventy thousand years ago, a herd of these creatures was foraging in a floodplain a few miles west of what is now downtown Waco. The landscape, in the waning millennia of the Ice Age, would have been prairies and lightly forested savannas populated with all sorts of vanished megafauna: camels, saber-toothed cats, ground-dwelling sloths that could rear up to twenty feet high, and massive, armadillo-like glyptodonts that shuffled along like living boulders.

There were a few juveniles in the mammoth herd, but most were adult females. A flash flood, roaring out of the ancestral Bosque River, caught them at the bottom of a steep-sided tributary. Perhaps a few members of the herd were able to scramble up the banks of the tributary and get away, but the rest were struck by a lethal blast of moving water. The positions in which the mammoths' bodies were found suggest that the adult females—in a protective gesture familiar to us from the behavior of modern elephants—tried to form a shield around the juveniles. But even full-grown mammoths could not keep their footing against the sudden velocity of the flood. Old and young drowned together as the water swept them away. Their bodies were then buried by subsequent deposits of soil and sediment and remained hidden from sight until 1978, when two Waco men, Paul Barron and Eddie Bufkin, came across what they thought was a mammoth bone exposed in the eroded wall of a ravine.

They knew they had found something interesting, but they didn't know how interesting until archeologists from Baylor University began to dig at the site and uncovered the remains of five mammoths. Later excavations revealed as many as nineteen more, as well as the bones of an extinct camel and a single tooth from a young saber-toothed cat. Taken all together, it was a mother lode—"the largest single-herd, non-human-related [Columbian] mammoth death site in the world," as John D. Bongino, a Baylor graduate student, described it in his 2007 master's thesis.

In 2009 the Waco Mammoth Site opened to the public, adding to the reputation for eclectic tourism that Waco already enjoyed with the Texas Ranger Hall of Fame and the Dr Pepper Museum. The site is located about four miles west of I-35, where the Brazos River makes a northeasterly bend at its confluence with the Bosque. There is a parking lot for fifty or so cars and a small welcome center and gift shop, from which visitors walk down a path toward the site of the tributary. "Follow me to the Mammoths," the signs read. High up on one of the light poles along the way, a ribbon marks the height of a Columbian mammoth. It's a simple but startling reminder. The day I visited, I stared up at the ribbon, trying to imagine the colossal beast whose shoulder muscles would have rippled along six or seven feet above my head.

Beyond the light pole is a steel bridge spanning a narrow ravine, the spot where the original bones were found. Most of the remains were removed years ago, encased in plaster jackets and stored in Baylor's Mayborn Museum. Of the roughly twenty-four mammoths found at the Waco Mammoth Site, only six are still there, and they are on spectacular display in the elegant building on the far side of the ravine.

The building is known as the dig shelter. I found it to be as airy and hushed inside as an art gallery; indeed, the first thing I saw as I entered was a pony-tailed artist named Lee Jamison, standing on a scaffold and surveying his work on an almost completed mural of a mammoth herd fleeing from a wall of water. Visitors to the dig shelter can view the mural and exhibit from a catwalk that is suspended from the ceiling. The gentle smell of overturned earth rises from about six feet below, where in situ bones of the remaining mammoths lie in a matrix of the alluvial soil that was deposited over many thousands of years by the slackwater floods of the Bosque River. The three deepest-lying specimens are part of the nursery herd, but the most complete and spectacular remains on display were found in shallower soil, which means that these animals were killed not in the flood that engulfed the nursery herd but in a separate event, ten thousand or twenty thousand years later, in more or less the same place, under probably more or less the same conditions.

"Mammoth Q" reads the label next to an impressive pile of sprawled and spavined bones near the entrance. Mammoth Q, a victim of the more recent flood, is the site's star attraction, the only bull found during the three excavations. One of his ribs had been broken, not in the flood but long before; there's a bulge where it had healed over. The beast's massive pelvic bone is in one compressed piece, and most of the material is flattened and scattered, the great toe bones lying there like the playing tokens from some inscrutable ancient board game, the skull a caved-in shambles. In spite of the wreckage, though, it's clear enough what this creature had been. All you need is one glance at the serpentine tusks growing out of the smashed skull, their tips curving emphatically toward each other. They're immediately distinguishable from the shorter tusks of a modern-day elephant or from the long, sabre-like tusks of the mammoth's slope-headed contemporary relation, the mastodon.

Scattered nearby are the bones of Mammoth R, a juvenile that was killed along with the bull. The younger animal was found in an interesting position, more or less athwart the bull's tusks, and this gave rise to speculation that the bull, in a noble final gesture, had tried to heave the younger animal up and out of danger as the waters rushed in. It's a touching thought, the idea of this prehistoric behemoth selflessly concerned with the safety of his young as he himself fought to keep from drowning. But more likely the receding floodwaters had simply trapped the body of the drowned juvenile against the tusks of its elder.

Nevertheless, at the Waco Mammoth Site the drama of that long-ago day is still eerily tangible. For me, there was something particularly poignant about Mammoth W, the female adult killed along with the bull and the juvenile in the later flood, whose bones lie forty or fifty feet away from theirs. I stood on the catwalk staring down at Mammoth W for a long time, at a heap of ribs and vertebrae and disarticulated leg and shoulder bones still half buried in the soil. The lower jaw had broken off and sat upright, so that I looked down upon the single enormous molar on each side of the mouth. The teeth were the size and shape of shoes, and the enamel striations on their surfaces created a pattern that made me think of astronaut footprints on the surface of the moon. Emerging from the ground next to the jawbone was the skull. It lay on its side, its occipital cavity still covered in dirt, the near tusk broken off, the other sloping down and disappearing into the earth.

The overall effect, though, was one of living cohesion. The bones were close enough to their original positions that you saw the creature whole, and once you saw her as whole you couldn't help but see her as real, something—someone—who actually existed, whose death agony had been caught in a geological freeze-frame almost as vivid as a photograph.

Texas is an especially good place for such Ice Age frissons, particularly if you're on the scout for *Mammuthus columbi*. In far north San Antonio, for instance, hidden among the new subdivisions and unfinished strip malls claiming the open land between Loop 1604 and Bulverde, there is a remnant strip of juniper and oak guarded by a locked gate. If you happen to be a homeowner in the Villas at Canyon Springs, standing at the window of your master suite in one of the houses that edge up to this oversized vacant lot, you have a backyard view of one of the continent's great prehistoric treasure troves. If you had been here twenty thousand years ago, you might have noticed a saber-toothed cat grunting and heaving as it dragged a baby mammoth down a sloping cave opening to its den.

The cat's den is still there, and for almost a hundred years scientists have been mining it for the bones of Pleistocene predators and their prey. The site is called Friesenhahn Cave.

"It's kind of like the La Brea Tar Pits of San Antonio," Laurence Meissner, a sixty-five-year-old biology professor at Concordia University, in Austin, told me on the day I joined his zoology class on a field trip. Meissner has been working at the site for thirteen years. Though he asked me to emphasize that Friesenhahn Cave is not a public site, it's clear enough that he regards it as a public treasure, a place whose secrets have only begun to be revealed.

The cave is small, with a single oval-shaped room sixty feet long, though Meissner has lately been doing electrical conductivity tests to determine if there are other chambers. The only entrance is a thirty-foot vertical shaft, covered with a steel grate. Before Meissner opened the grate to lead his students into the cave, he pointed out a shallow depression a few yards away to the north. This had been the original cave opening, he said, the sloping entryway down which the cats and other predators had hauled their kills. Ten to fifteen thousand years ago, it filled up with rubble, sealing the cave. Millennia later, the ceiling fell in, creating the other opening. But since this newer entrance is a sheer thirty-foot drop rather than a natural ramp, the cave was apparently never again used as a den for big predators.

The students put on hard hats and descended the ladder one at a time. When they reached the bottom, Meissner pointed out the spot where an entire skeleton of *Homotherium serum* (now on display at the University of Texas) was found in the early fifties. *Homotherium*, a species of saber-toothed cat, was tough and bandy, smaller than the iconic Smilodon, whose curving canines were often seven inches long and whose remains have also been found in Friesenhahn. But the abundance of *Homotherium* and immature mammoth bones suggests that this less imposing cat was particularly adapted to preying on young mammoths, no small accomplishment if we assume that mammoths, like modern-day elephants, were formidable protectors of their offspring.

Meissner ushered the students just beyond the natural spotlight created by the shaft, where an impacted mass of rocks and boulders indicated the location of the original entranceway. He shone a light along the wall, revealing what looked like a seam of friable rock but was in reality the protruding tusk of a young mammoth.

"And I'm pretty confident that's an adult mammoth tibia bone," he said, shining the light on a triangular-shaped object sticking out of the cave wall. Since it's unlikely that any animal could have dragged an adult mammoth down here, he speculated that it had been scavenged postmortem by a tiger or bear—not just any bear, but the extinct short-faced bear, which was almost twice the size of a modern grizzly.

"Ooh, look at this!" he called out to the students when he crossed the entrance chamber to the other side. Recent rains had washed away some of the soil at the bottom of the cave, revealing even more hidden material. "Look at this big bone! It's a leg bone!"

No sooner had he found the new bone than one of the students pointed out yet another lying nearby. "And look at that!" he almost yelped. He looked up at the students gathered around him, their plastic hard hats gleaming in the light from the entrance shaft, as he directed their attention to the bone that was just now emerging from the mud into human sight. "Christmas is coming!"

"Mammoth bones show up all over the place," Ernest Lundelius, professor emeritus of paleontology at the University of Texas, told me a few days later as he led me into the basement of UT's Vertebrate Paleontology Laboratory. "A tooth here, a tusk there, once in a while you get a bit more."

He flipped a light switch, illuminating an immense room filled with rows and rows of floor to ceiling metal shelves.

"This is where we keep the big stuff."

It took me a moment to process my amazement. It was as if I had taken a wrong turn in Costco and wandered into the prehistoric bone section. The warehouse-sized room was filled with tusks, femurs, and pelvic cradles from mammoths; skulls and arm bones from giant ground sloths, ancient rhinoceroses, and short-faced bears; and shells the size of industrial woks that had belonged to long-extinct species of turtles.

Lundelius, a vigorous, folksy man in his eighties, had personally extracted some of the material on these shelves from the ground. He pointed to a giant irregular lump of plaster that contained a mammoth skull he had found in Bee County. "God, that block was heavy," he recalled. "It took six of us to get that up on a little cart and drag it out of the gulley."

Lundelius indulged me while I browsed through his shelves a while longer, then we went back up to the first floor, where there were banks of tall specimen cabinets. He opened one that read "Friesenhahn Cave" and pulled out trays that held the jawbones and teeth of juvenile and baby mammoths.

"It's a neat system," he said as he traced with his fingers a series of ridges and valleys that made up the chewing surface of a paperweight-sized mammoth tooth. "There are three different substances here—enamel, cement, and dentine—that have three different hardnesses. It's a self-sharpening system. It's really nifty."

An older mammoth would have had only four such teeth in its mouth at a time. Over the creature's lifespan, which could reach eighty years, they would be worn out and replaced six times. Mammoths lived on grasses and woody vegetation. They ripped the grass up in tufts or stripped leaves off trees with their trunks, which at the tip likely had two gripping "fingers" delicate enough to pick flowers. A mammoth might have weighed ten tons, but it moved in a surprisingly light-footed way, almost on tiptoe, as the spongy tissue of its footpads expanded and contracted with each step.

The mammoth's elaborately corkscrewing tusks grew throughout its life, between one and six inches a year. They were used for protection from predators and in dominance battles with other mammoths, as well as for stripping the bark off trees and plowing up plants. These mighty tusks were rooted in the countervailing mass of the mammoth's skull. In its skeletal nakedness, its inscrutable blankness, the skull is almost supernaturally riveting, as I was reminded when Lundelius and I paused at a specimen on display in the Vertebrate Paleontology Lab's entrance hall. Viewed from the front, this skull was a sheer wall of bone, with an odd, oblong hollow near the crest. This had been the mammoth's nasal cavity, but its position at the front of the skull gave it the look of a disturbing all-seeing eye.

"The occipital orbits are here on the side," Lundelius said, "but the early guys in the Mediterranean thought this nasal opening was the eye hole, and it has been suggested that this is where the whole cyclops idea came from."

We know from cave paintings, ivory carvings, and the remains of huts that were supported by bones and tusks that mammoths and humans coexisted in Europe as far back as thirty-five thousand years ago. In North America, the evidence is not as abundant, but it's still compelling, and the best place to find it is at the Blackwater Draw site, a mildly picturesque declivity in a stretch of windblown farmland just across the Texas state line between Portales and Clovis, New Mexico. There is a little museum in Portales that showcases an impressive collection of the mammoth bones, Paleo-Indian tools, and spearpoints found there. But to get the full impact you need to drive another five miles, keeping an eye out for the easy-to-miss sign next to a lonely ranch gate. From there a dirt road leads to a no-frills visitors center.

Unless, of course, you regard mammoth bones as frills. There are plenty of them on display at the visitors center, including a towering femur and a pair of tusks long enough to rival the world's record holder, a sixteen-foot tusk found near Post, Texas, that's now in the collection of New York's American Museum of Natural History.

But it is not the bones themselves but what has been found with them that makes Blackwater Draw such an important site. It was here, eighty years ago, that archeologists first discovered the distinctive fluted projectile points that now bear the name Clovis, which established human occupation of this area back at least twelve thousand years, during the twilight time of the mammoths.

The Clovis people didn't just share the land with mammoths; they hunted them. Over the decades, the bones of twenty-eight separate mammoths have been found in Blackwater Draw. George Crawford, the site archeologist, told me as we headed down into the draw that eight or nine of them had been killed by humans.

How do we know this? "Because," Crawford said, "there were points found in and around the carcasses. Everybody feels pretty comfortable when you've got a lot of spearpoints like that. It's pretty clear that these mammoths were killed by people."

Crawford had to speak above a ferocious wind that came howling down off the Llano Estacado. Back in the thirties, during the time of the Dust Bowl, part of the site had been nicknamed Elephant Tusk Lake because of the mammoth remains exposed by that same ceaseless wind.

It is still a parched-looking place, though there is some greenery in the form of cottonwoods at the bottom of the shallow draw, and archeologists have planted native grasses and shrubs on the slopes to prevent erosion. But Blackwater Draw had been a small, bucolic lake once, thanks to an artesian spring that continued flowing until historic times, and the water had lured wildlife and people to its banks.

Not much remains to indicate the presence of that Ice Age watering hole to a casual visitor. Pleistocene-era dunes still stand on what was once the southern shore, but the draw was dried out by dropping water tables, scoured bare by wind, and in the sixties robbed of its prehistoric contours and no doubt many of its fossil treasures by a gravel mining operation. The miners, however, had helped uncover what the Portales museum boasts was "the largest known mammoth kill site in North America."

Five mammoths died here, killed—it seems likely—by the Clovis points that were strewn through the bone heaps. One mammoth, known as Big Momma, was found with four of those points, all of them lying in and around her rib cage.

How do you kill a mammoth if you're a prehistoric hunter? Various modern-day experiments have shown that Clovis technology was adequate to the task. Spears using replica Clovis points, for example, have penetrated the hide of living elephants from sixty-five feet away. But if mammoths traveled in nursery herds like elephants—as the Waco Mammoth Site seems to confirm—then they would also likely have been guarded by ill-tempered matriarchs who would have made any approach a lethal risk. In order to strengthen the odds in their favor, hunters may have dug pit traps or taken advantage of places like Blackwater Draw, where the mammoths, as they cooled themselves in the water of a now-vanished lake, would have been crucially less maneuverable.

"The mammoths that were killed here," Crawford said, "look like they were killed facing out toward the water. So the people here may have had a system—waiting for the mammoths to wade out into the water before they attacked."

Blackwater Draw is one of several drainages that cut through this part of the High Plains and provided a route for those ancient peoples as they ventured into the Brazos River valley to hunt or trade. It is still possible today to follow the draw all the way to Lubbock, a hundred miles away, where it joins with Yellowhouse Draw on the northwest side of town.

Highway 84, southeast out of Clovis, follows roughly the same route. I took the highway to Lubbock, and when it hit Loop 289 I found myself at another remarkable archeological site, the Lubbock Lake Landmark. Lubbock Lake is hard to miss, mostly because of a full-sized statue of a mammoth and her calf that overlooks a small museum and a walking trail leading past active archeological digs.

Lubbock Lake is a national historical landmark, a dry river valley like Blackwater Draw in which the exposed strata contain artifacts that neatly trace the human occupation of this part of the country from the earliest Paleo-Indians to nineteenth-century buffalo hunters. And, like Blackwater Draw, it may well be a kill site. The three mammoth carcasses that have been found in the deep Clovis sands here show evidence of human butchering when they were still freshly dead.

Eileen Johnson, the director of the Landmark, who has worked at the site since 1972, met me in her office at Texas Tech. With her curly dark hair, oversized glasses, and pleasant academic mien, she did not seem like a woman whose research interests include cutting up big game with stone tools. ("I've only butchered one elephant," she said. "I'd like to do more.") She said that the mammoths found at Lubbock Lake had definitely been butchered, but it was still an open question whether they had been hunted or merely scavenged.

"If an animal has been scavenged after it has stiffened," she explained, "the cut marks on the bone are different—they're wider, they're deeper. You may also see far more marks, because it's hard work. The carcass when it's fresh is easier to butcher."

Clovis hunters didn't just use mammoths for meat, she told me. They regarded a pile of mammoth bones the same way they regarded an out-cropping of flint, as a quarry to be exploited. They would take a leg bone, say, break it over a rock anvil, then select pieces to carry off to their camps to fashion into bone foreshafts for spears or into cutting implements that could be as sharp as stone knives.

Lubbock Lake and Blackwater Draw are two of the three possible mammoth kill sites on the Southern Plains. The third is in a wheat field a few miles outside Miami (pronounced "Miama"), a little railroad town tucked into the Panhandle Plains northeast of Amarillo.

"Hold still a minute," Larry Kaul told me the next day, as I struggled in the grip of a barbed wire fence that I had tried to climb, following his nimble lead. He carefully released the barbs, freeing me to fall into the dry chaff on the far side of the fence. I did my best to stanch the bleeding in my palm as we walked out into the wheat field. Kaul, springy and seventy-ish, owns a pest control business in Miami. Among his many jobs in the past was trapping coyotes for the Russian fur trade. (The Russians liked coyote fur, he said, because it doesn't collect frost.)

Kaul is also an amateur archeologist who has been looking for Indian artifacts since he was a teenager. He was present in the nineties when archeologists returned to this field to further investigate the original discoveries that had been made sixty years earlier.

"This low spot here is the center of it," he said, coming to a stop about a hundred yards before the farmland dropped down into a landscape of spidery breaks. This was where, in the early thirties, a farmer plow-ing deep furrows to keep the soil from blowing away in the Dust Bowl struck something solid. The bones he dragged up turned out to be those of at least a half-dozen mammoths that had died in what had once been a muddy sink. The evidence that humans had killed them came in the form of Clovis-era stone tools, including a broken spearpoint lying less than three inches away from a mammoth vertebra.

"The bison wallowed in these little lakes and the mammoth did too," Kaul said. "What happened here was the mammoth were pretty well half-mired in the mud and those Paleo people killed them with spears. That would be my opinion of it, anyway.

"This is a hide-working tool right here," he said, handing me a sliver of bone he had just picked off the ground. Then he found what he said was a piece of enamel off a tooth, then a piece of worked Alibates flint.

We drove in Kaul's pickup back to Miami and parked in front of the Roberts County Museum, where some of the bones found at the site are displayed in a kind of tableau that includes a stuffed sandhill crane and tufts of native grass. A backdrop painting depicts two Clovis hunters with spears in hand observing a mammoth as it approaches them across the infinitude of the broken plains.

Emma Bowers, who runs the museum, directed my attention to the mammoth vertebra that had been found near the spearpoint. She said the point is a replica. The original had been stolen. "We had the spearpoint in this case and all of a sudden it came up missing."

But she was proud of the display, secreted away in a back room of the surprisingly expansive museum, in a belowground extension that she described as a tornado-proof "'fraidy hole."

"Now look at that mammoth in that mural," she instructed. "Watch his eye. When you move, that eye follows you."

The mammoth's eye did seem freakily all-observant, in a probably unintended trompe l'oeil way. It gave the impression that this great beast still regarded itself as the presiding entity of the landscape, even though mammoths had disappeared from North America about ten thousand years ago, trailing along to extinction as the earth warmed. No one knows what the tipping point was. Mammoths may have died out from attrition as their browsable paradise of open grasslands and spacious woodlands gave way to dense forests. Or they may have been reduced to smaller and smaller pockets of congenial habitat, then hunted to extinction by a surging population of Paleo-Indians.

Mammoths are gone, but the human imagination is a long way

from relinquishing them. As I stared at the mural in the Roberts County Museum, I remembered another depiction of a mammoth eye I had seen, in a photograph of a startling millennia-old painting from Rouffignac Cave, in France. It was an image that was as haunting to me as an adult as that episode of *Science Fiction Theatre* had been to me as a child. In the painting, the mammoth is shown in profile, his right eye fixed on the viewer with a searching, intoxicating scrutiny. There is nothing prehistoric about it. It feels timeless and immediate, as if this long-extinct mammoth is looking at you, assessing you as you stand there in your own pocket of time, holding you in an unbreakable gaze as deep and ageless as a trance.

A TROUBLOUS LIFE

"I knew Jesse's brother."

My grandfather surprised my brother and me with this declaration one summer day in 1958. I was nine years old. We were standing at the grave of Jesse James in the Mt. Olivet Cemetery in Kearney, Missouri. The grave was marked by a ragged chunk of granite the size of a bowling ball, all that was left of a once-towering tombstone that had been chipped away by souvenir hunters.

My grandfather went on to explain that when he was a kid in Excelsior Springs, ten miles away, he had often talked to Frank James, who was by then a man in late middle age with nothing much better to do than while away afternoons on city benches entertaining children with stories of how Pinkerton detectives had blown off his mother's right arm in a botched raid on the James family farm. He had met Frank and Jesse's mother as well, he said, a frightening, one-armed old woman who gestured angrily at things with her empty sleeve.

He must have told us more, because I remember being hungry for details, startled by the idea that our soft-spoken, law-abiding grandfather, general manager of a Chevrolet dealership in Oklahoma City, had known one of the great outlaws of American history. It startles me even more today, because at this distance—more than fifty years after my grandfather's revelation and nearly 150 years after Frank James robbed his first bank—it seems impossible that the living roots of my own existence could reach so deeply into such a distant past.

If my grandfather related more details about his relationship with Frank James, I've forgotten them. From time to time, I've even wondered if he made it up to impress two young boys at a time when Jesse James fervor was at one of its periodic heights. (*The True Story of Jesse James*, the latest Hollywood version of the story, had been released the year before.) But the dates, as well as the locations, check out. My grandfather, born in 1895, would have been sixteen when Frank and Jesse's mother died in 1911, and twenty when Frank died in 1915.

Frank James was four years older than Jesse, but his routine life span, his mellowing temperament, and his colorless death have made him his brother's junior in the annals of criminal fascination. Nevertheless, because of our faint family connection, it was Frank who always stole my interest, as once or twice each passing decade Hollywood dependably recycled the James story. The various actors who played Frank—Bill Paxton, Stacy Keach, Sam Shepard, even Johnny Cash— had a natural air of horse sense and moral weariness, in contrast to the spell of mercurial menace cast by stars like Robert Duvall or Brad Pitt in the role of Jesse. Frank was always the ego to Jesse's id, the Dr. Watson to his Sherlock Holmes.

There is truth enough in that conventional paradigm. Frank seems to have been a more deliberate thinker than Jesse, and more capable of keeping his head down, his affairs in order, and his appetites in check when the brothers went separately into hiding after their disastrous final bank robbery together in Northfield, Minnesota, in 1876. Jesse's death six years later—at the hands of his own gang members—was sordid and sad, but it ended his story on a clarion note of treachery that helped seal his legend. Whereas Frank's story just went quietly on.

But until Frank cleverly slipped into retirement, his notoriety was never less than his brother's. Five months after Jesse was killed, Frank took a calculated risk and surrendered to Missouri governor Thomas Crittenden on October 5, 1882. Reporters who interviewed Frank in his jail cell in Independence, Missouri, and were determined to keep the James legend rolling, filled column after column with news about the appearance of this renowned criminal who had eluded their scrutiny for twenty years. The skinny, big-eared, weather-beaten man of thirty-nine seemed to herald some new development in human physiognomy. His face was "one among ten thousand, and one never to be forgotten." He had "a peculiarly-shaped head, being narrower between the eyes than any other man in America." His thinning hair was "so unruly that it infused a sort of earnest, positive, self-asserting aspect into the *tout ensemble*."

The James boys were the sons of a charismatic, college-educated Baptist preacher who perished on a quixotic journey to the California gold fields when Frank was seven. From Robert Sallee James both sons appear to have inherited a degree of dash, and perhaps that is one reason Frank made sure to end his outlaw career with a chivalric flourish, unbuckling his gun belt and declaring to the governor, "I want to hand over to you that which no living man except myself has been permitted to touch since 1861, and to say that I am your prisoner."

In the end, Frank's gallant pose paid real dividends. Astonishingly, this lethal character—who had been among the most remorseless partisans in the Missouri border wars, and who afterward preyed on banks and railroads and express companies and robbed and murdered innocent civilians—walked freely into a new life, the beneficiary of various dropped charges and two sensational murder trials that ended in acquittal.

His new life, after some wandering years and sputtering career steps, ultimately brought Alexander Franklin James back home to the farm in northwest Missouri where he was born in 1843. The farm had been a tourist site since shortly after Jesse's death, operated with an unsentimental eye for profit by Frank and Jesse's formidable mother, Zerelda James.

When Zerelda died, Frank took over the family business of showing curiosity seekers the place where he and Jesse were born. Sorting through a box of old family letters recently, I came across a striking postcard that my grandparents sent back to Oklahoma during a visit to Missouri in the early 1940s. On the front is a hand-colored photo of a white-bearded old man wearing a suit and bowler hat, standing in front of a farm gate. A caption declares this to be the "Last Picture of Frank

James, 'The Outlaw,' Taken at His Farm Near Excelsior Springs, Mo."
In the photo, a hand-lettered sign nailed to the gate reads "Home of the
James—Jesse and Frank James—Admission fifty cents each person."
Another sign—misspelled—warns visitors "Kodaks Bared."

The modern-day proprietor of the James Farm is Clay County, which
operates a museum that delicately interprets this famous cradle of law-
lessness. The site is only a few miles away from Jesse's grave, which now
bears a modest stone flush to the ground ("Born Sept. 5, 1847, assassi-
nated April 3, 1882") that replaces the desecrated tombstone I saw as a
nine-year-old boy.

It was a stupefyingly hot day when I returned to Jesse's grave as an
adult, paid whatever respects were due the memory of an unrepentant
robber and murderer, and continued down Jesse James Farm Road
through fields where the baled hay looked like giant loaves of bread
baking in the open-air oven that is Missouri in July. I paid my admission at the farm's visitors center, watched the obligatory short film, then
wandered through a much better than expected museum that briskly
chronicles the lives and times of the James brothers with admirable
objectivity.

It's a story that cannot be told without acknowledging the savage
regional violence that came on the heels of the Kansas-Nebraska Act
of 1854, and which only grew in intensity when Missouri, a nominally
neutral border state, cracked apart during the Civil War.

The Jameses were slaveholders and hardscrabble farmers. Like many
of the whites in northwest Missouri, they had strong Southern fealties.
Zerelda, a widowed mother of three who had lost much of her furniture
and farm equipment to her late husband's creditors, would have been
alarmed by the abolitionists who were flooding into neighboring Kansas in order to swing it into the free state column and further under-
mine her precarious solvency.

The dirty war between proslavery and antislavery partisans in Kansas naturally spilled over into Missouri after the Confederate attack
on Fort Sumter. Frank James, at eighteen, promptly joined the seces-
sion-minded Missouri State Guard and helped defeat Union forces at
the Battle of Wilson's Creek in August of 1861. It was a clear victory
but Missouri remained under shaky federal control, especially after the

bulk of the Confederate army in the region was defeated at the Battle of Pea Ridge. The result was an insurgent war against the pro-Union provisional government, a conflict that deteriorated to personal score settling between gangs of bushwhackers and rampaging militias.

Six months after Wilson's Creek, Frank was captured and allowed to return home under condition he not take up arms against the Union, but he brushed that obligation aside and joined up with freebooting guerrillas led by the opportunistic William Clarke Quantrill, who Frank later recalled was "full of life and a jolly fellow." It was in Quantrill's gang that Frank met a fellow bushwhacker named Cole Younger, who was later part of the James-Younger gang.

Though Frank was intelligent and supposedly a great reader who always had a Shakespeare quote handy, he was also rash and embittered and a ready participant in the depredations of this close-fought border war. He was part of Quantrill's horrific raid on the abolitionist capital of Lawrence, Kansas, which the guerrilla leader ordered "thoroughly cleansed" and in which almost two hundred men and boys were slaughtered. A few months later, Frank and Jesse—finally old enough, at sixteen, to get into the fight—fell under the deadly spell of the grandiloquent and perhaps psychopathic "Bloody" Bill Anderson, whose men decorated their horses' bridles with human scalps and who were responsible for, among other atrocities, the giddy execution of twenty-four unarmed Union soldiers at Centralia, Missouri, and for the slaughter and mutilation of almost 150 more who set out in reprisal.

Frank and Jesse's family endured their own trials. Zerelda and her submissive new husband, a doctor turned farmer named Reuben Samuel, were forced into temporary exile "for feeding, harboring and encouraging bushwhackers," and in 1863 Dr. Samuel was tortured by Unionist militiamen, who repeatedly strung him up on his own farm until he revealed the hiding place of Frank and his fellow bushwhackers. (Frank managed to escape.)

The brothers, though shot up at times, survived the Civil War but had no inclination to put it behind them. The conflict left the secessionists of Missouri defeated and disenfranchised, suddenly powerless in an occupied land. For Frank and Jesse James, and for the Younger brothers and other former guerrillas in their legendary gang, the seething resentments of the war melded smoothly into predatory self-aggrandizement. They seem never to have troubled themselves with the idea that there was a difference between righteous vengeance and outright robbery.

Their string of bank hold-ups, which began in 1866—possibly with a daylight assault on the bank in Liberty only a few miles from the James farm—were often marked by lethal shootouts with citizens and sometimes by cold-blooded executions of bank employees. After a few years of bank jobs, the gang began holding up trains. There were casualties in this new field as well—an engineer killed in a derailment, an express messenger brutally beaten—but passengers often reported that the robbers engaged them in jaunty banter, could sometimes be shamed into returning stolen goods, and that one of them even quoted Shakespeare.

Shortly after he began robbing trains, Frank married Annie Ralston, the daughter of a prosperous local farmer, a graduate of Independence Female College, and, according to one childhood friend, an excellent pistol shot. Her parents were horrified when she ran off with Frank, but it turned out to be an enduring marriage. Also a stressful one, no doubt, particularly after the calamity of the Northfield robbery, which netted the James-Younger gang $26.70 and turned into a street shootout and desperate manhunt that left all the outlaws except Frank and Jesse dead or captured.

After Northfield Frank had had enough. He adopted the alias Ben J. Woodson and lived quietly with Annie and their baby son in and around Nashville, where he worked as a teamster, joined the Methodist church, and raised hogs that he exhibited at county fairs. He made a point of making friends with prominent citizens and officers of the law, banking their good opinion against a time when his identity might be exposed. But his new persona wasn't entirely an impersonation. "My old life," he later wrote, "grew more detestable the further I got away from it."

The quiet life did not suit his younger brother. Jesse—under the name of J. D. Howard—lost money at poker and horse racing and made himself conspicuous by getting embroiled in lawsuits and bouncing checks. He put together a quarrelsome new gang and briefly enticed Frank back into the outlaw life. But after they robbed a train at Blue Cut, Missouri, Frank headed off with his family to Virginia, determined to slip back onto an upright path. A few months later, in April 1882, Frank was coming home from a walk when Annie met him at the door with a look of shock on her face and a newspaper in her hand: Jesse James had been shot in the back of the head by Bob Ford, who had conspired with his brother Charlie to kill Jesse for a ten-thousand-dollar reward.

After his surrender and acquittals, Frank did his best to follow his instincts and keep his head down, but celebrity and notoriety turned out to be lifelong distractions. "You ought to see how the women flock around him to buy dry goods," one observer wrote when Frank was working in a store in Dallas. He also sold shoes and worked as a door-man at a burlesque theater, as a race starter at the fairgrounds and even as an actor (a very poor one, apparently) in several plays, though he stipulated that "I will not have anything to do with a performance that idealizes law-breaking." In the end, he tried to have it both ways, forming a Wild West show with old friend Cole Younger—now paroled from prison—and cheekily playing the role of a passenger held up in a stagecoach.

In the James Farm museum I read the notation of Frank's birth that Zerelda had inscribed in the family Bible. I learned about Frank's beloved horse, Dan, who was buried on the farm and whose grave was included in the tours that he used to give curiosity seekers. (Probably, I thought, my grandfather had met Dan as well.) For a long time I stood in front of a portrait of the outlaw at age fifty-five. In it, Frank is impec-cably turned out in a wingtip collar and tie and is staring at the lens with the direct, suspicious gaze of a hostile neighbor.

I joined in as a James Farm guide led a small group from the museum along a boardwalk to a white clapboard farmhouse in a clearing a few yards beyond two commanding shade trees. This was the house where Frank had lived as a boy, where Jesse was born, and where the brothers hid out during their wild outlaw times in Missouri. It's also where Frank spent the last years of his life, making small talk with tourists and young boys like my grandfather.

The room we entered first was the sitting room Zerelda added onto the house in the 1890s, and which after her death became Frank and Annie's bedroom. Our guide pointed out samples of Annie's tatting dis-played on the walls and the business degree from Jones Commercial

College acquired by Frank and Annie's son, Robert F. James, who later built a three-hole golf course on the property. We learned that Annie maintained an eighteen-inch waist for most of her life and that Frank had an impressive library, at least by rural nineteenth-century Clay County standards. Frank inherited the books—fifty-four of them—from his erudite preacher father and kept them in a long wooden book chest with his name burned into the lid. The book chest was still there in the room, next to the bed in which Frank James had died.

We walked through the parlor, whose walls were decorated with James family photos, among them one of a youthful Jesse (supposedly made when he was near death from a bullet wound), a characteristically forbidding image of Zerelda, and a photo of Frank's lamented horse Dan. A telephone Frank installed in 1911 still hung near the entranceway to the kitchen.

Beyond the kitchen was the ancient heart of the house, a saddlebag log cabin (two rooms sharing a single fireplace) built in 1822. On the near side of the fireplace was Zerelda's bedroom. On the far side was what the guide referred to as the "Pinkerton kitchen"—named for the bungled nighttime raid on the farm in 1875 by Allan Pinkerton's detective agency. The raid was personal for Pinkerton; an agent he had sent to apprehend the James brothers the year before was found with a note pinned to his corpse that read "This to all detectives."

This time, Pinkerton's men, wrongly thinking that Frank and Jesse were hiding out with their mother, surrounded the house and tried to flush out the fugitives with an incendiary device they threw though the window, an iron ball filled with a liquid called Greek fire. But the device exploded, killing Frank and Jesse's eight-year-old half-brother Archie and mangling Zerelda's right arm so severely it had to be amputated.

The tour led us out through the kitchen doorway and into the backyard, where a replica of Jesse's original tombstone marked the spot where Zerelda first buried him. His body has been exhumed twice, once in 1902 when Zerelda had it transferred to Mt. Olivet Cemetery in Kearney, and again in 1995 for DNA testing to confirm that the remains were actually those of Jesse James. (They were.)

Standing next to the nine-foot-high tombstone, our guide told us how Zerelda used to sell tourists stones lying on top of her son's grave for twenty-five cents apiece, and then quickly replenish the supply from a nearby creek bed, and how she would carve his initials onto the handles of old pistols and sell them to particularly gullible visitors. As I stood listening, it occurred to me that this must have been the place where my grandfather, a century ago, had met Zerelda. He would have stood where I was standing now listening to this angry woman with the empty sleeve venomously lecturing him about the Unionist militia that tortured her husband, about the Pinkertons who maimed her and killed her eight-year-old son, about the murderous coward who shot Jesse from behind while he was adjusting a picture on the wall.

Frank himself died quietly at seventy-two, just another old man on his farm, felled by a stroke. He is buried—at least his ashes are—in nearby Independence, in a tiny cemetery surrounded by a stone wall at the edge of a rambling city park. Having seen his mother stand vigil over Jesse's resting place to ward off grave robbers, having watched his brother's tombstone chipped away by souvenir hunters, he had—true to character—planned carefully ahead. He left instructions for his remains to be cremated and kept safe in a bank vault until his wife's death, when they should be buried with hers.

He stipulated no religious service, though there was a simple funeral at the farm, with Frank's eulogy given by John F. Phillips, a federal court judge and one of the attorneys who secured his acquittal.

"I feel a positive conviction," Phillips said, "that the troublous, tragic life that befell him was neither of his liking or inclination."

Maybe so, though there are people who would eagerly disagree. Frank James's life can be easily seen as a chronicle of violence and hatred. But when you stand in this tranquil cemetery looking at his grave, it's more tempting to give him the benefit of the doubt and read his life as a testament to the power of cooling passions.

Here he lies: the older brother, the second banana, the faded outlaw legend. He shares a modest tombstone with his wife, but you would never know it was his grave unless you were somebody like me who had gone looking for it for his own wistful reasons. The surname "James" is carved at the top, but on Frank's side of the stone the name inscribed is technically correct but pointedly evasive: "Alexander F."

Frank James is still in hiding.

PART FOUR

WHERE IS
MY HOME?

WHAT TEXAS
MEANS TO ME

Lying in a feather bed, in the guest room of a friend's two-hundred-year-old house in western Massachusetts, I suffered a lapse of faith in Texas. I'm not sure what brought this crisis on. Perhaps it was simply the act of waking up, looking out the window at the syrup buckets hanging from the maple trunks, at the banked snow glistening in the sharp air, and realizing that Texas would never be that.

I could stand to live here, I thought. I would keep my cross-country skis propped by the front door, a bowl of apples on the kitchen table, a steady fire by which I would read during the dim winter nights.

But it was not just Massachusetts. The hard truth was that I was getting tired of Texas and was now able to imagine myself living in all sorts of places: on one of those minor Florida keys where a little strip of land containing a shopping center and a few houses counted as barely a riffle in a great sheet of translucent ocean; in an adobe house, even a fake adobe house, in the foothills of the Sangre de Cristos; or perhaps in a city like Los Angeles, which with its corrupted natural beauty seemed so much more likely a center for the development of urban chaos than Houston.

These were uneasy rumblings, and I was enough of a Texan to feel heretical in even allowing them access to my conscious mind. But my affection for Texas had gone unexamined and untested for so long that it was time to wonder just how much affection was there after all. There are certain people who are compelled to live in Texas, but I was never one of them. I am not a two-fisted free enterpriser, I have no fortune to make in the next boom, and my ancestral ties to the land itself are casual and desultory. Like a lot of other Texans, I am here because I am here, out of habit, out of inertia, out of a love of place that I want to believe is real and not just wished for.

Because I was born in Oklahoma and lived there until I was five, I missed being imprinted with native fealty for Texas. I don't recall having any particular image of the state when, on the occasion of my widowed mother's marriage to an Abilene oilman, I was told we were going to move there. But I did not much care to leave Oklahoma City, where my baby footprints were embedded in cement and where the world of permanence and order was centered. In the park behind our house was a sandstone boulder where several generations of children had scratched their initials. This boulder, whose markings seemed to me to have some ancient significance, like the markings on a rune stone, was one of my power centers, one of the things that persuaded me that I had not been placed arbitrarily on the earth but was meant to exist here, at this particular spot. In the same park was a little garden with a semicircular rock wall dominated by a bust of Shakespeare and brass plaques containing quotations from his plays. It was a place to ponder and reflect on the immortal bard, but its hushed and reverent aspect made me mistake it for a tomb. I had no real idea who Shakespeare was, only that he was one of those exalted characters like Will Rogers, and so it seemed perfectly appropriate to me that he would be buried in Oklahoma.

But all such reverberations stopped at the Red River. I filed them away, and with a child's tenacity I resisted letting Texas invade my essence. Abilene, Texas, had been named for Abilene, Kansas, and that fact was a convincing enough argument that it would be a dull and derivative place. Our house there had a dry, nappy lawn and a cinder-block fence. My brother and I attended a Catholic school that, in this west Texas stronghold of stark and bilious religions, was like a foreign mission. On feast days the nuns would show us western movies and serve us corn dogs. Nearby there was a dispiriting lake where drab water lapped at a caliche shoreline, and on the southern horizon were low hills—looking on a map now, I see they are called the Callahan Divide—that I longed to think of as mountains.

But I surprised myself by being happy there. I liked the excitement of being rousted from sleep on summer evenings and taken to a neighbor's storm cellar to wait out a tornado warning. Though I did not know what an oilman was exactly, I enjoyed visiting my new father's office, looking at the charts and drilling logs and playing with the lead dinosaurs on his desk.

"Well, they sure do grow 'em tall down there in Texas," my relatives in Oklahoma would say when we went back to visit, and I began to imagine they were right and to cultivate a little my Texan identity. In my heart I knew that I lived in Anywhere, USA, that I watched *Crusader Rabbit* after school just like the kids in Winnemucca, and that my image of my own environment came from the same sources that everyone else's did: from *Giant*, from *Davy Crockett*, from a thousand stray pieces of folklore and merchandising.

But even this stitched-together notion of Texas had its power. Everybody else seemed to believe that Texas children were out there on the raw frontier, riding horses to school and pumping oil in the backyard, so who was to blame us for believing it a little ourselves? Even the false image provided a certain pride of place and left one more open for the real but impalpable expressions of the land itself. It became easier to imagine that the trim suburban streets down which I teetered uneasily on my first bicycle had been the setting for trail drives and Comanche raids. And there were other times when the land was almost unbearably evocative. Riding home at night from one of those Oklahoma trips, with the windows open, the car smelling of spoiled fruit, and the seats strewn with comic books and cracker crumbs, I would allow myself to become hypnotized by the way the headlights illuminated the barbed wire and mesquite on the sides of the road, creating a corridor, an endless bower that led us on but seemed never to deliver us into the land's ghostly heart. And then we would hit some little nothing town and the headlights would fall on the bobbing pump jacks, whose rhythms were keyed to a languid, eternal pulse that seemed to be everywhere, in the swooping wingbeats of nocturnal birds crossing the road, in the pistons of the car, and in my own heavy blood.

"I can see Abilene," my father would say when we were still fifty miles from home. "I can see a fly sitting on the window of our house."

"Where?" I would say, peering hard through the windshield, believing it was possible to see that far, as far as Texas went.

When I was ten we moved to Corpus Christi and I found that the image of Texas I had been cultivating and was now at ease with did not apply to this semi-exotic coastal city with its manicured bay front. This was not cowboy land. It was a sultry, complicated place, although the agoraphobia induced by the stillness of the ocean was reminiscent at times of the west Texas plains.

For my first six months there I was virtually felled by the humidity. I moved about in a tentative, purposeless way, like the anole lizards that wandered around the yard.

It was not a seductive place, but once you had purged your mind of false expectations and your pores of the last lingering traces of dry west Texas air, you began to feel accepted and absorbed by it. And of course Corpus Christi had its traditional charms as well—beaches and such—that the people at the tourist bureau seized every opportunity to promote. They kept shoving into the public view Buccaneer Queens and Miss Naval Air Stations, who posed seductively among the sailboat rigging for brochures that advertised "The Sparkling City by the Sea."

A ten-year-old boy could tell they were trying too hard, but I secretly wished the boosters luck. Corpus seemed isolated not only from the world at large but from the conventional stereotypes of Texas. It was not until the TV show *Route 66* deigned to film an episode there that I felt I had been provided with convincing evidence that the city was real.

I remember going to the courthouse one day to watch the filming of a scene. Within sight of this spot, Alonso de Piñeda had passed on his great reconnaissance cruise in 1519. On this bay shore Zachary Taylor had brought in 1845 nearly half of the United States Army and encamped while waiting to provoke a war with Mexico. On this very spot, perhaps, stood the makeshift stage on which Lieutenant Ulysses S. Grant had reportedly played Desdemona during a production in that camp of *Othello*. I was ignorant of all that, but there on the courthouse steps strode Martin Milner, and it was as if the shadow of history had passed across me.

There were not many moments like that, and the study of Texas history in the seventh grade served only to confirm my suspicion that the state seemed somewhere to have gone flat. Texas history began with Indians, conquistadores, pirates, with revolutions and wars, but by the time the student reached "Texas Today and Tomorrow" in the history book he saw only pictures of sorghum fields, refineries, and official portraits of dowdy governors.

So as time wore on and the universal ill humors of adolescence began to work their magic, I slid deeper into the down cycle of what I fear may turn out to be a lifelong mood swing about Texas. Corpus especially rankled and galled me. As a college-bound high school graduate, I had a clear shot at leaving Texas for good, but when it came down to actually making a decision about where I was going to go to school I threw in with thousands of other freshmen who chose that year to go to the University of Texas at Austin. The quality of education I might receive there never entered my mind. I liked Austin because it was an exotic place, where students rolled about on skateboards and wore surfer shirts and water buffalo sandals; and I quickly adopted the smug view that Austin, with its "cultural aspects," was not really Texas at all. The lesson I failed to grasp, of course, was that it *was* Texas, and that I had not really wanted out of the state as much as I wanted to believe.

That was years and years ago, and in all the time since, I have never made a conscious decision that Texas was where I was to be. Texas always seemed right for the moment, and the moments grew longer and longer, and here I remained.

Now I was beginning to feel that those years of dawdling and indecision amounted to a subconscious investment, that I had built up without meaning to a certain ownership of place. That was one reason why the Massachusetts epiphany was so unwelcome.

I reacted to this crisis in a typically Texan way. I flew to Amarillo, rented a car, and took off driving. I had no plan really, just the raw desire to get out on the highway system and immerse myself in Texas. There were a few old haunts I wanted to see again and a few places I wanted to visit for the first time, but for the trip itself there was no excuse other than a self-prescribed saturation therapy. I was ready for the up cycle, ready to believe in Texas again, but I wasn't counting on that to happen. I had a vague apprehension that in some way I was laying it all on the line, that if Texas didn't "take" with me on this trip the clear inference would be that I really didn't belong here at all.

When my plane landed in Amarillo the man in the seat next to me nodded toward the window and said, "Pretty, isn't it?"

I'm afraid I gave him a rather blank look, because all I saw through the same window was a vast field of concrete and, far in the distance, the hazy Amarillo skyline, which at first I took to be a cluster of grain elevators.

"The weather, I mean," the man said, sheepishly. "The *weather* is pretty."

And the weather *was* pretty; it was a cool, capricious spring day, and every time the sun broke free from the ragged, thin clouds it seemed to deliberately spotlight some subtle facet of that monotonous land: the geometrical pattern of the crops, the sight of black cattle against a field of frost-white native grass, the occasional swales in the landscape that were no more significant than the furrows between rows of wheat, but toward which the eye gravitated hungrily for relief from the flatness.

At a McDonald's in Amarillo I noticed a framed poster on the wall that told the story of the creation of the High Plains. God had been working on the Panhandle one day when it got dark and He had to quit. "In the morning," He said, "I'll come back and make it pretty like the rest of the world, with lakes and streams and mountains and trees."

God came back the next morning and discovered that the land had "hardened like concrete overnight." Not wanting to start all over again, He had an idea. "I know what I'll do," He said. "I'll just make some people who like it this way."

It surprised me how kindly disposed I was to this country. It was good land to drive through, though I could see what a nightmare it must have been to Coronado, day after trackless day in an unbroken field of nothingness. He and his men found some relief in Palo Duro Canyon, which to a traveler in that region is a startling rift in the plains, an opening into another dimension.

I drove through the canyon and was impressed but not overwhelmed. Texas scenery is spectacular only to Texans. Palo Duro pales beside the

Grand Canyon, as the mountains of the Trans-Pecos pale beside the Rockies, as the coasts of Texas, its forests, deserts, hills, and even its cities, seem minor variations of grander and more definitive things in other parts of the country. Texas is a zone in which the stunning vistas more or less peter out, leaving us with only one great geographical distinction: size. The prudent and prideful Texan takes in the whole package while retaining an affection for the few component parts with the necessary spit and polish to be thought of as scenery. He develops an eye for breadth, along with an ability to look close and hard at the unlovely places and graciously accept them for what they are.

So I drove out of Palo Duro with a chauvinistic fondness for the place and kept heading south through the plains. Over the stripped cotton fields the dust rose almost vertically, and the wind riled the surface of the shallow, haphazard ponds that lay by the side of the road waiting to evaporate.

Soon the land gave way a little, and there was a miniature canyon where the Floydada Country Club golf course could be seen as a brilliant green strip beneath the eroded skirts of the mesas. After that, things were flat again for a while until the Cap Rock, where the ground buckled and broke all at once. Raptors suddenly appeared, patrolling the precipice. The change in the landscape was extreme and definite. Below the Cap Rock there were scraggly, alluring vistas, adorned with the supersaturated greenery of cedar and mesquite. That late in the season there were still beds of wildflowers, and soft, thick grass cushioned the banks of the minute creeks all the way to the waterline.

I drove through Matador, Glenn, Spur, Clairmont, and only then realized that I would be driving through Snyder, where my wife's parents lived. I came into town on State Highway 208 and passed through the town square with its windowless courthouse and its fiberglass replica of the white buffalo that had been killed near there in 1876. The buffalo was Snyder's totem, and though a drunken oil-field worker might occasionally knock a hole in the statue's head with a pipe wrench, most of the people I knew looked upon it with civic reverence.

It was dinner time when I arrived at my in-laws' house, and it went without saying that we would all go out to eat a big steak.

"How about if I order for you?" my father-in-law said.

"Fine."

"Bring him the Winchester. And we want an order of fried shrimp for an appetizer."

I ate three of these shrimp, each nearly the size of a potato, before the Winchester arrived. It was a big slab of beef, but I was hungry from driving and correctly calculated that I could put it away.

While we ate, my father-in-law complained with genial fervor about the state of the world. Since Reagan had been elected, he did not have quite so much to gripe about anymore. But even so, he had a few things on his mind. He was mad because the Democratic Congress wouldn't let the Republicans take a measly billion dollars from the synthetic fuel fund to stimulate the housing industry; mad because the British and the Argentineans were going to have a war over the Falkland Islands and guess who was going to have to go in there after it was all over with billions of dollars of foreign aid; mad because he had casually returned his YES token to the *Reader's Digest* sweepstakes and now he was being deluged with junk mail.

"There's something you should write an article about for your *Texas Monthly*," he said as we pulled out of the driveway of the restaurant, indicating a long-bodied motor home parked next to us. "These vans or whatever they are that block your view of the street when you're trying to pull out."

All of this good-natured grumpiness made me feel at home, and I lingered into the evening and finally ended up walking across the street to the high school with my mother-in-law to watch the production of *Ah, Wilderness!* that had recently won the state one-act-play competition. I was glad to have an excuse to see the high school where my wife had been a student, where she had edited the paper and written a column, under the name of Sonya Stifled, complaining about the Vietnam War and the lack of paper straws in the cafeteria.

The production took place in an immense auditorium that had been built with tax money from the great fifties oil boom. The play itself was minor O'Neill but showed Snyder High School's drama department to superlative advantage. One or two of the actors even managed very creditable New England accents. When the play was over and the audience was strolling out into the spring night, Snyder appeared less like a west Texas oil town than the idyllic Connecticut village that had been depicted in the play, a place with a tight matrix of tradition and community. It did not seem like the stifling place my wife had written about years ago, the place I might have glanced at contemptuously from the highway as I barreled through on my way to some hippie mecca in New Mexico. It seemed alarmingly like home.

The next day I got on I-20 and drove to Abilene, finding by dead reckoning the house we had lived in more than twenty years earlier. The owners had painted it yellow and put a ceramic burro in the yard, and the neighborhood itself was largely shaded from the searing sun I had known there by all the trees that had grown up and over it in the last two decades.

It was all so comfortable and congenial: the creeks were swollen with bright ocher water, the streets were lined with upscale shops and the great Danish modern cathedrals of the Protestant faith, and the movie theaters were showing *Deathtrap* and *Conan the Barbarian*. I wondered if I was feeling warm toward Texas again because it was more acceptable than I had thought or simply because it was familiar.

The land between Abilene and Dallas was unremarkable, but it held the attention of the practiced eye. In another month it would lose its verdant sheen; it would be dry and scruffy, and the very contours of the landscape would appear to recede and lose definition. But I had a fondness for that, too, tucked away somewhere.

In this accepting mood I surged through Dallas in the shadow of the Reunion Tower, which had always looked to me like the centerpiece to a bush league world's fair. But there was no city in the country that was honed to such a fine edge as Dallas, and you could sense its organic singleness of purpose, its obsession to project style and busyness. You were either on the team or not.

I was on the team that day, and I drove confidently through the streets, enjoying the familiar feel of the city. Then I headed south on I-35, going through Waco and Temple and past a wacky entrepreneurial jumble on the side of the highway that included a crumbling replica of the Matterhorn. Then on U.S. 183 to Lockhart, where I arrived in time to witness a reenactment of the Battle of Plum Creek. Bleachers were set up on the battlefield, microphones were planted into the ground. This epic, with its meager cast of dozens, required some thrifty stage management. A Texas Ranger would ride in on a horse and announce, "I been shot by one of them dad-blamed Indians," and his mount would then be led off the stage, shuttled around behind the bleachers, and ridden in from the other side by a Comanche with a beer gut.

The pageant served less to bring the past to life than to make the present seem anemic and unreal. But Plum Creek itself, several miles away, had not been milked of its drama. It was Edenic, and along with every other creek I passed that day on my meandering way south—La Parra, Agua Dulce, Papalote—it had a lush, overgrown, hummocky quality that made you understand why this part of the country had been the fertile crescent of Texas history.

Even further south, in the brush country of Jim Wells and Duval counties, the land was surprisingly green, so much so that the dilapidated, boarded-up main streets of the less successful towns looked as if they were in danger of being reclaimed by jungle. Swallows dipped ahead of my car in relays, and turkey vultures and caracaras fed together on dead baby armadillos that had been struck down on the highway in their earliest forays.

A friend's father was being buried in San Diego that day, and I had adjusted my itinerary so that I would pass through town in time to attend the funeral. The church stood across the street from a zocalo whose gazebo and benches had been overgrown with grass and whose function as the center of town had been usurped by the highway a block away. Inside, the church was stolid and secure, its walls painted a light blue. Beside the altar was a full-color pietà, with dark red blood trickling from Christ's wounds and Mary bent down on one knee, holding her son's body in a way that suggested both sorrow and verve. It was a fine, grisly statue, with that admirable Mexican trait of being on square terms with mortal matters, a trait that was not echoed in the liturgically trendy stained glass windows bearing happy cubist depictions of doves and chalices and unsplintered crosses.

The congregation was dressed in suits and pressed ranch clothes. The service moved along in an unflinching manner, its bone-deep rituals making death seem real but not necessarily final.

I got back into my car feeling sobered and transient, a little flicker of movement on the landscape. But soon enough my attention was drawn outward again. The country was full of arresting things, from the painted bunting I saw preening its iridescent body in a mud puddle in Swinney Switch to a herd of Brahman bulls that had gathered at dusk near the gate of a fence outside Floresville. In that light the bulls' hides were the color of marble; their pendulous scrotums swayed above the rich grass, and their curious humps twitched when they shifted their weight from one hoof to another. At the gate stood a man in a red cap. He was not doing anything, just standing there with the bulls, and they in turn seemed thoughtlessly drawn to him.

It began to grow dark, in a peaceful, sodden way, as if the air were absorbing darkness rather than relinquishing light. The radio said that the widow of Pancho Villa had died, but then the station disappeared in a flurry of static before I could hear details. I tuned in an ad for Diamond Head water troughs, followed by a self-conscious country song in which Hank Williams Jr. managed to drop the names of Willie and Waylon and Kris in lamenting the sad fact that nobody wanted to go out and get drunk with him anymore. The night deepened and the voices on the radio grew more desperate:

> You got to look that devil in the eye if you're sufferin' from satanic oppression. You got to say, "Devil, in the name of Jesus of Nazareth, take your hands offa my *finances*!"

> And Bob?
> Yessir.
> I just wanted to say something about this El Salvadorian business.
> Sorry. We're about out of time.
> I don't see why we just can't take one of them tactical nuclear bombs . . .
> Gotta go.
> Now, wait a minute. Put that bomb in downtown Nicaragua or wherever . . .
> Bye . . .

I coasted home to Austin on the strains of a song about a honky-tonk cowboy who was doomed to a life of loneliness because he couldn't dance the cotton-eyed Joe. I went to bed feeling glum and perplexed, having expected that by now all those images and impressions of Texas would have formed themselves into a single testament. But I was still at arm's length, still mildly estranged. I just couldn't dance the cotton-eyed Joe.

In the morning my five-year-old daughter was whiny and irritable when I took her to school, and after pacing around the house for a while in more or less the same mood I drove back to the school to pick her up.

"Where are we going?" she asked. "To the dentist?"

"No. To Enchanted Rock."

"What's that?"

"It's a special place."

"Oh. Like Disneyland."

We listened to her Little Thinker tape as we drove west through the LBJ country, where the roadside peach vendors were just putting up their stalls, and on through Fredericksburg, with its Sunday houses and German bakeries and relentless old-country quaintness.

The first we saw of Enchanted Rock was a bare salmon-colored nubbin erupting from the serene Hill Country vista ahead. The nubbin quickly loomed larger, until it was clearly a great stone mountain, so huge and abruptly *there* that all perspective dropped away and the rock had the one-dimensional clarity of a scene that has been painted on a panel of glass.

I felt an impatience to be there, to climb to the top. Enchanted Rock was perhaps my favorite Texas place, an immense granite batholith that the Indians had considered sacred. I had found it to be sacred too, and it was to Enchanted Rock that I used to come when I was in an especially powerful sulking mood.

We came quickly to the base of the rock, and above us, as we got out of the car, we could see the deep crease across its brow along which several minute figures crept upward.

"Wow," said my daughter. "Are we going to climb that?"

We were. We jumped across the half-dozen or so separate threads of water that composed Big Sandy Creek and followed the trail upward until it was lost in the expanse of solid rock. Then we walked up at a sharp angle, stopping about every fifteen yards so my daughter could rest and express disbelief at how far we had come. Near the top, where it was very steep, she got a little testy, so I picked her up and carried her to the summit.

"Boy," she said, as I staggered along with her in my arms, "mountain climbing is hard, isn't it?"

Finally I set her down next to a plaque that had been riveted into the rock.

"What does it say?"

"It says, 'Enchanted Rock. From its summit in the fall of 1841, Captain John C. Hays, while surrounded by Comanche Indians who cut him off from his ranging company, repulsed the whole band and inflicted upon them such heavy losses that they fled.'"

"What does that mean?"

"It means a guy had a fight with Indians up here."

"But Indians are nice now, aren't they? They only use their bows and arrows for practice."

Yes, Indians were nice now. Texas itself was nice, no longer a hostile country battled over by contentious spirits, but a reasonably representative American place, filled with familiar and ephemeral things: Wal-Marts, civic ballets, wind surfing, cable TV, Hare Krishnas. But Texas had not been wholly digested somehow, and in places like Enchanted Rock you could still get a buzz, you could still feel its insistent identity.

From the top the rock was as barren as the moon, and its vast surface canted forward slightly, so that there were two horizons, the rim of the mountain and, beyond it, the edge of the true world. I hoped this sight would take with my daughter; when her sisters were older I would bring them up here, too, so that Enchanted Rock could seep into their memories. I felt this place belonged to them, more than to me; they were native Texans, after all.

The lag, the missed beat I felt in my relationship with Texas, was something that I trusted would be corrected in future generations. And for the present, Enchanted Rock was every bit as much a power center for me as that sandstone boulder back in Oklahoma City. And there were others: a certain stretch of the Frio River, where after weeks of senseless brooding I had made up my mind to go ahead and be happy and get married; the lobby of the Menger hotel in San Antonio, where there was a plaque dedicated to the memory of Sidney Lanier and where you could find a gigantic Titianesque Nativity scene hung near a painting titled *Venting Cattle on the Frisco Range*; the Indian pictographs in Seminole Canyon; the mud flats and back bays of Laguna Madre; the old Shanghai Jimmy's Chili Rice on Lemmon Avenue in Dallas, where you were served chili by the man who claimed he had introduced that dish to China during the Boxer Rebellion; the Chinati Mountains; the Flower Gardens coral reef; the thick, suffocating Big Thicket forests, where you could find quicksand and wild orchids; any number of places that would give you all the barbecue you could eat for seven or eight dollars, where you could sit beneath a pressed-tin ceiling on a humid midsummer evening, give the baby a rib bone to gnaw on to help her with her teething, and pursue the illusion that life outside Texas would be bland and charmless. Texas for me was a thousand things like that, a thousand moments that in my mind had been charged with a special quality of place that I could not explain or understand. I only knew that the quality, and the place, was Texas.

A fault line ran across the back of Enchanted Rock like the stitching on a baseball. There was a sort of cave there, illuminated by the gaps between the collapsed boulders that had formed it, where we went to drink our apple juice. My daughter announced she wanted to play Indian.

"You be the daddy Indian," she said. "You can be taking a nap while I make the tea."

I closed my eyes obediently and felt the cool air of the cave on my face. I let the whole Texas question rest. "I'll just make some people who like it this way," God had said. I wasn't sure if I had been put on the earth with an inborn love for Texas, but I certainly seemed to have a high tolerance for it. Lying there in the cave, on the summit of an ancient and hallowed mountain, I still felt a mild longing to live someplace that was more exotic, or more ordinary; someplace that was not Texas. One of these days I might do that. Just not today.

THE SOUL
OF TREATY OAK

According to Stephen Redding, a mystical arborist who lived on a farm in Pennsylvania called Happy Tree, the Treaty Oak expired at five thirty in the afternoon on Tuesday, July 25, 1989. Redding felt the tree's soul leave its body. He heard its last words—"Where are my beloved children?"

Redding had read about the bizarre plight of the Treaty Oak in the *Philadelphia Inquirer*, and he had come to Austin to help ease the tree's suffering, to be with it in its terrible hour. The Treaty Oak by that time was an international celebrity. People in London, Tokyo, and Sydney had heard the story of how Austin's massive, centuries-old live oak— once showcased in the American Forestry Association's Tree Hall of Fame—had been *poisoned*; how a feed-store employee named Paul Cullen allegedly had poured a deadly herbicide called Velpar around the base of the tree in patterns that suggested some sort of occult mischief. It was an act of vandalism that the world immediately perceived as a sinister and profound crime. As the Treaty Oak stood there, helplessly drawing Velpar through its trunk and limbs, it became an unforgettable emblem of our ruined and innocent earth.

Stephen Redding—a big man with dark, swept-back hair and a fleshy, solemn face—was only one of many people who felt the tree calling out to them in anguish. Over the years Redding had been in and out of jail for various acts of civil disobedience on behalf of threatened trees, and he hinted darkly that the car wreck that had left him dependent on a walker may not have been an accident ("It was very mysterious—a dark night, a lonely intersection"). In preparation for his visit to the Treaty Oak, Redding fasted for six days, allowing himself only a teaspoon of maple syrup a day ("My means of partaking in a little bit of the life-blood of the tree kingdom"). On his second night in Austin, he put his hand on the tree's root flare and felt its slow pulse. He tied a yellow ribbon around its trunk and planted impatiens at its base. For almost a week he camped out under the tree, criticizing the rescue procedures that had been prescribed by a task force of foresters, plant pathologists, chemists, and arborists from all over the country. Finally Redding grew so pesky that the city decided to escort him away from the tree. That was when he felt it die.

"It was so intense," he told me in his hotel room a few days later. "I just kind of fell back on my cot without the energy even to sit. I felt like someone had dropped a sledge on my chest."

"I heard that you saw a blue flickering flame leave the tree," I said.

"I'd prefer not to speak about that. If you want to enter the rumor, that's okay. I don't want to confirm it. You could suggest that rumor has it that it looked like a coffee cup steaming. And if the rumor also said there was a hand on the loop of the coffee cup you could say that too."

I was surprised to realize, after an hour or so of hearing Redding expound upon the feelings of trees and the secret harmony of all living things, that I was listening not just with my usual journalist's detachment but with a kind of hunger. Anyone who went by to pay respects to the Treaty Oak in the last few months would recognize that hunger: a need to understand how the fate of this stricken tree could move and outrage us so deeply, how it could seem to call to each of us so personally.

When I read about the poisoning, I took my children by to see Treaty Oak, something I had never thought to do when it was in good health. The tree stands in its own little park just west of downtown Austin. Although in its present condition it is droopy and anemic, with its once-full leaf canopy now pale and sparse, it is still immense. It has the classic haunted shape of a live oak—the contorted trunk, the heavy limbs bending balefully down to the earth, the spreading crown overhead projecting a pointillistic design of light and leaf shadow.

The historical marker in front of the tree perpetuates the myth that Stephen F. Austin signed a treaty with a tribe of Indians—Tonkawas or Comanches—beneath its branches. The marker also states that the tree is six hundred years old, an educated guess that may exaggerate the truth by two hundred years or so. But the tree is certainly older than almost any other living thing in Texas, and far older than the idea of Texas itself. Stephen F. Austin may not have signed his treaty beneath the Treaty Oak, but even in his time it was already a commanding landmark. According to another legend, the tree served as a border marking the edge of early Austin. Children were told by their mothers they could wander only as far as Treaty Oak. Beyond the tree was Indian country.

It was a cool evening in early June when we went by Treaty Oak that first time. I looked down at the kids as they looked up at the tree and thought that this moment had the potential to become for them one of those childhood epiphanies that leave behind, in place of hard memory, a mood or a shadowy image that would pester them all their lives. The several dozen people who had gathered around the tree that evening were subdued, if not downright heartsick. This thing had hit Austin hard. In its soul Austin is a druid capital, a city filled with sacred trees and pools and stones, all of them crying out for protection. When my neighborhood supermarket was built, for instance, it had to be redesigned to accommodate a venerable old pecan tree, which now resides next to the cereal section in a foggy glass box. Never mind that Austin had been rapaciously destroying its environment for years. The *idea* of trees was still enshrined in the civic bosom. In Austin an assault on a tree was not just a peculiar crime; it was an unspeakable crime, a blasphemy.

"Oh, poor thing," a woman said as she stood in front of the ailing oak. Like everyone else there, she seemed to regard the tree as if it were a sick puppy rather than an implacable monument of nature. But you could not help personifying it that way. The tree's inanimate being—its very *lack* of feeling—only made it seem more helpless. Someone had left flowers at its base, and there were a few cards and brave efforts at poems lying about, but there was nowhere near the volume of weird get-well tokens that would come later. On the message board that had been set up, my children added their sentiments. "Get well Treaty Oak," my seven-year-old daughter wrote. "From a big fan of you."

Would it live? The answer depended on the experts you asked, and on their mood at the time. "The Treaty Oak was an old tree before this happened," John Giedraitis, Austin's urban forester, told me as we stood at the base of the tree a few days after Stephen Redding had declared it dead. "It's like an old lady in a nursing home who falls down and breaks her hip. She may survive, but she'll never be the same afterward."

Giedraitis was sipping from a Styrofoam cup half filled with coffee. "If this were a cup of Velpar," he said, holding it up, "about half of the liquid that's in here would have been enough to kill the tree. We think this guy used a whole gallon."

The Treaty Oak poisoning had thrust Giedraitis from his workaday position in an unsung city bureaucracy into a circus of crisis management. His passionate way of speaking had served him well in countless television interviews, and now when he walked down the street in Austin, people turned to him familiarly to inquire about the welfare of the tree. He replied usually in guarded language, in a tone of voice that betrayed his own emotional attachment to the patient. Two years earlier, Giedraitis had proposed to his wife beneath Treaty Oak's branches.

"There was never any question in my mind that Treaty Oak was where I would propose," he said. "That's the power spot. That's the peace spot."

"This is a magnificent creature," he said, standing back to survey the ravaged tree with its startling network of life-support equipment. A series of screens fifty-five feet high guarded the tree from the sun and made the site look from a distance like a baseball stadium. A system of plastic pipe, carrying Utopia Spring Water donated by the company, snaked up its trunk, and every half hour the spring water would rain down upon the leaves.

"You know," Giedraitis went on, "it's hard to sit here over the last six weeks like I have and think it doesn't have some sort of spirit. You saw those roots. This thing is pressed to the earth. This thing is *alive!*"

Giedraitis said he thought the tree might have been poisoned as long as five months before the crime was discovered. He first noticed something wrong on March 2, when he took a group of visiting urban forest-ers to see Treaty Oak and happened to spot a few strips of dead grass near the tree. The dead grass was surprising but not particularly alarm-ing—it was probably the result of a city employee's careless spraying of a relatively mild chemical edger at the base of the tree.

Treaty Oak seemed fine until the end of May, when a period of heavy rains caused the water-activated Velpar that was already soaking the roots of the tree to rise from its chemical slumber. On the Friday before Memorial Day weekend, Connie Todd, who worked across the street from the tree, noted with concern that its leaves were turning brown. She thought at first it must be oak wilt, which had been decimating the trees in her South Austin neighborhood. But when she looked closer at the leaves, she saw they were dying not from the vein out—the classic symptom of oak wilt—but from the edge inward. Todd called Giedraitis, who looked at the leaves and knew that the tree had been poisoned.

But by what, and by whom, and why? Whoever had applied the poi-son had poured it not only around the base of the tree but also in a peculiar half-moon pattern to the east. Giedraitis called in tree experts from Texas A&M University and the Texas Forest Service. Samples were taken from the soil to see what kind of poison had been used. Eight inches of topsoil were removed. Amazonian microbes and activated charcoal were injected into the ground.

When the lab reports came back on the poison, Giedraitis was stunned. Velpar! Velpar is the sort of scorched-earth herbicide that is used to eliminate plants and competing trees from pine plantations and Christmas-tree farms. Velpar does not harm most conifers, but it kills just about everything else. The chemical is taken up into a tree by its roots and travels eventually to the leaves, where it enters the chlo-roplasts and short-circuits the chemical processes by which photosyn-thesis is conducted. The tree's reaction to these nonfunctioning leaves is to cast them off and bring on a new set. But in a Velpar-infested tree, the new leaves will be poisoned too. The tree dies by starvation. It uses its precious reserves of energy to keep producing new leaves that are unable to fulfill their function of turning sunlight into food.

When Giedraitis and his colleagues discovered that Velpar was the poison, they immediately realized that Treaty Oak was in a desperate condition. As its tainted leaves fell to the ground and a deadly new crop emerged to replace them, outraged citizens called for the lynching of the unknown perpetrator from the very branches of the tree. They suggested that he be forced to drink Velpar. DuPont, the maker of Velpar, offered a ten-thousand-dollar reward for information leading to the conviction of the person who had so callously misused its product. The Texas Forestry Association chipped in another thousand dollars. Meanwhile a twenty-six-person task force bankrolled by H. Ross Perot convened in Austin and considered courses of treatment. The sun screens were erected, and the tree's upper branches were wrapped in burlap to prevent them from becoming overheated because of the loss of the leaf canopy overhead. Samples showed that the soil was contaminated to a depth of at least thirty-four inches, and so the dirt around the base of the tree was dug out, exposing the ancient roots that had bound the earth beneath the oak for hundreds of years. When the root system became too dense to dig through, the poisoned soil was broken with high-pressure hoses and sluiced away.

A Dallas psychic named Sharon Capehart, in Austin at the invitation of a local radio station, told Giedraitis that the workers had not dug far enough. The tree had spoken to her and told her what their samples confirmed—that there were still six inches of poisoned soil.

Capehart took off her shoes and crawled down into the hole and did a transfer of energy to the tree.

"It was a tremendous transfer," she told me. "But she needed it so much. It was like she was drawing it out of me."

Capehart had determined that Treaty Oak was a female. In another lifetime—when the tree was in human form—it had been Capehart's mother in ancient Egypt. The tree had a name, which it passed on to Capehart, stipulating that she could release it only to the person her spirit guides had revealed to her.

Meanwhile the vigil in front of the Treaty Oak continued. Sharon Capehart wasn't the only one beaming positive energy to the tree. To the protective chain that now cordoned off the Treaty Oak, visitors attached all sorts of get-well exotica: holy cards, photographs, feathers, poems ("Hundreds of you / Fall everyday / The lungs of the World, / by our hands taken down. / Forgive us ancient one"), even a movie pass to the Varsity Theater, made out in the name of Treaty Oak. People had set coins into the brass letters of the historical marker, and on the ground before it were flowers, cans of chicken soup, crystals, keys, toys, crosses, everything from a plastic unicorn to a bottle of diarrhea medicine.

All of this was so typical of Austin. Looking at this array of talismans, I was convinced anew that Austin would always be the never-never land of Texas. What other city would take the plight of an assaulted tree so grievously to heart or come to its rescue with such whimsical resolve?

There was a suspect. Sharon Capehart had an intimation of a "sandy-haired gentleman with glasses, around the age of thirty-eight," and that was about what the police turned up, though the man was forty-five. His name, Paul Stedman Cullen, had been put forward to the police by several different informants. Paul Cullen worked in a feed store in the nearby suburb of Elroy and lived alone in a truck trailer, where he read science fiction and books on occult magic with solitary fervor. According to the police, his arrest record—for drunken driving, for drug possession, for burglary—dated back more than twenty years. He had lived in California in the sixties, during the salad days of the drug culture, and now he drove a truck with a sign in the rear window that read "Apollyon at the Wheel" and was a self-confessed member of the Aryan Brotherhood.

Paul Cullen had poisoned the tree, the informants told the police, because he wanted to entrap its spiritual energy to win the love of a woman or to ward off a rival. They described the poisonous circle he had drawn at the base of Treaty Oak and mentioned the books—including one called *The Black Arts*—that he might have used as ritualistic manuals.

"Any pagan knows better than to kill a tree," an outraged Austin pagan known as Bel told me. "And *The Black Arts* is nothing but metaphysical masturbation. The reaction of the pagan community to this act is one of disgust."

Before Cullen could be charged with a crime, the tree had to be coolly appraised, using a complicated formula devised by the Council of Tree and Landscape Appraisers. The formula takes into account a tree's species, location, condition, historical value, and trunk size. (According to the guidelines, the current value of a "perfect specimen shade tree" is twenty-seven dollars per square inch of trunk cross section: "The cross section area is determined by the formula 0.7854D, where D equals the diameter measured.") When all the figures were applied, the mighty entity of Treaty Oak was judged to be worth $29,392.69. Because the tree's value was more than twenty thousand dollars, Cullen was charged with second-degree felony mischief.

"It's tree worship!" Cullen's attorney, Richard C. Jenkins, shouted at me over the phone as he proclaimed his client's innocence. "In my opinion, Paul is a political prisoner. He's being sacrificed in a new kind of witchcraft rite. He could go to jail for *life*! People have really jumped off the deep end on this one. Usually this kind of treatment is reserved for murder victims. Rape victims! Child-molestation victims! But a tree? Come on! I mean, it's a *tree*!"

Though the poisoned soil had been removed from the base of Treaty Oak, the tree was still full of Velpar, and the chemical crept slowly up its trunk and branches, killing off the leaves flush by flush. As a last desperate measure, the tree scientists drilled holes in the trunk of the tree and injected thirty-five gallons of a weak potassium-chloride solution, hoping that this salty flood would help the tree purge itself of the poison.

Sharon Capehart, in Abilene for a radio talk show, felt the tree weeping and calling out to her for another energy transfer. As soon as she was able, she got in her car and headed toward Austin. "Around Georgetown I could really feel her weeping and wanting me to hurry, hurry. I told her, 'Just wait. I'm putting the pedal to the metal. I'm getting there.'"

Capehart arrived at Treaty Oak wearing high heels, a tight black skirt, and a red jacket. Her blond hair was teased in a manner that made it look as if it were flaring in the wind. There were four or five other women with her, students and assistants, and they made a circle around the tree, holding out their hands and drawing the negative energy—the Velpar itself—into their bodies and then releasing it into the atmosphere. I was told I would be able to smell the poison leaving the tree, and I did detect an ugly gassy smell that may have been Velpar or may have been fumes from the Chevrolet body shop next door.

Capehart and her team did one transfer and then took a break, smoking cigarettes and waiting for their bodies to recharge their stores of positive energy.

During the second transfer the women each held a limb of the tree, and then they all converged on the trunk, laying their hands flat against the bark. Capehart's head jerked back and forth, and she swayed woozily as a couple of squirrels skittered around the trunk of the tree just above her head.

"Are we doing it, or what?" she called from the tree in triumph. "Two squirrels!"

Capehart's spirit guides had told her that I was the person to whom she should reveal the name of the tree. "Your name was given to me before you ever called," she told me in her hotel room after the transfer. "They let me know you'd try to understand."

She dabbed at her lipstick with a paper napkin and tapped the ash off her cigarette.

"Her name is Alexandria," she said. "Apparently Alexander the Great had started the city of Alexandria in the Egyptian days, and she was named after that. She was of royalty. She had jet-black hair, coal-black, very shiny. She was feminine but powerful. She had slate-blue eyes and a complexion like ivory."

Alexandria had been through many lifetimes, Capehart said, and had ended up as a tree, an unusual development.

"None of the guides or spirits I've communicated with have ever come up in a plant form before," Capehart said. "This is my first as far as plant life goes."

The energy transfer, she said, had gone well. Alexandria had told Capehart that when she began to feel better, she would drop her leaves upon the psychic's crown chakra. Sure enough, as Capehart stood at the base of the tree, she felt two leaves fall onto her head.

"There ain't no way that tree is dead. That spirit has not left that tree. She is a high-level being. They never leave without letting everybody notice."

Entrusted with the name of the tree, I felt compelled to visit it once again. She—I could not help but think of it as a female now—did not look to me as if she could ever recover. There was a fifth flush of

poisoned leaves now, and the tree's branches seemed saggy and desiccated. There was not much cause for optimism. At the very best, if
Treaty Oak survived, it would not be nearly the tree it had once been.

But even in its ravaged state it remained a forceful presence, a hurt
and beckoning thing that left its visitors mute with reverence. And the
visitors still came, leaving cards and crystals and messages. All of the
attention paid to the tree had created, here and there, a discordant
backlash. An anti-abortion crusader had left a prophecy, saying that,
because of all the babies "slaughtered without mercy" by the city of Austin, "the tree that she loved will wither and die. Tho' she care for it night
and day forever, that tree will not survive." Others complained, in letters to the editor, in press conferences, in editorials, that the money and
resources that had been bestowed on the tree should have been used for
the poor, the mentally ill, the Indians. They saw the circus surrounding
the tree as a sign of cruel indifference, as if this spontaneous display
of concern subtracted from, rather than added to, the world's store of
human sympathy.

I talked for a while to a man named Ed Bustin, who had lived across
the street from Treaty Oak for years and who used to climb it as a
boy, working his way up its steady branches to its spreading summit.
Another neighbor, Gordon Israel, had gathered up some of Treaty Oak's
acorns with his children a year before and now had some eight seed-
lings that in another five or six hundred years might grow to rival the
parent tree. A local foundry operator had put forth the idea to cast the
tree in bronze, so that in years to come a full-sized statue would mark
the spot where Treaty Oak lived and died. And there were other memorial acts planned: the Men's Garden Club of Austin would take cuttings
from the dying tree, and corporate sponsors were being sought out to
pay for an expensive tissue culture that would ensure genetically identical Treaty Oak clones.

"I hope you live so I can bring my children to see you," read a note left
at the tree by J. J. Albright, of La Grange, Texas, age nine. There were
innumerable others like it—from other children, from grownups, from
bankers, from pagans and Baptists, all of them talking to the tree, all
of them wanting in some way to lay their hands upon its dying tissue
and heal it. Perhaps this was all nonsense and I had just been living in

Austin too long to realize it or admit it to myself. But I was enough of a pagan to believe that all the weirdness was warranted, that Treaty Oak had some message to deliver, and that no one could predict through which channel it would ultimately be received.

My own sad premonition was that the tree would die, though not in the way Sharon Capehart had predicted, in an ascending glory of light. I felt that at some point in the months to come its animate essence would quietly slip away. But for now it was still an unyielding entity, mysteriously alive and demanding, still rooted defiantly to the earth.

Standing there, feeling attuned to the tree's power and to the specter of its death, I recalled with a shudder a ghastly incident I had not thought of in years. When I was in college, a young woman I knew slightly had burned herself to death at the foot of Treaty Oak. I remembered her as bright and funny, carelessly good-looking. But one day she had walked to the tree, poured gasoline all over her body, and struck a match.

The newspaper report said that a neighbor had heard her moan and rushed to her rescue with a half gallon wine bottle filled with water. By the time he got there she was no longer on fire, but her hair and clothes were burned away and she was in shock, stunned beyond pain. Waiting for the ambulance, they carried on a conversation. She asked the man to kill her. He of course refused, and when he asked her why she had done this to herself, she would not respond. But why here? he wanted to know. Why do it here at the Treaty Oak? For that she had an answer.

"Because," she said, "it's a nice place to be."

WISH I WERE THERE

During the autumn of 1849 the young novelist Gustave Flaubert and his friend Maxime Du Camp met in Paris to embark on a journey to Egypt that would become one of the most famous debauches in literature. Several days before they were to leave, Du Camp found Flaubert lying on the floor, on top of a black bearskin, overcome with anxiety and despair. "I have never beheld such a state of prostration," Du Camp wrote.

Flaubert, he reported, writhed on the bearskin rug in a fit of agony. "Never again will I see my mother or my country!" he cried. "This journey is too long, too distant; it is tempting fate! What madness! Why are we going?"

Flaubert awoke in better spirits the next morning, and he managed to work up his courage sufficiently to carry out his remarkably depraved tour of the fleshpots of the Orient. But for those of us who are likewise susceptible to homesickness, the image of Flaubert wailing on the floor is even more riveting than his later adventures with veiled harem girls and groping masseurs.

All my life, in all my travels, whether near or far, I have suffered from a chronic homesickness that, while not so wildly dramatic as Flaubert's, has often been powerful enough to take the starch out of me. I felt it when I was ten years old, sleeplessly spending the night at a friend's house, seriously considering opening the window and running through the darkness to my home, only two blocks away. I felt it at Boy Scout camp, standing in ankle-deep mud during a mountain rainstorm, my teeth chattering with cold and my heart almost breaking with the longing to be back where I belonged. I have felt it in impossibly faraway places like Madagascar or Borneo, with the strange hooting of lemurs in the trees and an alien star pattern overhead, and I felt it in a luxury hotel room only two hundred miles away from my own city—a room that was tricked out with amenities that surpassed even the comforts of home: a snuggly bathrobe, a complimentary chocolate chip cookie, and a soothingly bad Sylvester Stallone movie on the movie channel.

I embark on a trip with equal parts of anticipation and nostalgia. Part of my mind looks forward eagerly to the new sensations, tasks, and adventures that the journey promises, while the other part looks back at what I am leaving behind. And on a typical trip it is not long before that anxious, reflective side begins to hold sway. Say I'm going to be gone for a week. By day two I'm already mentally leapfrogging ahead, envisioning myself on the return flight home. It's no longer the experiences of the trip I crave but the relief of returning. The days of travel become merely an obstacle to reaching the goal of being back at home.

It's not that I am useless or even unhappy during this stretch of time; I'm energetic and fairly insatiable. If I'm working, I get my work done. If it's the rare pleasure trip, I practically sprint from one museum or historical site to the next. There are moments, when I'm standing in front of some glorious painting or on some windblown summit watching a hawk migration, when my soul begins to soar and I know that travel supplies some fundamental need for grandeur in my life, a need as compelling as that of family and home.

But even in these moments, there is a kind of background static I can never quite turn off. It's the realization that I am here and not there, that I have somehow left my real life at home and am now leading a kind of provisional existence. I begin to imagine the many calamities that could happen in my absence, calamities that could shatter my familiar life beyond repair and leave me stranded in the void.

"You know when I really get homesick?" my thirteen-year-old daughter confided as she steeled herself for summer camp. "It's when I go to sleep at night and dream I'm at home. Then I wake up in the morning and I'm just so sad."

I fully understood what she meant. I have had the same dream myself often enough: home appears as a shimmering, beckoning landscape, a harmonious world in which I am secure and in place. The fact that such a wondrous, uncomplicated abode could exist only in a dream does not lessen the sensation of being painfully banished from it. One's surrendering to this siren song, to this image of an idealized home, can make travel seem like exile.

We travel, I think, to probe not just the limits of the world but the limits of our own selves. We set forth into unfamiliar realms, feeling bold and expansive, but there is always that craven part of us that comes along as an unwilling passenger and that will bolt for home at the first opportunity.

From my own experience, I know that that fearful, stay-at-home voice begins to whisper in my ear whenever I lose focus or forward momentum. Fatigue, isolation, idleness: these are the great incubators of homesickness. The most homesick I have ever been was when I spent a month alone on a Caribbean island researching a book. I didn't really know anyone there, I had only my work to occupy me, and because it turned out to be a season of violent rainstorms I spent much of my time holed up uselessly in a motel room, staring at the plywood walls as my Rice-A-Roni simmered on the stove.

It was a dawdling, despairing time, and thoughts of home tormented me ceaselessly. But whenever the weather cleared, whenever I had somebody to talk to or something to do, my situation did not seem quite so purgatorial and I was able to regain my spirits.

In order to prevent myself from ever becoming becalmed in that way again, I have devised all sorts of mental tricks. When thoughts of home begin to invade my peace, I shove them out of my mind with all the brainwaves I can summon. I force myself to think about not what my distant family is doing at a given moment but what I am doing. I refuse to entertain thoughts of my homecoming. When I begin to feel lethargic, I grab a notebook and take a walk, writing down anything even mildly interesting—"old woman fishing alone off pier," "nose chipped on saint statue in cathedral niche"—as a way of tricking myself into feeling engaged.

The rituals of travel can help stave off homesickness. I take a peculiar comfort in the familiar objects I carry with me: a brown nylon duffel bag that I've used as a suitcase for fifteen years; a battered copy of Roger Tory Peterson's *A Field Guide to the Birds*; a stack of odd-sized reporter's notebooks I have to special-order from Virginia; an ugly but indestructible hat made of white cotton duck. I have traveled across the world with these touchstones, and by now their very presence can calm and console me.

Finally, of course, the best defense against homesickness is to feel at home. A wandering life is not necessarily a rootless one. Some of my friends are professional travelers, foreign correspondents, naturalists, or photographers who are often away for eight or ten months out of the year. On the occasions when I've traveled with them, I've envied their serene and unhurried manner. They talk about what they plan to do the next day, where they should eat that night, what old friends they can look up. I can't read their minds, but I'm certain they do not tick off the days as I am inclined to do or fall into a trancelike reverie of the home they were so foolish to leave. With every gesture—the way they pack their suitcases, the way they hand their boarding passes to the flight attendants, the way they stroll easily through the streets of a strange city—they are announcing that whatever place they happen to be in qualifies as their own territory.

I doubt that I will ever master the Zen of traveling to quite that degree, but I have managed to plant my flag here and there, have mentally colonized a few tiny parcels of the Earth, and in these havens I am generally free from homesickness. But I know I'll never have the confidence of a true nomad. I'm a homebody who only thinks he was born with a wandering soul.

THE EYESORE

The playhouse I built for my children when they were small was a monstrosity, a ramshackle assemblage of plywood and two-by-fours that, for some long-forgotten reason, I decided to paint an urpy shade of green. It's gone now, destroyed years ago by my own hand on the orders of my wife, but I can't quite put its memory to rest. Every now and then, when my brain is running at a nostalgic idle, I find myself recalling that ungainly playhouse with a distinct pang.

It was the only thing I ever built. Up to that point, my biggest construction project had been a plastic model of a space shuttle that I put together in an attempt to preserve my sanity while waiting for the way-overdue birth of our third daughter. I am not a carpenter. Nor am I a handyman. From time to time, I putter around the house, looking for a crack to caulk or a window screen to straighten, but I putter poorly and without conviction.

Years ago, however, a friend shamed me into buying a circular saw on the principle that it was one of those objects, like a pocketknife or a Dopp kit, that real men invariably and unthinkingly possess. That saw got the better of me. When I brought it home along with a commanding pair of plastic safety goggles, I felt an uncharacteristic impulse to create something—something out of wood. I thought about a big, plain, hulking table, but I knew my chances of getting the legs to come out the same length were remote. A deck was even further beyond my capabilities, and a sandbox—which I might have been able to pull off—held no allure. But one day, as I watched my five-year-old daughter and her friend having a tea party in a kind of bower formed by the interlacing ligustrum branches in our backyard, I decided that what my kids needed—and what I needed to build them—was a childhood sanctum. I wanted to make a structure as mysterious and serene as that leafy hollow where they were drinking their Kool-Aid.

I was ceaselessly in search of such places when I was a child. I draped sheets over rows of chairs to form dark tunnels that I could roam through like a gerbil, drenched in the strangeness, the infinite novelty of an altered environment. The forts and tree houses and hideouts that my friends and I constructed out of cardboard and scrap lumber had an appeal whose precise timbre eludes me after all these years, but I can still remember the intense satisfaction of simply sitting in these places, feeling impossibly remote and secreted away.

I never had a formal playhouse, although I remember waiting out the endless weeks for the arrival of a "log cabin" that I had begged my parents to order from an ad on the back of a comic book. The picture in the ad showed boys in coonskin caps, clambering in and out of the cabin through a stout wooden door in which the shafts of Indian arrows were embedded. When the log cabin finally appeared at my own door, however, it left me mute with outrage. The fabulous playhouse depicted in that comic book turned out to be merely a sheet of plastic printed with images of rustic, unpeeled logs; the directions said I was to drape it over a card table.

Was it to triumph over the memory of this childhood fraud that I threw my adult self so heartily into the construction of a bona fide playhouse? Off I went to libraries and bookstores, searching for schematics and specifications. But I quickly realized—looking at these plans for miniaturized versions of Queen Anne houses and Tudor mansions with their cute little dormers and gables and other intricate flourishes—that I could no more build one of these edifices than I could build a Saturn V rocket and fly it to the moon.

What I could build, I thought, was a big box. I knew my own capabilities well enough to understand that my playhouse would have no architecture, but perhaps, I wistfully reasoned, it would have some sort of style nonetheless. Awkwardly, I drew up the plans on a piece of graph paper. The playhouse would be a big square with an opening in front that was only two feet high to discourage trespassing adults. (An actual door was out of the question; I've never been good with hinges.) There would be three cutout windows and a ladder leaning against the inside of the back wall and leading up through a hole in the ceiling to a kind of roof garden, which I would enclose with a foot-high safe railing. And then my grand whimsical statement: a slide by which children could thrillingly descend from the roof to the ground.

As a writer, I am accustomed to the often great distance between the thing envisioned and the thing produced. This gulf grows immeasurably wider when you are not very good at your job. I don't recall how many afternoons and weekends I spent in my backyard, trying to wrestle those two-by-fours and sheets of plywood into some vague replica of the fantasy residing in my head. I do know that I was not a pleasure to be around. My children, excited at first at the prospect of watching their daddy build them a playhouse, soon learned to give a wide berth to the snarling goggle-eyed monster he had become.

But there at last the thing stood at the edge of the yard. Its faults— in terms of aesthetics and craftsmanship—were compellingly apparent. The windows, meant to be square, were somewhat trapezoidal. The railing around the roof was more than a crude stockade, and there was a conspicuous gap where the slide was supposed to be but wasn't. The gap, I soon realized, would always be there because I didn't have the slightest idea how to build a slide, and there was no store-bought slide that would match the peculiar dimensions I had thoughtlessly created. Overall, the playhouse looked less like the product of weeks of intense deliberation and labor than like some kind of eccentric emergency shelter.

On the other hand, it was strong. It did not wobble, as I had feared it might, when I leaned against it, and I could stand on the roof and jump up and down without the slightest fear of crashing through.

And the kids took to it. I like to think that if it had resembled the illustrations in the books I had consulted—a charming little junior cottage with wraparound porches and trellises and flowerpots under the windows—my children might have perceived it as something to be admired rather than explored. Instead, I believe, it aroused their sense of adventure. Not long after I built the playhouse they climbed up on the roof and took voyeuristic pleasure in observing our neighbor's backyard wedding. And I would eavesdrop on them as they flirted with imaginary danger on that same roof, daring one another to eat the "poison" berries from the swaying branches surrounding them or to leap up and try to grab the telephone line that ran high above their heads.

"When will the slide be here?" they kept wanting to know. From time to time, I would try to puzzle out how to follow through on this missing element, but my brain was just not mighty enough to wrestle with such a complex problem. For that reason, the playhouse always seemed unfinished to me, and I could not look at it without being overcome by a gnawing sense of my own limitations. At the same time, the satisfactions of watching my kids crawl in and out of its doors and windows or dawdle for hours on its rooftop were unexpectedly deep and abiding. I felt a thrilling sense of validation when a four-year-old school friend of one of my girls, visiting our house for the first time, walked into the backyard and said, "Wow!"

"Tell me again why you made me tear it down," I said to my wife the other night as I stared at the picture of the playhouse in one of our photograph albums.

"Why," she said, "because it was substandard."

She was not being cruel, although her observation did in fact shatter my fragile craftsman's ego. She had always feared, she gently explained, that a kid might fall through the railing I had built on top of the playhouse. Also, we had been in the process of moving and putting our house on the market, and she was worried that this big green eyesore in the backyard would diminish the value of the property.

No doubt she was right. And it is only fair to admit that, at the time of our move, the playhouse was three or four years old and, having lost its novelty, was neglected. Every few months, I had to grab a broom and knock down the cobwebs. So when I finally took a hammer and knocked the playhouse itself down, I had the sense that its time on earth had duly passed.

"You remember the playhouse, don't you?" I plaintively questioned our oldest daughter, a college junior now, when she walked through the living room that same night on her way to snag a cappuccino.

"The playhouse?" she said. "Of course I remember it. It was lime green—no, pea green. And it had a door that only children could fit through. And it had stairs inside going up to the roof."

With that brisk recitation, she opened the front door. Perhaps it was the vaguely crestfallen look on my face that caused her to turn on her way out and address me in a consoling voice.

"Oh—and one other thing," she said. "I remember being very impressed that you built it."

THE GOLDEN AGE
OF AUSTIN

Austin: It was grok at first sight.

This would have been the summer of 1963, years before I acquired a hippie vocabulary sufficient to describe the soul-claiming properties of Texas's modest little capital city. I was fourteen, and my Explorer Scout post was in the final leg of a hundred-mile canoe race. It began somewhere up on the Highland Lakes and followed the Colorado River to the finish line in downtown Austin. The actual paddling was done by my older brother and two other competitive-minded scouts. My place was on the support team, eating potato chips in the backseat of a pursuit car driven by my mother.

On a steep and winding two-lane road just west of town, she pulled into a turnout and parked the car on a high bluff overlooking Lake Austin. Far below, we could make out my brother's canoe struggling forward on the green water. We yelled and waved at the paddlers; they exhaustedly waved back. But my pretend interest in the canoe race had already been eclipsed by what can best be evoked by another word from that long-ago lexicon: a vibe.

I don't recall if I saw the city itself at that moment. There was no skyline then, nothing but the state capitol dome and UT Tower to be glimpsed beyond the treetops. What I saw were steely limestone cliffs accented by fissures and overhangs and shallow, inaccessible cave openings. Every irregularity in the rock cast a seductive blue shadow. Scrubby greenery covered the tops of the cliffs and the unending ranks of hills beyond. In the summer stillness I could hear the echoing sound of the canoe paddles slapping water hundreds of feet below.

The city of Austin, I would come to understand, is tuned to the pitch of the landscape I happened upon that day. There was nothing all that spectacular about those limestone canyons, just enough to impress a boy from the flat and humid coastal plains. But that's Austin for you: not grand, not goading, just quietly beguiling. There are plenty of places that are more exciting and excitable, places that rouse you to wonder or stir you to accomplishment. It has crossed my mind in the past forty-four years that I should have lived in some of them. But something in my nature responded to the welcoming torpor of Austin, responded so decisively—or so lazily—that I could never make a case for leaving.

I arrived from soporific Corpus Christi three years after that canoe race, one more bewildered college freshman in a madras shirt and scratchy polyester slacks. The city was just getting over the shock of the Whitman shootings, and there was a sense of other dark things patiently waiting to be revealed by history. I sat in polite attendance at a speech by Stokely Carmichael, congratulating myself on what an open-minded white boy I was. I went to rallies decrying the Vietnam War, but since I read only the movie reviews in the newspaper, I had no precise idea what was troubling the angry speakers who kept grabbing the microphone. I met a guy who claimed he had gotten high by smoking banana peels, but at that point his unlikely declaration represented my only firsthand acquaintance with the drug culture.

The big changes began to hit Austin soon after. Suddenly there was no longer any such word as "slacks." There were no more Beach Boys–style surfer shirts. You went to class—on those rare occasions when you went to class—in cutoffs and water buffalo sandals and the blue work shirts you bought at the Academy Surplus on sleepy little I-35.

I wore the costume, but I was unsuited and ill-prepared for a reign of chaos. I had the soul of a rule follower. At a time when rock was igniting the world, my puerile musical tastes (the Brothers Four, the sound track to *How the West Was Won*) were alarming even to me. The riots, the rallies, the angry hooting of the redneck clientele at Hill's Cafe, on South Congress, as we trooped in and picked up our menus ("Look at them goddam hippies!"): it was all mostly theater to me. I lingered at the edges of the whirlwind, too proud or too afraid to be drawn in. And what I remember most about those years is not the tear gas in the streets, not the ecstatic licentiousness in which I was too meekly reserved to play a part, but the staggering, unconscionable wasting of time: hour after hour, week after week, sitting on the floor of whatever falling-apart West Campus house I happened to be living in, watching other people smoke dope, watching them string beads onto necklaces while Frank Zappa or Buffalo Springfield or Steve Miller endlessly, feverishly emanated from the cheap turntable.

I don't recall arguing the great issues of the day. What was there to argue about? Everything was stultifyingly self-evident. The war was a criminal imperialist enterprise. Johnson, and then Nixon, were its evil masterminds. Godard's abrasive, unwatchable movies were works of genius. The 3-D image of the Stones on the cover of *Their Satanic Majesties Request* was far-out. I should have been climbing the walls, for within my breast a little baby bird of ambition was starting to flutter, but there was a kind of security in that lassitude that I seemed to need. The stasis I felt seemed to be confirmation that my life hadn't really started yet, nothing was yet officially at stake. I could safely reside in this cocoon of boredom until I worked up the nerve to stand up and declare myself.

Austin, of course, can be its own kind of cocoon, as generations of cheerful dead-enders can attest. I came of age as the city itself did, during what we can now arguably regard as its golden age. It wasn't much more back then than an overgrown, self-infatuated college hamlet. There was no traffic. There were always parking places in front of the feed stores and department stores on Congress Avenue. There were only a handful of movie theaters, each with a single screen showing fifty-cent matinees, though it was easy enough just to sneak in through the back door. The water in Barton Springs had not yet been debased by nutrient-rich runoff and had an arctic purity, so startlingly clear you could not believe what you were seeing. Rent in the ramshackle, roach-infested housing our integrity demanded we inhabit was forty-five, fifty dollars a month. The city itself was more or less self-contained, spilling modestly over Edwin Waller's original 1839 plat but still largely held in check by hills and creeks and other natural barriers. There was a Chinese restaurant, Lim Ting, way out near Ben White Boulevard; otherwise it seemed the only thing to eat in the whole city was chicken-fried steak.

But the joint was jumping. If you came here from Corpus Christi or Lufkin or Corsicana or Midland, Austin was Paris in the twenties. The city had an offbeat pulse of energy that was intoxicating. In an instant, you went from being a lonely, misunderstood soul in your provincial town to being just another face in a heaving hive of outcasts.

The place to go at first was the Vulcan Gas Company, a psychedelic hellhole located in an old dry-goods store downtown. Its specialty of the house was hard-core, electrified blues, a kind of music I tried earnestly to like but just found belligerent and screechingly loud. You would drop a tab of acid, or, if you were me, you would not, and sit on the concrete floor listening to Johnny Winter or Bubble Puppy while staring enraptured at a light show of throbbing paisley shapes. The light show was like an elaborate and endless version of the blistering images you saw on a movie screen when the film burned up in the projector. Why this was considered entertainment is a mystery that still haunts me.

I was more receptive to the Armadillo World Headquarters, a venue that was not nearly as claustrophobic and which was likely to showcase music born out of the great hippie-redneck détente of the early seventies. Listening to Willie Nelson, Commander Cody and the Lost Planet Airmen, Freda and the Firedogs, I could sometimes even hear the lyrics, an important consideration for someone who had just determined his mission in life was to compose obscurantist poetry. Planted cross-legged in my cutoffs on the floor, feeling the sticky spilled beer against my bare legs, I would stare at Jim Franklin's stunning painting to the left of the stage. It depicted the blues artist Freddie King, his face contorted in creative rapture, nailing down a decisive note on the neck of his guitar. Just at the moment the note was presumably sounding, an armadillo was bursting from the bloody center of King's chest. This explosive coronary embodied everything to me that was great about Austin. The armadillo was Austin's shy and absurd totemic animal, and even its timid spirit could not resist the harmonic magic that caused it to rocket out of its hiding place.

Austin was inspiring, but if you didn't watch yourself, it could be suffocating, too. The place had a native smugness, an insistence on its own laid-back wonder. It had enough of just about everything—music, eccentric culture, politics, scenery, scandal—to make you think you couldn't do better elsewhere. It was an incubator for itself; it kept a jealous hold on your dreams.

I was one of those who never made a break for it. I'm not sure why. After college, after a few years of dispiriting and low-paying jobs that would obviously lead me nowhere, it would have made sense for an aspiring writer to move on to someplace where aspiring writers moved on to. But I didn't know how to do that. I didn't know anybody except my fellow tadpoles in a slowly stagnating pond. I didn't have any money or any understanding of how anything more than a bare-subsistence income could be acquired.

But there was something else that kept me here: a feeling that if I left I would leave too much of my identity behind. All of that wasted time, all of that half passive participation in Austin's licit or illicit pleasures, had turned out to feel like a kind of sweat equity in a place that might just be on its way to finding its full expression. I was such a long way from being fully formed myself that the idea of starting over in another locale was terrifying. It could only mean moving from one holding pattern to another. I knew Austin, I knew I belonged here; it was just a matter of waiting for the two of us to grow up.

Austin's growth spurts have been something to behold these past few decades: Dell, IBM, Freescale, convention hotels, sushi restaurants, high-rise downtown condominiums, movie studios, crushing traffic, artfully rustic wineries, thousands upon thousands of networking hipsters with badges around their necks swarming into town for South by Southwest or video-gaming conventions or screenwriting conferences or social-networking seminars. The city that was once merely a modest provincial haven is now a premier destination. Austin's famous alternating current of energy and lethargy has been transformed into a steady buzz.

The surprising thing is, I like it even more now. One of the reasons

I don't bother to join in the carping about how much better Austin was in the old days is because in looking back I know I'll reencounter my old sluggish, formless, uncommitted self, the boy who caught the Austin vibe only to learn that it was a live virus, a strain of excitement that could mutate over time into terminal inertia. But in the new Austin the excitement feels genuine and lasting. For all its sprawling growth, its civic posturing ("Keep Austin Weird," "Live Music Capital of the World"), it's a real city now, edgier, less complacent, more demanding. The city that in the past could seduce you into a lifelong slacker's sleep is slowly gaining the power to jolt you into definition.

For most of my life, when people asked me where I was from, I would naturally craft an answer from the landmarks of my childhood: I might say Oklahoma City, where I was born and lived for five years; or the West Texas plains, where I lived until I was ten; or more likely the Texas coast, whose salt air and unrevealingly murky inland waters forever reoriented my imagination. But after living almost all my adult life in Austin, after writing almost every word of my professional writer's life here, after marrying here and having three children here and two grandchildren, maybe it's time to declare that Austin is not just my longtime home but my default natural place.

I remember one night, decades ago when the city was still new to me, when I allowed my friends to shame me into at least taking an inside glimpse at drug-induced reality. By this time my caution had become an obstinate pose rather than a conviction, and I knew I owed it to myself to see what this historical moment was all about. Otherwise I would be the armadillo who forever did not rupture forth from Freddie King's chest.

The drug might have been acid, it might have been synthetic mescaline. I don't think any of us really knew. Whatever it was, it was mild enough. No outright hallucinations, just an awareness that the borders and contours of every person and object I saw had a pulsating quality of expansion and contraction, that nature was coloring itself outside the lines. We piled into somebody's car, and some non-designated driver conveyed us in deep nighttime through the Austin streets. We walked into a UtoteM—an early iteration of 7-Eleven—and stared in wonder at the products in the aisles, at the lightbulbs and bottles of aspirin and racks of candy. We felt like archaeologists who had stumbled across the commissary of a previously unknown civilization.

A few hours before dawn we found ourselves trespassing in a housing development under construction above the lake, not far from the bluff where I had stood during that canoe race. We walked into a house site where the framing had just gone up and gazed in wonder at the empty open-air spaces that would one day be living rooms and kitchens and bedrooms. We were filled with cosmic insights about the transience of life and the mysteries of the time-space continuum, insights that the bourgeois suckers who were going into lifelong debt to build this bogus materialistic refuge could never fathom. I spotted a carpenter's pencil lying on the foundation, picked it up, and wrote on one of the studs, "By stealth of night we came." I remember guffawing at my wit. My drug-expanded mind somehow regarded this lame gesture as the greatest act of creative vandalism ever perpetrated upon a clueless world.

Every now and then I think about that house, with my scrawled sophomoric message hidden inside it, the cryptic wisdom that probably no one ever even noticed. That house has become my own secret time capsule, even though I have no memory of exactly where it is located. How many families have lived there in the past forty years or so? How many generations have passed through it?

Over the decades I've made my modest mark on Austin, though nothing commensurate with the colossal mark it has made on me. I've contributed to the economy by buying bogus materialistic refuges of my own, I've sent my children through the public schools, paid taxes, contributed to this or that election or initiative, served on boards, even helped raise money for the creation of statues—Philosophers' Rock, at Barton Springs; Angelina Eberly shooting off a cannon on Congress Avenue; Willie Nelson on Willie Nelson Boulevard—that were designed to become part of the everlasting iconography of the city. I am a minor aging burgher of this place, though still with a counter-culturalist's innate suspicion of the whole idea of civic-mindedness. If I have encoded myself anywhere, though, it's in the framework of that unknown house on what was once the edge of Austin, in the sealed-away handwriting of a young mind ablaze with anarchy and exuberance.

TEXANIC!

"I salute the Empire of Texas!" President Franklin Roosevelt proclaimed on a June day in 1936 to a crowd gathered at the newly named Cotton Bowl. He proclaimed it to the rest of the country as well, since his remarks were being broadcast nationwide. Texas, for once, was the place to be. The Texas Centennial Exposition, in Dallas—designed and built to celebrate a hundred years of revolution, nationhood, statehood, secession, and blustery regional identity—was the state's coming-of-age gift to the world and, more crucially, to itself. The frontier past was over, and all the marvels of the twentieth century were on spectacular display.

Among the proposed goals of the Centennial was to "Texanize Texans," and to create an extravaganza "bold enough to please the still hearts of Austin, Travis, and Houston, and big enough to mirror the accomplishments of Texas to all the sons and daughters of earth." The Exposition's moderne-inspired architectural style was labeled Texanic. *The Big Show*, a B movie starring Gene Autry, was filmed mostly on location at the Exposition, and if you watch it today you can get a sense of the scale and the self-conscious spirit of the event: files of marching Texas Rangers, a grand esplanade flanked by colossal buildings with stately symbolic statues, and the vast stage of the exposition's biggest attraction, the *Cavalcade of Texas*, a pageant in which the state's history was depicted in a flurry of galloping horses, ever-changing sets, and pioneers driving their wagons across the lonesome prairie. Elsewhere on the grounds were a replica of the Globe Theatre, full-size robotic dinosaurs, and attractions such as the "Streets of All Nations," which provided visitors with an anthropological excuse to watch a nude woman dive into a flaming pool of water. At the center of it all was the State of Texas Building, a somber palace consecrated to the noble idea of Texas. Former governor Pat Neff declared the building to be the "Westminster Abbey of the Western World."

Has there ever been a state that tried so poignantly hard, that wanted so desperately to believe in itself and to ensure that that belief was passed on to subsequent generations? We're a long way from 1936 and its high-water mark of Texas exceptionalism, but that please-notice-us legacy still endures. I've never been immune to it, and I don't think I've ever been exactly opposed to it, but because I came of age in a very different time—the counter-triumphalist sixties and seventies—I've always been squeamish and suspicious about the notion that Texas is, or at least has to be regarded as, the promised land.

It's an attitude that probably seeped into my identity as a father. I wasn't one of those proselytizing Texas dads to my three daughters, forever schooling them in the glories of their native state. I was too conflicted to play that role. But at the same time there was something I didn't want them to miss, the sense that they didn't just happen to live in Texas but were *from* here. There was just enough family history to justify some kind of aura of destiny. Though I was born in Oklahoma, somebody on my father's side of the family was said to have fought at, or been at, or been in the vicinity of, the Battle of Sabine Pass during the Civil War. Through my wife's family, the girls could trace their lineage back to a Georgia doctor named William McMath, who joined up in 1842 with the ill-advised Mier Expedition, an attempt by an army of piratical Texans to seize parts of northern Mexico. Some of the men were later captured and every tenth one was executed, their fate determined by whether they drew a white or a black bean.

I remember telling my children that they would not exist if some homesick, blindfolded guy rotting away in a Mexican prison in 1843 had not had the good fortune to pluck a white bean out of a jar, but they just gave me that please-do-we-have-to-stop-at-another-historical-marker look.

They were, I suppose, justifiably wary. If I put myself in their place, I had to realize that "Huh" was the only possible answer to a question like "Do you girls realize you're looking at possibly the last remaining Spanish mission aqueduct?"; or that when they innocently asked "What do you want for Father's Day?" they did not mean they were ready for a two-hundred-mile round-trip to inspect the original site of Washington-on-the-Brazos.

As they grew older, though, pride of place inevitably took hold. The younger girls, Dorothy and Charlotte, went to college in New York and then worked in the city at purportedly glamorous jobs for a few years afterward. It was the old story: they moved to New York for the excitement and opportunity, they moved back to Texas for the queso. Among the other things they missed badly enough to come home, they told me recently, were giant-sized iced teas in Styrofoam cups, swimming holes, long empty roads where the drivers in their pick-ups would give you a hi sign as they passed, and not having to explain to people what happened at the Alamo.

But you can't step into the same Texas twice. In the few years they had been gone, the state was a subtly different place: more and more strip malls and chain restaurants had continued to fill in the open highway stretches between cities; favorite hangouts and hideaways had either closed or exploded into unbearable hipster meccas; rent was up and jobs were scarce, though not as scarce as they were in the rest of the country in those recession years.

While they had been away, there had been a quiet shift in demographic history: the growing minority populations had finally overtopped the white non-Hispanic majority that had been calling the shots in Texas since 1836. This last fact was in vibrant evidence a few months ago when I went to my niece's law school graduation at the University of Houston. There was her name—Margaret Sharp—in the program, along with a hundred or so other Anglo-sounding names, but there were enough graduates with names like Aamir Shahnawaz Abdullah, Obiajulu Nnebuogo Enaohwo, Janie Ann Kunnathusseril and Innocent

Ifechukwu Obeta to make you wonder whether a singular Texas identity had already become a remnant notion, had already dissolved into a globalized future.

But it would be a mistake to think that the Texanizing of Texans is entirely a thing of the past. A few weeks after my niece's graduation, I was standing in the middle of the Odd Fellows Cemetery in San Antonio for a memorial service for my historian friend Kevin Young, who had died unexpectedly at the age of fifty-five. Kevin had been living in Illinois at the time of his death, but because he had lived so long in Texas and much of his work had been centered on the Texas revolutionary period, it was important for his friends to see him off someplace closer to home. They chose the cemetery where the ashes of some of the cremated Alamo defenders were said to have been buried.

We stood in the sun as two guys in cowboy hats strummed their guitars and performed "The Ballad of the Alamo" and "The Green Leaves of Summer." After the eulogies a group of re-enactors in 1830s clothing marched forward and delivered a twenty-one-gun black powder salute. As they reloaded, I noticed a teenage girl who was standing in front of me. She was wearing a tank top, and tattooed on the back of her bare shoulder were the closing words of William Barret Travis's famous letter of defiance from the Alamo. The rendering of his handwriting was exact. "Victory or Death," the tattoo read. "William B. Travis, Lt. Col. Comdt."

I remembered standing in front of a framed copy of that letter with my oldest daughter Marjorie when she was about the age of that girl in the cemetery. I had dragged the kids to the Alamo yet again, one of those dad-trips that they had learned to endure with sarcastic forbearance. But this time was different. Marjorie read the handwritten letter slowly, carefully—"Our flag still waves proudly from the walls. I shall never surrender or retreat"—and fifteen years later she named her second-born son Travis.

It wasn't just because of the letter. She and her husband, Rodney, had always liked the name Travis, she told me, just as they had liked the Texas-sounding name Mason for their older son. The sounds of those names, their accidental or on-purpose historical resonance, reinforced the idea that your destiny has something to do with where you're from and with the past that made that place what it is.

I took my two grandchildren on a field trip to the site of the Centennial Exposition, which had taken place seventy-six years earlier and was as far distant in the Texas past for them as the Comanche wars had been for me when I was their age. Fair Park, which encompasses the buildings of the Exposition, including the Cotton Bowl, is still a periodically thriving place, home to football games, the State Fair, the Children's Aquarium, and the Museum of Nature and Science. But in the middle of an uneventful June day, there was no one around as we walked up the stairs of the Exposition's long-ago centerpiece, the State of Texas Building—now known by the more imposing name, the Hall of State.

We stared at the massive bronze doors, and above them, *Tejas Warrior*, a gilded statue of an Indian drawing a bow, and above that, the soaring limestone pillars forming a semicircular portico. Four-year-old Mason was wearing a Handy Manny Halloween costume whose icky polyester fabric should have been unbearable on a blazing summer day, but his attachment to it was profound and unyielding. Travis, who was two, never went anywhere without his lime-green Kermit the Frog cap.

The two of them were an incongruous sight at this earnest shrine to Texas ideals past, but the truth is that anybody at all from our own time would have seemed incongruous at the Exposition grounds that day. They were so empty—and so, well, Texanic—that they looked like the ruins of a vanished civilization. In front of the Hall of State was the grand esplanade of the fair, featuring a reflecting pool whose fountains were programmed to dance in rhythm to "The Yellow Rose of Texas," and huge exhibition halls which had once demonstrated the coming marvels of electrical and automotive technology. The main buildings had all been restored, their heroic murals—depicting 1930s visions of space flight and medicine and farm productivity—uncovered and repainted, their rather hideous but also rather wonderful symbolic statues patched up or even recast.

We took all this in from our vantage point in front of the Hall of State and then walked through the bronze doors to the hushed gallery known as the Hall of Heroes, where Travis was lifted up to gaze indifferently at Pompeo Coppini's statue of his sort-of namesake, William Barret Travis, his sword unsheathed to draw his legendary line in the sand.

The Hall of State's purpose is sort of obscure. It is short on actual exhibits, though there is a small museum in one of its wood-paneled side rooms and there are display cases in the Hall of Heroes, one of which—nestled between the statues of Mirabeau B. Lamar and Stephen F. Austin—pays homage to Mariano Martinez, the Dallas inventor of the frozen margarita machine. Otherwise the building seems to be all about brute inspiration. When Mason and Travis entered the Great Hall, a four-story-high empty room adorned with massive murals featuring sinewy, stricken-looking Texas heroes, they gazed up in awe at a gold medallion as big as the sun on the far wall.

"What are those guys holding?" Mason asked me when he finally turned his attention to the murals.

"Guns."

"Why do they need those?"

Long story. How was I supposed to explain the Goliad Massacre to a four-year-old in a Handy Manny costume? He and Travis, two tiny little figures in this vast echoing chamber, were clearly working to take it all in, and I had the feeling they would be a long time sorting it all out. This 1936 vision of Texas—with its tonsured Franciscan friars, sinister conquistadors, muscle-bound Indians, gushing oil wells, and begowned women holding aloft symbolic torches—seemed even to me overwrought and otherworldly, less like a history lesson than some kind of collective anxiety dream.

After we left the Hall of State and the Fair Grounds, I decided—in case my grandchildren had not been imprinted with a big enough dose of Texas lore—to swing by Pioneer Plaza in downtown Dallas. This is the site not just of the city's oldest cemetery but also of a shock-and-awe art installation, a larger-than-life-size cattle drive sculpture depicting a group of wranglers driving a herd of seventy Longhorns across an artificial stream. We approached the sculpture through the old cemetery, which was full of broken granite slabs inscribed with the weathered names of the pioneer grandees of Dallas, and often their infant children. This prompted a battery of questions from Mason about death and burial that was interrupted when the boys discovered the bronze cattle herd making its sinuous way down a steep slope and across the river. Travis, gazing up at the statue of the trail boss, offered something appropriate from his vocabulary—"Yee-haw." Other than that, the boys did not seem to be particularly stirred. They had grown up with Handy Manny and *Yo Gabba Gabba!*, not as I had with Hopalong Cassidy and Davy Crockett.

"Why is he riding a horse?" Mason sincerely wanted to know. His idea of a solitary range-rider did not reach farther back than Lightning McQueen. I filled him in as best I could on the industrial revolution and then asked him why he thought all those cattle were crossing the river.

"Don't ask me! How would I know?"

We left it at that—no need to launch into a history of the Kansas railheads, or for that matter the slaughter of animals for food—and got back in the car and drove north on Griffin Street. We turned left on Elm and were heading toward Stemmons Freeway when I saw the white X in the middle of the street and realized I was driving them past the Texas School Book Depository and through its dark shadow.

I kept driving without saying anything to the grandkids, but the next day I went back by myself. It had been years since I had been to the Sixth Floor Museum or stood in Dealey Plaza looking at the assassination site. It was more of a touristy hub than I remembered, with self-appointed tour guides aggressively trolling for clients on the sidewalks, assassination theorists holding forth in front of tables laden with conspiracy books and DVDs and gruesome illustrations of the fatal head wound. A sign at the museum entrance read "Come Enjoy a White Chocolate Cherry Iced Mocha."

A tasteless yellow banner planted in the grass read "Grassy Knoll." I was standing in the pergola at the summit of this infamous slope when I noticed a big white horse-drawn carriage clomping up beside the front door of the building that had once been the School Book Depository. Riding in this fairy-tale conveyance was a Muslim family, the father stretched out, half reclining on one of the bench seats, his wife and an older woman sitting on the other, along with a girl who looked about ten. Both of the women wore hijabs but the girl was bare-headed, her hair cut into a fashionable-looking bob. I couldn't hear what the driver was telling them about the history of the assassination but saw that she was gesturing toward the middle of the street below.

Along with the family in the carriage, I followed her pointing finger and saw again the white X that marked the place where Kennedy had been struck in the head by the bullet from Lee Harvey Oswald's mail-order rifle. It occurred to me that the X stood for something else as well: the moment when that old idea of Texas—the unquestioned pride behind the Centennial Exposition—gave way to something murkier and less certain, a Texas that could not be so easily celebrated and passed down from parent to child without a haunted note of ambivalence.

If that X seemed to mark the birth of modern Texas, I had to remember it was modern only to someone my age, for whom the events of Dealey Plaza were still magically raw. Someday I would tell Mason and Travis what it felt like to hear my high school principal's voice come over the intercom and announce that the president was dead. I doubted, though, that I could really convey that sense of horrible amazement, the feeling that a trap door had just opened and I was no longer in my algebra class but alone and lost on some new plane of reality.

For my grandchildren, for that little girl in the Cinderella carriage, for the young couples who were born long after 1963 and were now drinking white chocolate cherry iced mochas in front of the School Book Depository, that long ago moment could only be the historical past, a trauma from a distant time heard about, read about, in the undying present. The cavalcade of Texas keeps moving on, a Centennial here, an assassination there. We may like to think that through it all there is something indefinably, steadily the same, something to hold on to. But that determination belongs to history, not to us. That is the way it has to be, the way it should be, and the way it shall be unto the Texas generations.

FADE IN, FADE OUT

Yesterday was a green-envelope day at our house. It happens probably seven or eight times a year: a green envelope will appear in the mailbox, and I'll pretend to be in no particular hurry to open it as I nonchalantly sort through the bills and catalogs and reminders from the vet that our deceased dog is due for a dental cleaning.

But beneath the affected calm, my heart is racing. For screenwriters who have been fortunate enough to have their scripts actually made into movies, a green envelope is a Pavlovian trigger. Green is the color that the Writers Guild of America, the screenwriters' union, uses when it sends out checks for residuals, which are the payments due to writers when their movies or TV shows are reshown.

On occasion during my thirty-year screenwriting career, the amount on these checks has been life-changing, enough money to buy a car or temporarily pay off our credit cards. But I don't really expect to see that kind of windfall again. I haven't had a movie made in eight years, and my current career status is somewhere between emeritus and irrelevant. Still, the check that came yesterday was a nice surprise. The total was $2,588.95. Included with the check was an itemized list of movies for which I had received sole or shared screenwriting credit and that had been shown again and again around the world. The biggest amounts were for *Cleopatra* ($716.41), a lavish and maybe-just-a-little-bit-cheesy ABC miniseries, and for *King of Texas* ($854.30), a western retelling of King Lear, with Patrick Stewart and Marcia Gay Harden, that had originally aired on TNT. A half-dozen other movies were on the list. They included a few boilerplate TV movies like *In The Line of Duty: Blaze of Glory* ($.56), an "inspired by a true story" bank heist movie starring those then-titans of the small screen Bruce Campbell and Lori Loughlin; a steamy Lifetime murder mystery called *Widow on the Hill* ($341.60), which remains the only thing I've ever written that my mother implied she would just as soon I hadn't; and *The Colt* ($122.53), a nicely rendered little Civil War movie that aired on the Hallmark Channel and that I had adapted from a seven-page short story by Mikhail Sholokov. The Guild statement provided scant information about which parts of the world embraced these movies most fervently, but I doubt that I'm far off the mark in imagining an unwatched TV screen in the back of a kebab stand in Kota Kinabalu.

Sholokov, Shakespeare, Campbell: such was my considerable range as a screenwriter for hire. Nowadays when I open a green envelope, if feels less like reaping a reward than confronting a feverishly hard-working and naively idealistic ghost of myself. By idealistic I mean that even when I wrote something like *In The Line of Duty: Smoke Jumpers* (sample note from NBC exec: "Can the Smoke Jumpers take their shirts off more?"), I never thought of myself as a TV movie hack. I wrote with the anguish and conviction of an uncompromising indie auteur. And by ghost I mean that it's pretty much all over. The kind of stuff I specialized in was, for the most part, Movies of the Week, known in the business as MOWs. They were called movies of the week because, in the days before reality television swept away the old scripted paradigm of TV entertainment, every broadcast network devoted at least one night a week to airing an original movie or miniseries. As a writer of what I call colon movies (such as *Beyond the Prairie: The True Story of Laura Ingalls Wilder*, or *Take Me Home: The John Denver Story*), the nineties were my golden decade. I was an A-list writer of B-list productions.

I had wanted to be a screenwriter since 1962, when I walked out of the Tower Theater in Corpus Christi, Texas, as a very different fourteen-year-old boy than when I had walked in. The movie was *Lawrence of Arabia*, and watching it was like being sucked into a wormhole and delivered to an alternate universe. The unworldly disorientation I experienced was due in large part to David Lean's direction, to his unprecedented sense of scale and pace and purpose, and to the Maurice Jarre score, which half a century later was still so haunting to me that I sometimes used it as the ringtone on my cell phone. But *Lawrence of Arabia* had another dimension, one that I had never really noticed before. For the first time, I was aware that movies were *written*, not just somehow fortuitously assembled. It was obvious that the dialogue—"The trick, William Potter, is not minding that it hurts" or "What attracts you personally to the desert?" "It's clean"—had to have been set down somewhere in cold print, rather than thought up on the fly. And it was more than the dialogue itself that made me take notice of the name Robert Bolt; it was the wordless action as well, the way the scenes steadily built and drew upon each other to produce such a satisfying impression of momentum and coherence.

That was who I wanted to be: not the guy behind the camera but the guy behind *him*, the one who created the story in the first place, who gave the characters words to say and destinies to fulfill. After *Lawrence of Arabia*, I fell into the habit of casually shaping and framing everything I saw, imagining daily life as a story I had written and that was now being filmed. But for a long, long time it was just a mental exercise. When I was in my early twenties I made a halfhearted attempt to write a movie about the sixteenth-century explorer and castaway Cabeza de Vaca—full of lines like "I claim this land for his Most Catholic Majesty Don Carlos of Spain!"—but I had no idea what I was doing and I soon gave it up for the greater dream of writing a novel, in which case the final product would be an actual physical object with my name on the cover, and not just the movement of light on a screen.

But there was a basic enchantment with the idea of writing a movie that I could never quite get out of my system. About ten years after that first attempt, my friend Lawrence Wright and I decided to take two weeks off from writing magazine articles to hammer out a screenplay. Neither Larry nor I had ever seen an actual script, and when we finally got hold of one we were heartened by the way the dialogue ran in a narrow, centered column in the middle of the page. There was so much white space! After years of grinding out margin-to-margin prose, we interpreted that white space as material that we didn't have to write. The screenplay whose form we were studying was less than 120 pages long. We figured we could write something similar in two weeks or even less.

We had a story in mind: an aging Apollo astronaut who has been to the moon and doesn't know what to do with the rest of his life falls in love with a younger female shuttle astronaut. It never occurred to us at the time, but this was essentially the plot of *A Star is Born*, set in space. We hammered it out on manual typewriters in Larry's basement office, one of us writing one scene, the other writing the next, leapfrogging like that all the way to our various alternate endings—the hero dying in one version, the heroine in another, and in yet another, both of them surviving to take care of some unfinished emotional business between the Apollo astronaut and his estranged daughter.

I can't remember what ending we finally tacked onto it when we sent it off to an agent we had met, but I do remember being on the phone a few days afterward and—in that era before call waiting—hearing the operator break into the conversation to declare she must put through an emergency call. It was the agent announcing that the script had been sold to the brand-new theatrical wing of CBS and that Sydney Pollack—whose most recent movie had been the blockbuster comedy *Tootsie*—was attached to direct it.

First-class flights to Los Angeles, rooms at the Miramar Sheraton, Larry's speculations about how maybe we ought to buy a six-story office building that was for sale in downtown Austin because we would need a place to work. . . . Our life as the hottest new screenwriters in Hollywood didn't all come crashing down exactly, but it did become clear in our meetings with Pollack that we had been the beneficiaries of beginner's luck and had no idea how to really write a screenplay. He wanted to know things like where the end of act two was and what the character's arc was. We didn't know characters were supposed to have arcs, we didn't know scripts were supposed to have acts, and in our guileless delight at having hit the big-time we certainly didn't know that the leading impediment to this project ever getting made would be our continued participation in it.

Moonwalker—that was the movie's name before Michael Jackson appropriated the title for his 1988 feature-length music video—never made it to the screen. It was the first of maybe thirty projects over the years for which I was duly paid but never had the satisfaction, or just as likely the horror, of seeing produced. Retitled *Ocean of Storms*, it was written and rewritten by other writers, bought and sold by other studios or producers, attached and unattached to other directors. The last I heard, Warren Beatty still owned it. If it's still in development somewhere, it has the distinction of having outlasted the space shuttle program.

Larry and I wrote several more scripts together, including a comedy for Jane Fonda that did not make her laugh, but none of them were produced, either, and we were still too green to realize what was wrong with them or to have any real point of entry into understanding how the movie business worked. No doubt it would have helped our careers to move to Los Angeles, but something kept me from going all in. I still wanted to be a book writer more than a movie writer, and I was cautious about uprooting my family, especially since I was becoming painfully aware that the progression from "Hollywood screenwriter" to "failed Hollywood screenwriter" could be alarmingly seamless.

As the movie industry's indifference to us mounted, the once-hot screenwriting team of Harrigan and Wright (or Wright and Harrigan— not sure we ever settled that) slunk back into the business of just-prose. But we each still dreamed and dabbled a bit on our own. Larry would eventually go on to write *The Siege*, the sadly prophetic 1998 Denzel Washington thriller about a terrorist attack in Manhattan. I first saw my name on a screen six years before that, when a script of mine was finally made for television by HBO.

The Last of His Tribe was the true (well, true enough) story of Ishi, the sole surviving member of the persecuted Yahi tribe of Northern California, who ended his days as a kind of living exhibit at the San Francisco Museum of Anthropology. Graham Greene was cast as Ishi and Jon Voight as Alfred Kroeber, the anthropologist who both shelters and unthinkingly exploits him. I had my own chair on the set, with my own name embroidered into it, a courtesy of rank I was soon to discover was a whopping anomaly for a screenwriter.

I had already written the script, so there was nothing for me to do on the set except sit in my special chair and eat red licorice from the craft services table while everyone around me was in urgent motion, often miserably trying to achieve some effect that I had thoughtlessly set down in my screen directions. "A raven lands on a rock" had cost me only a few keystrokes, but that mindless literary flourish translated into thousands of dollars of precious production time as a frustrated raven "wrangler" tried, in take after take, to make his trained bird hit its mark.

It began to dawn on me during the production of that movie that as much as I yearned to be part of the team, my real role was going to be that of lonely outlier. Screenwriters are less like filmmakers than like wedding planners: we work in isolation for months or even years making sure everything is ready, every detail is in place, but in the end it's just not our party.

The Last of His Tribe set a bar for mild cable television success that I could never quite vault over. When I think back on that script today its rookie limitations are glaring. It was a fluently written and well-constructed story, but it was full of the very clichés I thought at the time I was cleverly avoiding. (Emotionally closed-up scientist taught how to be fully human by saintly Indian—did I really go there?)

Nevertheless, I assumed I would climb inexorably to the next rung of the Hollywood ladder, that I would now write movies that would premiere not on television but in actual theaters, with popcorn and coming attractions. But few feature assignments came my way, and gradually word came down to me from my agent that I was lacking an edge. Nobody in the movie business can really explain what an edge is, but it is understood that to be without one is the direst of all creative assessments. It means that you are a mild-mannered craftsman who was put on earth to write not *Lawrence of Arabia*, not *Taxi Driver*, not *The Dark Knight*, but perhaps a "very special" installment of Hallmark Hall of Fame.

Maybe it was partly to advertise the edge that was visible to no one but me that I agreed to write *The O. J. Simpson Story* for Fox TV. This project was notorious at the time for presumably ushering in a new low for exploitative programming, since it was conceived as an almost instant TV movie, hurled into development mere days after the murders of Nicole Simpson and Ron Goldman in June 1994.

The national paroxysm created by the murders of Simpson's wife and her friend, as the prime suspect tried to make his escape in his famous white Bronco, was an out-of-nowhere phenomenon at the time, before helicopter freeway chases and wall-to-wall coverage of lurid crimes began to fill up the longueurs of twenty-four-hour news coverage. I was as transfixed as the rest of the country, though when Robert Lovenheim—who had produced *The Last of His Tribe* and bestowed upon me my screenwriter's chair—called me a few days after the Bronco chase to ask me to write the movie, I thought the idea was insane. Rupert Murdoch wanted it on the air in September, less than four months away. I wasn't sure it was even possible to make a movie that fast, even if there was already an approved screenplay in place. But there was no screenplay—that was what I was for. I would have something like three weeks to come up with an approach that would still be credible in the face of a daily torrent of new information, and then write a screenplay that was acceptable to the network, clearable by its army of lawyers, and palatable to me.

It wasn't the money that made me decide to take the job. I had another offer at the time, for another project that would have paid the same. As a magazine writer, I couldn't quite resist the crazy deadline involved, the chance to throw myself into a project that was weird and impossible and that directly addressed an urgent national obsession. And the character of O. J. had Shakespearean depth, even if the critics would eventually unite in agreeing that the screenwriter did not.

I started writing the script in late June and the movie went into production in Los Angeles in August. The average script that is made into a movie spends years in development, during which time it is rewritten at least a dozen times, usually after the original writer has been fired. So it was a strange new experience to sit at my computer and tweak dialogue or write entire new scenes, and to have the fresh pages almost instantly delivered to the actors who were waiting to say the lines.

The movie's air date was postponed, not because it wasn't ready, but because we had made it so fast that it would be broadcast before the trial even reached jury selection, thus possibly tainting the jury pool. When *The O. J. Simpson Story* was finally aired about six months later, it was a ratings success despite being the point-blank target of a critical fusillade. I think I recall reading a positive review from some lonely TV reviewer in the Midwest, but otherwise the critics universally chose to be appalled. ("This is another of television's scavenger productions, eager to pounce on the bare bones of any sensational story that might turn up a few gold fillings for the network bottom line." Tut-tuts courtesy of John J. O'Connor of the *New York Times*.)

It felt good, a little, to be reviled; I'm not sure why. Maybe because I had spent my whole career as a writer courting critical approval, there was something liberating about working on a project for which it was unachievable from the start. And I wasn't ashamed of the movie. The notion of an instant drama about O. J. Simpson had never struck me as unseemly in the first place, and I still maintain that as TV movies go (a low standard, I admit) the final product was triumphantly better than average. I was particularly fond of a scene I had written that really irritated Mr. O'Connor, in which the young O. J. Simpson gets a dressing-down from none other than Willie Mays.

But my reputation as a quality writer of noble Indian movies for HBO had taken a hit, and for my penance I had to turn down various lucrative but seedy assignments that came in the wake of O. J. until I could regain my middlebrow prestige.

There was no longer much of an incentive to try to break into features when the TV work was so steady. And in television the odds of actually getting a movie made were much greater, maybe along the lines of ten-to-one instead of a hundred-to-one. The budget for a typical TV movie was much smaller, the stars were less expensive since they were either on the way up or on the way down or, like me, static inhabitants of a realm of generally low expectations.

What I liked best about working in TV were the commercial breaks. A standard feature movie has three acts embedded into its structure, invisible pivot points that propel the action forward and help define the characters. When I started in the business, a network TV movie had seven acts—a decade or so later it was increased to eight. The acts were not implicit, as they were in a feature; they were glaringly apparent, because the end of an act was when the action stopped and the commercials came on.

The act breaks were crucial because the executives were always terrified that the viewers would change the channel and never come back to the movie. Act 4—or sometimes Act 5—was the all-important midpoint, or hour break. Some sort of crescendo or cliffhanger was essential here. At first I resented the crass audience manipulation that went into structuring the story in this way, but the more experience I developed the more I learned to love these restrictions and the challenges they presented. It was satisfying to hit my marks, to move the scene where the hero's girlfriend gets shot from page seventy-six to page fifty-two so that the audience would have to come back after the hour break to see whether she lived or died. Rolling up my sleeves to mull over the act breaks, I felt like a poet wrestling with some ruthlessly prescribed form, like a sestina or villanelle.

But I grew to learn not to think of myself as an author, as the creator of a stand-alone piece of writing. A screenplay is not a book, it's not exactly a text, it's not really even a thing. The physical form of a screenplay—120 or so pages held together by brass fasteners—is not to be taken seriously, because the script is in reality a sort of floating proposition, an ever-evolving set of instructions. The words "final draft" are eventually used, but since important changes are made all the way through the editing room, the idea of a final draft is notional. As a writer you are brutally reminded again and again that your script is not the end product; the movie is.

But that, too, was part of the fun, knowing that my contribution was crucial but not definitive, that an unproduced screenplay, no matter how brilliant I thought it was, was just an evolutionary dead end.

And there was always real pleasure in the work itself, in setting down dialogue and screen directions against that blessed field of white space, in endlessly wrestling with plot and structure, in discussing the next draft with producers and executives, who, with a few exceptions, were not brain-dead Hollywood sharks but thoughtful and intelligent people.

Sometimes I encountered the thrill of literally walking into a world I had created. That happened with *Beyond the Prairie: The True Story of Laura Ingalls Wilder* (by the way, that "true" in the title is more of a statement of intent than a guarantee). "Do you want to see your town?" Dori Weiss, my producer, asked when I arrived at the production office in Utah. I wasn't quite sure what she was talking about until we got in her car and drove to the set, which was the main street of the railroad town of DeSmet, South Dakota, circa 1881, where the author of *Little House on the Prairie* had lived as a girl. I had described the town in my script but somehow it had never occurred to me that it would actually be *built*. But here it was, real and three-dimensional, abruptly springing to life like an image in a child's pop-up book.

It was even more startling to arrive in Morocco during preproduction on *Cleopatra*, the thirty-million-dollar epic I wrote for the great Robert Halmi Sr., the Hungarian resistance fighter, balloon pilot, and *Life* magazine photographer who went on to become the king of television movies and miniseries. In the Moroccan desert he had built not only ancient Alexandria but ancient Rome as well, a set so grand that one of its temples could have swallowed up all of DeSmet.

That movie ended up being a tumultuous production. The original director was either fired or he stomped out on his own weeks before principal photography, and a new director was hired at the last moment. The new director brought in a new writer, Anton Diether, who had done an excellent adaptation of *Moby Dick* a few years earlier for Halmi. This was the first time since *Moonwalker* that I had been rewritten, but enough of my original work was left that I'm pretty sure it's me, and not Anton, who must bear the responsibility for what has been pointed out to me as the worst line of dialogue ever uttered in a miniseries. Julius Caesar has just aided the young queen Cleopatra in crushing a rebellion in the Egyptian capital. In the battle, though, the great library of Alexandria, the repository of all the world's wisdom and knowledge, has gone up in flames. As Cleopatra tends Caesar's wounds, he turns to her and whispers, "I'm sorry about your library."

I notice I've just written the phrase "he turns to her." After I had been in the business for awhile, I started to become aware of the word "turns," and the more aware of it I grew the more determined I was to outmaneuver it. It's the default word for the end of almost every scene:

"He turns"; "She turns"; "She hesitates for a moment at the door, then turns back to face him"; "He looks away, and when he turns back to her she notices there are tears in his eyes." It became my personal challenge to write an entire script without anybody turning, like that guy in the 1930s who once wrote a whole novel without ever using the letter E. But after a while I gave up. It was too hard, maybe even impossible. People in my scripts just naturally needed to turn to each other to button up a scene, to give it a proper note of finality. Trying to write a screenplay without using "turns" was like trying to write a pop song without using "baby."

Other screenwriting challenges were not nearly so frivolous. Even on the most forgettable of the TV movies I worked on there was a Manhattan-Project-like urgency and dedication, with sometimes a half-dozen people in the room with me throwing out ideas for how the story could be tighter, the characters clearer, the stakes higher. This was not the sort of gentleman's editing I was used to from the book world; it was an anything-goes deconstruct-o-rama. a tribunal that was convened not just once but every time I turned in a draft.

Most of the advice from these producers and executives was reasonably on-target—sometimes it was brilliant; but I discovered that good advice was something to be regarded with wariness as well as gratitude, since what seemed at first like a dazzling solution to a story problem could just as easily lead you into a trackless thicket of incoherence. Over time I learned I had to assume authority in those meetings, to be the strongest voice in the room, the one person who knew the script from the inside out.

I came to realize that what really matters in a screenplay are momentum and clarity. It was true that if you paid too much attention to the screenwriting gurus, with their how-to-write-a-screenplay books and seminars about plot points and inciting incidents and act breaks, you could end up with a script that was all skeleton and no heart. Sometimes you had to forget the rules even as you were slavishly following them, to give yourself a little room to improvise and explore. But the gurus had a consistent and undeniable point: the real writing was in the structure. Glittering dialogue meant nothing if it did not directly advance the plot; paragraphs of elegant screen description were merely ornamental obstructions that busy readers would impatiently skip over. Subtlety was too much like vagueness, and in a script nothing vague can survive.

You had to search and search until you found a story's irreducible thread: a man on the run from a killer, a young girl growing into a woman, a victim seeking revenge. If the movie was about one thing, it could be about many things. But if you started out determined to make it about many things, it would be about nothing.

Over the decades I wrote about forty movies on assignment, thirteen or fourteen of which were produced. Some of the movies were well reviewed, some were successful in the ratings, a few were both. *Beyond the Prairie* was watched by twenty-three million people on one night, though I don't think I ever actually encountered one of those viewers until a few years ago, when a college student told me that she had grown up watching the movie every Christmas with her family.

My ratio of produced-to-unproduced movies isn't bad. There are plenty of screenwriters who have worked steadily for years and years and never had anything at all made. Still, it can be disheartening to ponder, because among those twenty-odd movies that were never made is some of my best work. Of course, any screenwriter will tell you that his unproduced work is his best, because it is still pristinely preserved in his imagination and uncorrupted by budget realities or by the competing visions of directors or actors. In the category of never-were, among the real losses for me was a movie about the Donner Party that I originally wrote for CBS ("Just a thought," said the squeamish CBS execs. "Do we really have to mention cannibalism at all?"), which was later acquired by HBO, who hired me to rewrite it. ("It's a good script but it needs to be much darker. We want to see people gnawing on human bones.") The darker and better version was almost made, but at the last moment, for reasons I was too demoralized to inquire about, it was not.

I once wrote a movie for Robert Altman, a feature adaptation of S. R. Bindler's classic documentary *Hands on a Hard Body*, about a group of people desperately trying to win a contest for a Nissan pickup truck. Altman was close to the end of his run when I was hired. He had cancer, was undergoing chemo, and only had the energy to work a few hours a day. It was clear that, if it got made, this was going to be his last movie. But he was still full of renegade conviction and not in a mood to fret over the fine points of screenwriting. He had a bracing indifference to received wisdom about the primacy of character and story and was famous for running all over his writers, for throwing out their carefully wrought scripts and improvising. He just wanted to make a movie. Knowing that my contribution would be ultimately disposable proved strangely liberating for me. By that time I was tired of story and character myself, tired of scripted dialogue, aware that the traits I prided myself on—reliability, coherence, thorough craftsmanship—were the very traits that bored a visionary like Altman.

"Go ahead and write it the way you want," he told me with a conniving grin one afternoon in his Malibu living room, after I had ventured that it would be a good idea if we thought ahead of time about which of the twenty-four characters should win the truck. "Just remember that I'm going to double-cross you in the end."

I had more fun working with Altman than I'd had with anyone else. I sent in the final draft on a November day in 2006 and got a call from him a few days later. He sounded more revved up than I'd ever heard him, and he said the script was "brilliant and masterful"—which I knew meant he would take even more delight in completely ignoring it when the movie went into production. Among the actors who had agreed to play the people competing for the Nissan, he told me, were Meryl Steep, Hillary Swank, Billy Bob Thornton, Jack Black, Chris Rock, John C. Reilly, and Steve Buscemi. Filming would begin in three months.

A week later I got a call informing me that Robert Altman had died.

And then there was an adaptation of Hemingway's *The Old Man and the Sea* that was to star F. Murray Abraham. I won't even try to avoid the obvious comparison: writing that movie and not having it produced was like hooking into a 1500 pound blue marlin and fighting it for three days only to have it eaten by sharks.

Hands on a Hard Body, *The Donner Party*, *The Old Man and the Sea*, and various other stillborn projects were all heartbreakers for me. But maybe, in the end, my heart wasn't breaking enough. Even though writing movies was my line of work for three decades, screenwriting never struck me with the force of a vocation. I satisfied myself with a middling successful career because the work kept coming without me having to go in pursuit of it, and also because I was wary of that pursuit when I knew it might lead me permanently away from the sort of writing that mattered the most to me—novels that I could hold in my hand, that had no budget restraints, and in which my own voice spoke for itself.

Maybe my lack of an edge had something to do with that lack of all-or-nothing commitment. In the end, I think I loved the craft of screenwriting more than the art of it. But I really loved that craft: the well-turned line of dialogue, the well-placed act break, the meetings in which I would put the producers' fears to rest with a sudden clever solution to an intractable story problem.

As I said at the beginning, it's mostly over now, though there are still a few hibernating projects of mine out there with a just-detectable winter heartbeat. It would not take much to get me excited about them all over again. I remember, only a few years ago, sitting in a restaurant in Burbank, killing time before a meeting at the ABC offices on the Disney lot, about some forgettable, inspired-by-a-true-story Movie of the Week. The meeting was two hours away but I had arrived early because I didn't want to risk getting caught in traffic or lost on the Hollywood Freeway.

I was fifty-eight years old, probably almost twice the age of the executives I would be meeting. I had been doing this forever, but I was still an outsider, still an outlander. At my age the odds were growing slimmer and slimmer that I would ever write the next *Lawrence of Arabia*, but that didn't matter to me. I was content with my hard-won place on the B-team of American culture, happy to be sitting in a booth in Bob's Big Boy, psyching myself up for a meeting that after all this time still seemed to hold the promise of a dazzling new career in the movies.

WHERE IS MY HOME?

My grandmother made two kinds of kolaches. They were equally threatening. One had a prune-and-apricot filling, the fruit stewed together into a dark spackle that rested inside a shallow depression on top of the pastry. The other contained a poppy seed paste, hidden inside a plain mound of dough, that was even darker, even gunkier. The pungent smell of those kolaches, their suspicious texture and strong, complicated sweetness, were too much for a finicky young eater like myself. I tried them once or twice, and that was enough. It was not just the way they tasted but what they evoked: a world far older than my own, a dark age and a distant place that seemed to think it had some claim upon my soul.

My grandmother's married name was Gladys Berney, but she had been born Gladys Lednicky. Her parents had grown up in Czech villages only a few miles apart but did not meet until they had emigrated separately to America and settled in the Midwest, where they were married in 1885, in Buchanan County, Missouri. She was an industrious woman with cat-eye glasses who gave book reviews for local women's clubs and was once named Oklahoma's "Mother of the Year." I can remember her sitting at her kitchen table in Oklahoma City—where she and her husband moved the family in the thirties—talking on her red Bakelite telephone to her mother, gossiping rapidly in a baffling language she called "bohunk."

I don't recall being particularly curious about this language or why she would be speaking it. And for the next half-century or so I lazily remained indifferent. I knew more or less that my ancestors came from a region of the world that had once been part of Austria-Hungary, and after the First World War had coalesced into Czechoslovakia, and then after the fall of communism, in 1989, had become the Czech Republic. But as far as I was concerned, it was still a fuzzy, medieval-ish land. I grew up in midsized cities, not in roots-conscious big-city neighbor-hoods or rural communities. My world was a striving postwar America of blank cultural cohesion. Ethnically speaking, I had always felt like nobody in particular, a product of the casually mongrelized white middle class—in my case part Irish, part Scotch-Irish, and part murky middle European. To the degree I ever embraced any of these splintered identities, it was the Irish part—not the Czech—that had appealed most to my carefully cultivated, broodingly romantic soul. But DNA doesn't lie. When I looked in the mirror, I saw not some tortured black-haired Irishman but the generic round face, bald head, and mushy features of an Eastern Bloc apparatchik.

I don't think I ate a kolache between about 1954 and sometime in the mid-eighties, when my Uncle D. D. baked a batch for Christmas using my late grandmother's recipe and sent them around to the rest of the family. People use the word "Proustian" to describe the sort of sensation I had upon encountering these kolaches, but for the adjective to have real meaning, it helps to go back to the famous passage, early in the first volume of *Remembrance of Things Past*, where the author describes the experience of rediscovering the texture of his childhood through the taste of a madeleine cookie dipped in tea: "I feel something start within me, something that leaves its resting-place and attempts to rise, some-thing that has been embedded like an anchor at a great depth."

My uncle's kolaches were round, rather flat, formed irregularly by hand, and baked to a deep brown. They came in a cardboard mailing box, layer after layer of them—prune and poppy seed—wrapped in alu-minum foil. Unwrapping that foil released a smell, or rather an intricate tapestry of smells, that transported me instantly into the precognitive mist. I had just discovered the Dead Sea Scrolls of my childhood.

My way of pulling at the anchor was to begin making kolaches myself every Christmas. I worked from my grandmother's recipe, written in her own hand. It required some serious parsing and occasioned a few double takes. (The directions for one step read, "After they bake—put butter over top—I do + momma died.") The recipe, I was cautioned by my uncle, is a Lednicky secret, never to be published, though I think I can reveal that at one stage it calls for a box of crushed vanilla wafers.

I was able to approach but never quite attain Nana's standard. Making kolaches is hard. A famous Czech proverb, printed on pot holders and refrigerator magnets, confirms my own experience: "*Bez práce nejsou koláče*" ("Without work there are no kolaches"). First, there is the time-consuming process of making the dough, which involves an afternoon's worth of mixing flour and eggs and sugar, scalding milk, and melting butter, then kneading it, letting it rise, punching it down, letting it rise again, and rolling it out onto a floured surface, only to discover at the end of the procedure that you've left out a crucial ingredient—yeast, perhaps. There is also the filling to prepare, the endless stirring of the pot that holds poppy seeds and milk and flour and sugar as you wait—hope—for it to resolve itself into the proper speckled paste. Meanwhile, on another burner, the dried prunes and apricots stew together in a saucepan, a bubbling tar pit that you have to keep a careful eye on as it cooks down, until finally it is pliable enough to mush together with a heavy-duty whisk. Then you have to make *popsika*, the sugary, cinnamony, vanilla-y topping, and then comes the tedious, origami-like hand forming of the kolaches themselves, an art that I have humbly accepted I do not have the patience or remaining lifetime required to master.

For years I continued to make my kolaches without much encouragement. My children, when they were young, sampled them in the same grudging way I had. Now that they are grown, they claim they like them, but I know it's only a nostalgic tolerance. I've taken my kolaches to office parties and other sorts of gatherings, and the approbation I've received has been on the polite side. No matter: it's my own personal *recherche du temps perdu* thing, the hunt for something long misplaced, or something yet to be discovered.

What exactly is a kolache? Although a friend of mine recently confided that he thought the word referred to a type of shoe, this is not a question that needs answering so much anymore, particularly for people from Fayette or Lavaca or Caldwell or Austin or McLennan counties, or any of the other blackland prairie regions of Central Texas that were home in the nineteenth century to a steady influx of Czech emigrants. Throughout this territory, bake-offs and festivals and eating competitions have helped leverage the kolache from an obscure ethnic staple to a ubiquitous comfort food. Even if you're nowhere near the Czech belt, you've probably encountered chains like the Kolache Factory or the Kolache Shoppe or Lone Star Kolaches.

The word is a corruption of the Czech *koláč*. (The plural is *koláče*.) I can remember my grandmother pronouncing it the correct way: not "kuh-*lotch*-y," as we say it, but "*koh*-lotch." The Czech word from which it derives, *kolo*, means "wheel." Home-baked Lednicky kolaches were decidedly round, but most commercial bakeries these days squeeze the kolaches so close together on their trays that they bake into puffy squares.

As I understand it, "*koláč*" can be justly applied to many forms of Czech pastries, but at least here in Texas most people understand "kolache" to mean a springy mound of sweet dough with a declivity on top containing a dollop of some sort of fruit and a sprinkling of the streusel-like popsika. The fruit is almost always in plain sight, often sharing its little foxhole with a dab of cream cheese, but if it's a poppy seed kolache, the filling is usually tucked away within the dough. That's also the case with sausage kolaches, which are the best-selling variety in Texas.

For a long time I thought kolaches were more or less my family's secret—that's how blind I was to the Czech culture all around me. Then about fifteen years ago, my mother moved to Houston from Corpus Christi, and I began driving regularly from Austin to Houston on Highway 71 to visit her. I soon discovered that along the way there were several places to buy poppy seed kolaches, her favorite. I alternated between Weikel's, a little gas station-bakery combo on the outskirts of La Grange, and Hruska's, fifteen miles farther down the road in the tiny town of Ellinger. At that time Hruska's inventory seemed to be evenly split between kolaches and scrapbooking supplies, but when they put up a billboard proclaiming "Awesome Restrooms" and then began expanding by several thousand square feet, it became pretty obvious they were gearing up to fight the kolache wars in earnest. Weikel's responded by completely tearing down their building and replacing it with a truck-stop-sized kolache palace, with even awesomer restrooms featuring the best automatic hand-dryers in the Texas Czech Republic.

Although the kolaches I ate at Hruska's and Weikel's were perfectly respectable, they didn't carry the ancestral charge of the ones that my Uncle D. D. had made. Nobody likes a kolache snob, but that's what I had become. A part of me was resentful that the sacramental snack of my childhood had been so brazenly loosed upon the world, but another part of me was curious enough to learn more about what it had become—and why it mattered to me. I set out upon the kolache trail to find not merely the best but the most resonant, the most redolent—in a word, the most *Lednickyian*—kolaches on earth.

My first stop was—had to be—the little town of West, just north of Waco. West, Texas (locals refer to it as "West comma Texas" so they won't be perpetually misunderstood to be talking about the region of west Texas), is to kolaches as Lockhart is to barbecue: a pilgrim's holy ground. The town is home to the Village Bakery, the oldest and arguably best Czech bakery in Texas, to the newer but also impressively authentic Gerik's, and, of course, to the hegemonic Czech Stop, the mightiest of the gas-station kolache empires. Unsurprisingly, West also has one of the state's Czechiest populations and hosts the annual Czech heritage celebration known as Westfest.

The Czech Stop rules exit 353, siphoning off travelers along the I-35 Dallas-to-Austin corridor and luring them in with two separate storefronts, each with bakery cases filled with dozens of varieties of kolaches endlessly replenished by its 106 employees. It has been in existence since 1983, when it started out as a liquor store, selling kolaches on the side from a now-defunct local bakery. Selling booze next to the freeway at a time when the perils of drunk driving were beginning to incite alarm turned out to be the wrong business model, so the wholesome kolache took center stage.

Barbara Schissler, the CEO and president of the Czech Stop, sketched this history for me as we sat in a plastic booth in her establishment during a rare lull. Clerks in faux old-world Slavic vests waited on a handful of customers as polka music played over the speaker system.

"I don't have a clue," she said when I asked how many people stopped in for kolaches on a typical day. "It just never ends. One customer after another after another." She said she had a piece of paper in her office on which a former manager had once tried to calculate how many kolaches the Czech Stop sold per month. When she showed it to me later, neither one of us could quite decipher the exact totals, but the bottom line seemed to be in the neighborhood of 24,604. That's 24,604 *dozen*.

She took me on a backstage tour to see the giant rotating ovens, multiple proofing vaults, and walk-in refrigerators the size of suburban garages. Across the street in a separate warehouse was another enormous kitchen, with its own stock of industrial ovens and refrigerators, a forklift, and a customized golf cart for shuttling baked goods back and forth to the twin storefronts.

As for the kolaches themselves, I found the Czech Stop's to be consistently fresh and—given the demands of mass production—reasonably authentic, based on a family recipe that Evelyn Cepak, who manages the original storefront, bequeathed to the institution decades ago. But like the specimens from Hruska's or Weikel's, they were only glancingly familiar when I compared them with the kolaches of my childhood, which were not square and pillowy but dense, dark, and round. I'm not saying Nana's kolaches were objectively better, but their mojo had been so powerful it was hard not to think of any other kolache as merely a wad of dough.

Of course, there is a difference, or ought to be, between a commercial-grade kolache and one that is lovingly crafted at home. Last summer, I began musing about the idea of removing the Lednicky kolaches from the reliquary of my memory and bringing them into the sunlight of the Westfest kolache-baking contest. I had no illusions—well, I had a few illusions—that my once-a-year tradition would vault me into the Jedi ranks of amateur bakers. I had never quite succeeded in perfectly reproducing all the subtle notes in Nana's kolaches, but I had come close enough to think that I was ready to step into the arena.

It helped that the rules were not intimidating. There was no entry fee, and all that was required were six kolaches made from scratch yeast dough, all of average size and with the same filling. My entry would be my tried-and-true fruit mixture, three parts prune to one part apricot.

Out of the several dozen kolaches I made, I selected the six that were the most fetching and drove them on a hot, windy September Sunday to the West Community Center, a blank-looking building across the railroad tracks from the fairgrounds where Westfest itself was under way.

I noticed at once that my kolaches looked nothing like the perfectly shaped, evenly browned, fluffy entries I saw under plastic wrap on the folding tables, but the kindly ladies who accepted them into the contest betrayed no alarm.

Winners would not be announced until three in the afternoon, so I left the judges to their work and drove across the train tracks to Westfest. By the time I parked my car, a fierce wind was blowing dust and dead grass into the eyes of the festivalgoers and shutting down the carnival rides. Westfest is usually a massive three-day celebration, but because of the simoom-like conditions, the grounds were almost vacant, with few customers lined up at the food booths offering pork rinds and kettle corn and, of course, kolaches. The entrance arch that greeted visitors with the Czech phrase *"Vítáme Vás Na Westfest"* ("We Welcome You to Westfest") shuddered in the wind.

Along with most of the visitors, I sought refuge in a metal-roofed pavilion where a polka mass had just begun—liturgical music played to the sprightly accordion tempos of songs such as "The Huntsman's Waltz" and "The Happy Wanderer." When the mass was finished, I strolled over to the Czech genealogy booth, where a handful of harried volunteers fought to keep their documents from being swept away by the wind. Among the books on the table were passenger lists of nineteenth-century transatlantic ships.

I scanned the lists for John A. Lednicky, my great-grandfather. I didn't know much about him, only that he had died in 1931, almost two decades before I was born, and that he had emigrated to the United States as a young man from somewhere in what is now the Czech Republic toward the close of the nineteenth century. He would have been part of a steady surge of Czech migration that had begun in the 1870s, as rural cottagers found themselves unable to compete on their family homesteads with cheap American wheat prices and the mechanized farming that was changing the practice of agriculture. He made his way to Kansas and became fairly prosperous as the owner of several general stores throughout Brown County. He married twice, first to a Czech woman named Victoria (my great-grandmother), who died young, and then to another woman, also Czech, whom I dimly remember and who was known to several generations of the family as "Mommie." It was Mommie (the "+ momma died" of the recipe) who passed her kolache-making wisdom down to her stepdaughter, Gladys.

I didn't find a "John Lednicky" in any of the books at the genealogy booth. Which ship he took to America, what port he landed in, remained a mystery, though to call the details of my own Czech heritage a mystery was to give it a greater degree of urgency than I had ever really felt. Here at Westfest—where everyone else laughed heartily at the Czech wisecracks the priest had made in his sermon at the polka mass, where friends stood around a map of the Czech Republic comparing notes about the people they'd visited in their home villages—I felt like a fraud.

I continued to lurk around Westfest as the ferocious winds grew stronger and the festivities all but shut down. By mid-afternoon, I was back in the community center, waiting for the kolache judging to begin. I sat with about fifty other people on folding chairs as the judges finished their deliberations behind a plastic room divider. A teenage girl—Miss Westfest—stood off to the side, wearing the native Czech costume known as a *kroj*: a gauzy white apron over a long blue skirt, a blue vest over a puffy-sleeved blouse, and a flowery tiara with colored ribbons hanging down in the back. Almost everybody else was middle-aged, and their native costume was a T-shirt, a pair of shorts, and a ball cap. Nobody was talking much. Most of us just stared down at the linoleum, knowing that the next few minutes could bring either kolache glory or obscurity.

The room divider opened, and Mildred Dokupil, the Westfest associate director in charge of kolaches, announced that there had been 105 entries, the most ever. She was pleased about this.

"We're always looking for new contestants to challenge the people from this area and give them a run for their money—or a run for their dough."

She began to hand out the trophies, each of them decorated with a clay kolache she had made herself by hand. Somebody named Frank won first place for prune and apricot. Somebody else won second and third place. One by one other categories were called—hot link, cheese, cream cheese—and one by one the winners went up to the front of the room to receive their trophies while I waited in the back, increasingly aware that not only had I not placed but my outlier kolaches were going to be spared from coming in at 105th only because the judges would not have had the time or inclination to rank the entries all the way to last place.

"My God!" Mimi Montgomery Irwin exclaimed when I showed her a photo of the kolaches I had entered in the contest. She is the co-owner of the Village Bakery, which her family established in West in 1952 and of which she told me, "We're like Poilâne, in Paris. We have a standard to maintain. Someone has to maintain the classic tradition."

By the horrified look in her eyes as she stared at my kolaches, I had the impression I wasn't maintaining any standard at all. When I told her I smushed them down just before baking them so they would be flat, she actually gasped. She said the art of kolache-making was all about lovingly tending to the dough so it would rise, though she did concede the point that in the Czech Republic kolaches were usually on the flatter side.

We agreed that I needed an education in exactly how a Poilâne-grade kolache is manufactured, so a few weeks later I drove back to West, passing the Czech Stop at the freeway exit on my way to the Village Bakery, a modest little storefront in West's historic downtown. Mimi took me directly into the kitchen and introduced me to her beloved old Middleby-Marshall oven, a floor-to-ceiling contraption with a gas flame burning at the bottom and five or six baking trays rotating along the interior by means of a pulley system. She told me the oven had been bought in 1969 or 1970 and over time had been seasoned by use like a cast-iron skillet or a wine barrel. "It's a labor of love to keep it alive.

"We don't use convection ovens for kolaches," she explained. "They'll leave the dough too dark and raw in the middle. They don't give you that overall thorough beauty. And don't even get me started on electric."

The other equipment included three big Hobart industrial mixers for making the dough from scratch, sixty-year-old wooden tables for rolling it out, and the magnificent Eberhardt rounder, a steampunk dream of a device that presses down onto an unformed mat of dough and neatly transmutes it into several dozen perfectly formed balls that are the basis for the individual kolaches. With this machinery the Village Bakery creates between six hundred and a thousand kolaches a day, double that on Saturdays, and fills a steady stream of orders for special occasions.

"If someone prominent in town passes away, we bake, because we know people are going to be coming in from out of town and they're going to want to take something to the family. Same thing if there's a wedding. So you have to read the *West News* like you're an analyst for Paine Webber."

For several hours I observed some of the bakery's nonmechanical assets—their names were Jamie, Leslie, Lurethia, Louis, Rose, Linda, Debbie, Pam, and David—as they mixed the dough, peeled fruit by hand, boiled it down, cut up sausage, and performed a dozen other tasks with wordless synchronicity. Their craftsmanship was humbling when I compared it with my own sloppy technique, and the communal silence in which they worked was faintly unsettling, giving me the feeling once again that I was somehow an exile from a culture I had barely known existed.

After the dough had been mixed and balled and proofed and had risen twice, several of the women stood over the unbaked kolaches and poked them, creating the pocket that would hold the fruit. They all used two fingers, and Mimi said that she could recognize their individual fingerprints in the dough. "Every artist has a signature."

"Can you see why this is so important to me?" she asked. "It's a tradition that has to be preserved. It has to be."

She spoke in a tone of reawakened fervor, the result of having had a long career in the wider world as a New York–based fashion marketing executive. But after her father died, after she lost friends in 9/11 and spent three months cooking for firefighters in Lower Manhattan, and after her mother suffered a stroke, she came back home to West to run the family business.

Earlier in the evening, while we were waiting for the dough to rise, Mimi took me next door to the Village Shoppe—a dress store also owned by the family—so I could meet her mother, Georgia Morris

Montgomery. Mrs. Montgomery, a trim ninety-four-year-old woman in a red flowered blouse and brown slacks, told me that her father came to America before the First World War, sailing across the ocean with a summer sausage his mother had given him to eat on the voyage. He established himself in West, where he met his wife, whose family came from the Czech village of Frýdek-Mistek. He eventually started the Czechoslovak Publishing Company, which produced newspapers for the tight-knit Czech emigrant population in Texas.

To hear Mimi and her mother tell it, you couldn't really buy a kolache in Texas until the Village Bakery opened in 1952. People baked them at home, and they were served at weddings, funerals, and church bazaars just as they were back in the old country, but when it came to finding a kolache on the spur of the moment, Texas was a retail desert. "After a football game once," Mrs. Montgomery said, "our Catholic priest and two gentlemen who owned Ford dealerships in West and Mexia came to dinner at our house, and we happened to make kolaches. They dared us to start a bakery."

Mrs. Montgomery had her grandmother's kolache recipe. Her husband—whose family had been in Texas since the 1820s—had a master's degree in chemistry. It was his job to take the recipe and apply the food science necessary to make it work on a large scale.

Mimi thinks it was in the fall of 1953 when her father invented the sausage kolache. "He and my grandmother had been trying to make sausage bread, and my dad just said, 'Oh, why are we killing ourselves? Why don't we just take a link and put it in the dough?'"

They called the thing a *klobasniki*, which means "little sausage" in Czech and which is how the Village Bakery still refers to it. Mimi will say the words "sausage kolache" if she has to, but there is that standard to uphold. A Czech *koláč* is not a meat sandwich, it's a pastry. Therefore, the sausage kolache, like the chicken fajita, is an etymological contradiction and cannot technically be said to exist.

I sat in the dress shop talking to Mrs. Montgomery for another half hour or so. When I told her my grandmother had been a Lednicky, she nodded and repeated the name, but pronounced it "Lednitski." That was the way they said it in West, she said, where a Lednicky—Jerome J.— was chairman of the bank.

It sounded strange to hear my family name pronounced that way, a new note of dissonance that I recognized as being part of the slow-moving identity crisis that had begun decades ago when I unpacked that box of kolaches from my Uncle D. D.

For the next six months, I continued my statewide kolache blitz, driving anywhere there was a rumor of a good bakery: Temple, Hallettsville, Schulenburg, Zabcikville, Calvert, Hillsboro, Yoakum. I went to the Kolache Festival in Caldwell and hearkened to the yearningly titled Czech national anthem, "Kde Domov Můj?" ("Where Is My Home?"). I attended more earnest kolache judging ("And in the apricot division, our winner is Nicholas Faust from Snook!"). I visited the Texas Czech Heritage and Cultural Center in La Grange and talked about kolaches with their friendly and informed staff, and I probably would have visited the Czech Heritage Museum and Genealogy Center in Temple, the Burleson County Czech Heritage Museum in Caldwell, and the Czech Center Museum in Houston and talked about kolaches with their friendly and informed staffs as well if I hadn't started to think I was maybe overdoing it a little.

What was I looking for, really? What did I hope to find as I drove through all these Czech counties, ingested all these kolaches, and visited the famous painted churches in Praha or Ammannsville or Dubina that had been erected by homesick Czech emigrants to remind them of the ornate churches of their homeland? It couldn't really be about kolaches anymore, because the kolaches were all starting to look and taste the same. At every stop, I sampled an apricot one to keep my judgment consistent. I wrote down in my notebook phrases like "dough slightly salty—good or bad thing?" or "cute fruit pocket" or "intriguing popsika." But my criteria, I knew, were peculiar and unfair—and maybe I still didn't even really like kolaches that much. In my kolache quest, actual quality had become a side issue. I was not impartially looking for the best kolaches, I was looking for something else. Somewhere on earth, I reasoned, there must still be kolaches more like the ones my grandmother had made—not airy and perfect but unproofed, unrisen, somehow ancient.

The search continued to widen—really widen—until I began to realize it was leading me toward the ultimate destination, toward the fires of Mordor, where the original kolache was forged. Which was how, on a very cold day in November, I found myself on a train traveling east from Prague to Frýdek-Místek, which had been one of the centers of Czech migration to the United States. Mrs. Montgomery's father had been born there and, as it had turned out, so had my own great-grand-mother, Victoria Juřička. Ten miles or so away from Frýdek-Místek was Brušperk, the village that my great-grandfather had come from. Led-nickys still lived there, I was told. They had been informed that I was coming and that I had some weird thing about kolaches—and they were waiting to meet me.

On the train I reviewed an e-mail from Hana Michopulu, who writes a popular food blog in the Czech Republic. I had written to ask if she could recommend some bakeries where I could locate something along the lines of an ur-kolache, but she only confirmed the impression I had gathered from other people I had talked to. In the Czech Republic, there were no Kolache Shoppes or Kolache Factories. There were no kolache-industrial complexes like Czech Stop or Hruska's or Weikel's. Kolaches are still a closely held home tradition—some twenty per-cent of families bake them once or twice a week—but they have never exploded into a commercial phenomenon on their native soil the way they have in Texas.

Hana mentioned I should search out something called a *frgale*, which is a gigantic pizza-sized kolache. She also warned me off the mass-pro-duced kolaches that were available in grocery stores: "Pls don't eat this."

But I did anyway. The three-hundred-year-old inn where I spent the night in Frýdek-Místek was across the parking lot from a busy grocery store. In the bakery aisle I found two kolaches so tightly shrink-wrapped that I had to use my keys to pry them out. Everything was right about their appearance—right by my peculiar regressive standards, anyway. They were round, flat, and baked until they were dark brown, and the fruit on top was sort of smeared on rather than sitting elegantly in a deep pocket. That they tasted like the styrofoam tray with which they had been packed was immaterial. They were different enough from Texas kolaches, close enough to the Lednicky ideal, to sustain the belief that I was on the right track. I had arrived at the ancient birthplace.

Frýdek and Mistek used to be two different municipalities facing each other across the Ostravice River, which divides the Czech provinces of Moravia and Silesia. My hotel was on the Frýdek side of the river, and in the morning I took a stroll along a street lined with kebab restaurants and thrift stores and happened upon a bakery. I walked in hoping to find a kolache wonderland, but what kolaches they had on hand were casually displayed in bins with loaves of fresh bread and croissants and various kinds of rolls known as *rohlíky*.

"*Koláč, prosím*," I said to the woman behind the counter, a little thrilled to be ordering a kolache in the heart of Moravia and using two of the four words in my Czech vocabulary to do so. I pointed to a round poppy seed kolache that had been sliced along the sides to create a flower-petal shape, with a cherry on top. I also pointed to a more familiar-looking prune variety. They tasted okay, certainly better than the shrink-wrapped version I had tried the night before, but I was disappointed by the fact that they had not been given pride of place among the other baked goods. It made me wonder if we Texans, as is our way, had just up and created our own outsized preoccupation with kolaches, blowing them completely out of scale in a way that would bewilder our Czech forbears.

When I got back to the hotel, I met up with Martin Pytr, a guide and translator I had engaged through a Prague-based company called P.A.T.H. Finders, which helps people who are looking for information about their Czech ancestors. We got in his car and drove across the river, where he wanted to show me the one remaining street and town square of a village called Koloredov, which many decades ago had been enveloped by the larger town of Mistek, which had in turn been subsumed into Frýdek-Místek. Koloredov, he said, was where my great-grandmother had been born.

The old town square—the *náměstí*—was hidden behind modern apartment blocks and shopping centers, but we walked along a side street and up a stairway and soon emerged onto a beautiful urban clearing paved with cobblestones and surrounded by three- and four-story stone buildings painted in pastels and subtle shades of white. The businesses on the first floor of these buildings were modern, but the signs in the windows advertising burritos and tattoos did not seriously interfere with an impression of timeless calm. A statue of some saint with outstretched arms—neither Martin nor I could make out the eroded inscription at its base—anchored one corner of the square, and in the opposite corner rose the tower of the Church of St. James, with its oxidized pear dome. This was the church, Martin explained, where my great-grandmother had been baptized.

It was cold and we had an appointment in Brušperk, so we didn't linger. Anyway, my thoughts were too large. They kept circling back to Victoria Juřička. This woman was unknown to me except through her name and a photo I had seen of her grave marker in Kansas. She had been brought to this church as a baby, had grown up and sailed across the ocean to the American Midwest, had married and had children and died at the age of thirty-eight, and had bequeathed—among other things—my own future existence.

The village of Brušperk, the birthplace of her future husband, my great-grandfather Johann Adolf Lednicky—known in America as John—was only a twenty-minute drive away, through a rolling landscape at the base of the Beskydy Mountains, beyond whose northern summits lay Poland. A weather inversion had been bedeviling the Czech Republic all week, and haze from the steelworks surrounding the nearby industrial city of Ostrava weighed down on an otherwise enchanting pastoral tableau, with castle towers and fourteenth-century church steeples rising from the center of the villages we passed every three or four miles.

In the town square of Brušperk, a small cluster of my Czech kin were waiting for me. They were the descendants of František Lednicky, who had stayed behind in Brušperk when his brother Johann emigrated to America. I met them all in a confused rush, and there was no time to sort them out, because Marie Lancova, one of František's granddaughters and an insurance consultant who spoke excellent English, told me that we were expected in the mayor's office.

She ushered us into the municipal building facing the square and into a room where the mayor and the vice mayor greeted me at a conference table on which were arrayed three or four plates of kolaches. As Martin translated, introductions were made (distinguished visitor, member of the Lednicky family, well-known American writer, etc.), the Brušperk guest book was offered for my signature, and gifts were presented—lavish photo books, histories, brochures, maps, and some sort of local liquor.

As the mayor spoke, I looked at the kolaches in front of me, indecently eager to give them a try. Then I glanced around the conference table from one Lednicky face to another: Marie and her husband, Jaroslav, a retired coal miner; Marie's red-haired cousin Ludmila Zidkova; Ludmila's father (and Marie's uncle), Vaclav Sugarek; and Jan Krulikovsky, another descendant of František's, who seemed to have an encyclopedic recall of the family's history. The Lednicky resemblance was not immediately overpowering, but it was there: wide faces, straight noses, a characteristic mildness in the features.

When the mayor had finished welcoming me, Vaclav presented me with an idiosyncratic portfolio of the Lednicky family history. He was a vibrant, inquisitive man well into his eighties who spoke several languages, wrote poetry, and painted scenes of the American West—wagon trains and Indian battles—on pieces of bark from trees that had grown near a sacred spring in Brušperk.

"Uncle Vaclav was a steelworker," Marie explained, "but he"—she searched for the proper English expression—"he looked at the stars."

I turned the pages of the portfolio, which featured intricate hand-drawn genealogical charts, poems, photos, and reflections. I found my own name in the list of people descended from the young man who had left Brušperk in 1880 and, according to Vaclav, gambled everything on a new life in America. There were photos of family members going back generations. Some of them I knew about, like my grandmother's brother Victor Lednicky, who had moved to the Philippines as a young man, been imprisoned by the Japanese when they invaded, and survived to become a major industrialist. There were others I had never known existed: the soldier who had been conscripted into the Austrian army and died in an infantry attack against the Russians in the First World War, the partisan who had been murdered by the Nazis for acts of resistance and whose picture was displayed in a place of honor in the city hall.

We exchanged current family photos—"Ah," Marie said when she saw a picture of my two-year-old grandson, "he's a Lednitski!"—and then went on a walking tour of Brušperk, one of the many picturesque villages in the district, among them Příbor, the birthplace of Sigmund Freud, less than ten miles away. We followed a steep street leading upward from the town square to the top of a hill where the white-and-gray baroque tower of St. George's church commanded the view. St. George's had been standing in one incarnation or other in the center of the village since 1267. We walked through the cemetery next to the church, where generations of Lednickys lay beneath immaculate grave-stones. Beyond the cemetery wall was rolling farmland. An old white windmill, its blades missing but otherwise in respectable shape, stood all by itself in a field, surrounded by a sagging wooden fence. This had been Lednicky land once, Marie said, and this was the old Lednicky windmill. This was the home that my great-grandfather, in order to make a place for himself in the world, had decided to forsake.

Five miles away in the village of Stará Ves nad Ondřejnicí, where my ancestors had gone to school in a converted old castle with a draw-bridge, we stopped in at a local bakery called Pekařství Šeděnka. The manager, Jaroslava Máchová, told me that I should have come yester-day. That was the day they baked kolaches, a product that accounted for only about ten percent of their overall production. But she had heard from Martin that I was coming and had saved some for me from yesterday's baking, along with one of the pizza-sized *frgale* that Hana Michopulu had told me about.

I went back to my hotel in Frýdek-Místek carrying the big bakery sack. I meant to go to sleep early, but there was a wedding party going on downstairs and my room was vibrating with the pounding bass notes of "Hey Jude." Unable to sleep, I kept thinking of another wedding that had taken place long ago but that I had witnessed, in a way, earlier that afternoon. At St. George's church, in Brušperk, the local priest had met us at the gothic entryway, unlocked the doors, and led us inside. The church was empty of people but crowded with baroque flourishes, with painted statues of the saints and of the Infant Jesus of Prague and of Panny Marie, the Blessed Mother.

Marie had told me that it was here, in front of the main altar pre-sided over by a marble statue of St. George, that my great-great-grand-father—named, like his emigrant son, Johann Lednicky—had married Josefa Nováková, my great-great-grandmother. The wedding had taken place on February 14, 1854. The priest's name was Franz Thill. The groom had been twenty-seven years old and the bride thirty-two. After they had been pronounced man and wife, Marie said, the bride, if the playful custom had been upheld, would have turned from the altar and pretended to stomp on her husband's foot. Then everyone would have left the church for a wedding celebration, where tradition dictated that the guests would be served a ceremonial batch of kolaches.

Pretty soon, no doubt, they would be bringing out the kolaches at the wedding downstairs. I thought about sneaking in to grab one, but I was a stranger in town and not really the wedding-crasher type. Anyway, I had my own stash from the bakery in Stará Ves. I got out the bag and ate one of those flower-petal poppy seed numbers, and then part of an apricot one, and then absently sampled the giant prune *frgale* and—*zong!*—I was suddenly back in Oklahoma City circa 1953 as, half enticed, half recoiling, I took a bite for the first time of one of Nana's kolaches. It was the *frgale* that did it: the dark prune filling, the melting buttery latticework of *popsika*, the taste of the Old World that was now so stirringly close at hand.

The DJ downstairs began to play "Single Ladies." As I worked my way through the giant pastry and thought about the mountain of personal history I had just encountered, the Czech national anthem flashed into my mind and pushed out Beyoncé. "Where is my home?" the song asked.

The question had nothing to do with me. I knew where my home was, and until I was ensnared by my quest for the ancestral kolache, I had thought I knew who I was. But now I was not a Lednicky anymore, I was a Lednitski, all alone with my bag of kolaches in my strange new homeland, waiting for the band to stop playing so I could get some sleep.

—

ACKNOWLEDGMENTS

*T*he Eye of the Mammoth is, for me, a panoramic look backward. The essays collected in this book were written over a period of thirty-two years, and in reading them again I see straight through the prose to the young, inexperienced, and often despairing writer who was trying to teach himself what to look for and what to care about. I remember the countless nights spent in tents or motel rooms away from my family, the anxious scribbling in spiral-bound notebooks as I tried to write down what people were saying or what I was seeing, and afterward the heavy mental labor of trying to shape all that reportage into something coherent and meaningful.

But I also remember the companionship and generosity of the people I wrote about or called upon for their expertise. Many of these authorities are mentioned by name in these pieces, but many more just whisper in the background, often lending a credibility to my writing voice that I can't claim to possess on my own. Without the enthusiastic cooperation of these hundreds of people, I would have had very little to say.

Throughout my career as a magazine writer, *Texas Monthly* has been my home base. The magazine was founded by Michael Levy in 1973, making it possible for a Texas-based aspiring writer with very few contacts in the New York publishing world to make the transition from freelance yardman to freelance journalist. In the decades since, I've been fortunate to work with, and become friends with, each of *Texas Monthly*'s four distinguished editors: William Broyles, Jr., Gregory Curtis, Evan Smith, and Jake Silverstein.

I would like to thank them, and the other editors who helped guide me while I was writing the pieces included in this collection: Brian Sweany, John Swansburg, Jeff Salamon, David Grogan, Maggie Staats Simmons, Paul Hutton, and Linda Perney. And thanks also to my usual cadre of unofficial editors: Elizabeth Crook, Lawrence Wright, and James Magnuson. Charles E. Rankin and Byron Price of the University of Oklahoma Press graciously gave me permission to jump the gun on the publication of "The Last Days of David Crockett," which will be part of the press's forthcoming anthology about Crockett, edited by Paul Hutton and titled *Sunrise in His Pocket*.

I'm grateful to David Hamrick, the director of the University of Texas Press, for coming up with the idea of this wide-ranging collection, and to Casey Kittrell for editing it with both a sure hand and a light touch. And thanks also to Lynne Chapman, Jullianne Ballou, and Nancy Bryan. And of course to Nicholas Lemann for providing a foreword of such insight that on reading it I felt I was being introduced to my own work for the first time.